THE DIRECTORY OF Jobs & Careers Abroad

Edited by

Alex Lipinski

Distributed in the US by Peterson's Guides Inc.,
202 Carnegie Center, Princeton, N.J. 08543
Published by Vacation Work, 9 Park End Street, Oxford

First published in 1971
edited by Alison Garthwaite
Second edition 1975
Third edition 1977
Second Impression 1978
Fourth edition 1979
edited by Roger Brown
Fifth edition 1982
edited by Philip Dodd
Sixth edition 1985
edited by David Leppard
Seventh edition 1989
edited by Alex Lipinski

THE DIRECTORY OF JOBS & CAREERS ABROAD

ISBN 1 85458 013 2 (hardback)
ISBN 1 85458 012 4 (softback)
ISSN 0143 — 3482

Printed by Gibbons Barford Print, Wolverhampton, England

Contents

Specific Careers

Worldwide Employment

Overseas

South East Asia

Appendices

Preface

The Directory of Jobs and Careers Abroad is designed to help British men and women from all walks of life find suitable employment overseas.

While unemployment in the UK remains depressingly high, and while the standard of living here continues to be relatively low (see Appendix 4), the prospect of working abroad will attract many, including school leavers, graduates, skilled craftsmen, unemployed labourers and the highest paid executives. In order to address this extremely broad range of people, the Directory covers an expansive vocational and geographical spectrum — from six months nursing in the US to five year engineering contracts in Saudi Arabia, and permanent emigration to New Zealand.

This is now the seventh edition of *Jobs and Careers Abroad* and there have been a number of important changes on the international labour scene since it first appeared in 1971. In particular, stringent immigration and employment regulations have been introduced in several countries, such as the USA, Canada and Australia, which have traditionally been the focus of large scale British expatriate employment. These restrictions reflect both the exceptionally high level of worldwide emigration to those countries since the second world war, and the contraction of domestic labour markets following the general stagnation of the world economy since the oil crises of the 1970's. Each consecutive editition of the Directory has aimed to reflect the changing pattern of opportunities consequent upon these developments.

Closer to home, the European Community has embarked on a programme of creating a single European Market by 1992; this has implications for workers which are discussed below.

The careers with the best chances of getting work overseas, however, are still those which require special skills. Engineering and computing provide an extensive domain of opportunities, as do construction, petrochemical, teaching, nursing and secretarial work. Together with au pairing and domestic work, all these professions are eminently exportable.

This new edition retains the basic format of the previous edition, with a preliminary section on general approaches to overseas job-hunting, followed by two major sections, the first classified according to which career the prospective applicants is interested in, and the second according to which country he or she may wish to work in.

The section entitled *The General Approach* also includes a technique of finding work which will be unfamiliar to many readers, and which may consequently require a preliminary remark here. The method is called "the creative job search" and it works on the premise that there are a large number of "invisible" vacancies which job-seekers using the conventional approaches — also described in this section — are likely to miss. Invisible vacancies are those which are not publicly advertised through job centres, employment agencies or in the press. Recruitment for these vacancies does not operate through these conventional channels, but takes place instead through an informal "word-of-mouth" process, running along a network of contacts closely connected with the particular field of employment in which the vacancy has arisen. The task of those who are willing to follow this method is to become, as much as possible, a link in this chain of informal vacancy notification in order to tap the sources of employment potential which it offers. The chapter called *Getting the Job* provides some useful tips as to how to approach this task.

The first of the two main following sections, *Specific Careers,* is arranged by type of work.

A job in the Diplomatic Service, for instance, could take you to Hanover or Hong Kong, maybe both; as could jobs or careers in other fields of employment — engineering, education, banking and accountancy, computer services, journalism, law, medicine, agriculture, secretarial and interpreting, transport and tourism. International organisations require separate treatment, as do the armed forces and the police force, some branches of which cannot guarantee postings overseas. A chapter is also dedicated to voluntary work, which provides young people with a good introduction to work and conditions abroad — not merely in the developing countries, but also in Europe and North America.

The other main section — *Worldwide Employment* — is arranged geographically. It seems that most people who consider emigrating are most intent on improving their standard of living, and therefore choose one of the richer countries in Europe, the Middle East, North America or Australasia. These countries share a prominent position in *Worldwide Employment*, even though their present status as regards immigrants is, in some cases, far from promising. The US in particular is very sticky about work permits, but there is still a steady trickle of foreign labour to Canada, Australia and New Zealand. As for Europe, unemployment continues to strike hard, and some countries, like Norway and Switzerland, have virtually closed their doors to foreigners. However, the EC directives on free movement of labour permit us to look for work within the European Community, and to take up employment with a minimum of paperwork. This does not mean that work is easy to find there. The various other countries featured in this section, including for the first time, China, also offer employment prospects and have accepted numbers of British workers in recent years.

Each of the main specific country chapters also contains a section on short term working opportunities, designed to help those who may want to take up temporary work as a stepping stone to more permanent positions. A series of Appendices at the back of the Directory provides material on how to write a curriculum vitae, further reading, worldwide taxation and a rough guide to the standard of living in the countries dealt with here; while an index has been provided for ease of reference.

For the 150,000 or so who do go abroad to work each year, there are probably far more who never make it. Those that are not deterred at the planning stage by such obstacles as the trauma of permanent emigration or the effect of a period abroad on their pensions schemes, may find trouble in job-hunting because they do not have suitable qualifications. The need for unskilled, semi-skilled or inexperienced workers abroad is very slender, so school leavers, recent graduates or unskilled workers would be advised to spend a few extra years gaining further qualifications or relevant work experience.

As this book goes to press, there are some 2,500,000 people unemployed in the UK. In addition, there are thousands of people in work who feel that the quality of their working and private lives could be improved by a spell of work overseas. If it can help any of these people find appropriate work abroad, this book will have served its purpose.

Acknowledgements

Several people have contributed to this book, and I am grateful for their help. In particular I would like to thank Mr R. J. Anderton who wrote the chapter on Home Letting, Richard McBrien for writing the chapter on China and Tom Snow of the Oxford University Appointments Committee who provided the inspiration and some of the copy for the material on the creative job search. I am also grateful to Emily Hatchwell, Sarah Watson and David Woodworth for their assistance on various chapters of the book.

Alex Lipinski

Prices

The prices and exchange rates given in this book are intended as a guide only. While every effort has been made to ensure that they are correct at the time of going to press, fluctuations are inevitable, and no guarantee can be made as to their accuracy.

N.B. The editor and publishers have every reason to believe in the authenticity and correct practices of all organisations, companies, agencies, etc. mentioned in this book; however, they strongly advise readers to check credentials for themselves.

The General Approach

Discovering Your Employment Potential

Discovering your own employment potential is the first step on the road to job-hunting success. Whether you are still at school, have left school but have not yet decided which job to do, are considering a change of employment, or are thinking about working abroad for the first time, the importance of thinking hard about your career objectives cannot be overestimated. In particular, you have to think clearly and realistically about what kind of work appeals to you, and how you match up to its requirements. The decision you make now may influence the rest of your life.

Two useful reference books on careers which can be found in public libraries, are *Careers encyclopaedia,* edited by A. Segal, and *Equal Opportunities: A Career Guide,* by Anna Alston (see bibliography for details). In particular, the latter book includes information about opportunities for women in specific careers which is not often found in other books on the subject.

If you find that you are still uncertain about your choice of future employment, careers advice services exist to help you define and clarify your objectives.

PUBLIC CAREERS ADVICE SERVICES

Under the 1973 Education and Training Act, Local Education Authorities (LEA's) are obliged to provide a careers service to schools, Colleges of Further Education and Technical Colleges. Some Polytechnics and CFE's have their own Careers Offices, and students attending them do not have access to LEA careers services. University students can consult their own university's Careers or Appointments Board.

Your local Careers Office or Appointments Board is likely to have some kind of "vocational interests guide" which operates through a computerised databank to match the candidate's qualifications and requirements to potential specific vocations.

CAREER COUNSELLORS

As well as these publicly funded careers advice facilities, private career counsellors are also available to those who are able and willing to pay.

Career counsellors are related to management recruitment consultants (see below) in that they tend to deal with the top income bracket. However, their service is to the individual — executive, manager or other professional person — and the service provided is an analysis of his capabilities combined with a prognosis for the future of his career. They do not place people in specific jobs, but merely provide general guidelines compatible with the applicant's personality, achievements, qualifications, ambitions, family circumstances, etc. Obviously, this could include counselling on prospects for work abroad, and the applicant's suitability for this development in his career. As well as providing advice on the applicant's future career development, much emphasis is also laid on how best to present oneself when applying for vacancies — how to fill out application forms, interview techniques, etc. The theme of "marketing oneself" is recurrent in this field, and the attitude towards the whole operation recalls a sales or marketing project. Fees for the services vary widely, even within the different companies. The following are among the companies that fall into the category of career counsellors.

Career Analysts, Career House, 90 Gloucester Place, London W1H 4BL — a professional group of consultant psychologists offering career assessments and advice to applicants of all ages. Assessments include tests of aptitude, interest, personality and needs. The services range from schoolchildren to senior executives. Advice given on career direction as well as on the best career opportunities abroad. Free brochure available on request.

Chusid Lander Ltd., 35-37 Fitzroy Street, London W1P 5AF — career counselling, development and change, particularly for senior and senior middle managers and professional individuals.

InterExec SMI, Landseer House, 19 Charing Cross Road, London WC2H 0ES — Human Resource Management Consultancy, specialising in career management for senior and board level executives and career development services for the graduate or school leaver up to the age of 28.

Minster Executive Ltd., 28 Bolton Street, London W1Y 7BD — offer services to senior management comprising the full range of career counselling which includes not merely vocational guidance, but also assistance in marketing which involves Minster Executive with the client right up to the point where he or she embarks on a new career.

Percy Coutts & Co Ltd., 25 Whitehall, London SW1A 2BS — provides career counselling and full self marketing services at senior management level. Offices in Bristol, Birmingham, Manchester and Brussels.

Getting the Job

Introduction

One of the most frequently cited myths about the job market is that, because the current international unemployment situation is so bad, there are no vacancies available at all. This is a myth which is belied by even the most superficial examination of the facts.

Although there is considerable controversy concerning the exact extent and character of the present availability of work, both in the UK and overseas, there can be little doubt that there do exist sufficient vacancies to justify an attitude of realistic optimism on behalf of the determined job seeker. Despite the serious climate of worldwide unemployment, the number of international vacancies is enormous. Take the UK scene as an example. Although there were at least 2.5 million people unemployed at the time this book went to press, there were still some 25 million people, including self-employed and armed forces personnel, actively engaged in the UK labour force. That means that there are some 25 million jobs on the domestic market alone, of which up to 20% will be changing occupants each year.

Moreover, the number of vacancies being publicly advertised continues to run at an extremely high rate. In just one month, for example, the Department of Employment noted 250,000 new vacancies registered at local UK Jobcentres alone. Latest estimates suggest that Jobcentres are notified of one third of all jobs advertised publicly; this suggests close to 7 million jobs advertised annually in Jobcentres, newspapers, and through recruitment consultants and employment agencies. If this figure is extrapolated to take into account the numbers of overseas vacancies, we can begin to see just how extensive the international availability of work really is. And, as will become clear in the following sections, publicly advertised vacancies are by no means the only overseas vacancies available on the job market.

In spite of these factors, however, getting a job abroad can often be hard work in itself. Competition for work throughout a wide spectrum of career opportunities in many countries is now so intense that a reappraisal of traditional methods of job hunting seems necessary. It no longer appears realistic for job applicants to rely solely on the time-honoured methods of replying to vacancy advertisements in the press or on sending off speculative applications direct to firms and agencies. When the field is so competitive the job applicant can no longer be so passive. A more dynamic approach is required.

Apart from answering publicly advertised vacancies and making direct applications, there are two main methods of getting a long-term job overseas: you can get some organisation to do all the work for you; or you can set about using your own initiative and enterprise to find the job yourself. These two methods may be called the conventional and the creative approaches to job seeking. The most obvious difference between the two is that in the conventional job search, the applicant passively accepts the invisible hand of worldwide employment market forces, whilst in the creative job search, he or she actively engages in an energetic and imaginative campaign to find work which others, relying only on the traditional methods, will have missed. In this chapter we shall explore the merits of both of these methods of getting long-term employment abroad.

The Conventional Job Search

The conventional job search forms the backbone of the traditional methods of finding work, but because it is the traditional method, the vast majority of applicants will be following its path. What we are recommending is that job seekers follow this method, putting time and effort into chasing up the conventional avenues of possible employment outlined in this section, whilst at the same time vigorously exploring the potential suggested by creative job search, which is described in the next section. In general, the two methods go hand in hand, and neither should be favoured at the expense of the other.

ADVERTISEMENTS

Advertisements in the press work in two ways — Situations Vacant, and Situations Wanted. If you're interested in reading and replying to Situations Vacant advertisements, you will find a selection in all the national daily and Sunday papers. For specialist trades, you will find a greater concentration of suitable advertisements in specialist journals and magazines. A full list of these (not all of which carry advertising) is given in the *Trade, Technical and Professional Publications* section of the *Advertisers' Annual,* available in public reference libraries. Magazines that do carry advertising, and that can be ordered through any newsagent, or may be consulted in public libraries, include: *Architects' Journal, Building Today, The Caterer, The Certified Accountant, Chartered Surveyor, Contract Journal* (building and construction trades), *The Engineer, Flight International, The Lancet* (medical), *Nature* (science), *New Scientist, Nursery World, Nursing Mirror, Nursing Times, The Surveyor* and *UK Press Gazette.* In addition to these, there are many "in-house" publications, put out mainly by professional associations for circulation among their members, see the section *Jobs Which Are Not Publicly Advertised,* below.

In many ways, the best prospects are offered by the foreign press, especially if you want to go to a particular town or country. To focus your attention on the relevant area, a selection of the more prominent foreign papers are sold in the larger bookshops, or can be seen in public reference libraries, embassy and high commission reading rooms, or, for the best selection of all, the *City Business Library,* Basinghall Street, London EC2. Alternatively, you can arrange a subscription through your own newsagent; or through special subscription agencies such as *Bailey Subscription Agents Ltd.,* Warner House, Folkestone, Kent CT19 6PH; or direct through the newspaper itself; or, where relevant, through the UK agents (see next paragraph).

Situations Wanted advertisements can be placed direct with foreign papers, or indirectly through agencies, who will assist in your choice of paper, and, if necessary, help you with the wording and/or translations. The most practical reference source in this respect is *Benn's Media Directory* (the international volume), which gives the addresses of the main newspapers and a classified list of periodicals and specialist journals, with cross-coded references (where applicable) to the UK agents, or, in some cases, to the UK branch office of the newspaper itself. *Willings' Press Guide* gives much the same information. Willings lists each country's papers in straightforward alphabetical order (along with any relevant agents), but the lists themselves are more detailed than Benn's. Addresses of major foreign newspapers and UK agents can also be obtained from the *Advertisers' Annual.* All three of these books should be available in public reference libraries.

The agents for some of the most important newspapers are not listed here but under the heading *Newspapers* in the separate chapters of *Worldwide Employment.* In addition to the agents listed there, there are also a number of advertising consultancies, that act independently of the papers and can therefore offer free advice on your choice of medium, as well as helping you with the advertisement and placing it on your behalf. These consultancies are listed separately in the *Advertisers' Annual.*

DIRECT APPLICATION

There is never any harm in writing direct to companies or organisations abroad. Best results are obtained by enclosing an international reply coupon, a curriculum vitae, and full details of the type of work you are looking for. See *Appendix* 2 for advice on how to present your application to the best advantage. The main problem is finding the names and addresses of suitable contacts abroad. Using your local reference library as a starting point, consult the international trade yearbooks, which list companies worldwide. Such yearbooks include the *Advertisers' Annual, Bankers' Almanac and Yearbook, Flight Directory of British Aviation, Insurance Directory and Yearbook, Oil and Gas International Yearbook,* and many others in the same vein.

Other useful books in your library include the *Europa Yearbook,* which lists international organisations and each country's principal banks, universities, radio and TV stations, and newspapers; *The World of Learning* (also published by Europa) which gives learned societies, research institutes and universities; and the country-by-country tourist guides (such as *Michelin, Fodor's, Blue*), if you want to work in a hotel, restaurant, theatre, museum or art gallery.

Foreign telephone directories clearly offer the widest range of addresses. Embassies stock their own national directories, and a large selection is usually available for reference at major reference libraries, such as *Westminster Central Reference Library,* St. Martin's Street, London WC2; *Holborn Library,* 32 Theobalds Road, London WC1 and the *City Business Library,* Basinghall Street, London EC2, or those situated in Manchester, Birmingham, Sheffield and Glasgow. These libraries are a general source of all kinds of useful information, and hold a collection of *Kompass Registers,* which contain lists of the major commercial enterprises classified by country and by type of product. Another valuable collection of trade and telephone directories is held by the *Statistics and Market Intelligence Library* at the Department of Trade and Industry, 1-19 Victoria Street, London SW1H 0ET.

OVERSEAS SUBSIDIARIES

British Subsidiaries

The overseas branches or subsidiaries of British firms might be able to provide work in one of two ways. Direct application is one method. The other is to join the firm in Britain and then ask to be transferred abroad. A school leaver who starts as a managerial trainee has the best chance of eventually being posted abroad. A good knowledge of the language and local conditions is almost always a pre-requisite for such a transfer. Short lists of the major British enterprise in European countries are included at the end of their respective chapters in *Worldwide Employment,* but more complete and up to date lists can sometimes be obtained from the British Chambers of Commerce in these countries. Where such lists exist, either separately or as part of Chamber of Commerce Yearbooks, details are also given in the individual chapters of *Worldwide Employment.*

If you are unwilling to part with your money for these lists, consult the book *Who Owns Whom,* which is available in many public reference libraries. However, this book is not arranged by countries. Chamber of Commerce Yearbooks are sometimes included on general reference library shelves, but more likely sources are the special business libraries whose addresses are given above under *Direct Application.*

American Subsidiaries

The overseas subsidiaries of American parent companies might also be able to offer work, but the chances are not as good as with British firms. Because of the vast scale of US business enterprise abroad, subsidiaries have not been listed, but some American Chambers of Commerce publish lists, about which details are given in *Worldwide Employment,* wherever relevant. Lists of American parent and subsidiary companies are also published country by country, by the *World Trade Academy Press Inc.,* 50 East 42nd Street, New York, N.Y., 10017, at prices ranging from $5 to $30. They also publish the 2,500 page *Directory of American Firms Operating in Foreign Countries,* 10th edition for $175. Prices exclude postage. Addresses of American parent and subsidiary companies are also included in the book *Who Owns Whom,* available as above.

Foreign Subsidiaries in Britain

The British branches, subsidiaries, and affiliates of foreign based firms may also be worth approaching. Addresses of these British based foreign firms are available through the Commercial Section of the relevant Embassy in London, or through the relevant foreign Trade Centres and Associations, whose addresses may be found in the London Telephone Directory.

TRADE UNIONS AND PROFESSIONAL ASSOCIATIONS

Most unions will be able to advise their members on employment prospects and conditions abroad, and in some cases they may put you in touch with foreign employers or sister unions.

Similarly, most professional associations can offer some kind of help in the search for work abroad. Such help may include an appointments service that covers vacancies abroad; advice on foreign registration requirements or extra examinations that have to be passed; an "in-house" publication that contains advertisements for overseas jobs; an information service on working conditions abroad; or a service providing introductory letters to sister associations or even direct introductions to potential employers abroad. Most professional associations will offer some or all of this assistance to their members; very few go out of their way to help non-members.

For a comprehensive list of British professional associations, readers are advised to consult the book *Trade Associations and Professional Bodies of the United Kingdom,* edited by Patricia Millard. An equally useful source is *Professional Organisations in the Commonwealth,* edited by A. Tett and J. Chadwick. Both books are available in public reference libraries.

Information on some of these professional associations appears at the end of the relevant chapter in the *Specific Careers* section.

EMPLOYMENT SERVICE: THE ICV AND SEDOC SCHEMES

Britain is a member of the Organisation for Economic Co-operation and Development (OECD), which runs a scheme for the "international clearing of vacancies" (ICV) in conjunction with all EC countries and Austria, Norway and Sweden. Under this scheme, anybody seeking employment in these countries for at least three, and in most cases six or more, months can apply at their nearest Jobcentre in the UK.

Unfortunately, the Overseas Placing Unit of the *Employment Service* (address below), which co-ordinates the scheme through local Jobcentres, advises that, because ICV member states share serious unemployment problems in similar areas, chances of getting work through the scheme are currently slim. Only in cases where candidates have skills positively identified as being in short supply, relevant work experience and a good command of the local language, are they likely to succeed.

The employment services of the EC member states also co-operate in exchanging applications for, and offers of, employment within the EC (the so-called SEDOC system) which applies to jobs lasting six months or more. The employment services draw up and circulate a monthly list of vacancies in their own countries, together with detailed job descriptions, available at local Jobcentres. Prospects of work under the SEDOC system are better than those under the ICV scheme, provided that the applicant has the right qualifications.

The ES issues a free leaflet called *Working Abroad* outlining the ICV scheme, and containing tips on questions to ask before accepting job offers, available from local Jobcentres.

Although general information on both schemes is also available from the Overseas Placing Unit, Employment Service, PP4 Rockingham House, 123 West Street, Sheffield S1 4ER, particular inquiries should be directed to local Jobcentres, where an application form can be obtained.

Prospective applicants interested in particular towns or regions within the EC should contact the relevant National Employment Agency administrative head offices, which will supply lists of local employment centres. Addresses of these head offices are listed in the specific country chapters in the section *Worldwide Employment.*

The ES also runs the Professional and Executive Register (PER) for those possessing HNC diploma level qualifications or above. Enrolment is at local Jobcentres. PER issues a free weekly magazine, *Executive Post,* which contains hundreds of vacancy notices, including occasional notices for overseas positions. There are plans to privatise PER.

GOVERNMENT AGENCIES

Considering the worldwide unemployment situation, it is hardly surprising that most governments do not wish to promote immigrant labour. Therefore most embassies and high commissions in this country are unsympathetic towards job-seekers in their respective countries. However, some diplomatic missions act as intermediaries between employers and potential emigrants, or at least run information services and occasional recruitment drives. These include the Canadian, Australian and New Zealand High Commissions, for details of which, see these countries' separate chapters. Also, the embassies from some of the Arab States of the Middle East sometimes place advertisements in the national press. Below are some active missions in the field of recruitment:

Brunei High Commission
49 Cromwell Road, London SW7 2ED.

Nigeria High Commission (Recruitment Section)
9 Northumberland Avenue, London WC2N 5DX.

High Commission for Sierra Leone
33 Portland Place, London W1N 3AG.

High Commissioner for Malawi
33 Grosvenor Street, London W1X 0HS.

High Commissioner for the Republic of Zambia
Zambia House, 2 Palace Gate, London W8 5NG.

Hong Kong Government Office
6 Grafton St., London W1X 3LB.

Although needs obviously change from year to year, the most common personnel requirements are for experienced professionals for administrative and advisory positions both in government departments and in statutory corporations like railways, electricity supply commissions, etc.

The other governments that are interested in promoting imported labour are almost exclusively from the developing countries. The work is usually on two- or three-year contracts, since the ultimate plans are to phase out foreign staff in favour of native workers. Much of the recruitment for these countries is therefore for training and advisory appointments. Recruitment is usually channelled through appointed departments in Britain. Apart from the organisations listed below, organisations that only recruit teaching staff are listed under *Teaching*.

Staff designated by the British government to posts in the poorer developing countries are assured adequate renumeration and working conditions because of the supplementation schemes whereby the British government provides specific financial assistance.

The International Manpower Procurement Executive (Room 376) at the *Overseas Development Administration* (address below) can be contacted for a number of useful free booklets such as *Opportunities Overseas in International Organisations, Why Not Serve Overseas, Careers in the Geological Sciences, Associate Professional Officers Scheme* and *Opportunities in Education Overseas.*

Overseas Development Administration, Abercrombie House, Eaglesham Road, East Kilbride, Glasgow G75 8EA — the Recruitment Executive of ODA recruits mainly for public service posts in developing countries. Opportunities exist in various fields; agriculture, education, fisheries, accountancy, engineering, customs, mining, law, surveying, telecommunications. ODA tries to encourage people with suitable qualifications and experience to serve overseas (usually on 2-3 year contracts), as part of their professional careers.

The *International Manpower Procurement Executive* of ODA, at the above address, assists in the recruitment of British specialists for the field programmes of the United Nations and its specialised Agencies e.g. FAO and the International Labour Office.

Crown Agents for Overseas Governments and Administration, St Nicholas House, St Nicholas Road, Sutton, Surrey SM1 1EL — are a long established public body providing a recruitment service to over 100 governments and 200 public authorities mainly in the third world. Most appointments are in East and Southern Africa, the Middle East and the Western Pacific, and are normally for a tour of 2-3 years on a contract basis. Suitably trained and qualified professional and technical personnel are most needed in the fields of accountancy and audit, professional and sub-professional engineering (civil, electrical and mechanical), law, medicine and nursing, surveying and veterinary science. Vacancies are advertised as they arise in the national press, and in the appropriate technical and professional journals, although they do retain some lists of specialised staff seeking posts overseas.

The *Overseas Development Institute,* Regent's College, Inner Circle, Regent's Park, London NW1 4NS — runs the ODI Fellowship Scheme whereby recent graduates in economics and allied fields from British and Irish universities work for two years in the public sectors of developing countries in Africa, the Caribbean and the Pacific. Candidates must have (or be studying for) a postgraduate qualification and/or some relevant work experience. About 17 Fellowships are awarded annually. Application forms are available each September from ODI or from University Careers Advisory Offices.

The *Overseas Development Natural Resources Institute,* Central Avenue, Chatham Maritime, Kent ME4 4TE — is the scientific unit of the Overseas Development Administration. Formed in 1987 by the integration of the Tropical Development and Research Institute (TDRI) and the Land Resources Development Centre (LRDC), it provides technical assistance to developing countries through promoting the sustainable development of their natural resources sector. The operational staff of the Institute cover a range of specialist activities, the main ones being agriculture, entomology, food technology, engineering and economics. Recruitment is carried out by the Civil Service Commission, Alencon Link, Basingstoke, Hampshire RG21 1JB.

CONSULTANTS AND AGENCIES

The process of applying for long term overseas work through management recruitment consultants (MRC's) and employment agencies provides a better chance of success than any of the other methods of the conventional job search mentioned so far.

There is much discussion as to what constitutes an employment agency and what constitutes a management recruitment consultant. In some cases, the dividing line is hard to define, but the difference lies mainly in the types of personnel being recruited. Management recruitment consultants aim for the higher income brackets — executives, management and professional staff, particularly engineers and those in related trades; the usual age range is 25-55, often narrower, and the minimum qualification is HNC or equivalent. Agencies, on the other hand, find work for secretaries, nurses, domestic staff and au pairs, as well as temporary clerical and industrial workers. Also, there is usually a difference in the approach to the problems of recruitment: management consultants usually provide a much more thorough and complete service in matching the right person to the right job.

Agencies and consultants are all brought together under the Employment Agencies Act 1973, which came into effect in 1976. With some exceptions (see the *Au Pair and Domestic* chapter for details), this forbids agencies (and consultants) from charging a fee for finding someone a job. The agencies' clients must therefore be the employing companies, from whom the agencies are allowed to obtain money in exchange for providing staff. Management consultants have always adopted this policy, but the law has hit hard at some of the employment agencies which used to charge registration fees to job applicants. In many cases, particularly in the field of au pairs and domestic staff, employment agencies have either been forced out of business, or at least withdrawn from the international labour market, fraught as it is with the complications of raising money from companies or individuals based abroad. The Act obviously does not apply to foreign agencies, many of which, especially those involved in au pair and domestic positions, still charge fees to applicants.

The following section lists management recruitment consultants which cover a broad range of opportunities and cannot therefore be easily placed under the relevant chapter in the *Specific Careers* section. Employment agencies, alternatively, tend to be career-specific and will therefore be found in such chapters as *Au Pair and Domestic, Medicine and Nursing* and *Secretarial, Translating and Interpreting.*

Additionally, some of the more helpful foreign based agencies and consultants may be located under the individual country chapters in the section *Worldwide Employment,* along with a few British agencies that operate only in one or two countries.

Management Recruitment Consultants

Because management recruitment consultants (or "head-hunters") operate mostly on behalf of the company offering work, their approach to job applicants can vary considerably from one company to another. Since consultants have a steady stream of job offers on their books, many also have a permanent register of job applicants, so that they can match up the applicants on file with new vacancies as they arise.

Apart from keeping a register, very few consultants nowadays operate actively on behalf of the applicant. This is because, unlike employment agencies, their main task is to find people for the jobs and not jobs for the people. In a typical case, some 70% of their business is search/headhunting, the remainder being advertised positions. Moreover, those MRC's which do keep registers already have a disproportionate number of applicants on their books. For this reason, only candidates seeking positions at an above average level of management are encouraged to forward their particulars.

Below is a select list of those MRC's which still seek to encourage speculative applications for a broad range of overseas management executive positions. A full list can be found in the London Yellow Pages, under *Employment Agencies and Consultants.*

Angel ASB International Recruitment, 70-71 New Bond Street, London W1Y 9DE — offers contract and permanent job opportunities in accountancy, banking, catering and hotels, leisure, computing, engineering, insurance, law, medicine, nursing, commerce, office and secretarial, sales, marketing and media, teaching and lecturing, trade and industry, as well as travel. Contracts may vary from 3 months to 3 years, but the majority are for 2 years. Applicants are required to present a comprehensive CV.

Campbell Birch Executive Recruitment, Parr House, 52 Broadway,

Bracknell, Berks. RG12 1AG — recruits for international organisations in the commercial sector in the fields of electronic engineering, software engineering/programming, technical and sales support, research and development, sales and marketing, general management and technology consultants. Applicants must have several years experience.

Eagle Recruitment, Eagle Place, 210-212 Piccadilly, London W1V 9LD — specialises in multilingual recruitment for all types of permanent and temporary work — whether managerial, secretarial or technical — across a wide range of professional, commercial and media employment, mostly in Europe. Applicants combining language ability with technical or professional skills are matched against a large number of vacancies, and suitable candidates are offered an initial interview with a multilingual consultant. Assistance is also given on curriculum vitae presentation and interview techniques.

Echo Consulting Services Ltd., Braconash Road, Leyland, Preston, Lancs. PR5 1ZE — the UK recruitment agency for Al Hoty Establishment in Saudi Arabia, a service organisation to ARAMCo (Arabian American Oil Co). Echo also recruits for other Middle East companies on an *ad hoc* basis. All disciplines are covered except medical staff, for positions in the Middle East, Europe and internationally.

ERP International, 310 Chester Road, Hartford Northwich, Cheshire CW8 2AB — the overseas recruitment company associated with *John*

Courtis & Partners — a broad spectrum of opportunities, particularly in the Middle East, where appointments are covered for almost every commercial and industrial form of enterprise.

Executive Search International Ltd., 8A Symons Street, Sloane Square, London SW3 2TJ — specialise in Board, senior executive and middle management appointments worldwide.

J.G. Associates (UK) Ltd., 5 Market Street, Bridgend, Mid. Glamorgan, Wales CF31 1LL — worldwide procurement and contract specialists for professional construction staff, electronic engineers/computer staff, secretarial and medical staff. Contract periods range from 3 months to 24 months, with a one year renewable basis.

Sabre International Search, Seymour House, 17 Shouldham Street, London W1H 5AA — a general executive consultancy which is not restricted by industry or functional boundaries. Branch offices and sister companies are in North and South America, the Far East, and Europe.

F. J. Selleck Associates (UK) Ltd., Prospect House, 17 North Hill, Colchester, CO1 1DZ — recruits professional and technical staff on a contract basis worldwide, although the Middle East predominates. Contracts are renewable annually. Applicants must be 23/25 years or older and should have a BSc degree or City and Guilds Diploma.

Systematic Management Search S.A., Bahnhofstrasse 69, 8001 Zurich — specialists in the search for Top and Senior Executives on an international basis. Company owned subsidiaries in Düsseldorf and Los Angeles. Associated partner companies in Paris, London, Amsterdam, Brussels, New York, Chicago, Dallas, and Calgary.

J. Watson Sanderson Ltd., Moorings House, Heathfield Road, Woking, Surrey GU22 7JG — international recruitment specialists in the following disciplines: civil and chemical engineering, building and building service, computing, horticulture, hydrographic surveying, mining, petro-chemical, property development, on/off shore installations, and soil mechanics. Other related fields are to a lesser extent also catered for.

Further information on recruitment consultants and agencies dealing with overseas recruitment can be obtained from the *Federation of Recruitment and Employment Services Ltd.,* 10 Belgrave Square, London SW1X 8PH.

In addition, the *CEPEC Recruitment Guide,* produced by the Centre for Professional Employment Counselling, Sundrige Park Management Centre, Plaistow Lane, Bromley BR1 3JW, lists approximately 300 recruitment agencies and search consultants in the UK, about half of which will undertake assignments abroad. The guide is available in reference libraries or from the above address.

STUDENT WORKING EXCHANGES

Generally, student exchange schemes are either cultural or vocational in nature, although the distinction between these two types will become blurred where cultural exchanges lead to employment "spin-offs". Those interested in short term cultural exchange programmes, may contact the *Youth Exchange Centre, Seymour Mews House, Seymour Mews, London W1H 9PE* which can supply information about exchange schemes and grants. Cultural Youth Exchanges with the Commonwealth are handled by the *Commonwealth Youth Exchange Council,* 18 Fleet Street, London EC4Y 1AA.

This section deals with a number of vocation-oriented student exchange schemes, which provide opportunities for interested students to gain practical experience of working abroad. Details of the *British Universities North America Club (BUNAC),* and *Camp America* appear in the short term work section of the USA chapter. The *Project Trust* voluntary exchange scheme is referred to in the *Voluntary Work* chapter.

Details of the *International Farm Experience Programme* appear in the chapter on *Agriculture and Conservation;* and the CRAC exchange scheme with Australia and New Zealand is included under the *Specific Contacts* sections of the chapters on *Australia* and *New Zealand.*

AIESEC (International Association for Students of Economics and Management), UKIN House, 26 Phipp Street, London EC2A 4NR — arranges career orientated positions for students of economics, business and commerce related disciplines who are active members of the 28 local branches in the UK. Further information can be obtained from the address above.

The Central Bureau for Educational Visits and Exchanges, Seymour Mews House, Seymour Mews, London W1H 9PE — runs the Language Assistant Scheme which enables modern language students from Britain and over 30 other countries to spend a year working in a school or college in a country where their target language is spoken. Appointments as Junior Language Assistants are also available in France, the Federal Republic of Germany and Spain for school leavers intending to study French, German or Spanish at an institution of higher education.

European Community Young Worker Exchange Programme, Commission of the European Communities DGVC, rue de la Loi 200, B-1049 Brussels, Belgium — allows for young people aged 18-28 who are nationals of the European Community and have had vocational training, to take part in short-term (3 weeks — 3 months) or long-term (up to 6 months) projects in other member countries. Living expenses and up to 75% of travel costs are covered. Longer term projects also include language training.

UK applicants should apply to the Central Bureau, Vocational and Training Education Department, Seymour Mews House, Seymour Mews, London W1H 9PE.

GAP Activity Projects Limited, 7 Kings Road, Reading, Berkshire RG1 3AA — GAP arranges work overseas for school leavers during their "gap" year, i.e. after leaving school and before going to University, further education or a career. Some of the countries where they do have placements are Australia (work in schools and farm work), New Zealand (farm work), Israel (mostly work on kibbutzim), the Indian sub continent, and details of what GAP has to offer write to the Secretary of GAP in the autumn before your final examinations.

International Association for the Exchange of Students for Technical Experience (IAESTE), Seymour Mews House, Seymour Mews, London W1H 9PE — arranges an exchange scheme whereby penultimate year students of scientific and technical subjects can spend 8-12 weeks of the summer vacation gaining practical experience abroad. The scheme covers most of Europe, Australia and Canada, USA and several countries throughout the rest of the world. Students should apply through their own institutions which must be affiliated to IAESTE (UK).

Information on specific student-oriented exchange schemes within the EC is available in a useful pamphlet called *A Student's Guide to Europe,* available free from Henley Mailing Services Ltd., Tavistock Industrial Estate, Ruscombe Lane, Twyford, Berks.

Students interested in gaining short term practical experience in a wide range of employment categories in the USA should consult *Interships,* a directory which provides an excellent list of over 16,000 on-the-job training opportunities in everything from advertising to social services in that country, see the bibliography for details.

OTHER OPPORTUNITIES

Expats International Ltd., 62 Tritton Road, London SE21 8DE — An organisation which advises its members of jobs abroad, and recruitment agencies of expatriates looking for work abroad. A monthly magazine, *Home and Away,* is sent out to members, which includes a supplement listing jobs in Africa, Asia, Europe, the Far East, the Middle East and South America. The jobs cover all disciplines, although most tend to be on the technical side. A regularly updated list of overseas employers is also sent to members, together with their addresses and contact details. Expats International can also advise on legal and tax issues. The annual subscription charge is £60.

Leesons Employment and Accommodation Data Service, 4 Cranley Road, Newbury Park, Ilford, Essex IG2 6AG — provides an information service to those looking for work in Australia, New Zealand, South Africa, Canada and the USA. Although not an employment agency, LEADS can provide a list of names and addresses of companies and employment agencies/ consultants in any particular area in these countries, together with advice on work permits and help with the job application process. The cost for this service is £38 (£46 in Ireland).

The Creative Job Search

"The creative job search" is a phrase for an extremely effective way of getting a job. It is a method which requires a lot of skill, daring and panache. The technique originated in North America, and is particularly productive for those who are prepared to use it in the search for work abroad.

The success of the creative job search depends on the realisation that there are thousands of jobs available which are not publicly advertised. Recruitment for these jobs takes place on an informal basis, through a network of contacts who pass job availability information to each other by word of mouth. The objective of the creative job seeker is to make the most of his existing contacts whilst simultaneously building up a network of new contacts, through either of which he may be able to get work. Of course, the method is not a new one, but it's the difference of approach and emphasis which counts.

You have to become highly knowledgeable about yourself, your own abilities, aptitudes, interests and inclinations. Analysing your own employment potential requires a sustained introspective realism that most of us shy away from. The goals you are seeking are worth the sacrifice.

You also have to become extremely well-informed about a particular job area and, if you intend to concentrate your search on a specific country, you will have to learn its language, and come to understand its politics, economy and society.

In particular, you need to know what the overseas work you want involves, which abilities are needed, how recruitment in that field takes place and who is responsible for it. You have to place yourself within the network of contacts throughout which most "invisible" (i.e. not publicly advertised) recruiting takes place. You have to convince your contacts that you understand the special problems of that particular kind of work, and that you have the skills to solve them. These are not easily achieved objectives, but then neither is getting a long term job or career abroad an easy task. But if you follow the rules of the creative job search effectively, your chances of getting a permanent job abroad will be greatly increased.

Discovering your own employment potential (see chapter acquiring detailed knowledge about the particular field of w interests you are the first steps on the road to getting a job ab

The next step in the creative job search is to realise that, whilst the conventional methods outlined above may well be necessary conditions of success, they will rarely of themselves be entirely sufficient. This is because they presuppose two mistaken views about the character of the job market. The first is the view that all those jobs which are available are always publicly advertised; and the second is the mistaken belief that all such vacancies are given, and cannot, consequently, be created. The golden rule of the creative job search is that publicly advertised vacancies (including positions circulated through consultants and agencies) are just the tip of the job market iceberg.

JOBS WHICH ARE NOT PUBLICLY ADVERTISED

Every month, thousands of jobs become available which are never advertised in the national press or notified to Jobcentres, recruitment consultants or agencies.

Some of these vacancies appear in the House Journals or on the notice-boards of the various organisations which sponsor them. A typical example is the BBC's "in-house" newspaper, *Ariel,* which every week lists up to 50 journalistically oriented jobs which never appear in the national papers.

Many vacancies, however, are not even advertised on this restricted basis, but are circulated instead by word of mouth through a system of well established (and therefore more reliable) contacts. For many employers, advertising employment is an administrative and financial headache which they would rather avoid. Nationally advertised vacancies are not only expensive, but a lot of bureaucratic time and energy is spent assessing and replying to applications. The standard job interview itself is felt by many organisations to be a somewhat haphazard and ineffective means of selection.

Potential employers will therefore tend to by-pass the traditional methods of selection where possible, especially if they already have someone in mind whom they have met and know to be properly equipped, well-informed and enthusiastic about working for them.

JOBS WHICH ARE CREATED

Not all jobs, whether at home or abroad, actually exist before they are filled. Some are actually created, rather than offered.

Some managers are prepared to consider any constructive problem-solving ideas and to employ new people to execute them, provided they can be persuaded that they have chosen the right person. The potential scope here for the properly qualified and persuasive job seeker is enormous.

A good example of one way to create a job abroad is to convince an employer of the great advantages of taking on an English speaking person in order to promote his international trade. Such a case might arise in places like Hong Kong or Singapore, where English is the language of business and administration, and where there may not be many fluent English speakers of the right calibre in the labour market.

Even in countries where English speakers abound, the advantages of having an English accent could prove crucial in either getting or creating a job. An advertising firm in the USA or Canada might certainly be persuaded of the value of having someone with an English accent deal with prospective clients. Alternatively, a television station in New Zealand might decide that it was beneficial to have a newscaster who spoke the Queen's English. And a secondary school in Japan might be persuaded to hire an English born foreign language teacher as well as — or instead of — an American.

JOINING THE NETWORK

Once you have discovered your employment potential, and have realised the enormous number of "invisible" vacancies which are actually available, you will be in a strong position to begin the most vital stage of the creative job search — making visits and establishing contacts in your prospective area of employment.

Of course, this will be difficult if you are looking for work in Sweden, Greece or South Korea. The process of cultivating contacts is a slow one and you may have to take up temporary residence in the country of your choice while you undertake the task, see the section on *Short Term Work Abroad* for details.

There are three stages involved in the process of widening the range of people you can visit who may be in a position to offer you a job. First, you have to develop a network of intermediaries and referees who can put you in touch with your target contacts; then you must arrange to go and see these contacts; and finally, you have to know how to handle the meeting (or creative job search interview) with them, and how to follow it up most effectively.

Intermediaries and Referees

Draw up a select list of the people you want to contact. It's best if you can find a referee to go through-somebody who is known to both you and the target contact. When you ring him or her up you can say "your name was given to me by so-and-so (your intermediary) who said that you could give me some useful advice about the type of overseas work I am interested in". This approach means that if your target contact refuses to see you, he is also casting a bad light on your intermediary — and if the contact is worth anything at all this will be very unlikely.

But how do you find referees or intermediaries for jobs which are overseas? For conventional job seekers, the buck stops here. This is because the limits of their job search are the limits of their imagination. The creative job seeker, on the other hand, will actively exploit a host of possible connections in order to locate his target contacts. These include your:

* parents and relations
* friends and their parents and relations
* past or present school/college/university heads and subject teachers
* past or present school/college/university associates
* members of your church, political party, and fellow members of any social or sports club

* family doctor or solicitor
* bank/building society manager
* local councillor, MP or Euro MP
* past or present work boss or colleagues

When you see these people you can ask them "Can you help me get advice about working abroad? Do you know anybody who has been or, even better, is currently working overseas? Or do you know anyone who knows anyone who is"?

These intermediaries or referees may be able to put you in touch with target contacts who can help you get a long term job abroad. Such contacts, who may also of course be sought out directly, will typically include:

* members of foreign Trade Associations, for example, the Italian Trade Centre in London, or the British Chamber of Commerce for Italy in Milan (see the chapter on *Italy* for details)
* members of your local Chamber of Commerce who have connections with foreign based national Chambers of Commerce. Good examples include the Chambers of Commerce of Birmingham, City of Westminster, Wales, Leicester, London, Manchester and Southampton, which are all members of the Franco British Chamber of Commerce and Industry in Paris (see the chapter on *France* for details)
* members of foreign Residents' Associations, for example the Anglo-German Association, or the British Residents' Association of Switzerland (see the chapter on *Switzerland* for details)
* managers and employees of British based branches, affiliates and subsidiaries of foreign firms (see the section *Overseas Subsidiaries* above)

Visits and Contacts

The first thing to emphasise about arranging visits to potential employers or contacts (whose organisations do not advertise the vacancies you are ultimately seeking) is that they should never be presented as visits to obtain a job. They are initially and primarily visits to find out what the jobs you are interested in are like. Your prime objective is to get a personal interview with someone professionally involved in the field you are investigating. If you ask them for a job they may be unable to help you — and therefore unwilling to see you. But if you ask them for a few minutes of their time, at their convenience, to ask their advice about the work they are doing and how to go about looking for jobs in that field, then they are much more than likely to acquiesce. And if they don't, there will normally be somebody else in the same or a similar organisation who will be willing to see you.

Another golden rule for the creative job seeker is that sending off the c.v. and covering letter (see bibliography for details of books dealing with this) is a preliminary to the all important personal visit. If, as is often the case these days, the letter of enquiry is not answered within two weeks, make telephone contact with the target person and arrange to come and see him or her within a few days. Of course, the more aggressive and determined job seekers will begin the process with such a phone call, but it is always advisable to back it up immediately with a written enquiry. Either way, the potential contact has experienced you on two separate occasions and is therefore not as likely to have forgotten you when you arrive on his doorstep.

The Creative Job Search Interview

Unlike the ordinary job interview, the creative job search interview should be seen more as a discussion about the general possibilities of your getting work, rather than a specific application for a specific job. In this sense your meeting with your target contact will be something of a ruse: you have to give him the impression that, whilst you are very keen to get the kind of work which he or she is involved in, you appreciate that he may not be in a position to offer you a job immediately. There is a fine line to be drawn here, and presentation is the name of the game.

Nevertheless, once you've located the target contact and arranged an interview according to the procedure outlined above, you're already a sprightly step ahead of the competition and your chances of achieving your goals have multiplied inestimably. And that is real cause for the confidence needed at the interview.

You should arrive at the interview having properly researched both the organisation and the particular job in which you are interested so that your target contact perceives you as a knowledgeable and keen person over whom it is worth taking time and trouble.

You should press politely, but firmly, for specific details about the day-to-day aspects of the job. Ask your contact how he or she got their job and how their previous work experience may have helped them. What kind of educational or vocational qualifications did they think helped them get where they are today? Ask about the positive and the negative aspects of the job, and about promotion possibilities. What kinds of skill and attitudes make for a successful integration within the work environment?

These basic questions should keep your contact on his toes and impress upon him your genuine interest in the job. Towards the end of the discussion, if things have gone well, it might be worth enquiring how, if someone from your background was to apply, they would be viewed by prospective employers. From the answer to this question, you may be able to gather how closely you ought to keep in touch with this particular contact in the future.

Whether or not you do get a job as a result of your creative job search interview, it is vital that you collect from your contact a short list of other target contacts in your field of interest. From these you should be able to obtain still further contacts.

If you are working effectively, you should quickly know, and become known by, a large number of key people in your area of employment interest. In other words, you will have achieved in a very short time what takes most people years: you will have become a link in the chain of contacts through which non-publicly advertised vacancies are circulated. Writing thank you letters after each contact interview, and developing mentors by keeping in regular touch with a select number of helpful contacts will also increase your chances of success.

Further information about the methods of the creative job search is available in the book *What Color is Your Parachute?* — see the bibliography for details.

SHORT TERM WORK ABROAD

The really determined job seeker will be able to exploit, methodically and enthusiastically, the procedures of both conventional and creative job search methods outlined above. If he or she is in fact properly qualified for the job which is sought, a satisfactory overseas position will eventually be found.

For those who are prepared to leave the country before finding work (and for many this might be the only chance) however, there is a third and final way of getting work abroad. This is to apply the techniques of both conventional and creative job searches on the spot. The best way of doing this may be to take on some short term work in the country you are interested in so that you can support yourself and develop your network of contacts simultaneously.

Taking on a temporary job in a foreign country should, then, get you closer to the "permanent" job you are looking for. Job seeking in the EC countries can be easier than in most countries, because of the directive allowing UK citizens to spend three months in any Common Market member state looking for work. Very few other countries permit this, unless, of course, you are entitled to residence for other reasons.

Even if it is not in your own line of work a temporary job will at least get you in a position from which you can keep an eye on vacancies that are more suitable in newspapers and through employment agencies. Employers who would not consider summoning somebody from another country for an interview will look more favourably on someone who lives locally. You will also, of course, be able to improve your knowledge of the local language and get a taste of the way of life as well as getting some idea of how you can cope with being a semi-exile from home.

The majority of the short term jobs available to foreigners anywhere do not require any specific skills or qualifications except enthusiasm and, often, a willingness to work for less money than a local worker would expect and some knowledge of the local language. This sort of work is largely to do with agriculture, the tourist industry, or voluntary work: all of these are areas which call for large numbers of unskilled workers for a short time each year (often, but by no means always, in the summer). These jobs tend to survive despite high rates of local unemployment because they only offer a temporary solution to it. To use an example from Britain, an unemployed docker in Liverpool with a family to support will normally concentrate his energies on looking for another permanent job, rather than leave them for two weeks to go picking strawberries in nearby Cheshire for a minimal wage.

The business of finding temporary work is a complex one that is covered in detail in a series of books with self explanatory titles: *Summer Jobs Abroad, Work Your Way Around the World, The Summer Employment Directory of the United States, Working in Ski Resorts — Europe* and *Working Holidays,* etc., see the bibliography for full details. In this book we give brief details of the opportunities to be found in each country, and mention the main organisations that can help you to find work.

There are three basic ways in which you can find a temporary job: you can write directly to potential employers from home: you can contact employment agencies or organisations that can find a job for you; or you can go abroad, judge the current employment situation for yourself, and start knocking on doors. The *Specific Careers* section of this book covers those approaches to finding work that are applicable to several countries, such as writing to national tourist offices to obtain lists of hotels that may be able to offer employment, and lists those organisations that are helpful in more than one country. The chapters in the *Worldwide Employment* section cover those aspects of temporary work that are unique to that country: what and where the opportunities are, whether you will need a work permit or not, and tell you how to approach looking for work there.

Rules and Regulations

IMMIGRATION REQUIREMENTS

With worldwide unemployment reaching record proportions, very few countries actively encourage immigration, and most have very strict entry requirements which involve a lot of planning. Common requirements are that applicants should have a positive job offer, be able to speak the language, and have pre-arranged accommodation. Anyone seeking work abroad is strongly advised to request up-to-date information from the appropriate embassy in London, before making any plans. Addresses of embassies and high commissions are listed in the telephone directory.

Entry into the European Community

The European Community (EC), to give it its proper title, was set up in 1957 by the Treaty of Rome, signed by "the Six" — France, West Germany, Italy, the Netherlands, Belgium and Luxembourg, which established the European Economic Community (EEC) and the European Atomic Energy Community (Euratom). In 1967 these institutions were merged with the existing European Coal and Steel Community (ECSC) to create the European Community as it is known today. The UK, Ireland and Denmark joined in January 1973, Greece entered in January 1981, while the inclusion of Spain and Portugal in January 1986 brought the total membership to twelve. For the moment, no further expansion is envisaged until after 1992, when the single European Market will have been completed (see below), although Austria and Turkey have both expressed an interest in joining.

The aims of the EC are varied, but the most dominant is the creation of a free-trade zone enveloping all member states. This is of great importance to industries looking for an export market. More important, however, for the purposes of this book at least, are some of the secondary aims, and in particular the policy of free movement of labour, which cuts out the need for work permits and entitles foreign workers to the same employment conditions and benefits as nationals.

It should be pointed out that the abolition of work permits has not magically opened up a brand new labour market, and actually finding a job can still be as difficult, in Denmark and Italy, for instance, as it was before 1973. In addition, workers may find that their educational and professional qualifications are not automatically accepted outside the UK. This should change however; the signing of the Single European Act by the 12 member states in February 1986 has ratified the 1985 White Paper published by the European Commission, which set out the necessary programme to complete the European Market by 1992. By this date there should be no physical, technical or financial barriers to movement within the EC. Instead, an integrated market of some 320 million people will come into being, with equivalent legislation in each member country concerning the rules of trade, employment, and pay. Among other things, this will introduce mutual recognition among the member states of academic and professional qualifications, allowing professional people to practice in other EC countries as well, and also allow apprentices to obtain their vocational training qualifications anywhere in the EC.

At the moment negotiations between professional institutions of member countries have led to mutual recognition being established for architects, dentists, doctors, lawyers, midwives, nurses, pharmacists and veterinary surgeons. Freedom of movement has also been made easier in the mining, electricity, gas, oil and water industries, as well as in the fields of agriculture, forestry and horticulture. Members of other professions are advised to contact their trade association in this country for information on the acceptability of their qualificiations.

The free movement of labour within the EC applies only to "nationals of member countries". (For Spain and Portugal, the terms of accession to the Community mean that there will not be free movement to or from these countries until 1 January 1993, when the 7 year transitional period has ended).

The introduction of the 1981 British Nationality Act has complicated the issue somewhat by replacing the old category of "British national" with the new category of "British citizen". As a result of the Act, all earlier nationality laws have been replaced by three categories of citizenship:

1. *British Citizenship,* for people closely connected (i.e. settled here, or with a British mother or father) with the United Kingdom, the Channel Islands and the Isle of Man.

2. *British Dependent Territories Citizenship,* for people connected with the dependencies.

3. *British Overseas Citizenship,* for those citizens of the United Kingdom and Colonies who do not have these connections with either the United Kingdom or the dependencies.

The Passport Office advises that free movement of labour within the EEC is granted only to those with British Citizenship (Class 1), who have the right of abode in the UK. The only exception to this is for British Dependent Territories Citizens (Class 2) connected with Gibraltar.

In order to work within the EEC you must also have a valid British passport, not a British visitor's passport. The passport must be either endorsed *Holder has the right of abode in the United Kingdom* or, if issued after 31 December 1982, the passport must show the holder's national status as a British citizen.

Any queries on nationality from people resident in the United Kingdom should be addressed to the *Immigration and Nationality Department,* Lunar House, Wellesley Road, Croydon, CR9 2BY. People resident abroad should contact the nearest British Consulate or British High Commission.

Among the rights of a UK citizen in Europe is the right for his spouse and dependants to join him and enjoy the same privileges as him, including the right to take up employment.

The only other factor that might prevent entry into another member state is money. A foreign worker must show proof that he has sufficient funds to support himself and any dependants accompanying him. A definite job offer usually covers this, but people going to Europe to look for work have been known to be turned back.

Although work permits have become obsolete for EC countries, workers are still liable to the formality of police registration and the issuance of a residence permit. The regulations vary slightly from country to country and details are given in the respective chapter of *Worldwide Employment,* under the heading *Immigration.* One general ruling that applies to all EC countries is that residence permits may be refused unless the applicant has an offer of employment that will last at least three months.

SOCIAL SECURITY

Working in a foreign country normally means joining that country's social security scheme. There are many exceptions to this rule, however, and in certain cases contributions are still payable in Britain. Claims for national insurance benefits can also be complicated where more than one country's scheme is involved. The Department of Health and Social Security publishes a series of leaflets (described below) which are available from the *DHSS Overseas Branch,* Newcastle upon Tyne NE98 1YX. Leaflets CH 5 and CH 6, however, are obtainable from local DHSS offices, which may also be able to provide copies of leaflets NI 38 and SA 40/41.

Leaflet NI 38 *Social Security Abroad,* explains in general terms about cases where there are no reciprocal agreements involved. If you are claiming child benefit, ask for leaflets CH 5 *Child benefit for people entering Britain,* and CH 6 *Child benefit for people leaving Britain.* However, child benefit is only affected if the child goes abroad for more than eight weeks.

European Community Regulations

The rules concerning the EC Social Security Regulations are complex. Get advice from the Overseas Branch of the DHSS should you decide to live or work in another EC country. Details about medical treatment during visits to the other Community Countries are given in leaflets SA 40 *The traveller's guide to health — Before you go* and SA 41 *The traveller's guide to health — While you're away,* while leaflet SA 29 explains *Your social security and pension rights in the European Community.* The DHSS also issues a series of useful guides which explain in basic terms the Social Security arrangements of the other EC member states (a seperate booklet is available for most of the EC countries). Copies are available on application to the DHSS Overseas Branch, address above.

Other Reciprocal Agreements

In addition to the leaflets mentioned above, the following leaflets outline social security agreements between Britain and: *Australia* (SA 5), *Austria* (SA 25), *Bermuda* (SA 25), *Canada* (SA 20), *Cyprus* (SA 12), *Finland* (SA 19), *Iceland* (SA 24), *Israel* (SA 24), *Jamaica* (SA 27), *Jersey* and *Guernsey* (SA 4), *Malta* (SA 11), *Mauritius* (SA 38), *New Zealand* (SA 8), *Norway* (SA 16), *Sweden* (SA 9), *Switzerland* (SA 6), *Turkey* (SA 22) and *USA* (SA 33).

Health agreements covering tourists and short term visitors to a number of countries are set out in Leaflets 40/41.

UNEMPLOYMENT BENEFIT IN EC COUNTRIES

It is not widely known that someone who has been getting unemployment benefit in Britain for more than four weeks can arrange to receive their benefit abroad for up to three months while looking for work in another member country of the EC.

Those wanting to transfer their unemployment benefit abroad should first select the town where they intend to look for work and notify their local unemployment benefit office in this country of their plans. The unemployment benefit office will inform the Overseas Branch of the Department of Health and Social Security who will in turn supply a form, number E303, to be taken to the appropriate unemployment benefit office in the other country. Sometimes, depending on the country concerned, the Overseas Branch sends form E303 direct to the unemployment benefit office in the other country. Form E303 authorises the other state to pay your UK unemployment benefit.

This system involves, in effect, the exporting of UK unemployment benefit. Benefit is paid at the standard UK rate, which may not go far in a country such as Denmark which has a high cost of living. But it is also possible for people who have worked in another EC country and have paid contributions into its unemployment benefit insurance scheme to claim unemployment benefit in that country at that country's rate, which may well be higher than the British rate. The exact details, such as who administers the system and the length of time for which contributions must have been paid, vary from country to country.

Time spent working, and paying contributions, in one EEC country can be credited towards your right towards unemployment benefit if you move on to another EEC country — as long as you have worked and paid contributions in this other country. Thus, someone may work first in Britain and then in Germany, where he may lose his job and begin claiming unemployment benefit: if he then moves on to France he can continue to claim unemployment benefit there, but at the German rate.

TAXATION

The extent of the liability to United Kingdom tax of a person who is temporarily abroad depends on several factors, the principal one being whether the person is classed as resident in the UK for tax purposes. An outline of residence and its effect on tax liability is given in the Inland Revenue's leaflet IR20, *Residents' and Non-Residents' Liability to Tax in the United Kingdom.*

Where a person who is abroad remains resident in the UK for tax purposes, he may in some circumstances be liable to tax both in the UK and in the country which he is visiting. If this happens, however, he can normally claim relief, under a Double Taxation Agreement made between the two countries, from either one tax or the other. Details are given in the Inland Revenue's leaflet IR6, *Double Taxation Relief.*

A person who is abroad but remains liable to UK tax may be able to claim certain expenses of travelling. Details of the rules can be obtained from any local office of the Inspector of Taxes (to find the address of your local office, look in the Telephone Directory under Inland Revenue).

Inland Revenue leaflets are available from any local office of the Inspector of Taxes. Other general enquiries, claims and problems should be addressed to the *Inland Revenue Claims Branch, Foreign Division,* 1st Floor, St John's House, Merton Road, Bootle, Merseyside L69 9BL, or the *Inspector of Foreign Dividends,* Lynwood Road, Thames Ditton, Surrey KT7 0DP.

Learn the Language

Employment in foreign countries usually involves learning the language: many employers refuse to consider applications from prospective employees who speak only English, apart from the few jobs where no communication with people is necessary, in a factory for instance. Even so, it is a help to understand what you are told to do, and life in general abroad will be much easier and more enjoyable if you have some idea of what your neighbours are saying, and can join in conversations.

Some countries, such as Sweden, provide special courses and classes for foreign workers, and once abroad, most people pick up essential words and phrases. But if you want to learn the language before you go, here are a few ideas:

LOCAL COURSES

Most technical colleges, polytechnics and colleges of further education, workers' educational associations and adult education centres run part-time and evening courses in a number of foreign languages. These classes can be very cheap, but unless an intensive course is taken, learning can be slow.

CILT

The *Centre for Information on Language Teaching and Research (CILT),* Regent's College, Inner Circle, Regent's Park, London NW1 4NS, publishes a series of *Languages and Culture Guides* (price £3.50-£4.50), providing information on the available range of resources for many of the languages taught in the UK, including the courses available to learn the languages. The series also includes some of the less commonly taught languages about which information is often difficult to obtain.

PRIVATE SCHOOLS

There are large numbers of private language schools offering anything from correspondence courses with records to intensive (and expensive) four-week stays in the native land of the language, complete with private tutor. The following list is certainly not comprehensive, nor should it be thought specifically to recommend the schools mentioned.

Berlitz Schools of Languages Ltd., 79 Wells Street, 321 Oxford Street, London W1A 3BZ (and many provincial towns) — have native tutors to teach almost any language under the sun. Courses range from leisurely group tuition (up to eight students in a group) to the Total Immersion course. Private tuition can be arranged at times and schedules to suit the student, or given in the form of a crash course of six hours a day, five days a week. In-company tuition can be given to groups of up to 12 people in the same company, or executive crash courses can be arranged for groups of 3 or 4 people.

Euro-Academy (Outbound) Ltd., 77a George Street, Croyden CRO 1LD — offer a number of schools abroad where languages can be learnt on location. Vacation Courses and All Year Courses for young people (12-26 years) and adults at: Nice and Paris in France; Munich and Wiesbaden in West Germany; Malaga and Valencia in Spain; Florence in Italy and Lisbon in Portugal. Executive Crash Courses are also available at all levels.

Eurocentres, 56 Eccleston Square, London, SW1V 1PQ, is a non-profitmaking Foundation registered with the Charity Commissioners and provides language learning courses in various European countries for periods of 2 weeks up to 6 months. The minimum age is 16. There are centres for French in Paris, La Rochelle, Amboise, Lausanne and Neuchâtel; for German in Cologne and Lucerne; for Spanish in Madrid and Barcelona; and for Italian in Florence. All teaching is conducted in the language concerned with extensive use of language laboratories and computer assisted language learning, and audio-visual materials. All schools have multi-media learning centres with facilities for independent study to complement classwork. There are both intensive courses, some preparing for public examinations, holiday courses and special courses, and workshops for teachers. Accommodation is arranged in private households.

Inlingua School of Languages, 8-10 Rotton Park Road, Edgebaston, Birmingham B16 9JJ — offer a wide variety of courses in all the major Western European languages and many rarer ones, at centres all over Western Europe. Since there is such an extensive range of possible courses, prospective participants should, in the first instance, write to the Information Centre at the above address.

Polytechnic of the South Bank, Department of Modern Languages, 103 Borough Road, London SE1 0AA — as well as the conventional taught classes, a subscriber service is also available at an annual cost of £77. This is a flexible system which allows students to attend the Language Centre in their own time during the week. Students work at their own pace in a language laboratory and study with audio-cassettes, video-cassettes and computer programs. It is possible to start a course at any time, as there are no scheduled starting and finishing dates. Languages taught are French, German, Spanish, Italian, Russian, Arabic and Japanese.

Preparation and Follow up

As well as learning the language, it is also valuable to learn something about the culture and customs of the country you will be staying in. This is obviously most important if you are visiting a country whose culture and social climate is totally alien to ours, particularly if you intend to stay a long time, and where contact with native people is a vital factor to the work you will be doing. Many companies, and even government bodies, spend large amounts of money on briefing workers about to serve terms overseas; in return, these workers can then operate more efficiently and acclimatise themselves more rapidly to the new environment.

Less vital is the need for organisations offering follow-up and "rehabilitation" services to workers returning from abroad, but many companies will go to great lengths to see that returning staff settle easily back into the British way of life.

The organisations below each offer special services concerned with preparation and follow up for working and living overseas. None of them is in any way involved in recruitment or finding work.

The Centre for International Briefing, Farnham Castle, Farnham, Surrey GU9 0AG — the Centre runs about 50 residential courses per year to help people going overseas or coming to the UK, to work more effectively in their new environment. Each course briefs on one of over 100 countries and includes lectures and discussions about its history, geography, politics and economics, as well as the people and their culture. Visiting speakers discuss the business environment and many courses include intensive sessions on international negotiation skills. For those going to live overseas, social and domestic conditions are described. The Centre is an independent non-profit organisation, founded in 1953.

The Centre for Professional Employment Counselling (CEPEC), 67 Jermyn Street, London SW1Y 6NY — operates a careers counselling and resettlement service for professional expatriates returning to the UK. Their counselling service is either a one day programme (costing £500) or a more lengthy selective resettlement service, covering career, personal and financial matters to determine the client's career direction and options.

Women's Corona Society, 501-2 Eland House, Stag Place, London SE1E 5DH — a voluntary organisation with branches in the UK and overseas providing, among other services, either postal or personal briefing for any women about to live or work abroad. The postal briefing is in the form of a series of booklets (*Notes for Newcomers* — price £3) on over 100 countries, containing all the practical and domestic details needed to prepare for setting up home in an new country, including climate, clothing, educational and medical facilities, housing, household requirements, food, leisure activities etc.

The society also runs "Living Overseas," one-day courses with counselling on how to adapt to a new lifestyle and culture; held every two months in London (with possibilities in other centres) and special sessions on request. Lectures, medical advice, and a chance to meet someone with current knowledge of their country of destination giving participants (both men and women) good preparation for the life ahead. £40 per person (£55 for married couples.

Returned Volunteer Action, 1 Amwell Street, London EC1R 1UL — does not send people to work abroad but does give advice and information to people considering working overseas. It is an independent organisation of individuals who have worked overseas as project workers or volunteers in development projects. It works to ensure that the experience of volunteers is put to good use after their return, both through contacts with British community groups and through feedback to overseas development agencies and sending societies regarding the appropriateness of their programmes and methods.

There is an RVA network of local groups and contacts across the country who organise weekends for recently returned project workers, 'Questioning Development' days for prospective volunteers, and conferences, as well as providing a focus for those who want to participate in relevant activities at a local level.

RVA publishes a number of books on volunteering and development, and urges anyone considering working overseas to write for a copy of their pamphlet *Thinking about Volunteering?* (Send £1 + large SAE).

Home Letting

Any home owner who contemplates working abroad for more than a few months is faced with the decision of how best to dispose of his house — whether to let it during his absence or to sell it outright. If the stay abroad is to be permanent, then sale is obviously the best choice. Otherwise, letting is nearly always preferable.

The most significant approach to the problem is financial. If the upward trend in house prices continues, a period of only a year or two without a house could mean a loss of several thousand pounds. In addition, there are many ancillary costs associated with selling and buying property — solicitors' and estate agents' fees; purchase or storage of curtains, carpets, furniture and appliances; rental costs while looking for a new home; and modernisation or re-decoration of the new property. If a sale is decided upon, the investment of the proceeds after repaying the mortgage will rarely be sufficient to cover the ancillary costs, let alone the rise in house prices.

The arguments against letting are less concrete — fear of damage to the house or contents; non-payment of rent; inability to regain possession; and the understandable reluctance to accept someone else living in one's property. There are also certain specific circumstances in which letting is not a viable propostion, for instance property may be in poor condition or totally unmodernised, or it may be in an area where a suitable tenant cannot be found reasonably easily.

The home owner who decides to let his house while abroad should bear the following points in mind to ensure that the letting and management of the property is carried out satisfactorily.

The Agent

The importance of the agent cannot be under-rated. He must (a) advise as to all the relevant aspects about letting and values; (b) find a suitable tenant, not once but possibly several times over a number of years; (c) collect the rent and keep accurate accounts; (d) inspect the property periodically and carry out necessary repairs; and (e) ensure that proper contracts are drawn up and the home owner's interests are protected at all times.

Choosing a suitable and reliable agent is never an easy matter. An agent dealing with house sales, for example, is unlikely to have the experience, the staff or the interest to deal with the complexities of managing the property for several years. In fact, of the firms which should be approached (i.e. members of the Royal Institution of Chartered Surveyors, the Incorporated

Society of Valuers and Auctioneers, or the National Association of Estate Agents), only a handful can be said to be specialists in letting, collection and management.

Agreements

These should always be formal documents, individually drawn up to suit the client's circumstances. Various standard clauses should always be included, e.g. requiring the tenant to look after the house and garden. Also, it is absolutely essential (assuming the client is an owner-occupier within the meaning of the Rent Act 1977) to serve a notice on the tenant before he takes up occupation, notifying him that the owner might require possession of the house at the end of the agreement. If this notice is served, the courts must subsequently grant possession to the owner. Where the tenant has been carefully chosen, however, this type of action should not be required.

Rental Level

The most satisfactory rental level is the one at which a number of applicants will be attracted to the property, from whom a really good tenant can be selected. This rent might not necessarily be high enough to cover the outgoings (rates, repairs, mortgage repayments, etc.), as these may in some cases be far higher than would be reasonable in terms of rent.

Quality of Tenant

The cardinal rule of letting is that the tenant should be the best available in the rent range. Over a certain level, this will mean an executive from a multinational corporation, an embassy official or similar. If the property is not of the style to attract this type of tenant it is possible to find other tenants who are just as acceptable, but the range available will be very varied and therefore the care taken in choosing will be critical. References should not be the guiding factor, although naturally they will need to be satisfactory.

Services

These must always be transferred to the tenant, and never left in the owner's name.

Furnishings

Most property is let on a fully furnished basis, but this might sometimes be inconvenient. At certain levels of rental, it is possible to find tenants on a part-furnished basis, i.e. with a requirement for curtains, carpets, and possible some electrical equipment only. There is no variation in the protection afforded to the owner-occupier by the Rent Act 1977 in these circumstances.

Repairs and Decoration

Finally, do not expect the property to be the same after five years of occupation, since deterioration takes place irrespective of the occupant. It may be sensible to have a programme of decorations etc., during the letting period, the costs of which are tax allowable.

Specific Careers

Agriculture, Forestry and Conservation

This chapter deals with work in three areas that seem to be of growing importance to the future of the world. In the developing countries, an adequate food supply is a matter of life or death, and much work is done, both at research and practical levels, to increase the yields and maintain sufficient supplies of the staple crops. Development is also being carried out in areas where agriculture faces particular obstacles, such as deserts and jungles.

This work often goes hand in hand with the work of conservationists and ecologists, who aim to preserve aspects of natural life that are threatened by the encroachment of industrialisation, urban spread and capitalistic colonisation. Conservationists are perhaps best known for their efforts to preserve rare species of wildlife and areas of outstanding natural beauty.

AGRICULTURE AND FORESTRY

Agriculturists and foresters with recognised professional qualifications and experience are in steady demand in the developing countries in positions centred on research and development, education or rural administration and economy. Appointments will vary from tours of duty of only a few weeks to contracts for several years. A degree in agriculture or forestry is usually the minimum requirement, and applicants will be preferred who have post-graduate training and experience in a specialised field relevant to the work being offered.

Most of this type of work is handled by foreign governments, whose recruitment programmes are in the hands of voluntary organisations (see the chapter on *Voluntary Work*), the United Nations specialised agencies and development programmes (see *United Nations*); other official and international bodies (see *International Organisations* and the sections on *Government Agencies* and *Student Working Exchanges* in the chapter

Getting the Job); and management recruitment consultants (see the section *The Conventional Job Search*).

Opportunities in the industrialised nations are more limited, not so much because agriculture and forestry present no particular problems there but because most of the industrialised nations have enough of their own residents with suitable qualifications.

Hendrikson Associierte Consultants GmbH, Mergenthalerallee 51-59, Postfach 5480, 6236 Eschborn 1, West Germany — accept applications for overseas employment from well qualified and experienced livestock specialists, range specialists, agricultural economists, agricultural development banking specialists and financial controllers, for assignments (mainly in African and Asian countries) of short and long term duration.

The *International Agricultural Exchange Association,* NFYFC Centre, National Agricultural Centre, Kenilworth, Warwickshire CV8 2LG — arranges working visits to Australia, New Zealand, Canada and the USA for British and Irish agriculturalists. Applicants must be single, between 19 and 28 years with at least one year's practical farming/horticultural experience. Participants receive a wage, paid in accordance with local rates. The organisation arranges group air travel, full insurance cover, work permits, Information Meeting before leaving, Orientation Seminar and supervision in the host country.

The *International Farm Experience Programme,* NFYFC, YFC Centre, National Agricultural Centre, Kenilworth, Warwickshire CV8 2LG — arranges for young people who are making a career in agriculture and have worked in the industry for at least two years (minimum age 18) to obtain placements on farms overseas to broaden their experience. Work for three or six months is available in Austria, Belgium, Canada, Denmark, Finland, France, West Germany, Hungary, Netherlands, Poland, Sweden and Switzerland. Work training can also be offered in the USA.

Minster Agriculture, Belmont, 13 Upper High Street, Thame, Oxfordshire OX9 3HL — is a specialist agricultural consultancy operating exclusively overseas in the fields of agricultural development and related industries. Overseas employment prospects may involve short spells of only a few days or weeks, or longer projects of several years. The projects are mostly in the Middle East, Far East and Africa, and include all the normal range of agricultural services, as well as several specialised services, such as arid zone development, post-harvest technology, oilseed development, etc.

CONSERVATION

The field of conservation is one which includes agriculture and forestry, and also encompasses the whole concept of ecology. While the traditional spheres of agriculture and forestry are aimed at the most practical and economical use of land resources, the field of conservation also includes the ideology of protecting natural resources per se. Especially in the richer countries of the world, where industrialisation is threatening natural resources, wildlife and areas of natural beauty, there is a growing movement towards conservation on ideological rather than practical grounds. This threat does not exist on such a large scale in the developing countries, although the wealthier nations that are rich through their own natural resources (e.g. oil and minerals) are now seen to be going through the early stages of the industrialisation process. With conservation growing in importance in North America and Europe, it is also gaining momentum in South America and the Far East, where, in some cases, whole tribes and regions are threatened with extinction as the twentieth century moves in. It could well be that in a few years' time the concept of conservation will provide the basis for a counter revolution against the industrial movement.

The American *National Wildlife Federation,* 1412 Sixteenth Street, NW, Washington DC 20036, USA — publishes the annual *Conservation Directory* ($15.00 plus $2.75 shipping charge), which concentrates on listing American and Canadian organisations concerned with conservation, and also gives the addresses of conservation and environment offices of foreign governments.

A list of other opportunities in conservation work appears in the directory of *Internships USA,* a directory of on-the-job training opportunities for college students and adults, in the chapter on the environment (see bibliography for details). Positions are available on a short-term basis in America for students and other qualified individuals.

Au Pair and Domestic

The main source of recruitment for au pair, mother's help, and nanny vacancies overseas are the many employment agencies which specialise in this area. This chapter includes a select list of these agencies.

The advertising columns of *The Times, The Guardian, The Daily Telegraph, International Herald Tribune* and *The Lady* provide a very useful supplementary source for such vacancies.

Following an important change in the *Employment Agencies Act 1973,* some au pair agencies are now entitled to charge a fee of up to £40 to au pairs for finding them overseas posts when the services of an agent acting for them from premises abroad are used. Prospective au pairs are advised to check with the agency concerned before registration.

Those agencies which are particular to only one specific country are listed in the relevant country chapter.

Au pair positions are not really jobs — board, lodging and pocket money are given in return for part-time housework and looking after children; mothers' helps often work full-time around the house in exchange for a small wage; nannies are concerned with children and usually need some qualification in this field, such as the NNEB (National Nursery Examination Board) Certificate; further information may be obtained from the NNEB, Argyle House, 29-31 Euston Road, London NW1 2SD. Like governesses, who are usually engaged to teach children, nannies should expect a full wage. While au pairs and mothers' helps are usually girls aged 18-25, nannies and governesses can often be older. Private domestic positions for men, once rare are now becoming more common. In addition, some of the agencies below can occasionally offer work for footmen and butlers, for instance in British embassies abroad.

A word of warning is required concerning immigration regulations pertinent to au pair positions. Traditionally, au pair positions have tended to be exempt from work permit requirements, but this is now decreasingly so, and, even where work permits are not necessary, certain residence and immigration procedures usually have to be observed. Agencies should be able to comply with any regulations, but the warning is particularly apt for girls applying for au pair jobs independently, for instance in reply to advertisements. The normal minimum age for au pair and other private domestic posts is 18, but responsible girls of 17 are acceptable in Italy, Spain and Belgium.

It should also be pointed out that au pair positions are traditionally associated with opportunities for learning a second language, and that they are not therefore available for British citizens working in English speaking countries. Such positions are usually referred to as mother's help positions.

Those interested in opportunities in North America should note that the Canadian Immigration authorities have introduced measures enabling people to apply for permanent residence after the completion of two years as a mother's help. A work permit must be obtained, however, before working as a mother's help. Towards the end of the second year, your employers will provide time off for training, and contribute a certain amount each month towards courses. On completion of the second year, you will be free to undertake any type of employment in Canada for which you are qualified. Further information is available from *Childminders Canada,* address below.

For au pair work in the USA, opportunities are fairly limited, as the government does not issue work permits for this kind of work; such work is generally available only through special schemes such as those run by *Au Pair in America* and *CBR Au Pair* (see below).

More detailed information on au pair and nanny work can be found in *The Au Pair and Nanny's Guide to Working Abroad,* edited by Susan Griffith (see the bibliography for details), which contains a country by country guide to au pair and nanny regulations as well as listing the names and addresses of over a hundred employment agencies.

AGENCIES

Amitiés Internationales, 2 rue Ducastel, 78 100 St Germain En Laye, Paris, France — offers positions for au pairs, nannies and mothers' helps in France for a minimum of 6 months. Some French is required and the age limit is 18-30. Nannies should have some experience, for au pairs it is not necessary.

Anglia Au Pair and Domestic Agency, 37 Old Southend Road, Southend-on-Sea SS1 2HA — places au pairs, nannies and mothers' helps in Belgium, Denmark, France, Germany, Italy, Spain, Israel, Australia and Canada. Applicants should be between 18 and 27 (there is no upper age limits for nannies and mothers' helps). The minimum stay is 3 months.

The Au Pair Centre, 25 Kings Road, London SW3 4RP — has positions for au pairs, mothers' helps and nannies in most European countries. The minimum stay is 6 months, although most jobs are for a year.

Au Pair in America, 37 Queens Gate, London SW7 5HR — sends au pairs to the USA for 12 months. Medical insurance is provided, as well as the flight from London to New York and travel to the family. Applicants should have good practical experience, a full drivers licence and be non-smokers. The age limit is 18 to 25 years. No fees are charged; however £350 deposit is required which is refunded after successful completion of the year's contract.

Au Pairs Italy, 46 The Rise, Sevenoaks, Kent TN13 1RJ — places nannies, mothers' helps, governesses and au pairs in Italy for 6 to 12 months. Minimum age is 18. A deposit of £15 is required, refunded on request after completion of the arranged stay.

Au Pairs Universal, "The Dell" 180 Toms Lane, Kings Langley, Hertfordshire WD4 8NZ — can offer au pair and mothers' helps positions in France, Germany, Italy, Greece, Spain. Temporary summer positions available in all countries, otherwise minimum 6 months. Au Pair Universal has associate agencies in all of these countries. Include a stamped addressed envelope when writing.

Avalon Agency, 11 Abinger Road, Portslade, East Sussex BN4 1SD — specialises in the placement of au pairs in France, Germany, Italy or Spain. Basic knowledge of relevant language is essential. Minimum age 18 years, length of stay 6 months plus. A stamped addressed envelope should be included in the application.

CBR Au Pair, 63 Foregate Street, Worcester WR1 1DX — has run the Au Pair Homestay USA programme since 1986, under the auspices of the Experiment in International Living (EIL). Under this programme au pairs are placed in the USA for a year, with medical insurance cover and a back-up serviced provided by EIL. Child care experience is required, as well as a driving licence. Applicants must also be non-smokers and be 18 to 25 years of age. A fee of £500 is charged which includes the air fare and a £350 deposit refundable on completion of the contract.

Childminders Canada, 61 Woodlands Gardens, London N10 3UE — can place nannies and mothers' helps in Canada for a minimum stay of 1 year. Applicants should be at least 19 years old and have at least six months experience or a relevant qualification.

Helping Hands Au Pair and Domestic Agency, 10 Hertford Road, Newbury Park, Ilford, Essex IG2 7HQ — places au pairs in France, Italy, Germany, Austria, Greece, Belgium, and Spain. Minimum period six months.

Applicants must be aged between 18 and 27. Self addressed envelope to be enclosed when applying.

Home From Home, 1 King Street, Maidenhead, Berks. SL6 1DZ — places au pairs in France, Germany, Italy, Spain and Canada.

International Catholic Society For Girls, St. Patrick's International Youth Centre, 24 Great Chapel Street, London W1V 3AF — au pair posts (not restricted to Catholics) in Europe for a minimum of nine months. Applicants must be aged at least 18, have some relevant experience of child care and household tasks, and some knowledge of the native language. Include a self addressed envelope.

Jeeves & Belgravia Bureau, 35 Brompton Road, London SW3 1DF — recruits professionally trained nannies with at least two years child care experience for positions worldwide. Minimum contracts are for one year and applicants must be at least 21 and in excellent health. Driving licence preferred.

Just The Job — 11 Priory Road, West Bridgeford, Nottingham NG2 5HU — places au pairs in France, Spain, Germany and Italy for a minimum of six months and qualified nannies to Canada for 12 months.

Mondial Agency, 32 Links Road, West Wickham, Kent BR4 0QW — au pair posts available in Austria and France for a minimum period of six months.

Mrs Lines Employment Agency Ltd., 25a Kensington Church Street, London W8 4LL — offer opportunities abroad for various types of temporary and permanent domestic staff — butlers, cooks, nannies, mothers' helps, au pairs and dailies — for married couples or single people.

Paragon Now Ltd., PO Box 1, Sutton Scotney, Winchester, Hampshire SO21 3JG — has permanent positions for qualified nannies, mothers' helps, butlers, chauffeurs, housekeepers and cooks worldwide. Applicants must be 18 or older and some knowledge of the language of the resident country is preferred.

Relations Internationales, 20 rue de l'Exposition, 75007 Paris, France — handle six month au pair positions throughout France, as well as Belgium, Italy, Spain, Greece, and Israel; also 12-month mothers' help positions in Canada. Age limit 18-28 years.

Scattergoods Catering & Childcare Agency, Thursley House, 53 Station Road, Shalford, Guildford GU14 8HA — has positions for au pairs in France, Belgium, Netherlands, Germany, Spain, Italy, Greece, Israel, Norway, Denmark and the USA. Minimum stay is usually six months, but this can vary with the country involved. Applicants should be 18-30 except Belgium where the age limit is 17. For Germany, basic German is required. One year positions for nannies and mothers' helps are also arranged in Canada.

Students Abroad, Elm House, 21b The Avenue, Hatch End, Middlesex

HA5 4EN — au pair positions and mother's help positions in Europe (mostly Italy, France, Belgium, Spain, Germany, Greece and Holland); and mother's help posts for a minimum of 12 months in Canada. Long and short term (i.e. summer vacation) posts are available in Europe and Israel. Stamped addressed envelope essential.

Universal Aunts Ltd., 250 Kings Road, Chelsea, London SW3 5UE — can offer places for nannies and mothers' helps in European Community countries.

Universal Care Limited, Chester House, 9 Windsor End, Beaconsfield, Bucks. HP9 2JJ — offer au pair, mother's help and nanny jobs throughout Europe. Mother's help and nanny positions can also be arranged in Canada and Australia.

Westbury International Agency, 18 Sanderson Place, Heath Road, London SW8 3DG — arranges au pair, mother's help and nanny positions for 6-12 months all over Europe as well as Canada. Minimum age is 18 and a basic knowledge of the relevant language is required.

Banking and Accountancy

The field of finance offers scope for careers in three main areas:

commercial banking — private and company bank accounts
merchant banking — large scale company investments
accountancy — handling company finances.

Most of the recruitment for personnel in these spheres is carried out by the banks and companies themselves, but a list of recruitment consultants specialising in banking and accountancy positions is included at the end of this chapter. The international banking organisations, such as the World Bank and International Monetary Fund are dealt with in the chapter on the *United Nations.*

COMMERCIAL BANKING

Commercial banking as we all know it, is concerned with handling our personal bank accounts, arranging loans and generally helping with all financial matters. But the average High Street bank is also encroaching on the territory of the merchant bankers — handling company profits, investments and credit facilities and offering advisory services on taxation, insurance and unit trusts. International commercial banking is also greatly concerned with money transfers and exchanges.

While commercial banking is the largest recruiter of banking personnel, the overseas opportunities are still limited, since the majority of foreign banks are run and staffed by local workers and managers. Thus the most likely openings for Britons are with British banks that have foreign branches, and even so, only the senior management personnel will be expatriate Britons.

The Clearing Banks

The best chances of overseas banking positions are with the major "clearing" banks — especially Barclays, Lloyds, and Midland. The recruitment activities of their respective international divisions are detailed below.

Barclays Bank Plc, 54 Lombard Street, London EC3A 3AH — is the largest international banking organisation in the United Kingdom. It operates in more than 80 countries, with a staff of approximately 100,000. The Management Development Programme (Overseas) recruits about 30 graduates annually for a four year programme, which commences in the UK and normally includes at least one a year abroad. There follows a series of assignments, some overseas and some in the UK throughout the career.

Lloyds Bank Plc., 71 Lombard Street, London EC3P 3BS — together with its subsidiaries in the UK and in 45 other countries, employs 76,000 staff. Lloyds Bank runs comprehensive training schemes for graduates, which can include short periods overseas. Otherwise most positions are in the UK.

Midland Bank Plc, Global Banking, 110-114 Cannon Street, London EC4N 6AA — the Global Banking arm of Midland Bank deals with international and corporate business and there can be limited opportunities to work abroad during and after completion of the two-year graduate training programme.

Other British Banks

In addition, there are a number of British banks that are less well known in this country because they operate mainly overseas. It follows that they have a variety of overseas staff requirements. These banks include:

Australia and New Zealand Banking Group Ltd., (including Grindlays Bank Plc), Minerva House, Montague Close, London SE1 9DH.
Standard Chartered Bank Plc, 38 Bishopsgate, London EC2N 4DE.

Foreign Banks

The prospects of overseas employment with foreign banks are extremely slim, and are best for people with several years' banking experience. Finding work in the London branch of a foreign bank offers a slight chance of an eventual transfer to the home branch. The best prospects, however, seem to be for highly experienced bankers to apply direct to banks abroad.

Apart from the City of London, the main financial centres of the world are Zurich, New York and Tokyo. Because of the current Swiss immigration procedures, the chances of work in Zurich are restricted only to the most senior personnel.

There still seems to be a small demand for westerners in the Japanese banks; the list below includes the major Tokyo banks, and their London branches.

Bank of Tokyo, 6-3 Nihombashi, HongoKucho, l-chome, Chuo-ku, Tokyo (20/24 Moorgate, London EC2).
Daiwa Bank, 21 Bingomachi, 2-chome, Higashi-ku, Osaka 541 (Commercial Union Building, St. Helen's, 1 Undershaft London EC3A 8JJ).
Mitsui Bank, 1-2 Yaraku-cho, l—chome, Chiyoda-ku, Tokyo (34/35 King Street, London EC2).
Sanwa Bank, 1-1 Otemachi 1-chome, Chiyoda-ku, Tokyo 100, Japan (Commercial Union Building, 1 Undershaft, London EC3A 8LA).

MERCHANT BANKING

The merchant bankers originated as merchants, trading in goods, usually on an international scale. Gradually, they were elevated to the position of providing financial services to other traders, and this is the essence of their work today, although their services are offered not merely to traders, but also to industry, insurance companies, transport companies, in short, anyone with large amounts of money on their hands.

The services they provide may be conveniently grouped into banking, corporate finance, investment management and trading in securities; they include project finance, advisory services to governments and international corporations, leasing and financial futures dealing. The merchant banks all have head offices in the City of London and, being international businesses, are strongly represented overseas through subsidiaries, affiliates and representative offices.

In terms of numbers employed, the merchant banks are small in comparison with the clearing banks. The best opportunities are for graduates, preferably though not necessarily with degrees in economics, law or business studies.

Apart from the actual banking activities, there are also occasional vacancies for experienced and well qualified specialist staff, such as lawyers and accountants.

Recruitment is carried out by the banks themselves, all of which offer graduate training programmes lasting from six months to two years. The number of vacancies per year is low and competition stiff. Following the training course, the early part of a career will almost entirely be spent in London, but at the senior level, opportunities should arise for promotion, secondment or transfer to branches or agents abroad.

The most prominent merchant banks are the 16 main members of the British Merchant Banking and Securities Houses Association, whose London addresses are:

Baring Brothers & Co. Ltd., 8 Bishopsgate, EC2N 4AE.
Brown, Shipley & Co. Ltd., Founders Court, Lothbury, EC2R 7HE.
Charterhouse Bank Ltd., 1 Paternoster Row, St. Paul's EC4M 7DH.
Robert Fleming & Co. Ltd., 25 Copthall Avenue, EC2R 7DR.
Guinness Mahon & Co. Ltd., 32 St. Mary At Hill, 3C3P 3AJ.
Hambros Bank Ltd., 41 Tower Hill, EC3N 4HA.
Hill Samuel & Co. Ltd., PO Box 20, 100 Wood Street, EC2P 2AJ.
Kleinwort Benson Ltd., PO Box 560, 20 Fenchurch Street, EC3P 3DB.
Lazard Brothers & Co. Ltd., PO Box 516, 21 Moorfields, EC2P 2HT.
Samuel Montagu & Co. Ltd., 10 Lower Thames Street, EC3R 6AE.
Morgan Grenfell & Co. Ltd., PO Box 56, 23 Great Winchester Street, EC2P 2AX.
Rea Brothers Ltd., Alderman's House, Alderman's Walk, EC2M 3XR.
N. M. Rothschild & Sons Ltd., PO Box 185, New Court, St. Swithin's Lane, EC4P 4DU.
J. Henry Schroder Wagg & Co. Ltd., 120 Cheapside, EC2V 6DS.
Singer & Friedlander Ltd., 21 New Street, Bishopgate, EC2M 4HR.
S. G. Warburg & Co. Ltd., 33 King William Street, EC4R 9AS.

Further information regarding career prospects in merchant banking can be obtained from the *British Merchant Banking and Securities House Association,* Granite House, 101 Cannon Street, London EC4N 5BA.

ACCOUNTANCY

Accountancy is a well-respected and stable profession, and accountants are in demand throughout the world. School leavers and, more particularly, graduates who intend to take up accountancy as a career are faced with an awesome array of qualifications to aim for, each of which requires a period of practical experience (usually a minimum of three years), a preliminary or foundation examination (for non-graduates), and professional examinations. The different qualifications are offered by the various professional associations, some of which can offer their own members advice or assistance in finding work, at home or abroad, once they have qualified.

The various qualifications (and associations offering them) are listed below:

ACA — the Institute of Chartered Accountants in England and Wales, PO Box 433, Chartered Accountants' Hall, Moorgate Place, London EC2P 2BJ.

CA — the Institute of Chartered Accountants of Scotland, 27 Queen Street, Edinburgh EH2 1LA.

ACCA — the Chartered Association of Certified Accountants, 29 Lincoln's Inn Fields, London WC2A 3EE.

ACMA — the Institute of Cost and Management Accountants, 63 Portland Place, London W1N 4AB.

ASCA — The Society of Company and Commercial Accountants, 40 Tyndalls Park Road, Bristol BS8 1PL.

To qualify as a Chartered Accountant, training must be undertaken in a practising firm of accountants, combining work and study over a three year period. Cost and Management Accountants and Certified Accountants train within a specific company and are able to determine their own time frame with respect to obtaining their professional qualifications.

On qualification there are many openings abroad for Chartered Accountants; Certified and Cost and Management Accountants are slightly more restricted as their qualifications are considered to be more UK based. Many British accountancy firms have associated firms with offices overseas and transfers abroad are frequently arranged for qualified staff. The countries in which British accountants are most in demand are Australia, New Zealand, Canada, South Africa, the Middle East and Europe. The largest British firms with overseas associated offices are:

Arthur Andersen & Co., Surrey Street, London WC2R 2PS.
Coopers & Lybrand, Plumtree Court, London EC4A 4HT
Deloitte Haskins & Sells, 128 Queen Victoria Street, London EC4P 4JX.
Peat Marwick McLintock, 1 Puddle Dock, London EC4V 3PD.
Price Waterhouse, Southwark Towers, 32 London Bridge Street, London SE1 9SY.

Michael Page International, 39-41 Parker Street, London WC2B 5LH — specialise in the recruitment of financial personnel, from junior accountants to senior financial executives, for careers throughout the world.

RECRUITMENT CONSULTANTS

The activities of the recruitment consultants listed below are restricted totally to the field of finance. Other consultants with a wider scope of appointments are given in the section *Consultants and Agencies.*

ASA International, 69 St. Vincent Street, Glasgow G2 5JU — specialists in the recruitment of accountancy staff and financial management for overseas clients, both in the profession and in industry and commerce. Suitable applications are kept on file for matching with appropriate vacancies as and when they rise. Offices also in Edinburgh, Aberdeen, London and Birmingham.

BHMS Executive Search, 65 Queen Street West, Suite 2020, Toronto, Ontario M5H 2M5, Canada — a recruiting company in the banking and trust industry. Positions are not in Canada but specifically for the various tax havens throughout the world such as Nassau, Cayman Islands and the Channel Islands.

PROFESSIONAL ASSOCIATIONS

Banking

Career prospects in commercial banking — domestic and international — are greatly enhanced by passing the Chartered Institute of Banker's examinations, which include papers on law, accountancy, economic and monetary theory and practice of banking. The qualification is an integral part of special management trainee programmes offered by the major British banks. Details of the qualification — the Associateship of the Chartered Institute of Bankers (AIB) — are available from *The Chartered Institute of Bankers,* 10 Lombard Street, London EC3V 9AS.

Accountancy

The Institute of Chartered Accountants in England and Wales, PO Box 433, Chartered Accountants' Hall, Moorgate Place, London EC2P 2BJ, runs a recruitment service for its members which covers all countries.

Actuary

The Institute of Actuaries, Staple Inn Hall, High Holborn, London WC1V 7QJ, is able to provide a *List of Actuarial Employers,* setting out details of possible vacancies, including opportunities overseas.

Computer Services

THE COMPUTER INDUSTRY

Although the computer industry has now existed for some 40 years, it is really only over the last decade that computers have become an integral part of modern society, and their role in our lives will continue to grow at a remarkable rate. Computers can be utilised in just about every conceivable way; in industry, commerce, science and medicine, at home or in the office. A vast number of jobs can be performed with greater efficiency than ever before: credit card checking, plane seat reservations, wage slips for a whole company, medical diagnosis or the typesetting of this book.

In fact this increase in the computer's range of applications has given rise to the term *Information Technology (IT),* to reflect the fact that computers are used as much for information processing and communication purposes as for computing purposes alone.

Obviously jobs are lost, as computers replace humans, but to replace those jobs large numbers of staff throughout the world are required to programme and operate the computer systems springing up everywhere. There is a large market both in the UK and overseas, particularly in the Middle East and the USA; and more recently, in Europe (Germany and Holland especially). Computer skills are probably the most transportable in the world, since international computer languages are used.

The rapid rate of increase in computer technology means there are good prospects for promotion for suitably qualified people. To work in the computer industry, the basic requirement is not so much a scientific background or education, as the possession of a logical and flexible mind and a certain level of analytical intelligence. Working professionally with computers requires much more discipline than working with computers at home or in school, because of the greater complexity of the systems involved. Attention to detail must be combined with a responsible approach. This, together with an appropriate qualification, from GCSE up to degree standard, will help in obtaining a job in one of the various computer areas. These are:

1 — Systems design/analysis. The systems designer is called in to examine the way a company or a particular function is operating without a computer, and decides how best a system could benefit the situation. From this initial analysis, suitable methods must be devised for developing such a system. For this sort of job, prospective employees would either have qualifications up to a degree standard, or previous programming experience.

2 — Programming. The programmer is responsible for preparing sequenced instructions in the particular computer language in use, in other words the program, which will enable the computer to carry out the tasks required of it. An applications programmer handles programs for specific tasks; the systems programmer works on the basic functions allowing a program to be obeyed. Minimum qualifications here are usually GCSE and "A" level for applications programming, while the systems programmer is usually a graduate, highly experienced.

3 — Operations. Operators handle the day-to-day running of computers, acting as a link between user and computer. Within the operations field come a range of different activities: data preparation (turning data into an acceptable form for the computer); data control; operating (loading tapes etc); keypunch operators; right up to senior posts such as operations manager. Suitable qualifications in this area would be typing and office procedure experience, plus (for school leavers) five GCSE passes including English and mathematics.

4 — Hardware Design. Hardware is the actual machinery and electronics operating the computer, so this area applies to electronic and mechanical engineers, with knowledge of logic electronics a benefit. These are also posts for computer engineers who look after the maintenance and repair of computers.

5 — Sales. To convince a prospective buyer or user of the worth of a new computer, sales staff need good knowledge of computers and their uses. Most people move to sales from system analysis or applications programming.

To work abroad, it is absolutely essential to have relevant experience in one of the above areas. Qualifications count for little in the computer recruitment business, and applicants for any job should have an absolute minimum of two years' experience in their field before they even consider applying. That said, because of the high level of job mobility in the industry, those suitably experienced should have little difficulty finding work overseas, as is borne out by the recent mushrooming of computer recruitment agencies.

A valuable reference book available in all good reference libraries is the *Computer User's Year Book* which contains useful lists and addresses of recruitment agencies throughout Britain, in addition to extensive lists of the various training courses available at all levels, plus salary surveys for each job area.

The weekly journals *Computing* and *Computer Weekly,* also available in reference libraries, advertise vacancies in the computer industry, including vacancies abroad.

COMPUTER RECRUITMENT AGENCIES

The following organisations are particularly involved in recruiting staff for overseas jobs; it must be re-emphasized that only those with relevant experience should apply for work through these agencies. In addition, other opportunities are listed in the section *Consultants and Agencies* and the chapters *Oil, Mining and Engineering, International Organisations, United Nations,* and *British Government Departments.*

Abraxas Computer Services Ltd., 357 Euston Road, London NW1 3AL — can offer employment to well qualified computer software specialists with skills in Data communications, Telecommunications and related disciplines worldwide.

ASA International, 69 St. Vincent Street, Glasgow G2 5JU — provides career advice and assistance in finding employment for experienced computer personnel with two years or more experience in all computer related jobs.

Austin Knight Ltd., Knightway House, 20 Soho Square, London W1A 1DS — offers positions to marketing executives, customer support engineers, computer engineers and field service engineers in Saudi Arabia and the Middle East generally.

Benny Electronics Ltd., 1A Telford Road, Ferndown Industrial Estate, Wimborne, Dorset BH21 7QN — employs systems analysts and programmers on a contract basis, and under agency for other companies both in the UK and overseas.

Computer Careeer Consultants, Chiltern House, Oxford Road, Aylesbury HP19 3EQ — deals with Manufacturers, Distributors, Software houses, Systems houses and Value Added Resellers (not with End Users). All the positions handled are permanent. Their overseas placements are in the USA, Canada and in the Middle East for experienced computer staff, and each candidate is interviewed in-depth to ascertain his or her technical competence, experience and requirements.

EDP Systems Ltd., 31 Palace Street, London SW1E 5HW — long established agency (started 1965) dealing exclusively in computer staff. Active in Continental Europe for both permanent and contract positions. Most contracts are medium to long term; minimum experience requirement is two years, but generally more.

Exchange Resources, 28 Milsom Street, Bath BA1 1DP — an agency which places people in socially useful employment. It is developing an equal opportunities policy for encouraging women, ethnic minorities and people with disabilities to take part in working with technology. Exchange Resources provides permanent and contract staff in computing, electronics and other technologies in Europe and the USA.

Focal Point Consultancy & Recruitment Ltd., Stuart House, 43-47 Crown Street, Reading, Berks. RG1 2SN — supplies contract and permanent placings within the Data Processing industry around the world.

James Duncan & Associates, 8 St. John's Road, Tunbridge Wells, Kent, TN4 9NP — maintain a large register devoted to computer staff, mainly for data processing work. Contracts range from one year programming to senior data processing management. Operations are mainly in the UK, Europe

(Netherlands and Belgium) with some outlets in the Middle East for well qualified Data Processing professionals.

Hexagon Computer Services, Hexagon House, 145 Wardour Street, London W1V 3TB — has a steady supply of contract staff to Europe, and occasional openings in the Middle East and the USA. Contracts vary between three months and a year, and cover most areas of computer activities, particularly real time and data base analysts, systems designers and programmers. Applicants with 2-3 years' full time commercial experience can contact the External Resources Division.

I.C. Software A.G., Artherstrasse 5, 6300 Zug, Switzerland — a Europe wide agency which assigns computer professionals to client application software development projects or technical and real-time projects on a freelance, consultancy or permanent basis. Project durations are usually 6 months to 2 years, extendable in some cases. Applicants should have at least 3 years experience (preferably 5 years) in any of the above areas of computers. Foreign languages are not always essential as most multinational companies use English as the common language. However, where appropriate, language sessions can be arranged. I.C. Software can also offer guidance on tax planning and social security questions relating to the country of employment, as well as details of local economic/social conditions and temporary and permanent accommodation.

Ingineur Ltd., Pendicke Street, Southam, Warks. CV33 0PN — Europe-wide agency for electronics professionals. Contract assignments (usually 6-24 months duration) and permanent positions for managers, design engineers and other specialists in the electronic hardware, telecommunications, aerospace and semiconductor industries. Usual requirements are a degree, at least two years relevant experience and some knowledge of a European language.

Knight Programming Support Ltd., Royalty House, 72 Dean Street, London W1V 5HB — offers contract work of between 6-12 months duration as well as permanent positions worldwide for all data processing staff, especially programmers and analyst programmers. A minimum of four years' experience is required. Other offices are based in Manchester, Birmingham, Amsterdam, New York, Los Angeles, Dallas and San Francisco.

Kramer Westfield Associates Ltd., 5 The Avenue, Egham, Surrey TW20 9AB — specialist recruitment consultancy for the communications and semiconductor industries. Particular geographic areas include Europe, North America and Far East and disciplines covered are general management, sales and marketing, engineering and applications.

Modus International, Kingswood House, Heath and Reach, Leighton Buzzard, Bedford LU7 0AD — recruits all types of computer personnel, from programmers and technical authors to systems analysts and software engineers, for positions in Europe and the USA. Permanent and short term contracts are available. Applicants should be graduates with at least three years experience.

SD Scicon, Centrum House, 101-103 Fleet Road, Fleet, Hants. GU13 8PD — recruits systems engineers and programmers for permanent posts in Belgium, West Germany, Italy and the Netherlands. Graduates with at least two years experience are preferred.

Systems Support Services Ltd., Systems Support House, Wembley Hill Road, Wembley, Middlesex HA9 8BU — handle analyst programmers, analysts, operating staff, programmers and consultants (not data preparation). The company specialises in contract work and contract support for all types of hardware, both mini- and mainframe. Average contracts are between 3 and 6 months, and cover Holland, Germany, Switzerland and Eire (expansion is taking place into the Middle East and the USA). Minimum three years' relevant experience.

Targa Computer Recruitment, MDA House, The Grove, Slough, Berks. SL1 1RH — has openings for computer staff with good experience in Europe, the Middle East, the Far East and the USA. Targa deals with permanent positions abroad while contracts (from 3 to 12 months) are handled by their associated company *Data Scene International,* at the same address.

PROFESSIONAL ASSOCIATIONS

The British Computer Society, 13 Mansfield Street, London W1M 0BP — cannot help computer personnel to find work, but does produce a useful booklet dealing with careers in computing, and sets qualifying examinations.

The Institution of Analysts and Programmers, Gibson House, 39-41 Fourth Cross Road, Twickenham, Middlesex TW2 5EL — can only offer assistance to its members. However it does produce a Directory of Members (£19 to non-members), listing the names and addresses of members in over 60 countries to whom enquiries can be made.

Journalism

In comparison with the numbers of aspirant journalists, openings are few and therefore fiercely contested. Promotion and advancement are slow procedures, so journalists usually have to spend several years working in this country before becoming eligible for postings overseas.

Despite these considerations, however, journalism is one profession where the methods of the creative job search outlined in the section, *The General Approach,* are most likely to succeed. This is because recruitment is frequently undertaken by word of mouth and through a network of personal contacts. The advice of one newspaper personnel officer sums up the whole aproach: "go to the local or national newspaper offices and start banging on doors".

BRITISH PRESS

Working for a British newspaper will only bring an overseas appointment if you are employed by one of the national daily or Sunday papers: several years experience on a national paper are usually necessary before you will be sent abroad — and full-time staff positions abroad are few and far between. The *Guardian,* for instance, has only eight full-time staff members abroad — in Brussels, Cyprus, New Delhi, Jerusalem, South Africa, Moscow and two in Washington.

But for those who are exceptionally determined and sufficiently motivated, it may be possible to earn a very basic living as a freelance foreign correspondent, although the importance of already having some domestic journalistic experience, and of having a network of contacts on the foreign desks of Fleet Street cannot be over-stressed. The section on *Stringers,* below, discusses this in more detail.

The requirement that prospective Fleet Street journalists have three years experience on one of the 1,300 provincial newspapers used to be part of a strict agreement between the National Union of Journalists and the Newspaper Publishers' Association. At the moment there is no such national agreement, but all the papers tend to follow the old rule, except where someone of unusually specialist knowledge is required. Journalists should also have passed the Proficiency Certificate for Journalists which is set by the National Council for the Training of Journalists. Details of this training is available from: *The Newspaper Society,* Training Department, Whitefriars House, 6 Carmelite Street, London EC4.

Journalists who wish to break into Fleet Street, and who have already served their time in the provinces (or who are prepared to risk the "back door" approach) should apply direct to one of the Editors of the daily or Sunday papers:

Daily Express/Daily Star/Sunday Express, 121 Fleet Street, London EC4P 4JT.
Daily Mail/Mail on Sunday, Northcliffe House, Tudor Street, London EC4Y 0JA.
Daily Mirror/Sunday Mirror/Sunday People, Holborn Circus, London EC1P 1DQ.
Daily Telegraph/Sunday Telegraph, Peterborough Court, South Quay, 181 Marsh Wall, London E14 9SR.
Financial Times, Bracken House, 10 Cannon Street, London EC4P 4BY.
Guardian, 119 Farringdon Road, London EC1R 3ER.
Independent, 40 City Road, London EC1Y 2DB.
Observer, Chelsea Bridge House, Queenstown Road, London SW8 4NN.
Sun/News of the World, 1 Virginia Street, London E1 9XR.
Times/Sunday Times, 1 Pennington Street, London EC1 9XN.
Today, Allen House, 70 Vauxhall Bridge Road, Pimlico, London SW1V 2RP.

BRITISH RADIO AND TELEVISION

As with the press, broadcasting jobs are all highly contested, and those that involve overseas work are, in any case, extremely rare. The BBC, for example, employs only 28 full-time overseas correspondents: 16 in radio, seven in television and five in the External Services.

Within the radio and television companies, the main route to the top jobs is via internal promotion. Thus the present producer of a popular radio programme may have started his or her radio career ten or 15 years ago recording cows and tractors for the Archers.

Within broadcasting, the only long-term overseas posts are for correspondents, representatives and engineers. Other jobs may entail occasional overseas travel for varying periods, sometimes at short notice. These include news reporters, film crews and production staff, together with associated staff (make-up, costume, film, etc.). Radio producers may also undertake brief spells of duty abroad.

The BBC also seconds a small number of its staff to other broadcasting organisations to assist in training or development in fields such as news, general radio or television programme production and engineering.

Enquiries about BBC employment should be addressed to Corporate Recruitment Services (or, for openings in engineering, to the Engineering and Technical Operations Recruitment Officer), *British Broadcasting Corporation,* Broadcasting House, London W1A 1AA.

The BBC's weekly house magazine, *Ariel,* contains dozens of positions which are not advertised in the national press.

Employment in independent radio or television is handled by the individual stations whose addresses can be obtained from the *Independent Broadcasting Authority (IBA),* 70 Brompton Road, London SW3 1EY.

FOREIGN PRESS

Apart from field reporters and photographers, the foreign press also offers opportunities for editorial and management staff, but only experienced personnel will be considered. Those seeking work for overseas newspapers and journals will find few openings in foreign language publications, but many countries have English-language newspapers for their English and American resident populations. However, staff on these is always small, so vacancies are rare.

The most practical way of finding work on a foreign paper is direct application. Addresses of newspapers will be found in *Willing's Press Guide,* the International Volume of *Benn's Media Directory,* or the blue pages of the *Advertisers' Annual.* All three directories should be obtainable in local public reference libraries. In addition, *Writers' and Artists' Yearbook* (see bibliography for details) lists the addresses of newspapers and magazines in the English-speaking world.

OVERSEAS RADIO AND TELEVISION

Vacancies are even rarer in overseas broadcasting companies than in the foreign press. The major companies in the English-speaking world (Australia, New Zealand, the USA and Canada) can usually fill their own needs internally, and will advertise any other specialised vacancies in the British press. Unsolicited applications will rarely be successful, so the addresses of the individual companies are not included here. They can be found in the *World Radio and Television Handbook,* available in public reference libraries or through bookshops.

There are many non-English-speaking countries that have English language broadcasts, usually as part of their external services, rather like the BBC World Service or Voice of America. Naturally, there are a few openings for native English-speaking personnel to produce, direct and broadcast these services. Full details of English language broadcasts are also given in the *World Radio and Television Handbook.*

STRINGERS

The international news system is so structured that most of the foreign news in the British press and media originates either from news agencies or from individual "stringers", and not from permanently based expatriate reporters. "Stringers" tend to be people already based overseas who, for a retainer and/or commission, will feed stories from their part of the world back to Britain. Stringers thus function on a part-time, freelance basis, and their work — while providing a valuable source of extra income — is usually secondary to a full-time career (often as a reporter or editor for a local paper). If you have journalistic experience and are going abroad to another job, you could always offer your services as a stringer to one of the national papers.

There are considerable opportunities for the dedicated foreign stringer which do not, however, fall into any of the conventional categories discussed so far. A foreign stringer need not be restricted to finding the occasional news story for the national and international press. If he or she really knows the market, opportunities for writing travel, sociological, and current affairs features for national and specialist magazines and newspapers abound. Contact likely sources of publication before setting off to ensure the best chances of success. *Writers' and Artists' Yearbook* contains useful information on newspapers and magazines across the world, while the *UK Press Gazette,* the weekly newspaper for journalists, sometimes contains advertisements from sources looking for foreign freelance contributions. Prospective foreign stringers will also do well to advertise their availability for occasional or one off contributions in those columns.

NEWS AGENCIES

All in all, the news agencies offer the best chance of working overseas, but nevertheless, most British staff will remain based in Britain. A list of the news agencies in Britain, and the services they provide, is given in *Benn's Media Directory,* under the heading *Agencies and Services for the Media Industry.* It will be noted that most of these agencies operate solely within the United Kingdom. Career structures in the larger agencies are unlikely to include more than the occasional trip or tour of duty overseas. The major exception to this pattern is Reuters.

Reuters Ltd., 85 Fleet Street, London EC4 — an international news organisation which supplies news of political, economic, financial, general and sports interest to the media and business communities in most countries of the world. It also produces a wide range of computerised data retrieval services, combining both news and statistical data, using the latest technology to supply banks, brokers, financial institutions and major corporations worldwide with up to the minute information on international money rates, securities, commodoties and all factors affecting these markets.

Reuters has one of the largest private communication systems in the world and is a major user of minicomputers to service over 25,000 subscribers in some 150 countries. Its extensive real-time data retrieval networks are among the most sophisticated and reliable in operation, interfacing with high speed communication links and making use of satellites, cables and high frequency radio.

Reuters employs some 9,500 staff including over 1,000 full time journalists. It recruits about 10 graduates each year for training in journalism, about 18 graduates for training in a wide range of management disciplines, and about 4 graduates for training in accountancy. Some Computer Science graduates are also taken on for a technical management career. Successful candidates will be expected to have at least a Second Class Honours Degree. In addition, applicants for the journalist training scheme will be required to speak three languages, one of which should be English. Applicants for the other three schemes should have a good knowledge of at least one foreign language. All four schemes offer opportunities for posts at home and abroad.

Applications in writing to the Assistant Staff Manager at the above address before 30 December each year.

The Law

Like Banking and Accountancy, the law is a highly reputable and well established profession, and opportunities exist for qualified British lawyers in many countries throughout the world.

SOLICITORS

Despite the wide difference between the legal systems throughout the world, which might seem to restrict opportunities to move from one legal system to another, a variety of opportunities exist for solicitors to practise or work abroad. Some of the larger solicitors' firms have offices abroad, particularly in Europe, the USA and the Middle East. Also a number of solicitors have positions with local lawyers' firms or as legal advisors employed by local or international industrial and commercial companies abroad. Because of the common law roots of their legal systems, many solicitors seek admission in the United States, Canada, Australia and New Zealand, although increasingly, immigration restrictions reduce these opportunities.

There are solicitors on the staff of various international organisations such as the institutions of the European Community, the European Patent Office, the Council of Europe and the United Nations, undertaking legal and administrative work or acting as translators and interpreters. Others work as legal draftsmen or in other capacities in Commonwealth countries under schemes run by the Commonwealth Fund for Technical Co-operation or by other Commonwealth institutions.

Finally, there are also a number of opportunities for professional exchanges for those solicitors interested in gaining practical experience of other legal systems for short periods. Details of the Young Lawyers' International Associations Scheme and of national schemes are available from The Law Society's International Relations Department (address below).

The training to become a solicitor is lengthy and exacting. A would-be solicitor must normally first pass either a qualifying law degree or a subject other than law, in order to take the "Common Professional Examination". He or she must then attend a one-year preparatory course at an approved college or polytechnic and pass the "Final Examination", before serving a period of articles (or apprenticeship) under the supervision of an established solicitor. The CPE may also be taken by mature students who have not graduated, although they are then required to attend a course of two years leading to the CPE rather than the usual one year course attended by graduates. School leavers wishing to qualify as solicitors must serve a minimum of five years in articles and pass the "Solicitors' First Examination" and the "Final Examination". Full details of how to qualify as a solicitor are available from The Law Society's Education & Training Department.

BARRISTERS

The Senate of the *General Council of the Bar,* 11 South Square, Gray's Inn, London WC1 advises that, in many overseas countries, the distinction between the work done by a barrister and that performed by a solicitor does not exist, since the professions are merged. It follows that much of the information describing opportunities for solicitors also applies to working prospects for barristers. The main exception is that there are no official professional exchange schemes for barristers.

The Bar Council advises, however, that overseas vacancies for British barristers are more common in the Commonwealth and North America than in most other countries. Intending overseas barristers are advised to contact the Bar Association of the country in which they are interested, addresses available on request from The Law Society library, 113 Chancery Lane, London WC2A 1PL or from the information offices of the relevant embassy in London.

There are three stages in the process of becoming a barrister. A student must (1) be admitted to an Inn of Court, (2) satisfy the educational and training requirements of the Inns and, finally (3) be called to the Bar. He or she should also usually hold a degree from a British or Irish university. Full details appear in *A Career at the Bar,* available from the Bar Council at the above address.

Recruitment Consultants

Recruitment consultants dealing with legal appointments abroad include:

Reuter Simkin Ltd, 26-28 Bedford Row, London WC1R 4HE.
Law Personnel, 95 Aldwych, London WC2B 4JF.

See also the section on *Consultants and Agencies* in the chapter *Getting the Job.*

Professional Association

The Professional Association for solicitors in England and Wales is *The Law Society,* 113 Chancery Lane, London WC2A 1PL.

The Law Society's *Appointments Registry* assists in placement of solicitors, both in England and Wales and abroad.

Medicine and Nursing

There is always a demand overseas for people with medical, paramedical and nursing qualifications, although many of the first world countries may require candidates to pass their own examinations, or undertake a further period of training, before British qualifications can be accepted.

This chapter sets out the major employment possibilities in a wide range of medical and hospital careers. Other substantial references to this type of work will be found in many of the chapters in *Worldwide Employment,* also in the chapters on *Voluntary Work, United Nations* and *Military Service.* Agencies dealing with nannies and nursery staff for domestic positions are dealt with in the chapter *Au Pair and Domestic.* Other employers and recruiters might also be found in the chapters *Getting the Job* (especially *Government Agencies*); *Oil, Mining and Engineering;* and *Transport and Tourism* (under *Merchant Navy* and *Tour Operators*). Appointments in medicine and hospital administration are also within the scope of most of the management recruitment consultants in the section *Consultants and Agencies.*

AGENCIES

The bulk of agencies in the general field of medicine are interested primarily or solely in nurses, but the list below includes a few that offer a wider scope of appointments.

ARA International, Edman House, 17-19 Maddox Street, London W1R 0EY — serves the requirements of private and public sector hospital staffing mainly in the Middle East and has vacancies for all levels of medical personnel.

BNA International, 3rd Floor, 443 Oxford Street, London W1R 2NA — have vacancies for qualified nurses in many countries around the world. Registration and language requirements vary with location. Specialist nurses are particularly welcome. Appointments are available for short term and long term contracts in Holland, Switzerland, South Africa, USA and the Middle East and Europe.

PMR International, 87 Jermyn Street, London SW1Y 6JD — coordinates the design, construction and staffing of hospital projects, especially primary health care clinics in developing areas.

Rand Medical Recruitment International, 37/38 Margaret Street, London W1N 8PS — deal with appointments for doctors, paramedical staff and nurses, as well as administrative, technical and all supporting staff for hospitals; posts are mainly in the Middle East.

Universal Care, Chester House, 9 Windsor End, Beaconsfield, Bucks. HP9 2JJ — a registered nursing agency which can advise and assist staff on nursing vacancies abroad.

HOSPITAL MANAGEMENT ORGANISATIONS

A number of organisations — American and British — are responsible for the entire management and staffing of hospitals or chains of hospitals. The main staff need is for medical, para-medical and nursing staff, but it also follows that there is a demand for engineering and maintenance personnel, where these cannot be recruited locally.

Allied Medical, 12-18 Grosvenor Gardens, London SW1W 0DZ — a British organisation requiring a wide variety of personnel for their health care projects in the Middle East.

HCA International Ltd., 49 Wigmore Street, London W1H 9LE — an American-owned organisation with offices in Sao Paulo, Sydney, Panama, Riyadh and London. Owns or manages over 4,000 hospitals worldwide, notably in the USA, Australia, Brazil, UK and one in Saudi Arabia, the King Faisal Specialist Hospital and Research Centre. All types of highly qualified medical, nursing and para medical personnel are required. Contracts are for one or two years.

International Hospitals Group (IHG), Stoke Park, Stoke Poges, Slough, Berkshire SL2 4HS — UK-owned and based group specialising in consultancy, management and operation of hospitals worldwide.

PROFESSIONAL ASSOCIATIONS

Professional associations are most useful for their advisory and information services, which, in some cases, are even available to non-members. Some associations are also active in helping their members to find work abroad. The associations below rank among the most helpful.

The *Society of Chiropodists,* 53 Welbeck Street, London W1M 7HE, can advise trained chiropodists about the prospects of working abroad.

The *International Dental Federation,* 64 Wimpole Street, London W1M 8AL, publishes the *Handbook of Regulations of Dental Practice,* which lists the licensing authorities of over 100 countries and the regulations and qualifications relating to each.

The *British Medical Association,* Tavistock Square, London WC1H 9JP has a Commonwealth and International Medical Advisory Bureau, which can give advice and information to members wishing to work abroad.

The *Institute of Medical Laboratory Sciences,* 12 Queen Anne Street, London W1M 0AU, can refer its members to the equivalent professional body in the appropriate country, or to members resident abroad. The Institute's monthly journal *IMLS Gazette* (£1.50 per issue for non-members) usually contains advertisements for overseas posts.

The *Medical Women's Federation,* Tavistock House North, Tavistock Square, London WC1H 9HX, has an Appointments Service which can circulate to interested members any information on vacancies in Britain and overseas. They warn, however, that they hear of very few vacancies, either in Britain or overseas.

The *Royal College of Nursing,* Cavendish Square, London W1M 0AB, provides an advisory service for members who wish to seek employment or undertake grant-aid study visits overseas.

The *British Association of Occupational Therapists,* 20 Rede Place, London W2 4TU, can refer members to the national professional associations in the other 34 countries belonging to the World Federation of Occupational Therapists.

The *British College of Optometrists,* 10 Knaresborough Place, London SW5 0TG, can offer advice and assistance to qualified and registered members.

The *Royal Pharmaceutical Society of Great Britain,* 1 Lambeth High Street, London SE1 7JN, cannot help in finding employment, but overseas vacancies are advertised in their publication, the weekly *Pharmaceutical Journal.* Registered pharmaceutical chemists applying for a position abroad are advised to contact the society for information on pharmaceutical practice in the country concerned. This is particularly important for those seeking work in countries where no reciprocal recognition of qualifications exists.

The College of Radiographers, 14 Upper Wimpole Street, London W1M 8BN, offers qualified radiographers assistance and advice relating to jobs overseas and in particular negotiates reciprocal arrangements with certain other countries enabling British radiographers to practice there.

The *British Association of Social Workers,* 16 Kent Street, Birmingham B5 6RD, can put its members in touch with other member associations of the International Federation of Social Workers.

FURTHER INFORMATION

The best sources of information on work prospects abroad are the professional associations (see above), which will also be able to give advice on the acceptibility of British qualifications in foreign countries.

Information on training and careers in Nursing is also offered by the *ENB Careers,* PO Box 356, Sheffield S8 0SJ. The department is not, however, in a position to answer specific enquiries about working abroad.

Oil, Mining and Engineering

As less developed areas of the world learn to benefit from modern technology, the biggest demand is for engineers, mainly in civil projects, building roads, bridges, dams, schools, hospitals and other constructions that fit in with large scale development programmes. There is also a steady demand for electrical, gas, marine and other specialised engineers. Most of the work available at present is in the Middle Eastern countries, which can afford development on a massive scale, thanks to the revenue from oil. But there are also opportunities in the less developed countries of Africa, Asia and Latin America, as well as the more developed countries of Europe, Australasia, and North America.

OIL AND GAS COMPANIES

Oil and gas companies have a constant demand for a wide variety of engineers, and an additional need for other types of personnel from the exploration stage (pilots, aerial photographers, geologists and cartographers) through to production (geochemists, petrochemists), as well as a variety of support staff. The breakdown of professional staff within a typical oil or gas company might be: engineers — 30%; geologists, geophysicists — 25%; computer programmers — 10%; accountants — 10%; administrators, researchers, analysts — 20%; with the remaining 5% made up of lawyers, doctors, nurses and others.

The main overseas opportunities occur in the Middle East, North Africa, North America, Venezuela, Australia and several European countries. The large international oil companies themselves are pressured into recruiting local staff as much as they can, and senior posts abroad are often filled by internal transfer or promotion. Vacancies are therefore highly competitive and only those with the highest qualifications should apply.

Employment in the petrochemical industry is frequently handled by management recruitment consultants: these are listed in the section *Consultants and Agencies.*

Details of the world's oil and gas companies and their activities, are given in the *Oil and Gas International Yearbook* available in public reference libraries. *The UK Offshore Oil and Gas Yearbook* gives detailed information on the production and exploration licensees in the British, Norwegian, German and Dutch sectors of the North Sea, as well as lists of the contractors and companies actively involved in providing services to the North Sea oil and gas industries.

The Personnel Departments of major national and multinational oil companies are worth contacting to obtain details of their current recruitment programmes. The UK offices of the principal companies are:

British Petroleum Co., plc, Britannic House, Moor Lane, London EC2 9BU.
Conoco (UK) Ltd., Park House, 116 Park Street, London W1Y 4NN.
Kuwait Oil Co., 54 St. James's Street, London SW1A 1JT.
Mobil, 54-60 Victoria Street, London SW1E 6QB.
Phillips Petroleum, Philipps Quadrant, 35 Guildford Road, Woking, Surrey GU22 7QT.
Shell International, Shell Centre, London SE1 7NA, (see below).
Texaco, 1 Knightsbridge Green, London SW1.
Total Oil Marine plc, Berkeley Square House, Berkeley Square, London W1X 6LT.
Umm-al-Jawaby, 33 Cavendish Square, London W1.

The companies listed below are representative of the type of recruitment being carried out in the petrochemical field, and include the companies most interested in employing British staff:

HeMan (Middle East) Ltd., 4 The Promenade, Castletown, Isle of Man — recruits engineers and technicians for the oil and gas, petrochemical, engineering and construction industry in the Middle East and Far East. All disciplines are covered, including civil, structural, mechanical, electrical and instrumentation, for all categories of engineers, designers, supervision and technical staff. Contracts range from six months to three years. For senior grade positions, degrees are essential; however, for intermediate positions HNC/HND will normally suffice.

Petro-Canada, PO Box 2844, Calgary, Alberta, Canada T2P 3E3 — is one of Canada's major corporations. It is organised into two divisions: Petro-Canada Resources explores for and produces crude oil, natural gas and natural gas liquids; Petro-Canada Products refines, distributes and markets petroleum products. Petro-Canada employs over 7,000 professional, technical, clerical and secretarial staff.

Pan-Canadian Petroleum Ltd., Pan Canadian Plaza, PO Box 2850, Calgary, Alberta, Canada T2P 2S5 — operates oil and gas wells in Western Canada, and has active interests in the USA. Professional requirements are in the fields of engineering, geology, geophysics, accounting, administration and computer services.

Shell International Petroleum Co. Ltd., Shell Centre, London SE1 7NA — offers career prospects in the Exploration and Production Function for exploration geologists, geophysicists, petroleum engineers and field engineers

— all of which will involve a considerable amount of time overseas. Shorter overseas assignments may also be included in a general career pattern in other branches of the company, e.g. manufacturing and refining, marketing or research. Support staff most often recruited in Britain include teachers and nursing sisters to work in staff schools and hospitals in the remoter areas of operation.

T.E.A.M. Services (Technical Engineering Administration & Management Services), Macklin Ave., Cowpen Lane Industrial Estate, Billingham, Cleveland TS23 4BZ — recruit qualified engineers and inspectors in design, construction, commissioning/hook-up, production, maintenance and development projects. For engineers, the minimum requirements are HNC plus 5 years relevant experience; for supervisors, City & Guilds plus 7 years relevant experience. An extensive register, constantly updated, is maintained. Contracts are for 1 year, renewable, and geographical locations covered include the European continent, the Middle East, the Far East, Canada and North Sea offshore. Clients are principal oil and gas companies, major contractors and selected vendors.

Addresses of the UK offices of other petrochemical and gas companies can be found in the Central London Yellow pages under *Oil Companies* and *Oil and Natural Gas Exploration Companies.*

Pipelines

One area where personnel are constantly required is pipeline work: contracts of two to three months require an enormous amount of labour. Although it is better to possess some kind of specialised skill (digger, driver, welder or crane operator), there is also work for the unskilled on fencing, cooking or just general labouring.

Although you could contact the major companies in this field, it is unlikely that this would be of much use, since you must have prior knowledge of when and where contracts are due to take place. The quickest and simplest way to discover these details is to obtain a copy of *Pipeline Digest,* available from PO Box 55225, Houston, Texas 77255, USA, at a cost of $5 (or $45 for 24 issues). This excellent publication contains lists of all the major contracts planned throughout the world, including the name of the main contractor with telephone number, and the start-up and completion dates. With this information, those interested in this kind of work can contact the correct main contractor, and in addition find out from that source the firms involved in sub-contract work.

MINING

Whether it be coal or gold, mining offers employment in most of the countries of the world. Areas particularly rich in minerals include North America, Australia, Malaysia, South and Central Africa, Nigeria, Sierra Leone and Thailand. The core of the mining personnel are geologists, metallurgists, geophysicists, etc., but the operational and back-up staff cover a broad spectrum of professions.

Mining Associations

The *Mining Association of the United Kingdom* (formerly the Overseas Mining Association), 6 St. James's Square, London SW1Y 4LD, is an association of mining companies operating mainly abroad. Recruitment is carried out by the individual companies,a complete list of which is available from the association. Applicants will find, however, that the overwhelming tendency is towards recruitment of local staff. Senior professional staff with a great deal of relevant experience are the only British applicants likely to be offered employment.

The *Mineral Industry Manpower and Careers Unit,* Prince Consort Road, London SW7, can offer advice on professional courses in the various mineral technologies, including mineral processing, mining engineering and petroleum engineering. The unit can also offer guidance on employment prospects for such graduates within the UK and overseas.

Mining companies

A complete, worldwide list of mining companies will be found in the *Mining International Yearbook,* available in public reference libraries. Those that express an active interest in employing British staff include:

British Columbia and Yukon Chamber of Mines, 840 West Hastings Street, Vancouver BC, Canada V6C 1C8 — publishes and distributes a free list of the major mining operations in British Columbia, Yukon Territory and Northwest Territories.

Gencor Recruitment, 30 Ely Place, London EC1N 6UA — a South African mining finance house, has openings for mechanical, electrical and chemical engineers, as well as for chemists, geologists and metallurgists.

ENGINEERING

Engineering covers a wide field of specialities and in addition to the opportunities listed below, references to engineering work will also be found in most of the other chapters of this book, notably: *Getting the Job, Voluntary Work, International Organisations, United Nations, British Government Departments, Military Service,* the section *Consultants and Agencies,* and the chapters in *Worldwide Employment.* This section also overlaps with the other two sections in this chapter where the main needs are for engineering and technical staff.

Engineering & Construction Companies

The number of engineering companies operating large-scale projects abroad is obviously immense, and a complete listing would be a futile task. The following selection includes a cross-section of the types of company that are interested in British applicants, and is representative of the broad scope of work available to those with the relevant qualifications.

W. S. Atkins Group Consultants, Woodcote Grove, Ashley Road, Epsom, Surrey KT18 5BW — a British-based engineering/management consultancy operating internationally and covering a wide variety of engineering (civil, structural, transportation, offshore, process) as well as project management, industrial and economic planning, research and development, testing and inspection. Employment is on permanent career terms, based in the UK, with the probability of overseas assignments on a short or long term basis (one to two year contracts for specific contracts overseas).

Kennedy & Donkin, Westbrook Mills, Godalming, Surrey GU7 2AZ — provide consulting engineering services particularly for projects for the supply and generation of electric power but also for building services and transportation. Many projects are overseas and offer short term visits and residential appointments.

John Laing International Ltd., Page Street, London, NW7 2ER — is involved in construction contracts in Jordan, Egypt and the Gulf area. In most instances, tradespeople are recruited directly in the country concerned, but categories of Trades Foreman, Site Engineers and construction staff of a supervisory nature are generally filled by expatriates.

Sir M. MacDonald & Partners, Dementer House, Station Road, Cambridge CB1 2RS — the MacDonald group of consulting engineering works on multi-disciplinary projects worldwide. Staff is recruited at all levels, on a permanent and contract basis. The firm generally employs graduates in civil, mechanical and electrical engineering; some staff have post-graduate qualifications in disciplines such as hydrology, economics, water resources engineering and management. The majority of the work, about 85%, is overseas and there are currently offices in 25 countries. At any one time 65% of the staff is operational abroad.

Survey and Development Services, 3 Hope Street, Bo'ness, West Lothian EH51 0AA — are land surveyors involved in topographic mapping by ground and aerial techniques. Their overseas involvement is currently confined to the Middle East and specifically Saudi Arabia where the company has an associate office with Al Jalahima and Al Amoudi Company (JATCO) in Dammam, Saudi Arabia. Survey and mapping using computers compatible with the UK office is becoming an increasing part of the work, together with survey engineering control. Personnel for overseas tours are either seconded or taken on for specific contract periods.

Ward, Ashcroft and Parkman, Cunard Building, Liverpool L3 1ES — operate as consulting engineers in Nigeria, Kenya, Uganda, Indonesia and other countries in East Africa and the Far East. Personnel requirements are for chartered civil and mechanical engineers with experience in water supply, public health, irrigation and highway design.

Recruitment Consultants

The companies listed below are among the many management recruitment consultants involved principally or solely in the field of engineering and technology. Consultants with a broader range of interests (usually including the engineering disciplines) are listed in the section *Consultants and Agencies.*

ARA International, 17-19 Maddox Street, London W1R 0EY — recruit a wide range of experienced/qualified engineers, managerial, professional and technical personnel for major developments in oil, petrochemicals, telecommunications, marine and defense, throughout the Middle East and in many countries around the world.

Assistance Teknica Ltd., York House, Borough Road, Middlesbrough, Cleveland TS1 2HP — an operational and management consultancy, providing technical assistance to Western Europe, North Africa, Middle East, West Africa and the Far East; the main interest centering on the iron and steel industry with oil mining and the engineering industry playing a secondary role. Technical personnel with a minimum of ten years experience are deployed, the contracts usually involving operation and maintenance of various plants. In addition short term consultancy work is available on an *ad hoc* basis, this usually extends from a few days to two to three months in duration.

Benny Electronics Ltd., 1A Telford Road, Ferndown Industrial Estate, Wimborne, Dorset BH21 7QN — employs personnel on a contract basis, and under agency for other companies, both in the UK and overseas. Categories of personnel recruited include draughtsmen/draughtswomen, engineers, technicians, electricians, petrochemical engineers, electronics and mechanical engineers, instrument mechanics, etc.

Davy Services Ltd., 250 Euston Road, London NW1 2PG — part of Davy Mckee (London) Ltd., a worldwide engineering and construction company. The company recruits suitable project or engineering candidates for contract assignments worldwide.

Devenco (UK) Ltd., Collingham House, Gladstone Road, London SW19 1QH — have an overseas division dealing with appointments in civil engineering, petro-chemical engineering, construction, mechanical engineering, electrical engineering and accountancy in all categories from graduates to artisans. Territories covered are Africa, Europe and the Middle and Far East.

Employment Placement & Training Ltd., 44-48 Hide Hill, Berwick-upon-Tweed, Northumberland TD15 1AB — an employment agency servicing the requirements of the construction industry. The following disciplines are covered: engineers (all types), detail and design draughtsmen, tradesmen and inspection personnel, and managers and administrators.

Inspectorate Site Services Ltd., Haig House, 15 Young Street, London W8 5EH — operate mainly in the petrochemical, offshore and heavy engineering/ construction industries, providing technical manpower on a contract hire basis overseas.

Inter Engineering (Consultancy) Ltd., 22/24 Buckingham Palace Road, London SW1W 0QP — is part of an international engineering organisation operating in the petrochemical, chemical, nuclear, aircraft and automotive industries, and recruit British personnel for contracts both in the UK and overseas.

McQ International Services, 12 West Street, Portadown, County Armagh, Northern Ireland — recruits construction managers for client companies mainly in Africa and the Middle East. Of particular interest are civil engineers and quantity surveyors. Applicants should be degree qualified and be 25-45 years old. Contracts usually have a duration of two years (renewable).

Personnel Strongfield Services, 151 Great Portland Street, London W1N 5FB — have placements for contract and permanent staff engineers in the aerospace and electronics industries, mainly for positions in Europe. For contracts over 12 months duration, degree level qualifications are expected.

PMR International, 87 Jermyn Street, London SW1Y 6JD — operate extensively overseas, particularly in the Middle East and Africa. Files are kept on executives and management applications, and an Overseas Appointments Register covering professional and qualified staff in the fields of civil engineering and building.

Survey Data Services Ltd., 49-57 High Street, Droitwich, Worcs. WR9 8EP — specialists in the hire of site engineering staff — site engineers, agents, land surveyors, to consultants and the construction industry. Associated companies, Survey Data Ltd. and Survey Data Nigeria Ltd. are involved in land and engineering surveys in the UK and overseas.

Thomas Telford International Recruiting Consultants, Thomas Telford House, 1 Heron Quay, London E14 9XF — is the official recruitment consultancy of the Institution of Civil Engineers and the Institute of Chemical Engineers. The consultancy is structured to serve the following industries and specialisations: civil engineering and construction, chemical engineering and process industries, and the oil and gas industry. The company serves the staff requirements of clients across the whole spectrum of engineering positions, both in the UK and overseas.

PROFESSIONAL ASSOCIATIONS

The Appointments Bureau of *The Royal Institute of British Architects,* 66 Portland Place, London W1N 4AD, handles UK and overseas appointments (mostly in Africa and the Middle East), for experienced Architects and Architectural Technicians. The RIBA International Directory of Practices gives details of British Practices with overseas branches.

The *Royal Institution of Chartered Surveyors* has an Appointments Service at 12 Great George Street, Parliament Square, London SW1 3AD. Over 5,000 of its qualified members are serving in over 100 overseas countries including the Middle East and North America. Interested applicants should approach the Appointments Service direct.

The *Institution of Electrical Engineers,* 2 Savoy Place, London WC2R 0BL — provides a professional brief for its members, called *Working Overseas,* which contains general information on living and working abroad. Its monthly newsletter, *IEE News,* also contains a job vacancy supplement, which sometimes includes overseas positions.

The *Institute of Metals,* No 1 Carlton House Terrace, London SW1Y 5DB, can offer its members advice on employment problems and prospects, through branches and individual members overseas.

Secretarial, Translating and Interpreting

SECRETARIAL

Opportunities for properly trained and linguistically fluent secretaries abound in many countries and organisations abroad. Apart from the employment agencies listed below, prospective secretaries should consult the chapters on *International Organisations, United Nations, Voluntary Work* and *British Government Departments.* Those agencies which specialise in secretarial vacancies in one specific country are listed under the relevant country chapter. The branches, affiliates and subsidiaries of British companies overseas, listed at the back of each country chapter, may also be worth contacting. In general, any sufficiently qualified secretary who speaks the local language should be able to apply successfully for work on the spot.

As well as opportunities with the agencies below, senior secretarial positions are handled by several of the companies listed in the section *Management Recruitment Consultants,* above.

Inspectorate Site Services Ltd., Haig House, 15 Young Street, London W8 5EH — a worldwide recruiting agency, mainly in the engineering field, although there are occasions for bilingual secretaries.

International Secretaries, 174 New Bond Street, London W1 — can help experienced secretaries with shorthand and typing skills (and, where relevant, knowledge of the country's language) to find work in the Middle East, Europe and the Far East.

Manpower, Manpower House, 270/272 High Street, Slough SL1 1LJ — the world's largest temporary office employment agency, offering secretarial work to experienced, linguistically fluent secretaries in offices throughout Europe. They have offices in Ireland, France, Germany, Holland, Denmark, Belgium, Luxembourg, Spain and Portugal, as well as in Israel, Latin

America and the Far East. Addresses available from their headquarters at the above address.

Multilingual Services, 22 Charing Cross Road, London WC2H 0HR — selects experienced bilingual secretaries and, to a lesser extent, professionally qualified technical translators, for permanent posts in EC countries.

Polyglot Agency, Bank Chambers, 214 Bishopsgate, London EC2M 4QA — a specialist employment agency for linguists that recruits experienced bilingual secretaries and qualified translators for positions in Belgium, France and West Germany.

TRANSLATING AND INTERPRETING

Overseas work for translators and interpreting does exist for properly qualified British personnel, though recruiting often takes place on a less formal basis than for secretarial jobs abroad. Prospective applicants in this field are advised that it is very much a cottage industry, with most of the work going to locally recruited freelance operators. Many organisations, particularly those dealing with the prospering area of technical translation, demand very high standards. Professional translators' qualifications should also be held and some experience in the commercial or technical sphere is usually required.

Interested applicants should consult the organisations listed in the chapters on *Transport and Tourism* (especially the *Tourist Trade* section), *International Organisations* and *United Nations.* See also the organisations dealing with international work in the London *Yellow Pages,* under the heading *Translators and Interpreters.*

Berlitz Translation Service, Berlitz schools around the world often recruit freelance translators and interpreters from the locally based English community. A list of Berlitz schools is available on request from Berlitz's office at 321 Oxford Street, London W1A 3BZ. Particular queries should be addressed direct to the individual schools. General information on work for translators and interpreters is available from *Berlitz Corporate Worldwide Headquarters,* 866 3rd Avenue, 31st Floor, New York, NY 10022, USA.

Interlingua TTI Ltd., Imperial House, 15-19 Kingsway, London WC2B 6UU — is the world's largest translation company with offices in the USA, Switzerland, Hong Kong, Singapore, Spain, France, West Germany and Canada.

Institute of Linguists, Mangold House, 24A Highbury Grove, London N5 2EA — cannot find employment but does offer general advice on careers with languages, how to make use of qualifications already held, and details of qualifications required for specific jobs connected with languages.

Teaching

There are generally good opportunities for qualified teachers to work abroad, although this will depend on the subject being offered. For professional teachers, over-training in the first world countries has led to some slackening of demand for long term opportunities; however there still appears to be a steady stream of short term openings. In the developing countries there is always a shortage of qualified teachers, particularly in higher education and specialist training. Vacancies are widely advertised in the national press, particularly in *The Times Educational* and *Higher Education Supplements*.

Local education authorities subscribe to the teacher exchange schemes described below. Apart from these two schemes, however, there is no longer any possibility for teachers who apply for positions abroad to obtain secondment from their LEA, and therefore there is no longer any guarantee of employment when you return.

Working abroad might have an adverse effect on social security (enquire at your DHSS office) and superannuation contributions (enquiries to the *DES,* Pensions Branch, Mowden Hall, Staindrop Hall, Darlington, Co. Durham DL3 9BG).

The DES issues a free leaflet (721 Pen.) which gives information about the arrangements which exist whereby a teacher may pay combined contributions for a period of absence from reckonable service, available from the Pensions Branch.

When looking for work abroad, whether in the first world or in the developing countries, some sort of qualification is usually necessary. For those who are unqualified and wish to teach, a most useful qualification is the diploma in teaching English as a foreign language (TEFL). The growing demand for English teachers throughout the world has led to a growth market in the field of TEFL and there is therefore no shortage of jobs for those with this qualification. The diploma is awarded by the Royal Society of Arts after four or five weeks of study full-time and is available in many institutions throughout the UK. Alternatively, graduates can attend a one year Postgraduate Certificate in Education (PGCE) course.

The British Council's *English Teaching Information Centre (ETIC),* 10 Spring Gardens, London SW1A 2BN, provides information to members of the public on all aspects of English language teaching (ELT). ETIC also produces various publications, including a free leaflet entitled *Brief List TEFL/TESL Academic Courses.*

The unit is also responsible for compiling the *English Language Teaching Profiles,* a series of country-specific papers which describe the present state of English Language Teaching in these countries. A valuable source of reference for ELT teachers, these profiles are available free on request from the Information Centre at the above address.

Apart from the prospects outlined on the following pages, teaching posts are also featured in the chapters on *Voluntary Work* and *British Government Departments,* and under the separate country chapters. Teacher recruitment also forms the bulk of the activities of many organisations listed under *Government Agencies* in the chapter *Getting the Job.*

TEACHER EXCHANGE SCHEMES

The Central Bureau for Educational Visits and Exchanges, Seymour Mews House, Seymour Mews, London W1H 9PE — arranges Assistantships for junior teachers and university students on an exchange basis (apply at the beginning of the penultimate year). Contracts are for one academic year, and posts are available in about 40 countries in Europe, Africa and Latin America.

The League for the Exchange of Commonwealth Teachers, Seymour Mews House, 2nd Floor Suite, 26-37 Seymour Mews, Wigmore Street, London W1H 0AA — arranges for British Teachers with at least five years' experience, aged 25-45, to exchange their post for one year with a teacher from another Commonwealth country. Included in the scheme are Australia, Bermuda, Barbados, Canada, Hong Kong, India, Jamaica, Kenya, Singapore, New Zealand and Trinidad. Full UK salary is paid, and cost of living and travel grants are awarded.

BRITISH COUNCIL

Apart from the teaching and other posts within the British Council (see under *British Goverment Departments),* the Council is also active as a recruiting agency for teaching and educational advisory posts in foreign governments and institutions. Most vacancies are senior English teaching positions at all levels of education, so the necessary requirements are usually a degree or diploma in education, or a TEFL qualification. Teaching experience is always required, except for lectureships and assistantships in Eastern European countries. Apart from English teaching, jobs available through the Council are mainly for technical instructors in colleges and secondary schools. The scope of the appointments is worldwide, but concentrated in non-English speaking countries. Most contracts are for two years and renewable.

Further details from the Overseas Educational Appointments Department, *British Council,* 65 Davis Street, London W1Y 2AA, from whom the free booklet *Teaching Overseas* is available.

PRIVATE SCHOOLS

The European Council of International Schools, 21B Lavant Street,

Petersfield, Hants GU32 3EL — an organisation of over 150 independent international schools in Europe, but with Associate Members in many other countries round the World. Teachers must be fully qualified and are ordinarily required to have had at least two years full time experience. Current individual membership is £80 (first time) and £55 (renewing). Subscribers receive a periodic Newsletter, the twice-yearly International Schools Journal (otherwise £8 per annum) and the annual Directory (which costs £13) which, apart from giving details on all members also gives information on some 750 independent international schools throughout the World. Individual members of ECIS are also entitled to make use of the Council's placement services, which match applications to current vacancies, circulating professional dossiers to appropriate schools.

Gabbitas, Truman & Thring Services Ltd., Broughton House, 6/7/8 Sackville Street, Piccadilly, London W1X 2BR — recruit on behalf of overseas English speaking schools and institutions for teachers with qualifications and experience, aged 25 and over.

Worldwide Education Service, Strode House, 44-50 Osnaburg Street, London NW1 3NN — recruits teachers for some 80 schools all over the world. In addition, Worldwide Education Service also operates MASON (Master Access to the Source of Names), an international databank of teachers and schools for matching suitable applicants with existing vacancies abroad. This service deals with primary and secondary level teaching and administrative posts, including nursery teachers, private tutors and TEFL teachers.

LANGUAGE SCHOOLS

Native English speakers are required by language schools abroad. The direct method of teaching is universally used, so knowledge of the country's language is unnecessary. However, a qualification in TEFL is always required, and some schools insist on teachers completing their own course before offering them a job. These courses (except the free Berlitz course) must be paid for by the candidate, and no guarantee is made that a job will be offered at the end of it.

Berlitz School of Languages Ltd., 29 rue de la Michodiere, 75063 Paris — have a few vacancies at their schools in Paris. Preference is given to locally recruited English native speakers. Staff must be aged 23-45 and undergo a free training course of variable duration (usually 12 days). Berlitz schools around the world also occasionally recruit EFL teachers. Applicants should apply direct to these schools, addresses available from Berlitz's office at 79 Wells Street, London W1.

Inlingua Teacher Service, 28 Rotton Park Road, Edgbaston, Birmingham B16 9JL — each year recruits approximately 150 teachers of English as a Foreign Language to work in one of its 180 associated schools abroad. Vacancies occur mainly in Spain, Italy, West Germany and Singapore. Candidates must have a degree and teaching experience would be useful. Prospective applicants should write to the Recruitment Officers at the above address.

International House, 106 Piccadilly, London W1V 9FL — offers TEFL posts in its 80 affiliated schools in Europe, the Middle East, North Africa, South America and the Far East. The minimum qualification for appointment is an RSA Certificate in TEFL with a Pass Grade B. Most recruiting is carried out in spring or early summer in preparation for the beginning of the academic year. However some posts are available at other times of the year. Contracts in Europe are normally for 9-12 months, while those further afield tend to be for two years. Contracts are normally renewable by mutual consent. Travelling expenses and settling-in allowances are paid. For further details, contact the Teacher Selection Department at *International House.*

International Language Centres Ltd., 1 Riding House Street, London W1A 3AS — employ teachers in their overseas centres on a full-time basis. Contracts are normally for one year (two years in Japan). They also have vacancies in their Summer Schools in July and August. Candidates should be graduates and hold the RSA Prepatory Certificate in TEFL. For many of the posts, including the Summer Schools, teachers must have some previous experience. Air fares are paid at the beginning and end of contracts; salaries are reviewed annually. Further details from their Personnel Department at the above address.

OTHER OPPORTUNITIES

The *Centre for British Teachers,* Quality House, Quality Court, Chancery Lane, London WC2A 1HP — employs qualified teachers to teach in Brunei, Germany, Malaysia and Oman.

Christians Abroad, 11 Carteret Street, London SW1H 9DL — recruits graduate teachers on behalf of overseas employers, mainly in Africa and the Caribbean.

The Embassy of the People's Republic of China, Section of Education, 51 Draycott Gardens, London W13 — has an exchange scheme for English teachers to teach in China (see the chapter on *China*).

International Language Services, 14 Rollestone Street, Salisbury, Wiltshire SP1 1ED — recruits teachers for Sweden and Italy. Applicants should be between 21 and 40 with a degree and/or diploma in education. Applicants who do not hold either a Cert.Ed. or PGCE cannot be considered. Single teachers are preferred; exceptionally, married couples who both teach can be considered.

The *Japanese Information Centre,* 9 Grosvenor Square, London W1X 9LB, runs the Japan Exchange and Teaching (JET) programme. See the chapter on *Japan* for further information.

Mozambique Information Office, 7A Caledonian Road, London N1 9DX — launched a recruitment programme in 1975 at the request of the government of the People's Republic of Mozambique. Teachers of EFL, science and maths subjects, primary school teachers for the International School (English medium), and University teachers are currently included in the primary categories of recruitment.

The programme's aim is to enable people with relevant skills to assist and participate in the transformation of Mozambique from an under-developed country into a modern, independent, socialist state. Minimum requirements are the relevant professional training and at least two years post-qualification experience in the intended area of work.

The *Service Children's Education Authority* engages over 1,800 teachers in schools catering for children of British Army, Navy and Air Force servicement and Ministry of Defence civilian staffs employed overseas.

About 100 schools are in operation abroad, over three-quarters of them in Germany. There are also schools in Cyprus, Hong Kong, the Netherlands, Belgium, Denmark, Italy, Norway, Gibraltar, Brunei, and Nepal.

Applications are considered from qualified teachers who have completed their probationary teaching service and have recent experience in the UK, including at least two years in a post similar to that for which they are applying. The upper age limit for applicants is 47.

Appointments, which are renewable or transferable, are for three years. Teachers are civilians but with the status of officers regarding travel and accommodation. Pay is at Baker rates plus special allowances which are largely tax free. Classes are often smaller than in the UK to ensure that the children do not suffer educationally through the frequent moves of their parents.

For further details, contact the *Service Children's Education Authority,* Teachers Appointments Section, Headquarters, Director of Army Education, Court Road, Eltham, London SE9 5NR.

The *Sudan Cultural Counsellor's Office,* Sudan Embassy, 31 Rutland Gate, London SW7 1PG — occasionally has positions for English teachers in Sudanese schools as well as Khartoum University and Polytechnic.

HIGHER EDUCATION

The Association of Commonwealth Universities, John Foster House, 36 Gordon Square, London WC1H 0PF — provides facilities for any member university (and for certain other institutions) to invite applications and assess candidates from outside its own region for vacancies on its staff. The service is most frequently used by universities in Australia, New Zealand, Papua New Guinea, the West Indies, Botswana, Lesotho, Swaziland, Zimbabwe and Malaya. The Hong Kong Polytechnic, the City Polytechnic of Hong Kong, and certain colleges of advanced education in Australia also make use of the Association's Appointments Service.

Vacancies are advertised as they arise in the UK national press, and details are circulated to university registrars and careers advisory services in the UK.

SOURCES OF INFORMATION

All the organisations above provide brochures and information on their prospects abroad. If you want to apply direct to schools abroad, telephone directories are a good starting point, and some cultural institutes can provide lists of possible employers. A number of relevant reference sources will be found in the *Specific Contacts* sections of the various chapters in *Worldwide Employment.*

Those who wish to make direct applications to foreign universities, academies, colleges, learned societies and research institutes, will find a very comprehensive listing of addresses in the book *The World of Learning,* published by Europa and available in public reference libraries.

Detailed information about universities in all Commonwealth countries is contained in the *Commonwealth Universities Yearbook,* (1987 edition £83) which is published by the Association of Commonwealth Universities (see above) who also publish the biennial *Scholarships Guide for Commonwealth Postgraduate Students* (1987-89 edition £11.50), which gives information about awards open to graduates of Commonwealth universities who wish to undertake postgraduate study or research in another Commonwealth country; and, also biennial, *Awards for Commonwealth University Academic Staff* (1988-90 edition £12.50), which gives information for university teachers who wish to research, study or teach in another Commonwealth country. These books are available for consultation in academic and public reference libraries, and in many British Council offices.

Jobs in Japan, by John Wharton (see bibliography for details), describes many openings for English teachers in Japan.

The *Nigerian Universities Office,* 180 Tottenham Court Road, London W1P 9LE can be contacted about university teaching appointments in Nigeria.

Useful free booklets on careers and work prospects in teaching overseas include:

Teaching Overseas, by the British Council, 65 Davis Street, London W1Y 2AA.

Opportunities in Education Overseas, by the Overseas Development Administration, Abercrombie House, Eaglesham Road, East Kilbride, Glasgow G75 8EA.

Transport, Tourism, and Catering

The tourist and transport industries form a vast source of employment for millions of people worldwide. However, while the jobs described in this chapter may take you literally around the world, most of the work will still be based in Britain. Whether you work as an airline pilot or a lorry driver, your overseas experience will only be seen as a series of excursions from home base. Apart from the seasonal or permanent foreign-based staff of British tourist companies, opportunities for positions actually based abroad are rare.

Merchant Navy

Following a period of retrenchment, which has seen a continuing decline in the number of ships in the Merchant Navy, shipping companies now appear to be recruiting again. There are currently vacancies for appropriately qualified applicants for training as deck and engineer officers as well as ratings. Enquiries should be made direct to individual shipping companies, a list of which appears in the Yellow Pages of the major seaport areas, under *Shipping Companies and Agents*. The Department of Transport has recently announced a scheme of assistance for training Merchant Navy officers. A list of companies participating in the scheme may be obtained from the scheme's coordinating agent, which is located at the General Council of British Shipping (see the section on Further Details).

OFFICERS

(1) *Deck and Engineer Cadets:* these schemes provide training for future deck and engineer officers in the Merchant Navy. Minimum entry requirements are the possession of 4 GCSE passes (or equivalent), including

mathematics, a physical science, English and one other subject. Candidates for the deck department must have perfect form and colour vision.

(2) *Radio/Electronic Officers:* candidates are required to complete a 3-year course of training for the Home Office Marine Radio General Certificate and Radar Certificate before employment. Employment opportunities for sea-going radio officers are limited. Enquiries should be addressed to one of the maritime radio departments situated in colleges of further education in major seaport areas.

(3) *Pursers, Purserettes (including Stewardesses, Nurses etc.):* these categories of employment are normally only available on passenger ships. There are very few ships in this category and the companies normally recruit direct. There are likely to be long waiting lists.

(4) *Former Merchant Navy Officers and Ratings interested in re-entry:* there are relatively few vacancies for officers and ratings who have left the Merchant Navy to re-enter although opportunities do occur from time to time and approaches should be made to individual shipping companies.

RATINGS

Entry as a junior deck or catering rating is generally restricted to young persons aged 16-17½. AB certificates are issued after successfully sitting the qualifying examination and complying with regulations regarding periods of service and pre-sea training. Details of the many certificates that can be gained by merchant navy ratings are given in the relevant Merchant Shipping Notices (see under *Further Details,* below).

POSITIONS ON PASSENGER SHIPS

The openings described above apply equally to both passenger and freight vessels. In addition an extremely limited number of vacancies occasionally become available on passenger ships only. Competition for these posts is very tight, and there are absolutely no trainee schemes. Direct application should be made to those shipping companies who operate large passenger vessels (lists available in the *Journal of Commerce*). The following are the most usual specialist staff areas:

a) *Assistant Purser/Purserette* — secretarial, clerical and reception work. Candidates should be 21-30, with GCSEs in English and maths., shorthand at 120 w.p.m., typing at 55 w.p.m. and have a pleasant manner.

(b) *Children's Host/Hostess* — responsible to the purser for children on board (organising games, entertainments etc.). Candidates, aged 25-35, should possess the relevant qualifications and experience for working with the under 12 age range. (Some ships also take on Nursery Stewards/Stewardesses, who may be younger, but must have an NNEB Certificate or Certificate of Nursery Training College).

(c) *Social Host/Hostess* — plays host to passengers, especially the old and lonely, and organises general passenger entertainment. Candidates, aged

26-34, should combine a high educational standard with a sympathetic manner and good organisational ability.

(d) *Telephonist* — maintains a 24-hour service on a duty rota. Candidates should be aged 24-35 with GPO training and first class hotel switchboard experience. Knowledge of at least one continental language is preferable.

(e) *Hairdresser* — must hold a recognised hairdressing diploma and be fully trained and qualified in styling, beauty culture and manicure.

(f) *Retail Assistant* — must have several years retail experience.

Allders International (Ships) Ltd., 84/98 Southampton Road, Eastleigh, Hampshire SO5 5ZF — recruits retail staff and beauty therapists/hairstylists, both with a minimum of three years experience, for their retail concessions on board cruise ships worldwide and also UK ships and ferries. Candidates must be at least 23 years old and are required to work on board ship for a period of six months, which is followed by one month's leave.

FURTHER DETAILS

The *General Council of British Shipping,* 30-32 St. Mary Axe, London EC3A 8ET, can supply names and addresses of companies and other organisations which are sponsoring trainees under the Government-assisted training scheme.

The *Department of Transport,* Marine Directorate, Sunley House, 90 High Holborn, London WC1V 6LP, issues a wide variety of Merchant Shipping Notices, including explanations of the regulations regarding examinations, qualifications, periods of service etc. required for attaining different ranks. A list of current Merchant Shipping Notices is available from the Department in the guise of Merchant Shipping Notice No. M. 1287; this is revised on an annual basis with a change of number.

The *Southampton Institute of Higher Education,* East Park Terrace, Southampton SO9 4WW, can supply information on appointments and training requirements for radio officers. Enquiries should be addressed to the Department of Systems and Communications Engineering, Faculty of Technology, which also runs courses in electronics and communications.

The *National Sea Training College,* Denton, Gravesend, Kent DA12 2HR, is able to provide further information about recruitment opportunities for ratings.

Youth Employment Offices and Mercantile Marine Offices will give information and advice to all those contemplating a career in the Merchant Navy.

HMSO Publications

Relevant HMSO publications include:

Certificates of competency in the Merchant Navy — two volumes: *Deck Officer Requirements* (£6.60) and *Marine Engineer Officer Syllabuses &*

Examination Papers (£6.30) published by the Department of Trade.

Handbook for Radio Operators (£4.50) with Amendment 1 (20p), published by the Post Office.

These publications are available from the *Government Bookshop*, 49 High Holborn, London WC1V 6HB (mail orders: PO Box 276 London SW8); or from the Government Bookshops in Belfast, Edinburgh, Birmingham, Bristol and Manchester; or through any appointed bookshop.

Civil Aviation

Civil Aviation is a constantly expanding industry, which each year offers career possibilities to a growing number of people.

Unfortunately, air traffic controllers, airport staff, and other ground crew personnel can rarely obtain a position abroad; on British airlines, all foreign-based personnel, with the exception of a few top-rank administrative officials, are recruited locally; and foreign airlines prefer to recruit their own nationals in their home country. Even the developing countries, which, in the past, have relied on experienced personnel from Britain and other western countries, are now becoming more independent of our help. For these reasons, this section is devoted almost entirely to two careers: pilot and cabin crew. Even in these jobs, personnel will mostly be based in Britain (usually at one of the London airports), but will be travelling internationally in the course of their duties.

PILOTS

In 1979, British Airways decided to suspend their Pilot Training Scheme, the only sponsored cadetship available in Britain, providing training for young men and women to the standard necessary to obtain the Civil Aviation Authority Commercial Pilot's Licence and Instrument Rating. At present, British Airways and one or two other leading airlines offer limited sponsorship; applicants should apply to the airlines direct.

The essential requirements for applicants are being reviewed but are likely to be as follows:-

Academic: Five subjects including two at GCE "A" level, one of which must be Mathematics. At GCSE level, Physics and English Language will be mandatory. For Scottish candidates: Five SCE subjects including three at Higher Grade, one of which must be Mathematics. At Ordinary Grade, Physics and English Language will be mandatory.

Age: When training commences the pilot cadet must be at least 18.

Medical: A high standard of physical fitness is required. The only schools which run CAA approved courses for the Commercial Pilot's Licence and Instrument Rating are:

Air Service Training Ltd., Perth Aerodrome, Perth PH2 6NP
Bristons Helicopters, Redhill Aerodrome, Redhill, Surrey RH1 1SQ
Oxford Air Training School, Oxford Airport, Kidlington, Oxford OX5 1RA
Trent Air Services, Cranfield Airfield, Bedford MK43 0AI

Further information can be obtained from the Public Relations Department, *Civil Aviation Authority,* CAA House, 45-59 Kingsway, London WC2B 6TE.

CABIN CREW

The work of air stewards and air stewardesses (or hostesses) is very demanding: during one flight they can expect to fulfil the roles of receptionist, clerk, nurse, waiter/waitress, nanny, guide and companion. While experience in any of these occupations is obviously an advantage, a more important qualification is the ability to discharge all these duties and retain an unruffled appearance and a pleasant humour throughout.

Although applicants are normally required to have reached a GCSE standard of education, and fluency in at least one foreign language is preferred, the selection procedure is based far more on the applicant's disposition and ability to converse pleasantly, freely and reassuringly, in English. An above average intelligence and general awareness are essential.

Good health is another deciding factor; there are also height and weight limitations, since, especially for air stewardesses, a neat appearance, including a good figure, is most important. The minimum entry age is 18, but most successful candidates are in their early to mid-twenties.

FURTHER DETAILS

Apart from the sponsored pilot training schemes discussed above, applicants for appointments with British airlines, and with private air charter and helicopter services, should contact companies direct; a full list can be found in the *Flight Directory of British Aviation* (under *Commercial Aviation*) available in most reference libraries, and which also contains a list of foreign and Commonwealth airlines with offices in Britain.

General Publications

Leaflets on careers in Civil Aviation occasionally pass through the hands of local Careers Offices.

The Civil Aviation Authority publishes a number of books and pamphlets, including some that are of interest to prospective air and ground crew members. A catalogue is available from the *CAA, Printing and Publication Services,* Greville House, 37 Gratton Road, Cheltenham, Glos., GL50 2BN.

Road Transport

There are opportunities for drivers with relevant HGV licences and several years experience in this country, to drive lorries on international routes, mainly within Europe, although a few companies operate on routes into Asia and North Africa. Knowledge of a few foreign languages is obviously helpful. Most of the international companies prefer to employ drivers for a trial period of several months in this country before sending them abroad.

Since most companies employ only a few drivers for their foreign routes, applicants should enquire about prospects with more than one company, in order to learn of the best chances of foreign travel. A wide variety of companies — removal and freight — are listed in the major cities' Yellow Pages under *Road Haulage.*

If you are employed as an international trucker, or if you are running a haulage firm that operates on international routes, you are advised to consult the publication *Your Lorry Abroad — Guide for British Goods Vehicle Operators Making Journeys Overseas,* available from the *Department of Transport,* International Road Freight Office, Westgate House, Westgate Road, Newcastle upon Tyne NE1 1TW.

The road transport trade associations may also be able to help with enquiries about international work, and have lists of all the main British companies in the field:

The *Road Haulage Association,* 104 New Kings Road, London SW6 4LN.

The Freight Transport Association, Hermes House, St. Johns Road, Tunbridge Wells, TN4 9UZ.

The Tourist Trade

TOUR OPERATORS

The overseas requirements of conventional tour operators are mainly seasonal, and are usually limited to two types of personnel: couriers and representatives. Coach tour operators also need coach drivers. While the coach drivers and couriers work from a home base, representatives are based in towns and resorts abroad, and are sometimes either recruited locally or selected from among the permanent staff in Britain. The requirements for the different types of work are: a PSV licence and coach driving experience for drivers; fluency in at least one European language for couriers and representatives, who must also have the ability to organise their tour members, liaise with hotels, etc., and cope with any problems that might arise; representatives also need a good knowledge of the town or area which they are to work.

Apart from the overlanders (whose staffing needs are discussed in a separate section below) the tour operators' scope of recruitment widens the further the tours deviate from the norm. Those that cater largely for families, for example, will require children's representatives to organise itineraries, activities, entertainments and baby-sitting. Tours for the disabled will need a quota of nurses and doctors; sports and activities holidays will need relevant instructors and supervisors; camping holiday organisers need people to erect, maintain and dismantle tents; chalet girls are needed for chalet skiing holidays.

Recruitment for the summer season usually takes place at the beginning of the year, and from May for the winter season. Short training courses are given for couriers and representatives. Nowadays, the winter season also offers an abundance of opportunities for couriers and representatives. The following conventional and specialist tour operators are among those that carry out regular, but mostly seasonal, recruitment.

A much fuller list can be found in the book *Summer Jobs Abroad,* see *Bibliography* for details.

Best Travel Ltd., 31 Topsfield Parade, London N8 8PT — recruit about 200 summer staff for Greece, Spain, Portugal and Yugoslavia and about 50 winter ski resort staff for Switzerland and Austria, including representatives, cooks and resort managers.

Bladon Lines, 56-58 Putney High Street, London SW15 1SF — well known for their winter skiing holidays, they also have a summer programme. In winter they employ around 300 staff for Switzerland, Austria, Italy and France including representatives, cooks and chalet girls. The summer staff of around 50 are usually recruited from the winter staff. The summer staff comprises representatives beach hotel personnel and watersports instructors.

Canvas Holidays Ltd., Courier Department, Bull Plain, Hertford, Herts. SG14 1DY — need residential couriers (graduates and undergraduates) for the summer season in Austria, France, Italy, Spain, Germany, Switzerland and Yugoslavia.

Carefree Camping, 126 Hempstead Road, Kings Langley, Herts. WD4 8AL — need staff at the beginning and the end of the season to set up and dismantle campsites in France as well as couriers to look after clients.

Club 18-30 Holidays, Academic House, 24/28 Oval Road, London NW1 7DE — recruits overseas representatives, airport transfer representatives, general administrators, accounts administrators and entertainers from November till January for the following summer season. Applicants should be single and under 30 years of age. Recruitment for winter work is carried out from amongst the summer staff.

Club Cantabrica Holidays Ltd., 146-148 London Road, St. Albans, Herts. AL1 1PQ — require couriers, resort managers, maintenance staff and childrens activities couriers (SRN or NNEB qualified) to work on campsites in France, Greece, Italy, Portugal, Spain and Yugoslavia in the summer. They also recruit for 'Snowcoach', a winter sports operation.

Club Méditerranée, 106-108 Brompton Road, London SW3 1JJ — runs holiday villages in France, Greece, Israel, Mexico, Morocco, Portugal, Romania, Spain, Tahiti, Tunisia, Turkey, Yugoslavia, the French West Indies and China. Summer staff needs are for qualified and experienced instructors in golf, scuba-diving, sailing, water-skiing, riding and tennis, as well as hosts/hostesses, nurses, playgroup leaders and restaurant, boutique and administrative personnel. Ski instructors and resort personnel are also recruited in the winter. Applications should be submitted in January and February. Basic requirements are fluency in French, single status, age between 21 and 30, and availability to work from May to October. Applications should be made direct to the head office in France: Recruitment Service, Club Méditerranée, 25 rue Vivienne, 75002 Paris.

Contiki Travel (UK), Wells House, 15 Elsfield Road, Bromley BR1 1LS — specialises in touring holidays by coach, in Europe, Australia, America,

New Zealand and Great Britain. Tour managers and drivers are employed on a seasonal basis (April-October). Drivers should be PSV qualified and aged between 23-35. Tour managers should be outgoing and be capable of taking charge of a group throughout their holiday. Applications should be made in writing before December for interview in January.

EF Educational Tours, EF House, Farman Street, Hove, Sussex — need tour operators to lead groups of North American students around Europe over Easter and in June and July. Employment is for the duration of the tour, which may be from nine to 35 days.

Intasun Ltd., Intasun House, 2 Cromwell Avenue, Bromley, Kent BR2 9AQ — require overseas representatives for the summer season (from April-end of October).

Keycamp Holidays, 92 Lind Road, Sutton, Surrey SM1 4PL — recruit couriers to look after clients on French campsites between April and September.

Next Travel Division, Edmundson House, Tatton Street, Knutsford, Cheshire, WA16 6BG — recruit campsite representatives for the summer season on sites in Austria, Belgium, France, Italy, Germany, Spain, Switzerland and Yugoslavia.

PGL Sunsport Holidays, 874 Station Street, Ross-on-Wye, Herefordshire HR9 7AH, run adventure holidays in the South of France. They require canoe and sailing instructors, couriers, group leaders, kitchen, site and store assistants, drivers, fibreglassers, nurses and administrative assistants from May to September.

PGL Young Adventure Ltd., at the same address, operates barge holidays in the Netherlands and need couriers/group leaders to accompany groups on each departure from London for eight to 12 days mainly during July and August.

Ski Supertravel, 22 Hans Place, London SW1 — take on a winter staff for France, Switzerland and Austria of about 160, including representatives, odd-job men, ski guides, cooks and chalet girls.

Sun Living Ltd., 34-36 South Street, Lancing, West Sussex — require a variety of staff around the year for the children's adventure holidays they organise around the year through their four component companies. Tops Holidays operate adventure courses in France and Spain for school groups; Dolphin Holidays organise American-style summer camps in the UK; Music World run European tours for school choirs, orchestras and bands, and Snow World offer a range of winter sports holidays at 20 European ski resorts.

Thomson Travel, Greater London House, Hampstead Road, London NW1 7SD — comprises Britannia Airways Ltd., Lunn Poly Ltd., Thomson Holidays, and Portland holidays. They need couriers, representatives and children's representatives, mostly from April to October. Applicants should contact Overseas Personnel at the above address.

Village Camps, Inc., Chalet Seneca, CH 1854 Leysin, Switzerland — recruit summer camp counsellors and winter ski counsellors for their children's holidays in France, Austria and Switzerland.

Mark Warner, 20 Kensington Church Street, London W8 4EP — require kitchen staff, sports instructors, chalet girls, handymen etc. for the summer holidays they organise in France, Turkey and Greece and for the winter ski holidays they run in France and Switzerland.

In addition, those who wish to work as instructors in holiday centres abroad can contact *Outdoors Unlimited,* PO Box 75, Hereford HR1 1NU, the national staffing bureau for outdoor pursuits instructors. Positions are at all levels of experience, and are usually residential positions, with board and lodging included.

OVERLANDERS

The overland tour companies differ from the regular tour operators in two main aspects: the places they go to, and the way they do it — travelling some of the worst roads in the world in order to reach the remotest spots in the world. Some companies operate all year round, others just in summer. The type of work involved is very rigorous, but one of the maim aims is participation on the part of all the travellers. Thus, many tours are run by one leader/driver, who is in charge of route planning, itinerary, driving, mechanical problems and any other problems (medical, legal, etc) that might arise. For insurance purposes, drivers must be aged 25 or over and have a HGV or PSV licence, depending on the type of vehicle used. They also need linguistic, mechanical and organisational abilities. Most companies prefer their drivers to work for two years (or two summers) as a minimum. Training of one form or another is always given, and the first tour might be as an unpaid assistant driver. Some of the less rugged tours are manned by more than one; but three — a driver, a leader and a cook — is perhaps the upper limit.

The list of overland tour operators given below is by no means exhaustive (the number of companies in this category probably runs into three figures), but is intended to give an idea of the scope of operations and recruitment policies. Other companies will be found by looking through the advertisements in *Trailfinder,* published thrice yearly by Trailfinders Ltd, 46/48 Earls Court Road, London W8 6EJ. *Trailfinder* is available on subscription for £6.00 for four copies.

Dragoman Adventure Travel, Riverside, Framlingham, Suffolk IP13 9AG — drivers and leaders are required to conduct expeditions across Asia, Africa and South America. Applicants should be aged between 25 and 30, and preferably have a PSV or HGV driving licence. Positions are available throughout the year for at least 18 months. Applications to the Operations Director at the above address.

Encounter Overland Ltd., 267 Old Brompton Road, London SW5 — operate treks, safaris, expeditions in Africa, Asia and South America. Vehicles used are safari trucks. Groups of 20 people from around the world participate between the ages of 18 and 40. Employment is for leader drivers. Full time job for about three years. Applicants between 22 and 29. Should have leadership abilities and mechanical aptitude. PSV is required but can be obtained during training.

Exodus Expeditions, 100 Wandsworth High Street, London SW18 4LE — need leaders for overland expeditions operated in Asia, Africa and South America. HGV driving and mechanical experience required, with minimum 2-year commitment. They also employ trek leaders on their walking holidays, although usually on a short term basis.

Guerba Expeditions Ltd., 101 Eden Vale Road, Westbury, Wiltshire BA13 3QX — employ a number of expedition leaders for treks, specialising in Africa. Most leaders are full time and spend a greater part of the year in Africa: applicants should have an HGV or PSV licence, be over 25, have experience of organisation and of handling groups of people, some basic ability in French, an aptitude for mechanics, a cool head and some knowledge or interest in Africa.

Hann Overland, 268-270 Vauxhall Bridge Road, London SW1V 1EJ — a relatively small, but well-established company. Employs three full-time drivers for the shorter Middle East runs, and Turkey. Internal India tours run between April and February.

Journey Latin America Ltd., 16 Devonshire Road, Chiswick, London W4 2HD — operates overland tours in South America throughout the year, ranging from Mexico to Tierra del Fuego at the tip of South America. Approximately 12 new tour leaders are taken on each year, the main requirements being (ideally) a good working knowledge of the languages involved (Spanish or Portuguese), experience of South American and experience with groups or organising people (e.g. teachers). Tour leaders do not need to be drivers, since transport is organised locally.

Sundowners International, 267 Old Brompton Road, London SW5 9JA — operate coach trips between London and Kathmandu. Couriers and drivers. Drivers must have PSV and mechanical aptitude. Couriers need leadership and organisational ability, experience of this work preferred.

Top Deck Travel, 131-133 Earls Court Road, London SW5 9RH — tour operators running double decker buses to Europe, overland to Asia, India, North Africa, as well as escorted tours around South East Asia and overland through Africa. They have road staff: drivers, cooks and couriers, of around 150 men and women. All road staff must be aged between 23 and 35, and drivers must hold a current PSV Class 1 licence. Top Deck also have substantial maintenance division comprising mechanics, electricians, spray painters, panel beaters, carpenters and detailers. The retail division of the company have up to 20 travel and flight consultants.

Tracks Africa Ltd., Tracks Europe Ltd., 12 Abingdon Road, London W8 6AF need drivers/couriers and cooks for their extenesive range of camping tours in Europe (Russia, Scandinavia) and Morocco. Drivers must hold English PSV licences; minimum age for all positions is 25. Driver/leaders are also required for overland safaris and expeditions in Africa. Drivers require HGV licences for the four wheel drive expedition vehicles.

Expeditions

It is perhaps misleading to include a section on expeditions in a directory of jobs and careers: almost without exception, participation in expeditions involves no financial payment and no employer-employee relationship. This section is therefore restricted to mentioning a few organisations that run or sponsor expeditions, and a few self-help organisations that offer advice, assistance or even financial awards for independent expeditions.

Expeditions are organised, often at very irregular intervals, by schools, universities and various associations with leaders and crew members generally being appointed internally. Since most expeditions have a scientific bias, the staffing needs are for science graduates with relevant degrees in geology, biology, botany, etc., as well as photographers and leaders. Cooking, driving, etc., are usually shared duties. On schools expeditions, the scientific staff will also be required to teach.

None of the organisations below offer employment in any normal sense of the word. Most of them offer an interchange of ideas and information.

British Schools Exploring Society, at the Royal Geographical Society, 1 Kensington Gore, London SW7 2AR — organises annual expeditions (about 6 weeks in duration) to arctic, sub-arctic or tropical regions, between July and September. Expeditions of up to one hundred people (age 16½ to 20) from schools and colleges are led by experts in the field from universities, the Services and industry. Applications should be made in September of the previous year to the Executive Director.

Earthquest, 54 Sunderland Terrace, Ulverston, Cumbria LA12 7JY — organises a range of overseas expeditions each year, run by voluntary leaders for young people aged between 17 and 30. There are usually a few vacancies on each year's operations for volunteer scientific leaders, volunteer support staff members and volunteer adventure task leaders. Leaders and support staff are provided with subsidised flights and subsistence, but it does expect a financial contribution (which varies according to the operation) from each volunteer. Work opportunities last from six weeks to six months. Team building and training events are provided for all volunteer staff.

The *Expedition Advisory Centre,* at the Royal Geographical Society, 1 Kensington Gore, London SW7 2AR — run jointly by the Royal Geographical Society and the Young Explorer's Trust, aims to advise and assist individuals and groups in planning expeditions. The Centre provides information on all aspects such planning, and organises annual seminars and symposiums. In addition a number of publications are available, including *The Expedition Planners' Handbook and Directory.* While the Centre does keep a list of all planned expeditions, it is not in a position to place individuals on these. Occasionally there are requests from leaders for specialists with either scientific or medical skills, preferably with past expedition experience, and for this a register of personnel available for overseas projects is maintained. Those who do have a particular skill to offer and wish to be included on this register should send a stamped, self-addressed envelope to the Centre for the appropriate form.

The Globetrotters Club, BCM/Roving, London WC1N 3XX — exists mainly for independent travellers and non-institutional groups. Membership costs £7 for one year, £12 for two years. The principal benefit of membership is an interchange of information, ideas and hospitality through a directory of the worldwide membership. The bi-monthly newsletter *Globe* (circulated free to members) includes a "Mutual Aid" section in which free advertisements can be placed for travel companions, expedition members or travel information.

The Scientific Exploration Society. The Powerhouse, Alpha Place, Flood Street, London SW3 5SZ — has run 12 major scientific expeditions (including Operation Raleigh from 1984-1988) since its foundation in 1969. The Society's aim is to organise scientific expeditions (if judged to warrant it) by universities, schools, services and individuals. All society members are eligible to take part in expeditions if they can prove their worth.

WEXAS International (World Expeditionary Association), 45 Brompton Road, London SW3 — provides members (£22.23 a year) with advice and information through *The Traveller,* a magazine which is published three times a year. It also publishes *The Independent Traveller's Handbook,* arranges discount flights, car hire, and offers financial assistance to selected expeditions through its annual award programme.

Catering

Catering, often referred to as the "hospitality" industry, incorporates accommodation and the food and drink services, and includes hotel work, restaurant work and institutional catering, (staff canteens, hospitals, schools etc). In the UK, it is the second largest employer in the country and, subject to language restrictions, there are plenty of career opportunities for catering staff to work abroad (for example 10% of the Hotel Catering and Institutional Management Association's members work abroad in over 90 countries).

Hotel and restaurant work is also a popular choice for seasonal or temporary work. This is because hotels and restaurants need large numbers of extra workers to look after clients at the height of their tourist seasons perhaps only for a few weeks. Such seasonal workers need not always have previous relevant experience, or even a knowledge of the local language. But such jobs only represent part of the potential work, as there are many hotels and restaurants that function at more or less the same level of business all the year round; work with them will involve long term employment. To obtain permanent employment in the catering industry abroad you will need better qualifications, more experience and superior language skills than would normally be required of seasonal staff; for a fairly responsible position such as a floor manager, receptionist or reception clerk, a catering qualification would be a great advantage.

For information on career prospects, the *Hotel Catering and Institutional Management Association (HCIMA),* 191 Trinity Road, London SW17 7HN, can supply various brochures. Those interested in exchange schemes in the catering trade should contact the *British Hotels, Restaurants and Caterers Association,* 49 Duke Street, London W1.

FM Recruitment, 6 Conduit Street, London W1R 9TG — specialises in the field of financial management recruitment in the hotel and leisure industry, UK and abroad. Positions handled vary from junior accounts trainee to group financial director, although FM Recruitment tends to handle more senior positions. Applicants should have financial or systems exposure within the hospitality and leisure industry.

However, for anyone with experience and/or qualifications in catering there is little need to go through an agency for the usual catering jobs. By getting hold of a suitable hotel guide for the country in question and writing speculative letters to the larger establishments a positive result is the likely outcome, as there is a worldwide shortage of catering workers, and British qualifications are highly regarded around the world.

Seasonal Work

Jobs in the Alps, PO Box 388, London SW1X 8LX — arrange jobs in alpine resorts in Europe, both during winter and summer. Summer positions are generally for three months, while winter jobs last from December to April. Some knowledge of French or German is preferable. The jobs arranged include waiters, kitchen helpers, hall porters, barpersons, receptionists etc, and all applicants are interviewed to assess their suitability. Contact the Director at the above address for further information.

See *Summer Jobs Abroad* and *Working in Ski Resorts — Europe* for addresses of hotels and restaurants which employ seasonal staff.

Voluntary Work

Although voluntary work is generally associated with the poorer nations of the Third World — in Africa, Asia and Latin America — there is also a need for volunteer labour in the more developed countries, although the type of work involved is obviously quite different. A volunteer can most easily be defined as an unpaid worker — but this is obviously an over-simplification. In some cases a worker may actually be paying to take part in a particular project; volunteers at the other end of the scale might receive free board and accommodation in addition to a regular 'allowance' which could easily surpass the local average wage.

A volunteer might be equally accurately described as someone who works without the primary motive of financial or material gain. As well as the pure altruists with true missionary zeal, this definition also encompasses those whose motive is to gain practical experience, whether in the nature of the work itself, or merely in the opportunity to travel and meet people from different backgrounds and cultures.

The Developing Countries

Attitudes to Third World development have changed enormously over the past decade and the emphasis is now placed on helping developing countries to help themselves through guidance and example, rather than supply unskilled labour of which the Third World has an endless source. The volunteer demand is for skilled professionals, principally in the fields of finance, administration, education, agriculture, medicine and engineering. Volunteers are usually needed for terms of at least a year with the predominant exception of disaster relief services. This means that volunteers can become more deeply involved in a project as well as being more economical for the sending societies who often pay travel and other expenses.

Work in the developing countries, whether voluntary or professional, is difficult to find, unless you have much needed training or skills. Even so, the selection process can be extremely rigorous. There are other obstacles in the way, not least of which is the general restriction of work permits imposed by many governments, even when skilled workers are desperately needed.

Recruitment is mainly carried out by organisations based in Britain and Europe, which fall into two categories: religious and secular.

DENOMINATIONAL CHRISTIAN ORGANISATIONS

Since there are over 200 denominational missionary societies in the UK, a complete listing has not been possible here, but the list includes the main recruiters of lay personnel. It is assumed that ordained clergymen wishing to serve abroad know how to get in touch with their own missionary society.

The following Christian societies require skilled lay workers in the fields of agriculture, engineering, education and medicine. Although membership of the religious denomination in question is not actually specified, applicants with religious backgrounds, or at least a sympathy for the cause, are always preferred. The countries in which these societies operate vary slightly, but Africa and Asia are common ground, especially former British territories. Some also operate in the Caribbean and South America.

Baptist Missionary Society, 93/97 Gloucester Place, London W1H 4AA — accepts long-term ministers, graduate teachers, technical workers, doctors, nurses (RGN, RM), some builders and the occasional secretary. A minimum service of two years is necessary, plus training, except for volunteers of 20 plus, who are accepted for six months, needing to pay their own fare. Workers are needed in Zaire, Brazil, Bangladesh and Nepal.

Catholic Institute for International Relations (CIIR), 22 Coleman Fields, London N1 7AF — runs an Overseas Programme which places workers in development projects in Central and South America, North Yemen, Somalia and Zimbabwe. CIIR workers provide technical support — in agriculture, health, social communication, education and other skills — for local organisations that are tackling the causes of poverty in their communities. They welcome applicants who are skilled in such technical areas, and who are available for a two year work contract on a basic, single person's salary. CIIR's Overseas Programme is secular, open to people of any religious beliefs or none and is not restricted to British citizens. CIIR's activities are detailed in their Annual Review and the British Volunteer leaflet which, together with a vacancy list, are available on request from the above address.

Catholic Medical Mission Board (CMMB), 10 West 17th Street, New York, NY 10011 USA — places volunteer medical doctors, registered nurses, dentists and, far less frequently, ASCP certified medical technologists, licensed practical nurses, optometrists and physical therapists at independently operated medical mission institutions in Africa, the Caribbean, Central and South America, India and Oceania. Duration of service may be short-term (one month-one year) or long-term (at least one year, preferably two). Board and lodgings are provided free of charge. Long-term volunteers receive a modest monthly allowance. Applicants must be fully qualified members of the medical, nursing or dental professions, with work experience. Contact the Rev. J. J. Walter, President and Director, at the above address.

Church Missionary Society, 157 Waterloo Road, London SE1 8UU — offers medical, teaching, pastoral, administrative and agricultural opportunities in various countries in Africa and Asia. CMS short-term volunteers are accepted for periods of two to three years. Missionaries go overseas for a minimum of two three-year tours.

Church of Scotland, The Board of World Mission and Unity, 121 George Street, Edinburgh EH2 4YN — places accountants, administrators, agriculturalists, ministers, teachers, technical staff and all kinds of medical and para-medical staff in Africa and Asia, usually for a minimum of three years. *Operation Youth Share* also offers young, qualified and experienced people between the age of 18 and 30, the chance to spend up to a year working abroad on church based projects.

The Council for World Mission, Livingstone House, 11 Carteret Street, London SW1H 9DL — an international organisation serving different churches which recruit Missionaries for specialised ministries, teaching, medical and administrative work in Zambia, Papua New Guinea, Samoa, Kiribati, Taiwan.

Mennonite Central Committee, 21 South 12th Street, Akron, Pensylvania 17501, USA — is a voluntary relief and development agency that places about 1,000 volunteers a year in 50 countries in Asia, Africa, Latin and North America, usually in conjunction with other agencies. Experience and/or qualifications are necessary relevant to work in the following fields: agriculture, economics, technology, health, education etc. Applicants must be Christian. Expenses are paid. No restriction on nationality.

Methodist Church, Overseas Division, 25 Marylebone Road, London NW1 5JR — recruits Christian teachers, doctors, midwives and nursing tutors to work with partner churches in Africa and Asia. Tours last two to three years or more.

Papua New Guinea Church Partnership, Partnership House, 157 Waterloo Road, London SE1 8XA — supports the work of the Anglican Province of Papua New Guinea, and has an occasional need for people with special skills and abilities, such as priests, nurses, teachers, administrators, etc.

Quaker Peace & Service, Friends House, Euston Road, London NW1 2BJ — sends a small number of suitably qualified workers, mainly teachers, medical and development workers, to various projects in Africa, Asia and the Middle East (two year appointments). Quaker or Quaker-oriented volunteers preferred for all posts.

The Salvation Army, National Headquarters, 101 Queen Victoria Street, London EC4P 4EP — operates a Service Corps for the placement of qualified lay workers, aged 21 plus, in centres overseas. There is a continual need for nurses (SRN, SRN/midwifery, SRN/SCM) and other medical staff in Africa, Central and South America, South and East Asia. Agriculturalists, doctors, teachers, hospital and school managers, are also needed periodically. Christian commitment, or a sympathy with the Movement's evangelical programme, together with acceptance of its life-style of teetotalism and non-smoking, desired. Period of service — three years. Remuneration equivalent to that of Salvation Army officer. Application should be made to the Administration Officer at the above address.

Short Term Evangelical Projects (STEP), The Evangelical Union of South America, High Rising, Linton, Ross-on-Wye, Herts. HR9 7RS — sends around 100 young Christians to help with community based tasks in support of the Latin American church in Brazil, Peru and Bolivia. Jobs are varied and period of work ranges from two to six months. Applicants should be 17-30 and committed Christians. Travel expenses are not paid.

OTHER CHRISTIAN ORGANISATIONS

The following societies are non-denominational, but they recruit mainly for overseas churches and Christian institutions, and therefore prefer applicants with a Christian background.

The Medical Missionary Association, 244 Camden Road, London NW1 9HE — was founded "to encourage and assist suitable Christian men and women who desire to give themselves up to medical missionary work". Their own recruitment programme consists of the OYSTER (One Year's Service To Encourage Recruitment) scheme, providing a limited number of grants for registered medical practitioners to serve for one year (usually the year immediately after registration) in Christian missions in the Third World. The MMA also acts as a clearing house for most of the Protestant missionary societies, and can provide details of openings for doctors, nurses and para-medical workers in Protestant projects in the developing world.

Tear Fund, 100 Station Road, Teddington, Middlesex TW11 8QE — is a Christian relief and development agency that recruits committed Christians who are suitably qualified in their profession with appropriate work experience. Usable skills include the provision of clean water, health care, agriculture and forestry programmes, administration and training for employment. Assignments overseas are usually for two to four years.

Volunteer Missionary Movement, Shenley Lane, London Colney, St. Albans, Herts. AL2 1AR — recruits professionally or technically qualified people to work, for a minimum period of two years, in development projects linked with the local churches of Africa and Papua New Guinea. Volunteers required include: teachers, doctors, nurses, pharmacists, agriculturalists, builders, mechanics, carpenters and other tradespeople. Minimum age 21.

OTHER ORGANISATIONS

Action Health 2000, International Voluntary Health Association, 35 Bird Farm Road, Fulbourn, Cambridge CB1 5DP — is concerned with the promotion of appropriate health care in developing countries and operates in India, Bangladesh, Tanzania, Zimbabwe and China. Applicants should be fully qualified and registered doctors, midwives, nurses or other health workers and willing to do long-term work. Those staying for more than two years have all their expenses paid. Applications considered any time of year, but preferably 12 months notice is required.

British Executive Service Overseas (BESO), 116 Pall Mall, London SW1Y 5ED — recruits retired volunteer business executives with professional, technical or specialised management skills for assignments in developing countries. The length of placement averages two to three months.

British Red Cross Society, 9 Grosvenor Crescent, London SW1X 7EJ — keeps a register of doctors, nurses, administrators, mechanics, engineers, agriculturalists, development advisors and other field delegates with relevant professional experience who are willing to go abroad on short-term assignments of three to six months, to assist victims of disaster situations. Longer term development projects are occasionally undertaken. 25-50 age group is required and airfares and allowances are provided.

The Institute of Cultural Affairs, 41 Miranda Road, London N19 3RA — is a registered charity involved with village development projects in India, Korea, the Philippines, Jamaica, Brazil, Egypt, Zambia and Tonga. Volunteers are taken on for a minimum of nine months. No specific requirements are necessary but experience in health or teaching is an advantage. Expenses are not paid.

International Voluntary Service (IVS) Overseas, 3 Belvoir Street, Leicester LE1 6SL — like IVS Britain, seeks to tackle the causes of deprivation and underdevelopment. It operates as an agency sending qualified, skilled personnel with a minimum of two years' experience to Botswana, Lesotho, Mozambique and Swaziland, as required by the governments and communities. About 60 such placements exist at any one time. Those skilled in the following are most often requested: medicine, agriculture, civil, mechanical and water engineering, architecture, planning, construction, forestry, English language teaching and community development. Volunteers should be aged between 21 and 65, able to work

for a minimum period of two years, single (or applying with a partner who can be placed in an IVS Overseas post), without children or dependants and eligible for permanent right of residence in the UK or Ireland. *IVS Overseas* provides return airfares, accommodation, language training, medical cover, National Insurance contributions and equipment grants. Applicants should send a short CV to the Recruitment/Selection Unit at the above address.

Nicaragua Network, 2025 I Street N.W., Suite 212, Washington D.C. 20006, USA — raises funds for their humanitarian aid programme in Nicaragua and recruits volunteers for coffee harvesting, tree planting and house building brigades. These brigades stay for two to four weeks, over the summer and winter, according to the work. Minimum age 16. Apply to the Office Manager at the above address.

Paschim Banga Samaj Seva Samity, 191 Chittatanjan Avenue, Calcutta — 700 007, India — maintains hospitals, health clinics and other social institutions in India. A wide variety of jobs are available. Around 300 volunteers are recruited for three to four weeks from January to February, June to July, and October to December. Applicants should be English speaking and aged 16-28. Write to the Treasurer at the above address for further details.

United Nations Association International Service (UNAIS), 3 Whitehall Court, London SW1A 2EL — sends a small number of health workers, agriculturalists, water engineers and other skilled and experienced people for a minimum of two years to posts in Burkina Faso, Cape Verde Islands, Mali, the West Bank, Gaza, Brazil, and Bolivia. Expenses are paid and various allowances given.

United Nations Volunteers — work in the developing countries under the auspices of the United Nations Development Programme for a period of two years. Travel to and from the country of assignment is provided for each volunteer and dependants are authorised to accompany him or her. A modest monthly allowance is provided at either single or dependancy rates, along with a settling-in grant to set up housekeeping. UNV candidates must possess skills and qualifications needed by developing countries. Appropriate academic or trade qualifications in a particular profession are required, along with a minimum of two years' working experience in that field. UK applicants should contact the Enquiries Unit VSO/UNV, 9 Belgrave Square, London SW1X 8PW.

Project Trust, Breacachadh Castle, Isle of Coll, Scotland PA78 6TB — aims to further the education of school leavers by sending them to work overseas for a year. The work projects take place in Australia, Central America and the Caribbean, Eastern and Southern Africa, Sri Lanka, and the Far and Middle East; they mainly involve social service, farming or teaching. Each volunteer must bear a portion of the total cost of his trip. Volunteers must be UK nationals between the age of 17½ and 19, and in full time secondary education up to the time that they go abroad. Once abroad, they receive free board and lodging, and pocket money. Applications must be in by the 1st January for those going overseas in September and by the 1st May for those leaving in January.

Voluntary Service Overseas (VSO), 9 Belgrave Square, London SW1X 8PW — is a registered charity that recruits volunteers to live in local communities and pass on their skills and experience to colleagues in developing countries. The areas involved are: Africa, the Pacific, the Caribbean and Asia. About 600 volunteers a year are sent to work for a minimum of two years. About half are placed in schools, teacher training colleges and vocational training centres; the rest work in crafts, trades, engineering, the health services, agriculture and specialist fields such as librarianship and small business development. Volunteers should be aged between 20 and 65 and be qualified and experienced in the relevant fields. VSO provides fares, training, various grants, National Insurance contributions; the overseas employer provides accommodation and a salary based on the local rate for the job. Those interested should contact the Enquiries Unit at the above address.

Projects in the First World

WORKCAMPS

Voluntary work in the more developed countries is usually organised into workcamps, which accept unskilled, short-term labour and are therefore very popular with young people as working holidays. Workcamps can be purely physical labour (construction or agriculture, for instance), but the work often has a more social bias (playschemes for deprived or mentally handicapped children, hospital work, or community development etc.). Financial arrangements vary considerably from one organisation to another. In some cases, volunteers are provided with board, lodging and pocket money; in other cases, it is quite common for the volunteer to have to make a substantial contribution towards costs. Travel expenses are usually the responsibility of the volunteer.

British applicants should normally apply for foreign workcamps through a British-based organisation, but in the case of independent organisations abroad the applications must be made direct. Due to the enormous number of associations that recruit for workcamps at a local or national level, only a selection has been included below. Reasonably comprehensive lists of these organisations will be found in the relevant publications mentioned under *Sources of Information,* below.

Within Europe, and to a lesser extent further afield, there is a major effort to co-ordinate workcamp programmes, so each intended volunteer should, where possible, address his application to the appropriate body in his own country or to a centralised international headquarters abroad. When writing to an organisation dealing with international exchange programmes, the applicant should state the country or countries in which he or she wishes to work and any preferences as to the type of work, location and time of year. Information can be obtained either direct from the organisation or from the addresses listed under *Sources of Information,* below.

American Hiking Society, Volunteer Vacations Programme, 1015 31st Street, N.W., Washington D.C. 20007, USA — organises camps involved with outdoor work, maintaining trails, helping as fire lookouts, wildlife observers, historical researchers etc. The minimum age is 16 and the period of work is generally two weeks.

Christian Movement for Peace, Bethnal Green U.R.C., Pott Street, London E2 0EF — sends young volunteers (aged 18 and over) on workcamps in East and West Europe, the USA, Canada and Morocco. Camps are usually of two to six weeks' duration and take place between June and September.

Committee of Youth Organisations of the USSR (KMO), Bogdan Khmelnitsky 7/8, Moscow, USSR — organises international voluntary workcamps in the USSR. Around 350 volunteers are needed to help with agricultural, construction and conservation work. Camps are held during the summer and last for two weeks. Minimum age 18. Contact the *Co-ordinating Committee for International Voluntary Service,* 1 rue Miollis, 75015 Paris.

Concordia (Youth Service Volunteers) Ltd., 8 Brunswick Place, Hove, Sussex BN3 1ET — in conjunction with similar foreign organisations, recruits for voluntary work in several Western and Eastern European and North African countries. Applicants must be aged 18-30 and only British citizens are accepted.

Ecumenical Youth Council in Europe, Youth Unit, British Council of Churches, Inter-Church House, 35-41 Lower Marsh, London SE1 7RL — organises workcamps for study, manual labour and social development in most European countries, lasting two to three weeks in the summer. The aim is to promote Christian understanding and faith. Minimum age is 18.

Frontiers Foundation, 2615 Danforth Avenue, Toronto, Ontario M4C 1L6 — organises summer workcamps, usually in Indian communities in the isolated areas of Northern Canada, for applicants who are over 18 and can work for eight weeks. Expenses are paid.

Internationale Bouworde (International Building Companions), International Secretariat, rue Notre-Dame de Graces 63, March-en-Famenne, Belgium — runs two to five week workcamps to assist in socially useful building projects in Austria, Belgium, France, Germany, Italy, Netherlands, Portugal and Switzerland.

International Voluntary Service (IVS) Britain, Upper New Walk, Leicester LE4 0QG — runs a Workcamps Programme which co-ordinates approximately 50 short-term camps a year in Britain, and sends British volunteers to take part in projects in about 25 countries, in Western and Eastern Europe and North America. In some countries the projects take place with branches of *SCI (Service Civil International),* the movement of which IVS is a part; in others, *IVS* cooperates with other workcamp organisations. Most projects last between two and four weeks, and take place between June and September. A list of summer projects abroad is available in April. Send a SAE to the above address for information on *IVS*. Applicants must be over

18. Those interested in medium- or long-term work overseas see under *IVS Overseas,* above.

Quaker International Social Projects (QISP), Friends House, Euston Road, London NW1 2BJ — recruit for several workcamp organisations in Eastern and Western Europe, Turkey and North Africa. Camps are run all year round in some cases, although the majority are during the summer. Duration is two to four weeks in general and the minimum age is 18. Disabled applicants and families are welcome.

Tahoe Rim Trail Fund Inc., P.O. Box 10156, South Lake Tahoe, CA 95731, USA — was formed in 1983 to build and maintain a 150 mile trail around the ridge of the Lake Tahoe Basin in California. 400-1,000 English speaking volunteers are needed a year, in all seasons, for all aspects of the project. Volunteers may specify length of service. Minimum age 16. Accommodation is not usually provided.

Union REMPART (pour la Rehabilitation et L'Entretien des Monuments et du Patrimonie Artistique), 1 rue des Guillemites, 75004 Paris, France — takes on about 4,000 volunteers over the spring and summer to restore and maintain old buildings, villages, etc. of cultural importance.

United Nations Association (Wales) International Youth Service (UNAIYS), Temple of Peace, Cathays Park, Cardiff CF1 3AP — recruits young British people to work for two to three weeks on projects run by sister organisations in Europe, the USA, some African countries and India.

The Winant Clayton Volunteer Association, 43 Trinity Square, London EC3N 4DJ — places UK volunteers on community projects with the elderly, adolescents, children and psychiatric rehabilitation. The projects are based in New York, Boston and Washington. Volunteers work for eight weeks and have four weeks for individual travel. Minimum age 19, period of work mid-June to mid-September. Applications accepted only from UK residents and should be in by November 30th.

CAMP COUNSELLING

Looking after a campful of schoolchildren during the summer vacation may not be everybody's idea of fun, but with hundreds of children spending at least part of their summer at a camp, the staff needs are naturally high. Most camps are staffed on an international basis by male and female camp counsellors — often without special skills or experience — who provide leadership, assist in organisation, and take part in the activities of the camp. Camp activities vary widely and include all kinds of sports, handicrafts, artistic and educational pursuits. Sometimes counsellors are chosen for their special skills, particularly the ability to instruct in one of the camp's chosen activities. As well as general camps, there are also special camps, e.g. for the disabled or mentally retarded.

YMCA (National Council), 640 Forest Road, London E17 3DZ — organises camp counselling programmes, in America, for anyone between the age of 19 and 26. Camps last nine weeks and time is given for individual travel. Flights are paid.

YWCA, Clarendon House, 52 Cornmarket Street, Oxford OX1 3EJ — runs a number of playschemes for the dependants of those serving in the British Army on the Rhine. Recruitment takes place in April/May. Volunteers aged 18-30 are needed. Travel expenses are paid.

KIBBUTZIM AND MOSHAVIM

Kibbutzim and Moshavim are both unique to Israel. There are about 300 Kibbutzim in all parts of the country. They began in 1909 as agriculturally based collective villages, but collective industry has also become a major concern. They represent the ultimate in commune life, the ideal of communism put into practice — all the means of production are owned by the community as a whole. Division of labour is decided according to ability, the division of wealth according to need. Long-term members of a Kibbutz must undergo a trial period of a year, but temporary workers from abroad are also welcome. Due to the enormous demand among young people of Western Europe and America, visits arranged by special agencies are preferable. There are vacancies throughout the year although these are limited in July and August. Visitors are expected to work eight hours a day, six days a week, with a few days holiday each month. The minimum period of work is usually one month. Board and lodging is provided, together with other allowances.

Moshavim are family based settlements which, like the Kibbutzim, were originally agricultural but are now turning to industry as well. Unlike the Kibbutz, the Moshav allows for private enterprise and members have their own land and property. Volunteers are given accommodation and a small wage by the family for whom they work. Visitors are expected to share in the social and cultural activities of the village. The wage volunteers receive, the slightly longer working hours and the greater personal involvement with the family makes life on a Moshav quite different from that on a Kibbutz.

The following organisations offer positions for Kibbutz and/or Moshav visitors. In addition to the registration fees, visitors are also required to pay for their travel to Israel.

Kibbutz Representatives, 1A Accommodation Road, London NW11 8ED — run regular visitor schemes throughout the year both for groups and individuals. Minimum period of five weeks, maximum of one year by special arrangement. Applicants must be in good physical and mental health. Audio-visual film and orientation interview given to everyone. Groups meet together before departure, and transport directly to the kibbutz is included. Registration fee for everyone is £24. SAE to above address will bring booklet and application forms by return.

Project 67 Ltd., 36 Great Russell Street, London WC1B 3PP — offers working holidays on Kibbutzim for periods from five weeks to three months (or up to a year by special arrangement), with travel arranged in groups on pre-set dates; also working holidays on Moshavim where volunteers work with an Israeli family on a communal farm. Age limit is 18-35. There are departures scheduled for every week of the year.

Worldwide Student Travel Ltd., Israeli-Egypt Dept., Priory House, 6 Wrights Lane, London W8 6TA — arranges Kibbutzim and Moshavim working holidays for a registration fee of £50 and £45 respectively. This covers local hospitalisation insurance and also transfer from Tel Aviv airport (for Kibbutz only, Moshav volunteers must make their own way). Minimum stay of six weeks for Kibbutz and two months for Moshav volunteers. Age limit: 18-35.

ARCHAEOLOGICAL DIGS

Although the work is usually extremely hard, participation in archaeological digs tends to be the most expensive form of voluntary work, as there is rarely an unlimited budget backing projects of this kind. Not only must volunteers pay for their own travel expenses to and from the dig, they nearly always have to pay for their day-to-day living expenses as well. Obviously, *ad hoc* arrangements can be cheaper if you have your own tent and arrange your own meals.

Archaeology Abroad, c/o Institute of Archaeology, 31-34 Gordon Square, London WC1H 0PY — provides three information bulletins annually (available by subscription) about opportunities for archaeological field work and excavations abroad. Information is also supplied to organisers of expeditions who wish to recruit personnel. Information on digs to be carried out in Britain is given in *British Archaeological News,* available from the *Council for British Archaeology,* 112 Kennington Road, London SE11 6RE. (Send SAE for subscription details). This information is relevant since inexperienced diggers are advised to work on at least one or two British digs before applying for positions abroad.

Concordia (Youth Service Volunteers) Ltd., 8 Brunswick Place, Hove BN3 1ET — can offer work to students of archaeology on projects in Spain and France. Only British volunteers are accepted.

Project 67 Ltd., 36 Great Russell Street, London WC1B 3PP — arrange organised participation in selected archaeological projects in Israel. Time off is given for sightseeing. Work is open to anyone over 18 and no experience is necessary.

Details of other Israeli excavations seeking volunteers are sent out on request by the *State of Israel Ministry of Education and Culture,* Department of Antiquities and Museums, PO Box 586, Jerusalem 91004, (please mark envelopes *Volunteers).*

LONG TERM OPPORTUNITIES

Although it is not always the case, those doing long-term voluntary work may be more likely to need specific skills besides the fitness and enthusiasm which are generally sufficient for short-term work. In addition, a greater degree of dedication is required since a long posting abroad could mean a complete break from a secure job at home.

Arbeitskreis Freiwillige Soziale Dienste, Stafflenbergstr. 76, 7000 Stuttgart, Germany — offers one year's voluntary work on social projects in the Evangelical Church. Applications must be made at least one year ahead and volunteers should be between 18 and 25 years old. The scheme operates throughout West Germany, including West Berlin, and all participants must be able to speak fluent German. Travel expenses are not paid.

ATD Fourth World Voluntariat, 48 Addington Square, London SE5 7LB — is an international movement operating in Europe, the USA, Canada, Africa, Asia and Central America. Their purpose is to help those in disadvantaged communities fulfil their roles as parents and citizens. Fourth world families are involved with the planning of projects. Minimum age for volunteers is 18, they must be in good health and work experience is desirable. *ATD* also organises three month Short-Term Volunteer Schemes and summer workcamps in the UK and France.

Brethren Volunteer Service, 1451 Dundee Avenue, Elgin, IL 60120, USA — runs a programme that aims at peacemaking, advocating social justice and meeting human needs. Volunteers help with counselling, community development and refugee work etc. Minimum period of work is one year in the USA or two years abroad. Minimum age 18; specific requirements may apply to some placements.

The Camphill Village Trust Delrow House, Hilfield Lane, Aldenham, Watford WD2 8DJ — runs schools and communities for mentally retarded adults and children in Austria, Brazil, Finland, France, Germany, the Netherlands, Norway, South Africa, Switzerland and the USA. Volunteers work for a minimum of six months. Applications should be sent to the Secretary at the above address.

The Missions to Seamen, St Michael Paternoster Royal, College Hill, London EC4R 2RL — requires volunteers to assist port chaplains in their work of caring for seafarers of all nations. The work involves ship and hospital visiting, befriending seafarers and welcoming them to the mission club, organising social events and sharing the general duties of running the club. Opportunities exist in Europe, the USA, Africa, the Far East and Australia. The length of service is one year. Applicants must be between 18 and 24, and must have a car driving licence. They must be practising Anglicans or Christians prepared to participate fully in Anglican ministry and worship. Travel and medical expenses, board and lodging, laundry and pocket money are provided. Enquiries to the Assistant General Secretary (Ministry), at the above address.

Volunteers in Mission, The Presbyterian Church (USA), 100 Witherspoon, Louisville, Kentucky 40202, USA — offers opportunities to people of all ages who are willing to live at subsistence level while helping to meet social needs around the world. Volunteers should be church members with some specialist training, such as medicine or teaching. Volunteers are often posted for a year although some summer camps are arranged.

Sources of Information

Bureau for Overseas Medical Service, Africa Centre, 38 King Street, London WC2E 8JT — keeps a register for all types of health workers who wish to work in developing countries and acts as a co-ordinator for the sending agencies it services. Placements are for six months to two years. Qualified people only should apply. The Bureau also produces a list of posts available.

The Central Bureau for Educational Visits and Exchanges, Seymour Mews House, Seymour Mews, London W1H 9PE — publishes: *Working Holidays,* a guide to short-term paid and voluntary jobs available throughout the year in the UK and abroad; and *Volunteer Work,* a guide to voluntary work and service with information on over 100 organisations recruiting volunteers for medium and long-term projects all over the world.

Christians Abroad, 11 Carteret Street, London SW1H 9DL — is an ecumenical body which exists to help those who are thinking about work overseas and provides an information and counselling service about opportunities abroad for people of all ages. Information leaflets are available about a wide variety of occupations. *Opportunities Abroad* — a list of vacancies through over 30 mission, volunteer and aid agencies — is published every six months. In addition, teachers are recruited on behalf of overseas employers, mainly in Africa and the Caribbean. Sometimes accountants, agriculturalists and civil engineers can be placed in development and relief projects. Christians who will be working or studying abroad are invited to get in touch if they would like an introduction to the church abroad, or help with preparation.

The Coordinating Committee for International Voluntary Service, UNESCO, 1 rue Miollis, 75015 Paris — issues lists of workcamp/long-term voluntary service organisers by country and publishes on a regular basis directories of short-term and long-term voluntary service throughout the world. A list of CCIVS publications and their costs is also available from the above address.

International Liaison of Lay Volunteers in Mission, P.O. Box 29149, 4121 Harewood Road N.E., Washington, D.C. 20017-9149, USA — acts as a reference centre for various agencies and programmes and potential volunteers. They refer a wide range of volunteers to organisations which send them on programmes in all parts of the world. Most positions are long-term (one to three years), but not exclusively.

The National Council for Voluntary Organisations, 26 Bedford Square, London WC1B 3HU — has an International Affairs department, the head of which can sometimes suggest suitable contacts for people wishing to work in other countries.

The *Overseas Development Administration (ODA),* issues the free booklet *Why not Serve Overseas?* available from the Procurement Executive, Room

376, *Overseas Development Administration,* Abercrombie House, Eaglesham Road, East Kilbride, Glasgow G75 8EA.

The Panos Institute, Third World Development Information Agency, 8 Alfred Place, London WC1E 7EB — publishes a bimonthly magazine, *Panoscope,* which contains articles describing projects taking place in developing countries; they are written by journalists from those countries and would be a useful insight for those considering work in the Third World. For information on subscriptions send SAE to the above address.

Returned Volunteer Action, 1 Amwell Street, London EC1R 5UL — does not send people to work abroad but does give advice and information to people considering working overseas. They publish a pamphlet, *Thinking about Volunteering?* (Send £1 plus large SAE).

Third World Publications Ltd., 151 Stratford Road, Birmingham B11 1RD — stock a wide range of background material and publications with information on developing countries, but nothing specifically on work. Catalogues are available on request. Write to the above address or the London office: Africa Book Centre, 38 King Street, Covent Garden, London WC2E 8JT.

Vacation Work Publications, 9 Park End Street, Oxford OX1 1HJ, publish *The International Directory of Voluntary Work,* a comprehensive, worldwide guide that lists over 400 organisations and covers all types of work; *The Directory of Work and Study in Developing Countries,* which includes information on short and long term voluntary work in over 100 Third World countries; *The Directory of Summer Jobs Abroad* which gives details about voluntary projects, from conservation to care of the elderly, taking place all over the world; and *Kibbutz Volunteer,* which gives information on 220 individual kibbutzim and kibbutz work, as well as practical guidelines and hints on archaeological digs and other work in Israel.

International Organisations

Employment opportunities in the United Nations — the largest of all international bodies — are treated separately in the next chapter. The international organisations included in this chapter recruit on a much smaller scale, but have a steady intake of British personnel, particularly the most highly qualified professionals and administrators. With the exception of the rare posts that require English as first language, the vast majority of personnel, particularly in secretarial and clerical grades, are recruited on a local basis.

The organisations singled out below merely provide examples of the scope of work available, and it is not intended as a complete list of the international organisations that recruit in this country. A fuller list of the world's major international organisations and associations is given in Volume I of the *Europa Yearbook,* available in public reference libraries. The most comprehensive list of all is in the *Yearbook of International Organisations,* published by the Union of International Associations in Brussels, and also available in public reference libraries.

THE EUROPEAN COMMUNITY

Constitution

The European Community is composed of the European Economic Community (EEC); the European Coal and Steel Community (ECSC); and the European Atomic Energy Community (EURATOM). Together, the three Communities share the following common administrative, legislative and judicial institutions.

Commission of the European Communities, 200 rue de la Loi, B-1049 Brussels — is responsible for the implementation of treaties enacted by the Communities; it also acts as an advisory body to the Council and Parliament.

Council of Ministers of the European Communities, 170 rue de la Loi, B-1048 Brussels — has the two-fold responsibility of ensuring the co-ordination of the member states' general economic policies, and of taking the decisions necessary to implement the treaties.

European Parliament. Centre Européen, Boite postale 1601, Luxembourg — supervises the executive bodies of the three communities.

Court of Justice of the European Communities, Kirchberg, L2920, Luxembourg — ensures that in the interpretation and officiation of the treaties establishing the European Communities the law is properly observed.

Economic and Social Committee of the European Communities, 2 rue Ravenstein, B-1000 Brussels — an advisory body on European legislation.

Recruitment

There are opportunities for Britons to work in these institutions at all grades. Personnel grading for all institutions follow the same pattern:

Grade A — degree-level administrative staff
Grade L/A — degree level linguists/translators/interpreters
Grade B — secondary education level administrative staff
Grade C — clerical officers, secretaries, shorthand/typists
Grade D — skilled workers.

The Commission, Council, Parliament, and Economic and Social Committee all share the same method of recruitment: vacancies are filled by open competition following published notices. Advertisements of these notices are published in the national press, although the notices, giving more detailed information, are not; they are published in the *Official Journal of the European Communities,* the availability of which is decribed under *Information* below. Candidates who are successful in the open competitions form a reserve recruitment list and may be offered positions as they become vacant. Success in a competition is not, therefore, a guarantee of employment.

Enquiries concerning competitions should be addressed to the Personnel Division of the institute concerned, address given above. Those interested in interpreting and translating for the Commission can obtain further information from the Joint Interpreting and Conference Service (or The Translation Service, *Resources and Professional Development Service*), Commission of the European Communities, 200 rue de la Loi, B-1049 Brussels. Information concerning scientific posts can be obtained from the Directorate-General for Science Research and Development, Joint Research Centre, Commission of the European Communities.

Apart from the normal recruitment channels outlined above, the following special schemes also exist:

The European Parliament has two training schemes: one for holders of Robert Schumann scholarships in research and documentation; the other for linguists to spend periods of 1-6 months in the translating and interpreting departments. Attendance on these courses in no way guarantees permanent employment. Applications for Robert Schumann scholarships should be addressed to the Director General for Research and Documentation at the European Parliament; applications for the translating and interpreting courses should be sent to the Director of Translation and Terminology or the Director of Interpretation.

The Commission of the European Communities and the Economic and Social Committee run a five-month *stagiaire* training course for graduates seeking Grade A posts; enquiries to the Personnel Department, Training Division, at either organisation.

The Court of Justice recruits independently of the other institutions of the European Communities but on a similar basis. All vacant posts are advertised in the national press, as and when they arise.

There are also two satellite bodies of the European Community, the *European Vocational Training Centre* in Berlin (Bundesallee 22, 1000 Berlin 15) and the *European Foundation for the Improvement of Living and Working Conditions* in Dublin (Loughlinstown House, Shankill, Co. Dublin) which occasionally have vacancies. Enquiries should be addressed to the Head of Administration in both cases, although again prospective applicants should be highly qualified/experienced.

Information

The Personnel and Administration Department of the Commission of the European Communities produces a free booklet entitled *A Career in the European Communities,* explaining the Commission's recruitment procedure and employment conditions.

Apart from the separate institutions themselves, the main sources of information on the European community are the four British offices of the Commission of the European Communities. These are at:

8 Storey's Gate, London SW1P 3AT;
7 Alva Street, Edinburgh EH2 4PH;
4 Cathedral Road, Cardiff CF1 9SG;
Windsor House, 9/15 Bedford Street, Belfast.
There is also an Irish office at 39 Molesworth Street, Dublin 2.

The London office of the European Parliament is at 2 Queen Anne's Gate, London SW1H 9AA.

As far as notices of competitions are concerned, the *Official Journal of the European Communities* can be consulted at these offices, as can copies of all Community documents and publications. They can also be consulted at any of the 47 British public, university and polytechnic libraries that are designated as either European Documentation Centres or European Depository Libraries.

Copies of the *Official Journal* and other European Community publications can be bought from the *Government Bookshop,* 49 High Holborn, London WC1V 6HB (mail orders: PO Box 276, London SW8); or the Government Bookshops in Belfast, Edinburgh, Birmingham, Bristol and Manchester; or through any appointed bookshop.

OTHER ORGANISATIONS

The Commonwealth Fund for Technical Co-operation (CFTC), Marlborough House, Pall Mall, London SW1Y 5HX — is a multilateral agency set up in 1971 within the Commonwealth Secretariat to provide technical assistance (advice, experts and training) to Commonwealth developing countries. The Fund's General Technical Assistance Programme provides experts such as accountants, agriculturists, architects, auditors, bankers, economists, engineers, lawyers, librarians, managing directors, medical officers, quantity surveyors, statisticians, and specialists in broadcasting, education, industrial development, telecommunications and tourism. An Industrial Development Unit provides assistance to Commonwealth governments on the planning of new industries. It identifies suitable projects from data supplied by countries and international studies and it undertakes more detailed profiles of the prospects of these industries and provides specialised help on such aspects of implementation as finance and technical expertise. The Export Market Development Programme supports a wide range of activities geared to the promotion of exports, both commodities and manufactures. They include market surveys, trade fairs and missions, the setting up of institutions for export development, product modification, designs, packaging, standards, and staff training in market analysis, marketing and trade negotiation. A roster is maintained of experts who wish to be considered for field assignments; experts have been drawn from 29 Commonwealth countries.

The *Consultative Group on International Agricultural Research (CGIAR)* is sponsored by three United Nations agencies (FAO, UNDP and the World Bank), and consists of 32 governments and 11 internatonal bodies concerned with specific agricultural problems, such as maize, wheat or rice improvement, tropical agriculture, animal diseases and farming in dry areas. Details of the work of CGIAR and the addresses and aims of the 11 organisations involved, are given in the book *International Agricultural Research,* available free from the UNDP, Palais des Nations, 1211 Geneva 10.

The *Council of Europe* 67006 Strasbourg, France — 'Europe of the 21' periodically recruits graduates for general administrative posts at the secretariat in Strasbourg, with an initial contract of two years. The essential requirements are a good university degree, excellent drafting ability in English and very good reading knowledge of French. Two years' administrative experience is desirable. Upper age limit normally 35 years. Application forms available from the Establishment Division at the above address. Recruitment by written examination and interview of shortlisted candidates. Specialist vacancies also occur notably for practising lawyers, subject to the same age limits. In addition, English Language secretaries are recruited regularly, with good 'O' and preferably 'A' levels (with good grades in English and French) and 110/50 wpm minimum shorthand/typing (Pitmans/RSA or equivalent), age limit 35 years. Occasional freelance work for fully-qualified conference interpreters with bilingual English/French, capable of translating from

German or Italian. Translator competitions — postgraduate translation diploma and experience essential.

The *European Association for Cooperation* Europe Centre, rue Archimède 17A, 1040 Brussels, Belgium — is an organisation set up and financed by the Commission of the European Communities to recruit and subsequently manage specialised personnel for technical assistance and cooperation projects financed by the EEC in the developing world.

The specialisation required is very wide and varied, but a constant need exists for development economists, civil engineers (construction, water-resources, roads, ports, dams, airfields, etc.) and tropical agronomists (cash crops of all types, cattle etc.). Frequently vacancies occur for mining experts, veterinary surgeons, geologists, human resource experts, wild-life experts, etc.

Candidates should normally possess a minimum of five years professional experience in their particular discipline or speciality, a minimum of four years of which should have been spent overseas in a developing country.

A working knowledge of French, Spanish, Portuguese or Arabic may be an advantage for posts in certain countries where any of these languages is commonly in current use.

The *European Organisation for Nuclear Research (CERN),* 1211 Geneva 23, Switzerland — accepts applications from nationals of member states (including the UK) for their fellowships. Most appointments are in the field of experimental and theoretical subnuclear physics, however there are some openings in applied physics, electronics, computing and engineering. One-year fellowships (extendable for a second year) are granted to young post-graduates usually having just completed a doctorate; or occasionally to more senior scientists (up to age 33) with post-doctoral experience.

Associateships in the fields listed above are available for research scientists of any nationality, who will normally be on leave of absence from their parent institute during the tenancy of the associateship (maximum duration one year). Scientific associateships for collaboration in CERN laboratory work are usually supported financially by parent institutes but there are a number of paid associateships to enable scientists to join an existing project.

Applications should normally be made six to twelve months before the expected starting date. Details of the application procedure and further information may be obtained from: Fellows and Associates Service, Personnel Division, CERN, 1211 Geneva 23, Switzerland.

The *European Space Agency (ESA),* 8-10 rue Mario Nikis, Paris 15e, France — has its headquarters in France, its Space Research and Technology Centre (ESTEC) in the Netherlands, its Space Operations Centre (ESOC) in the Federal Republic of Germany and its Information Retrieval Service (ESRIN) in Italy. The agency was created in 1975 to control European satellite and launcher activities (formerly the responsibility of ESRO and ELDO respectively). ESA's purpose is to provide for and to promote, for exclusively peaceful purposes, cooperation among European States in space research and technology and their space applications, with a view to their being used for scientific purposes and for operational space applications systems.

There are occasionally some vacancies for engineers, mathematicians and scientists, preferably with experience in aerospace fields. These are mainly with ESTEC in the Netherlands. Copies of vacancy notices may be obtained from the *UK Delegation to ESA,* Space Branch, Department of Trade and Industry, 29 Bressenden Place, London SW1E 5DT. Candidates may also apply direct to the Head of Personnel Management at the ESA headquarters, where their applications will be studied for whichever centre appears most suitable.

The *Intergovernmental Committee for Migration (ICM),* with headquarters in Geneva (33 member governments and 18 observer governments, among which is the UK) has, since 1951, carried out the migratory movements of refugees and nationals on a worldwide scale. In 36 years of operations, ICM has processed and moved over 3.8 million migrants to resettlement countries.

In addition to providing services and assistance to refugees, the Committee's task is to assist qualified technicians and professionals to ensure transfer of technology in order to promote the economic, social and cultural advancement of developing countries. In this connection ICM carries out Migration for Development programmes such as Return of Talent, Selective Migration, Integrated Experts, and Intraregional Cooperation among Latin American countries. Through its Selective Migration Programme, ICM provides such services as: recruitment, selection, transfer, placement and integration of high-level manpower according to the specific needs of Latin American countries, in close cooperation with the national labour authorities.

Although the UK has only observer status with ICM, British nationals possessing the required professional qualifications are not excluded from the Selective Migration Programme.

For details on these facilities, interested persons may contact ICM, Geneva Office for Latin America, 17 route des Morillous, 1211 Geneva 19, Switzerland.

The *International Telecommunications Satellite Organisation (Intelsat),* 3400 Internat Drive NW, Washington DC 20008, USA — has as its main objective the development of the global satellite system required for international public telecommunications. The staff at Washington has 609 members, including nearly 400 professionals and some 200 general staff members. While the general staff is recruited locally, the professionals are recruited locally and from the member countries on an international scale. Candidates must be highly qualified scientists with experience in space research and/or telecommunications.

The *North Atlantic Treaty Organisation (NATO),* 1110 Brussels, Belgium — have vacancies for professional and administrative posts, which are filled either by secondment from member nations' civil service and diplomatic service staff, or by direct hire. These posts generally require several years graduate experience together with a good knowledge of the two NATO official languages, English and French. There is also a need for secretarial and linguistic staff; examinations are held regularly for the recruitment of translators and interpreters.

The *Organisation for Economic Co-operation and Development (OECD),* 2 rue André-Pascal, 75775 Paris 16, France — recruits for civil service types of jobs at their secretariat in Paris. Applicants must have strong economic qualifications, plus experience in one of the organisation's spheres of activity; social affairs, labour, education, environment, science, industry, agriculture and fisheries, energy, finance and public management. Fluency in one of the official languages of the Organisation (English and French) is required. A good command of both is desirable.

Applications are handled by the International Manpower Procurement Executive, *Overseas Development Administration,* Abercrombie House, Eaglesham Road, East Kilbride, Glasgow G75 8EA.

Save the Children Fund, Mary Datchelor House, 17 Grove Lane, London SE5 8RD — has 140 paid expatriate staff in 30 developing countries, involved in long-term primary health care programmes and short-term relief and emergency programmes. The funds needs are for qualified and experienced nurses, doctors, health visitors, midwives, nutritionists, physiotherapists and administrators; one year contracts are offered, linked to Whitley Council Scales.

The *South Pacific Commission,* BP D5 Noumea Cedex, New Caledonia — employs two main categories of staff: specialists and support staff. Most of the latter are recruited, whenever possible, locally. Occasionally, support service vacancies arise which cannot be filled locally.

The South Pacific Commission is a technical and developmental organisation which provides training and assistance in social, economic and cultural fields, with particular emphasis on rural development, to twenty-two countries of the region it serves (The Pacific region). The Commission's role is advisory and consultative. Its programmes are closely co-ordinated with those of the countries and territories of the Pacific for which it works. The Commission's integrated work programme responds to regional and subregional needs as well as to the expressed needs of the small Pacific countries.

The Commission has 105 staff members based at SPC headquarters in Noumea, New Caledonia, 30 in the Community Education Training Centre, Plant Protection office and Regional Media Centre in Suva, Fiji and 6 in Sydney, Australia. The official languages of the Commission are French and English.

Fields of activity include Food and Materials (Agriculture; Plant Protection), Marine Resources, Rural Management and Technology (Conservation and Environment Management; Rural Health, Sanitation and Water Supply; Rural Employment; Rural Technology), Community Services (Community Education Training; Youth and Adult Education; Women's Programmes and Activities; Family and Community Health Services; Public Health), Socio-Economic Statistical Services (Statistics Section; Economic Section; Information, Research, Advisory Services and Training; Services in Population Data and Utilisation), Education Services (English Language Programmge; Media Unit), Information Services, Regional Consultation, Awards and Grants (Short-term Experts' and Specialists' Services;

Assistance to Applied Research, Experiments and Fieldwork; Inter-Country Study Visits and Travel Grants).

The *Universal Esperanto Association,* Head Office, Nieuwe Binnenweg 176, Rotterdam 3015 BJ, Netherlands — collects and files information on opportunities for paid and voluntary work within the worldwide Esperanto movement; and offers a small amount of work, mainly clerical, at the head office. Fluent knowledge of Esperanto is essential.

World Vision of Britain, Dychurch House, 8 Abinger Street, Northampton NN12 2AJ — World Vision is an international and inter-denominational Christian relief development organisation, begun in 1950, which works through local churches and community leaders in close cooperation with the United Nations and other international relief agencies.

World Vision has support offices in Australia, Austria, Britain, Canada, Finland, Hong Kong, Ireland, New Zealand, The Netherlands, Singapore, Southern Africa, Switzerland, West Germany and the USA, as well as field offices in 80 countries around the world. Child care sponsorship is an important part of World Vision's work, with over 400,000 children being currently cared for in 2,200 projects in 43 countries.

Requirements for positions vary, but the UK office has openings for 12 month contracts in Chad, Kampuchea, Mali, Mozambique, Senegal and Mauritania in the following disciplines: doctors, nurses, administration/finance managers, project managers, agricultural engineers, budget and accounting officers, and agricultural economists. Personnel should have Christian commitment.

United Nations

The United Nations Organisation has 159 countries as members. Employment of varying types can be found at the UN secretariat headquarters in New York; at overseas offices and missions directly subordinate to the secretariat; and in the Specialised Agencies, which are independent in most activities, including personnel recruitment. Vacancies are open to nationals of all member countries, and at the professional level attempts are made to maintain a proportional geographical distribution of personnel. Britain is a member of the UN and all the agencies, so UK nationals are eligible for employment in any branch. However, Britain is at present heavily over-represented, so prospects are not good.

The main personnel need is for specialised professional staff, particularly in economics and related fields. Preference is always given to applicants with a knowledge of both English and French, the official working languages of the UN. A knowledge of one of the other four official languages — Arabic, Chinese, Russian and Spanish — is also an advantage.

A general source of information is the *United Nations Information Centre* at 20 Buckingham Gate, London SW1E 6LB, which can supply a list of addresses for recruitment offices of the United Nations and its specialised agencies, and any other information on request.

An active role in the recruitment of United Nations field personnel is played by the *International Manpower Procurement Executive, Overseas Development Administration,* Abercrombie House, Eaglesham Road, East Kilbride, Glasgow G75 8EA. Free booklets *Opportunities Overseas in International Organisations* and *Opportunities with UNESCO* are available from the ODA at the same address.

SECRETARIAT

The United Nations *Secretariat* includes the United Nations Headquarters in New York, the United Nations Offices in Geneva and Vienna, the United Nations Conference on Trade and Development (UNCTAD) and the Office of the United Nations Disaster Relief Co-ordinator (UNDRO) in Geneva, the United Nations Centre for Human Settlements (HABITAT) in Nairobi, the peace-keeping missions, the more than 60 information centres throughout the world and the five economic commisions of the UN.

The United Nations has a steady need for competent staff in various fields. While it is impossible to list in detail the different types of positions for which the Organisation recruits, the major categories are listed below. The majority of professional posts in the Secretariat are closely related to the nature of the work required by the resolutions of the General Assembly and its principal bodies. As a result, the need is largely for specialists in the major fields of administration, economics, information science, statistics and in providing technical assistance to developing countries in the areas of economic and social development.

The United Nations is particularly interested in those candidates with international experience in more than one of these major areas which will enable them to follow an integrated and interdisciplinary approach to problems in development and administration. In the area of economics, demand for specialists is expected to arise in accounting, business administration, development planning, econometrics, financial and industrial planning and administration of economic programmes. In statistical work, vacancies may arise in census and demography, industrial labour and trade statistics, national accounts and training of personnel in statistical methodology. In the fields of energy and natural resources, experts are needed in geothermal, petroleum and mineral exploration, energy systems planning, solar energy development and water managment. Other experts are required in traffic planning, transport engineering and port management. In the field of housing and planning, professionals in construction, environmental planning and urban, rural and regional planning are sought. In data processing, specialists in computers, computer systems analysis and information science are likely to be needed.

There is a continuous need for *stenographic and clerical staff* and for high-speed conference typists in the six official languages of the United Nations (Arabic, Chinese, English, French, Russian and Spanish) to serve in large typing pools.

United Nations *field service staff* is responsible for servicing various United Nations field missions and is comprised of security officers, vehicle mechanics, radio technicians, radio officers and secretaries.

Guides are recruited usually once a year for a period of two years and their service as Guides does not carry any expectation of career employment with the Organisation.

Recruitment of *translators/précis-writers* and *interpreters* is by competitive examinations. Apart from their own language, which must be one of the six official languages, candidates should have knowledge of at least two of the other languages.

Librarians should have an advanced degree or equivalent professional qualification, and working knowledge of at least two official languages, together with several years practical library experience.

The United Nations is especially interested in recruiting women with a combination of skills and experiences acquired in an international setting which will enable them to assume administrative responsibilities.

Grade levels correspond to certain age limits and these are taken into consideration when evaluating candidates for professional posts. Professional requirements include an advanced university degree and ability to work easily in either English or French. Knowledge of one of the other official languages of the United Nations may also be desirable.

Staff may be expected to work at United Nations Headquarters in New York or at any of its main overseas offices in Addis Ababa, Bangkok, Baghdad, Geneva, Nairobi, Santiago (Chile) and Vienna.

Requests for further information about posts in any of the above job areas should be addressed to the *Recruitment and Placement Division, Office of Human Resources Management,* United Nations, New York, NY 10017, USA.

OTHER OFFICES AND MISSIONS

The United Nations Office at Geneva is the largest United Nations office outside Headquarters in New York. The work done there encompasses primarily conference and other international meetings, specialised economic activities, administrative and related functions. The United Nations Office at Geneva always gives careful consideration to applications from persons well qualified for employment. Secretarial staff are recruited locally and priority is normally given to candidates who already have familiarity with the function of the Organisation, and to those whose names have been put on a waiting list. Applications for all types of work should be addressed to: the Secretariat Recruitment Section, Personnel Service, Palais des Nations, CH 1211 Geneva 10, Switzerland. However, due to the current financial crisis faced by the organisation, all external recruitment has been suspended until further notice. Vacancies that do arise will in the first instance be filled through internal redeployment.

Application forms for internships are obtainable from the applicant's own university or from the United Nations Information Centre in London.

The International Trade Centre UNCTAD/GATT — an organisation in the United Nations system that carries out technical cooperation activities with developing countries in trade promotion. ITC's headquarters staff currently number about 240. In addition, ITC recruits approximately 700 experts each year for its projects in developing countries. Such consultants work in the areas of institutional infrastructure for trade promotion, export marketing, specialised trade promotion services, import techniques and training. Inquiries should be addressed to the Director, Division of Programmes, Finance and Personnel, International Trade Centre UNCTAD/GATT, Palais des Nations, 1211 Geneva 10, Switzerland.

United Nations Environment Programme: UNEP, like UNCTAD and UNIDO, is a part of the Secretariat, but carried out its own recruitment. The Programme's work is based on environmental problems, and experts in this field are occasionally needed. Applications should be addressed to *UNEP,* Personnel Service, PO Box 30552, Nairobi, Kenya.

United Nations Department of Technical Co-operation for Development: Development Programmes, financed by the UNDP and in conjuncton with overseas offices or specialised agencies, need technical assistance experts in the areas of finance, transport, statistics, electric power, mineral resources, economic development, public administration and social welfare. Candidates should have reached high professional standing in their fields, after long experience — usually at least 15 years. Junior candidates are very rarely accepted. UK nationals wishing to apply for these posts should address their enquiries to the International Manpower Procurement Executive, *Overseas Development Administration,* Abercrombie House, Eaglesham Road, East Kilbride, Glasgow G75 8EA.

Economic Commissions: The UN maintains five regional economic commissions, aimed at the economic and social development of the areas they represent. The five commissions are the ECE (for Europe), in Geneva; ESCAP (for Asia and the Pacific), in Bangkok; ECLA (for Latin America), in Santiago, with a branch office in Mexico City; ECA (for Africa), in Addis Ababa, with a branch office in Dakar; and ECWA (for Western Asia), in Baghdad. Staff recruitment in all these offices is limited to specialists experienced in economics, statistics and sociology. Applications should be addressed to the Chief of Professional Recruitment, *Secretariat Recruitment Service,* United Nations, New York, NY 10017, USA.

Information Centres and Field Missions: The UN maintains 64 small information centres around the world and a number of field missions. These offices have no vacancies to speak of, since administrative posts are filled by internal reassignment, and secretarial staff are recruited locally.

Military Personnel: Military observers and UN peace-keeping forces are not recruited by the UN, but are selected from the armed forces of member countries.

Associated Projects: There are several projects under way in the developing countries, which began under the auspices of the UN or one or more of its agencies, and which are now largely autonomous. Such a project is the Mekong Project, whose headquarters are at ESCAP in Bangkok. It is largely funded by UNDP. Positions at the Secretariat in Bangkok, and for field work — mainly for professional engineers and socio-economists — are dealt with by the *Interim Mekong Committee at Mekong Secretariat,* c/o ESCAP, United Nations Buildings, Sala Santitham, Rajdamnern Avenue, Bangkok 10200, Thailand.

Voluntary Work: The opportunities for voluntary service under UN schemes are covered in the chapter on *Voluntary Work.*

SPECIALISED AGENCIES

The United Nations specialised agencies recruit their own staff, both for work in their head offices, and also on projects and development programmes abroad, especially in the developing countries. Secretarial and clerical staff are invariably recruited from local sources, and the only vacancies to be filled internationally are for fully qualified and well experienced professionals in the fields with which the agencies are concerned. Details of only a few agencies are given below, on the understanding that agencies' recruitment programmes differ only in the type of professional staff they employ; further information can always be obtained from the agencies themselves.

In general, unsolicited applications to any of the agencies below are unlikely to be considered; nor do many agencies maintain files or candidates. Instead, details of vacancies are forwarded to the appropriate departments in member states, who are invited to advertise the vacancies, hold interviews, and return a short list of suitable candidates. Thus the ICAO will notify vacancies to the British Civil Aviation Authority; the UPU will inform the Post Office, and so on. These departments in turn are responsible for recruitment, and many of them maintain selective files of candidates already screened, who would be likely to fill the type of vacancies that might arise. Applications for post in the developing countries under the auspices of UNDP, ILO, FAO, UNIDO, IMO and HABITAT (based in Nairobi) should be addressed to the International Manpower Procurement Executive, *Overseas Development Adminstration,* Abercrombie House, Eaglesham Road, East Kilbride, Glasgow G75 8EA.

Food and Agriculture Organisation (FAO), Via delle Terme di Caracalla, 00100 Rome, Italy — employs some 2,000 people in over 130 developing countries and over 3,000 at Rome headquarters. Over 2,000 professional staff divided roughly evenly between headquarters and other duty stations, work in some 2,700 field projects in developing countries. Most of the work is in the fields of agriculture, fisheries and forestry, and related subjects such as soil and water resources, nutrition, economics, marketing, statistics, and project evaluation. Most positions require a minimum of five years' professional experience after university. However, there are a limited number of junior level openings for candidates with less experience. (Applications to the Overseas Development Administration).

International Atomic Energy Authority (IAEA), Wagramerstrasse 5, PO Box 100, A-1400 Vienna, Austria — recruitment is usually for professionals with experience in nuclear sciences, reactor physics and engineering, spectrometry, and the application of radioisotopes in agriculture, biology, industry and medicine. Applications direct to IAEA headquarters.

Applications for secretarial and clerical positions in the General Service category should also be submitted direct to the IAEA, and are generally assessed for local recruitment.

International Bank for Reconstruction and Development (IBRD), 1818 H Street NW, Washington DC 20433, USA — operates closely with the *International Development Association (IDA)* and the *International Finance Corporation (IFC)* (both based at the above address). Together they are known as the *World Bank Group;* recruitment is carried out both separately and jointly.

The World Bank Group differs from other agencies in that its professional staff (which numbers 1,800) are usually given an initial assigment to headquarters, from where they may be expected to travel extensively; only 5% of the staff are stationed outside Washington.

Qualified, experienced economists are most in demand, the preferred age being 30-55. Applied experience is required in one of the fields in which the Bank operates, such as development economics, transport, agriculture, industrial problems, commodities, international trade, or fiscal affairs. The Bank's predominant concern with loans and the investigation of schemes put forward for loan approval, leads to the employment of two further categories of staff: those with specialised knowledge or experience of the various aspects of investments and loans; and those experts who can investigate schemes requiring loans — including agriculturalists, agricultural and irrigation engineers; power, telecommunications and water supply engineers; road, port and railway engineers; architects, planners and educationalists. (Applications to the Overseas Development Administration).

Candidates aged under 30 with a recognised master's degree or equivalent in economics, management, public administration, law and related fields, can apply for employment under the Young Professionals Programme, which involves 12-18 month tours of duty. Selection is on a competitive basis and takes place three times a year.

International Labour Organisation (ILO), 4 route des Morillons, 1211 Geneva 22, Switzerland — the experts employed by ILO need long experience in employment and development (manpower planning, alleviation of rural poverty, small scale industry development); vocational or apprentice training; sectoral activities (development of co-operatives and training for the hotel and tourism industry); work study and industrial relations. (Applications to the Overseas Development Administration).

International Monetary Fund (IMF), 700 19th Street NW, Washington DC 20431, USA — employs qualified economists, as well as accountants, administrators, computer systems officers, language specialists and lawyers. Nearly all staff members are based in Washington although the Fund also maintains small offices in Paris and Geneva. A few staff members are also stationed for varying periods in member countries as resident representatives. In addition, work assignments frequently require travel to member countries to study economic problems and lend technical assistance. Recruitment is either through direct appointment to the regular staff (or by appointment for a fixed term, usually two or three years), or through the Fund's Economist Programme, which is open to well educated graduates below 33 years of age, who may not have previous relevant work experience. The Economist Programme operates twice a year, in April and October. Enquiries to the Recruitment Division. For direct or fixed term appointments, applicants usually have significant prior experience in a government department or academic or financial institution.

International Telecommunication Union (ITU), place des Nations, 1211 Geneva 20, Switzerland — vacancies at headquarters (which are rare and very competitive) and in the developing countries are advertised internationally through the co-operation of the telecommunications administrations of the member countries. British applicants should address enquiries in the first instance to the *Department of Trade and Industry,* Telecommunications and Posts Division, Room 529, Kingsgate House, 66-74 Victoria Street, London SW1E 6SW. Specialist posts are open to qualified engineers with several years' experience in one of the fields of telecommunications.

United Nations Development Programme (UNDP), One United Nations Plaza, New York, NY 10017, USA — the agency which co-ordinates and finances the field programmes of the United Nations and the various specialised agencies. The annual total of US $540 million is spent on about 8,000 projects in the developing countries. Field offices in over 100 countries supervise the implementation of development projects in the spheres of agriculture, industry, transportation, education, training and research. UNDP staff requirements are for people with postgraduate qualifications, preferably in the social sciences (e.g. economics, sociology and public administration). Permanent staff are expected to spend most of their careers on four year tours of duty in field offices to in the developing countries. (Applications to the Overseas Development Administration).

United Nations Educational, Scientific and Cultural Organisation (UNESCO), UNESCO House, 7 place de Fontenoy, 75700 Paris, France — has a constant need for specialists to work on projects in the UNESCO Field Programme in the developing countries. Most field appointments are for one or two years, but some may be even shorter. The Field Programme requires highly qualified people already established in a specific field of education (particularly in the areas of science, engineering and technology), and with a substantial amount of teaching experience at university, college of education or technical college level; experience in curriculum development, teacher training and educational organisation, administration and research are common prerequisites. Occasionally, vacancies also arise for experts in educational broadcasting, audio-visual aids, mass media, librarianship and documentation.

United Nations Industrial Development Organisation (UNIDO), P.O. Box 300, Wagramerstrasse 5, A-1400 Vienna, Austria — has been a specialised agency since 1986. The main professional requirements are for economists and engineers who have specialised in problems related to industrial development. The recruitment for the headquarters' posts is carried out by UNIDO's Recruitment Section, Personnel Services Division, and for technical assistance field assignements by UNIDO's Project Personnel Recruitment Branch. Applicants interested in technical assistance assignments should contact the Overseas Development Administration, Foreign and Commonwealth Office, Abercrombie House, Eaglesham Road, East Kilbride, Glasgow G75 8EA. The main professional need in this area of activity is for highly qualified experts with at least five years professional experience who have specialised in problems related to industrial development. UNIDO's secretarial staff in normally recruited locally and candidates who are in Vienna, even on a temporary basis, are allowed to sit for the qualifying tests. Enquiries about these posts should be addressed to UNIDO's Recruitment Section.

World Health Organisation (WHO), 20 avenue Appia, 1211 Geneva 27, Switzerland — main staff requirements are for highly quailfied medical personnel to work on health projects in developing countries. The staff includes: senior medical officers, nursing administrators and sanitary engineers, to act as advisers to governments on broad health programmes; nurse educators, sanitarians, sanitary engineers and other medical personnel to teach or supervise teams of instructors in schools and institutes; specialists in paediatrics and child health, serology, entomology, bacteriology, biochemistry and epidemiology: hospital administrators, radiologists, X-ray technicians and dieticians: and fully qualified doctors with experience in malaria, tuberculosis, nutrition, leprology, venereal diseases and treponematoses. Vacancies at the WHO head office are rare, but the Geneva headquarters also recruits on behalf of the regional head offices in Brazzaville (covering Africa). New Delhi (Asia), Copenhagen (Europe), Alexandria (Eastern Mediterranean), and Manila (Western Pacific).

Other specialised agencies include:

General Agreement on Tariffs and Trade (GATT), Centre William Rappard, 154 rue de Lausanne, 1211 Geneva 21, Switzerland.

International Civil Aviation Organisation (ICAO), 1000 Sherbrooke Street West, Suite 400, Montreal, Canada H3A 2R2.

International Fund for Agricultural Development (IFAD), 107 Via del Serafico, 00142 Rome, Italy.

International Maritime Organisation (IMO), 4 Albert Embankment, London SE1 7SR.

United Nations Children's Fund (UNICEF), 866 United Nations Plaza, 6th Floor, New York, NY 10017, USA.

Universal Postal Union (UPU), Weltpostrasse, 3000 Berne 15, Switzerland.

World Intellectual Property Organisation (WIPO), 34 chemin des Colombettes, 1211 Geneva 20, Switzerland.

World Meteorological Organisation (WMO), 41 avenue Giuseppe Motta, 1211 Geneva 20, Switzerland (UK address: c/o Meterological Office, London Road, Bracknell, Berks. RG12).

SUB-CONTRACTS

In many cases the work of the United Nations and its specialised agencies consists of financial assistance to complete a particular project, rather than carrying out the project alone. The money is then used to procure the relevant services throughout international bidding for contracts. Sometimes a contract is only for supplies and equipment, but there are also cases where a complete project, including personnel, is involved. Of course, the familiar pattern will evolve — all but the most specialised and highly qualified personnel will be recruited locally. But there is still scope — at the upper levels — to work for one of these subcontractors.

Details of contracts being offered are given in the fortnightly newspaper *Development Business,* published by the UN. Information on subscriptions is available from *Development Business,* United Nations, PO Box 5850, GCPO, New York, NY 10163-5850, USA.

British Government Departments

DIPLOMATIC SERVICE

Appointments in the Diplomatic Service normally provide a career rotating between tours of duty at British Diplomatic Missions in over 100 countries abroad and in the Foreign and Commonwealth Office in London. An officer can expect to spend up to two-thirds of his/her career overseas serving in:

1. High Commissions and Embassies, based in capital cities, of Commonwealth and foreign countries.
2. Consulates, usually situated in major cities outside capitals, primarily concerned with commercial or consular work.
3. United Kingdom delegations to international organisations such as the UN, NATO or the EC.

There are special nationality rules governing entry into the Diplomatic Service. Full information can be obtained from the Civil Service Commission but in broad terms candidates are eligible provided they are British citizens with at least one parent who is (or was) also a British, or Commonwealth citizen or citizen of the Irish Republic for 30 years or more prior to their appointment. Close connections with the United Kingdom taking into account such considerations as up-bringing and residence are also required.

Career Openings

Career openings are available in the following branches, for which recruitment is undertaken by the Civil Service Commission:

Administrative Branch (Diplomatic Service Grade 7D and 8): On entry members fill middle grade posts at home and abroad, working on political or commercial matters, rising during the course of a career to the highest positions in the Service. Graduates aged 20-32 with at least second-class honours degree in any subject, are eligible to enter the tripartite selection process, comprising qualifying tests (assessing verbal numerical and logical abilities), a two-day series of tests and interviews and, if short-listed, a final interview before a Board. Overall, there is an annual intake of about 20. In addition, there are occasional opportunities for older candidates with specialised experience in relevant fields, e.g. international relations, economics, hard and rare languages. These competitions are advertised separately as and when they occur.

Executive Branch (Diplomatic Service Grade 9): At home and abroad members deal with consular, commercial, political and administration work. The functions of this and the Administrative Branch overlap considerably, especially at the senior levels, and promotion prospects are good. Candidates for the executive branch should either be graduates or hold at least two "A" levels; the selection is on the basis of a two-stage process: an objectively marked qualifying test and a final interview. All applicants must be under 50. There is also a separate competition confined to school leavers, aged between $17\frac{1}{2}$ and $19\frac{1}{2}$ years.

Clerical Grades (Diplomatic Service Grade 10): Members are responsible for all kinds of office work, from routine filing to junior administrative posts. Promotions lead into the Executive Branch. About 100 applicants are accepted annually, to work in London in the first instance, but with the expectation of overseas service after 2-3 years. Candidates should have five GCSE passes (including English Language and Mathematics) or equivalent, and be aged under 20.

Legal Advisers: There are a small number of legal advisers in the Diplomatic Service, most of whom are based in London, though there are a few opportunities for work in the larger missions abroad. Applicants must be barristers or admitted solicitors, aged 22-32. Vacancies are advertised as they occur.

Research Department: Members compile information on the history, politics and current affairs of certain foreign countries, and prepare reports to serve as bases for official foreign policy. Candidates must have a good honours degree, an aptitude for foreign languages and special qualifications in a relevant field, e.g. history, economics, political studies. Vacancies are advertised as they occur. The Department is based in London, although there are occasional opportunities for members to be posted overseas.

The following recruitment is undertaken directly by the Foreign and Commonwealth Office:

Communications Branch: Posts are filled by applicants with specialised experience of radio-operating or technical qualifications in telecommunications. Vacancies are advertised as they occur, but applications are accepted at any time.

Secretarial Branch: Applicants with shorthand at 100 wpm and typing at 30 wpm are recruited to work as secretaries or shorthand-typists at home and abroad. A GCSE level qualification in English Language is desirable though not essential. Selection is by tests and personal interviews. Applications are accepted at any time.

Queen's Messengers: Usually based in London, members of this branch are responsible for delivery of the diplomatic bags containing official correspondence to and from posts abroad. Candidates must be between 40 and 50. Vacancies arise infrequently.

Security Officer Branch: Positions are open to those with relevant security experience, aged 35-50 and prepared to serve only at missions abroad. No applications are accepted except during advertised recruitment campaigns.

Recruitment

Diplomatic Service Grades 7D/8; 9 and 10: recruitment to permanent posts in these mainstream Diplomatic Service grades is carried out by the Civil Service Commission. Full details of the recruitment regulations and selection process are contained in booklets available from the *Civil Service Commission,* Alencon Link, Basingstoke, Hampshire RG21 1JB.

Other grades: general information about recruitment for other Diplomatic Service grades, Research Department, Legal Advisers and the Secretarial Branch is available from the Recruitment Section, Personnel Policy Department, *Foreign and Commonwealth Office,* 4 Matthew Parker Street, London SW1H 9NL.

Communications Branch: further information can be obtained from the Personnel Officer, Communications Administration Department (FCO), Hanslope Park, Milton Keynes MK19 7BH.

Queen's Messengers: Prospective applicants should write to the Superintendent of Queen's Messengers, Communications Operations Department, *Foreign and Commonwealth Office,* King Charles Street, London SW1A 2AH.

Security Officers: application forms for Security Officers are available from the Personnel Operations Department, *Foreign and Commonwealth Office,* 3 Central Buildings, Matthew Parker Street, London SW1H 9NL.

BRITISH COUNCIL

The Royal Charter of the British Council defines its aims as "promoting a wider knowledge of our United Kingdom and the English language abroad and developing closer cultural relations with other countries." Financed by public funds, it is non-profit-making and works non-politically in over 80 countries. The Council has a network of 120 offices employing 4,500 staff, well over half of whom work overseas.

The Council's work is divided as follows:

English language teaching and educational aid: every year the Council recruits several hundred British teachers for overseas universities, teacher-training colleges and schools; and provides an advisory service to Ministries and Departments of Education abroad.

Personal contacts and co-ordination: Council staff in Britain and overseas make contacts with, and arrange tours and meetings for, leaders in educational, scientific and cultural fields, to encourage international co-operation and knowledge.

Library work: the Council runs and supplies 126 British reference and lending libraries abroad, and holds over 250 British book and magazine exhibitions annually.

Arts and sciences: the Council promotes scientific contracts and advises on scientific and medical education available in Britain. Tours are arranged for British theatre, ballet and opera companies, especially in countries where such visits are rare: and paintings and sculptures by British artists are sent to international festivals.

Other activities: the Council supplies information on aspects of British cultural life, arranges lectures, film shows, concerts and play-readings, and conducts British examinations abroad.

Recruitment

Overseas Career Service: Applicants should have three years' work experience and preferably postgraduate qualifications in either TEFL, linguistics, management, teaching, librarianship, information science, accountancy, engineering science or education. Overseas experience such as VSO is valuable and linguistic ability desirable.

Recruits can expect to spend two-thirds of their career overseas, mostly in the Third World, and not necessarily in countries of their choosing.

Advertisements for the OCS appear in the national press in September. Further details can be obtained from Head of Recruitment, Personnel Management Dept., 65 Davies Street, London W1Y 2AA.

Overseas Educational Appointments: Since its foundation the British Council has undertaken the recruitment of British staff for overseas appointments as part of its educational and cultural activities. Within the broad field of education, English Language Teaching (ELT) has always been a particularly important area for the Council. Of some 1,100 Council-recruited teachers and advisers who are overseas at present over 700 are engaged in ELT.

Nearly all overseas employers insist on at least one to two years' experience. Occasionally, however, a Postgraduate Certificate in Education or a qualification in the teaching of English as a second or foreign language without subsequent experience is acceptable. For example, since 1982 the Council has recruited newly qualified teachers of science and mathematics for secondary schools in Botswana.

The Council's role in much of its recruitment is that of an agency. A substantial part of its work in that capacity is on behalf of the Overseas Development Administration (ODA). Under the Key English Language Teaching (KELT) project, financed by ODA, it recruits specialists on contract to the Council to work within the educational systems of developing countries and offers them professional support at post. The Council also recruits and employs on contract teachers and directors of studies for its own Direct Teaching of English (DTE) operations in 26 countries (see the chapter on *Teaching*).

For information, contact OEAD, 65 Davies Street, London W1Y 2AA.

BRITISH GEOLOGICAL SURVEY

The Survey is concerned with geological mapping and mineral investigations in Great Britain and its continental shelf and in developing countries overseas. The overseas component is administered by the Survey's Overseas Directorate as part of the Overseas Development Administration's aid programme.

All scientific members of BGS have the opportunity of serving overseas either as members of geological teams working on specific technical assistance projects or on secondment as members of geological survey departments of emerging Commonwealth countries.

The work of the Overseas Directorate is administered through four Regional Units dealing with Africa, Asia, Latin America and the Caribbean, and the Pacific. Much of the work overseas now involves BGS specialists in the field of hydrogeology, geophysics, geochemistry, engineering geology, etc.

Further details on employment and career prospects can be obtained from the *British Geological Survey,* Keyworth, Nottingham NG12 5GG.

Military Service

The British Armed Forces

Although there are British military bases scattered throughout the world, cuts in government defence spending have reduced the numbers of personnel at these bases. At present there are Army bases in Belize, Cyprus, the Falklands, West Germany, Gibraltar and Hong Kong.

Eligibility

The following points should be noted before an application is made.

Marital Status — Single and married men are generally eligible, as are single women. But married women are rarely considered, and if their applications are taken, they will not normally be accepted without signing a declaration to the effect that their marital duties will not interfere with their work. Employment within or in support of the armed forces is exempted from the conditions of the Sex Discrimination Act (see section 85 of the Act).

Nationality — An applicant must be, and must have been at all times in his or her life, a Commonwealth subject or a citizen of the Republic of Ireland; must have been born within the Commonwealth or the Republic of Ireland; and both parents must have been born within the UK, the Commonwealth or the Republic of Ireland. These regulations are sometimes stretched, but only with the special permission of the Secretary of State for Defence.

Political Bias — No-one while a member of the Armed Forces may take part in any political activity.

Age — The minimum age for entry into the armed forces is school-leaving age, i.e. 16½. Parents' consent is needed for entrants under 18. Upper age limits vary.

Health — All applicants must pass a strict health examination. Applicants for some branches may be refused on the grounds of their height, hearing or eyesight.

Information

The functions of recruitment and careers advice for military personnel are the responsibility of the regional Army, Navy and RAF Information Offices, situated in most large towns in Britain (addresses given in telephone directories). Although the London addresses of the Ministry of Defence departments are given in their respective sections below, applications and requests for information received there are usually sent back to the appropriate regional offices. Teachers, nurses, and other personnel should write direct to the relevant London addresses.

ARMY

Most soldiers serve at one time or another in Germany, and there are also opportunities to travel to many other countries.

Commissioned Service

Most commissions must be obtained through the Royal Military Academy, Sandhurst, to which entry is achieved in any of the following ways:

Young Entry — candidates aged $17\frac{3}{4}$-22 with five GCSE passes, two at "A" level, including English language, maths, and either a science or a foreign language, are considered for Regular and Special Regular Commissions.

Scholarship Scheme — army scholarships are awarded to boys and girls aged 16-$16\frac{1}{2}$, to enable them to take the "A" levels necessary for Sandhurst entrance.

Welbeck College — boys aged 16-$17\frac{1}{2}$ with GCSE in English, maths, physics, and preferably other science subjects, can take science "A" levels at Welbeck to qualify Sandhurst. They will mainly be commissioned into one of the Technical Corps.

Graduate Entry — open to graduates or those with certain professional qualifications. The upper age limit is 25 (29 or 30 in some cases).

Undergraduate Cadetships — open to men and women aged $17\frac{1}{2}$-22 who are at, or about to go to, university. An undergraduate cadet is commissioned as 2nd Lieutenant on probation. He cannot normally resign his commission within 5 years of graduation.

Bursary Scheme — similar to the Cadetship, open to women as well. They cannot normally resign their commission within three years of receiving it.

Middle Entry — open to men aged 22-26 (or up to 29 in some corps) seeking Special Regular Commissions. They must have 5 GCSE levels, including English Language and Maths.

Short Service Commissions — available to holders of 5 GCSE levels, including English language. Candidates must be over 18, and normally no older than 26 (29 in some cases).

The length of training at Sandhurst is 12 months. The method of entry also affects the ultimate choice of commission — Regular, Special Regular or Short Service.

Professional Arms — commissions are granted to appropriately qualified men to serve in the Royal Army Chaplains' Department, Royal Army Medical Corps, Royal Army Veterinary Corps, Royal Army Dental Corps and Army Legal Corps. Commissioned entry into these departments is on a four week course via Sandhurst. Medical and dental cadetships are available.

Non-Commissioned Service

(a) Technical, Arms and Corps Apprentices — various technical apprentice colleges offer 1-2 year courses for boys aged $15\frac{2}{3}$-$17\frac{1}{2}$ on entry. Basic military training, education, general subjects, and many specialist employments are taught.

(b) Junior Leaders — boys aged 16-17 may join a Junior Leaders unit in the corps of their choice, and take an educational and military course lasting 12 months.

(c) Junior Soldiers — boys aged $16\frac{1}{2}$-17 can enter as Junior Troopers, Gunners, Signalmen, Guardsmen and Infantrymen, also Junior Drummers, Buglers and Pipers in the Infantry. No qualifications required.

(d) Junior Bandsmen — boys aged 16-$17\frac{1}{2}$, preferably with musical experience, can train as bandsmen. They must be auditioned and accepted by the Corps, Regimental Director of Music or Bandmaster. Training lasts two years, and those with special aptitude are given a further 12 month course at the Royal Military School of Music.

(e) Adult Entry — unqualified men aged 17-25 (sometimes 30) may enter one of the 92 employments in the Army. Men aged 23-30 who have served an apprenticeship in a mechanical, electrical or electronics employment, and have reached ONC or equivalent standard, are also accepted.

Length of Service

Entry into the ranks is on the terms of a notice engagement. Enlistment is initially for 3, 6 or 9 years (the longer you enlist for, the higher your scale of pay). Junior entrants (under 17) and young soldiers can only opt for the 6 or 9 year engagement (to date from their 18th birthday or the end of their training, whichever is later), but at the age of 18 they can revise this to three years. However, some of the longer training courses rule out the option of the three year engagement. Entrants under the age of $17\frac{1}{2}$ are allowed to leave the army within the first six months if they find themselves unsuited to the army life. A full career in the ranks is reckoned as 22 years, but 12 months notice can be given at any time so long as the initial period of enlistment has been served.

Further Details

Army Career, at your local Army Careers Information office, listed in the phone book under "ARMY".

Ministry of Defence, DAR 1, Empress State Building, Lillie Road, London SW6 1TR — for information on training at Sandhurst, and all kinds of commissioned service.

WOMEN'S ROYAL ARMY CORPS

The WRAC is a permanent army corps, whose function is to replace men in work which can be done as well by women. This includes technical trades in transport and communications; administrative and clerical work; catering, and other jobs. Not all jobs qualify for service abroad.

Commissioned Service

Candidates over 18½ are considered for officer training, having fulfilled the entry requirements. Candidates for short service commissions are also accepted with 5 passes at GCSE and two "A" levels. They are also accepted under the Direct Entry Scheme for Graduates.

All candidates are trained at the Royal Military Academy at Sandhurst on a 28 week course.

Non-Commissioned Service

Women aged 17¼-33 and medically fit may enlist in the ranks. Six weeks of basic training is given at the WRAC Centre in Guildford, following which specialised training is undertaken in a variety of jobs including catering, postal and clerical work, technical trades, transport, signals, storekeeping, and a variety of other jobs including kennelmaid, bandswomen, provost and stewardess.

Length of Service

Commissioned service as in the army. Service in the ranks is for an initial three years (18 months notice can be given any time after the completion of the first 18 months), with a full career lasting 22 years. Women may leave all branches of the armed services when they marry.

Further details

Corps Recruiting and Liaison Officer, WRAC Centre, Queen Elizabeth Park, Guildford, Surrey GU2 6QH.

ROYAL NAVY

The Royal Navy provides extensive opportunities to serve abroad both on ships and at shore bases situated all over the world.

Commissioned Service

Scholarships and reserved places in the Engineering and Seaman branches are available to young men aged 15-17 with five GCSE passes or equivalent. Some scholarships are given to help schoolboys take "A" levels. Graduates may join all branches, and some University Sponsorships are offered.

Short Career Commissions are available for appropriately qualified young men in seaman, pilot or observer positions, or in mechanical and electrical engineering. Doctors, dentists, and instructors all enter initially on Short Career commissions. Age limits vary from branch to branch; and training courses depend on qualifications already obtained.

Non-Commissioned Service

(a) Junior and Adult Entry — men aged 16-33 with no educational qualifications may enlist in most branches except Medical Technician and Artificer Apprentice.

(b) Artificer apprentices (Engineering Technicians) — boys aged 16-21 with GCSE or equivalent including maths, English and an acceptable science may be accepted for a five year apprenticeship. Applicants who do not hold the required academic qualifications can take the MOD (N) Artificer Apprentice written examinations. Subject to passing these examinations, applicants will be considered for entry.

(c) Medical Technicians — candidates aged 17-33 with five "O" levels may apply to specialise in radiography, physiotherapy, laboratory technician, Environmental Health Inspector or Pharmacy Dispenser. "A" levels are required for some specialisations.

(d) Direct Entry Technicians — medical technicians (under the age of 33), with suitable qualifications and experience may be accepted subject to availability and approval by a professional board.

Length of Service

There are three types of commission: Full Career (pensionable), Medium Career and Short Career (8-12 years, transferable or renewable, pensionable after 16 years). The minimum period of service for most commissions is normally 4-5 years, but sometimes longer, depending on the type of training undertaken.

Royal Naval Recruits are entered for 22 years service from age 18 or date of entry if later. There is a minimum commitment of 4 years trained adult service if premature release is not sought.

All ratings automatically have the right to claim discharge on giving 18 months' notice at any time after completing two years six months' service from age 18, or after completion of initial training, whichever is later.

For details of service, pay rates, etc., contact the Director of Naval Recruiting, *Ministry of Defence,* Old Admiralty Building, Spring Gardens, London SW1A 2BE. Those trying for a commission should write to the Officer Entry Section, Naval Careers Service, at the same address.

ROYAL MARINES

The Royal Marines are a moderately autonomous arm of the Royal Navy, and today provide Britain's only Commando force; special training for jungle, desert, snow and mountain warfare is given in Malaysia, Borneo, the Arctic, Norway, Canada and Scotland.

Commissioned Service

(a) Royal Marines Scholarship Scheme — for boys aged 15-17 with 5 GCSE/GCE acceptable grades (or equivalent). The scheme provides education leading to at least two "A" levels.

(b) Direct Entry — for candidates aged 17½-22 with 5 GCSE acceptable grades (including two at "A" level); short-service entrants aged 17½-23 with the same qualifications; and candidates aged under 25 with a degree. University Sponsorships are also available.

Non-Commissioned Service

(a) Junior Marine — open to boys aged 16-17½ who pass the medical and selection tests.

(b) Junior Buglers — boys aged 16-17½ are accepted for 20 months' training at the Royal Marines School of Music at Deal.

(c) Junior Musicians — boys aged 16-17½ who can play an instrument are accepted for a three-year training course at the School of Music in Deal. Promotion to Band Sergeant is possible from the age of 26. There are also limited openings for direct entry for trained musicians aged 17½-28.

(d) Adult Entry into the General Duties or Technical Branch — for men aged 17½-28.

(e) Cooks and Clerks — for men aged 16-28. A Marines recruit training is completed before the necessary specialist courses.

Length of Service

RM recruits are entered on a Long Service and reserve Engagement, i.e. 9 years' service over the age of 18, or to the age of 27 if entered before reaching the age of 18, followed by service in the Royal Fleet Reserve for the residue of 12 years reckoned from the date of entry.

Further details

The Director of Naval Recruiting, *Ministry of Defence,* Old Admiralty Building, Spring Gardens, London SW1A 2BE.

WOMEN'S ROYAL NAVAL SERVICE

The WRNS are an integral part of the Royal Navy, whose members serve in naval establishments, shore bases and air stations in Britain and abroad.

Commissioned Service

The direct entry scheme is open to candidates aged 20½-26½, with degrees, diplomas in social science, teacher training, professional secretarial or catering qualifications and experience. Training courses are given at the Royal Naval College at Dartmouth, and service is in the following branches: secretarial; administrative; quarters and catering; communications; and computers.

Non-Commissioned Service

WRNS must be between 17 and 28 on entry. Following five weeks of general training at HMS *Raleigh* at Torpoint, East Cornwall, specialised training there or elsewhere is given, in one of the categories open to WRNS. These cover technical, secretarial, supply, communications and weapons analysis; other posts include education and training support, dental surgery and hygienist assistant, telephonist.

Length of Service

Commissions are all for eight years, with options to leave after five years, or to transfer to a permanent commission. Non-commissioned WRNS entrants join for a 15 day probationary period, during which they may claim their release if they do not feel suited. They subsequently enter on a nine-year engagement which commences either from age 18 or from date of entry, whichever is later.

Further Details

The *Directorate of Naval Recruiting,* Old Admiralty Building, Spring Gardens, London SW1A 2BE.

ROYAL AIR FORCE

Although the number of RAF bases abroad has been reduced for economic reasons, the prospect of overseas service is still good. The Women's Royal Air Force is not a separate force and so is not listed by itself — unlike the other two services many of the jobs are interchangeable.

Commissioned Service

University cadetships are available to applicants aged under 23, who have a university place or at least good prospects for one. The scheme is designed to help entrants obtain a degree.

Direct Entry — entry into commissioned service is via the RAF College at Cranwell. Men aged 17½ and women over 18, with 5 GCSE level passes, can be considered for Officer Training; "A" level and graduate applicants are preferred. The upper age limit varies with branch and can be up to 39, however entrants for General Duties (Pilot) must be under 24 at start of training.

Professionally qualified men and women up to age 30 may enter via a shortened course at RAF College Cranwell into the Medical, Dental, Chaplains and Legal branches.

Scholarships are available for boys aged 15-17, for "A" level studies this includes approximately 30 hours flying tuition. Recipients are expected to enter the RAF on either a Short Service or Permanent Commission on completion of their "A" levels.

Non-Commissioned Service

(a) Apprenticeships — engineering technician apprenticeships are offered to boys aged 16-18½ (exceptionally 21) with a minimum of 4 GCSE level passes, including Mathematics and an appropriate science subject.

(b) Ground Airmen and Airwomen — men aged 16½-39 and women aged 17-39 can be considered for vacancies which arise in the following trade groups: aircraft engineering, air electronic engineering, general engineering, ground electronic engineering, mechanical transport, security, air traffic control, general service, telecommunications, aerospace systems operating, surface and safety, photography, medical, dental, accounting and secretarial, supply and movements (men only), catering, and music (men only).

Length of Service

Commissions are in two types — permanent commissions can last until the age of 55, but may be terminated at the 38/16 point, i.e. at the age of 38 or after 16 years service if you enter after the age of 21, whichever is the later. Short service commissions are for three to six years, for ground branches and 12 years, with an option of leaving after eight years, for aircrew. Fixed engagements for non-commissioned service are either six or nine years for airmen. Airwomen enlist on a notice engagement for nine years with the option to leave earlier.

Further details can be obtained by writing to your nearest RAF Careers Information Office, address in the telephone directory under RAF.

Ancillary Services

NURSING AND WELFARE

Whichever service the student or registered general nurse chooses to join, prospects of an overseas posting are good. There are service hospitals wherever large numbers of servicemen and their families are based, and nurses are constantly in demand.

Queen Alexandra's Royal Army Nursing Corps

Registered General Nurses aged 21-38 may apply for a Short Service Commission in the QARANC. This is an eight year commission, a minimum of 2 years to be spent on the active list and the balance on the Regular Army Reserve of Officers. If they wish a full career in the Corps they may apply to convert to a Regular Commission.

Direct entry is also available for SEN's and for untrained women aged at least 17, to train as nurses, medical clerks, dental clerk assistants, ward assistants, laboratory or pharmacy technicians. Minimum service is for 3 or 4 years dependent on training undertaken. If wished, on completion of training, the period of service can be extended up to 22 years.

The nurses' training courses (5 GCSEs are needed for the RGN course) conform to the same standards as those required by civilian hospitals.

For further details contact the Corps Recruiting and Liaison Colonel QARANC, Ministry of Defence (DAR 2), Empress State Building, Lillie Road, London SW6 1TR.

Queen Alexandra's Royal Naval Nursing Service

Registered General Nurses with at least two years' nursing experience, and preferably an extra qualification, may enter direct as an officer on a five-year short-term commission. The maximum age on entry is 33.

Girls aged 18-28, with GCSEs may train for RGN training, five passes are required (English Language compulsory).

For further details, contact the Directorate of Naval Recruiting, Old Admiralty Building, Spring Gardens, London SW1A 2BE.

Princess Mary's Royal Air Force Nursing Service

Registered General Nurses aged 23-35 with a minimum of one year's post-registration experience and a second qualification may enter on a 4 year short service commission for up to 8 years or transferred to a permanent commission.

For further details contact the *Director of Nursing Services (RAF),* Room 811, Ministry of Defence, First Avenue House, High Holborn, London WC1V 6HE.

Enrolled Nurses aged 21 to 40 may enter the PMRAFNS on a three year engagement. Limited opportunities for further service are available to suitable candidates.

RGNs may be accepted for entry as staff nurses between the ages 21-39 years; however, the preferable age group is 21-26 years. Candidates do not require a second qualification nor is any post registrational experience necessary. Opportunities exist for further managerial and professional qualifications and suitable candidates may be selected for commissioned service. Initial period of engagement is nine years.

Further details can be obtained from *RAF Careers Information Offices* or by contacting The *Inspectorate of Recruiting (NLO),* Government Buildings, London Road, Stanmore, Middlesex.

Soldiers', Sailors' and Airmen's Families Association

The SSAFA Overseas Community Health Service provides Community Health Care for families of Servicemen of overseas stations in Germany, Holland, Belgium, Gibraltar, Cyprus and Hong Kong.

SSAFA recruits Health Visitors who have had a minimum of two years post-graduate experience working in a Health Authority. There is also a Community Midwifery Service, but recruitment into this service is restricted to the wives of Servicemen who are qualified Midwives.

The scope of the work covers Health Visiting, School Health, Ante-natal and Post-natal work and Health Education. The Service has developed to include the two specialists, Health Education Officer and In-Service-Training Officer.

The SSAFA Social Work Service provides qualified social work with Service families in similar conditions overseas.

For further details contact: The Director of Community Health, or: The Director of Social Work, *SSAFA,* 16-18 Old Queen Street, London, SW1H 9HP.

St John and Red Cross Joint Committee

The Service Hospitals Welfare Department of the St John and Red Cross Joint Committee employs about forty welfare officers in service hospitals both in Britain and abroad (in West Germany, Cyprus and Hong Kong). Welfare Officers are responsible for the general welfare of service patients, their families and civilian patients in service hospitals. Their duties include the upkeep of hospital libraries and the organisation of diversional handicrafts and general activities for the patients.

Applicants aged 22-35 will be considered, who should have a good standard of education, plus initiative, tact, and the ability to mix with all types of people.

For further details, contact the Director, *St John and Red Cross Service Hospitals Welfare and VAD Department,* 4 Grosvenor Crescent, London SW1X 7EQ.

ROYAL FLEET AUXILIARY

The RFA is a civilian manned fleet owned by the British Government and with merchant navy status. Its main tasks, however, are to supply Royal Navy ships with fuel, food, stores and ammunition; it also provides sea transport for army personnel and equipment. As a civilian operation, the conditions of entry and service are as laid down for merchant shipping (see chapter on *Transport and Tourism),* but for specific careers information, contact the Careers Office, *Royal Fleet Auxiliary,* Room 504, Empress State Building, London SW6 1TR.

Foreign Armed Forces

National armed forces are usually open only to citizens of that country. However, some countries welcome alien residents into their ranks. Other countries, like the USA, insist on foreign residents signing up, although at present active service is not obligatory.

The Middle East states are among the countries prominent in recruiting well trained personnel for their armed forces. The following companies are involved in recruitment for Arab forces:

Saudi Arabia Support Department, British Aerospace Plc, Warton Division, Warton Aerodrome, Preston, Lancs PR4 1AX — some vacancies on defence support contracts with the Royal Saudi Arabian Air Force.

Airwork Ltd., Bournemouth (International) Airport, Christchurch, Dorset BH23 6EB — deal with positions in the Sultanate of Oman, for all aspects of aircraft work, from engineering through to storekeeping, teaching, administration and medical posts. Also deals with positions in Zimbabwe for aircraft engineers only.

FRENCH FOREIGN LEGION

The French Foreign Legion, immortalised by Beau Geste and Laurel and Hardy, was created in 1831 and is a semi-autonomous unit under the French Ministry of Defence. Although the legionnaire is idealised in fiction and the recruitment leaflets, it can in real life be very lonely and austere, and the chances of getting out before the end of the five-year contract are slim.

Entry Requirements

Applicants should be aged between 17 and 40 (average age is 24) and physically fit. Beyond this, the only requirement is complete loyalty to the legion, whose motto *legio patria nostra* (the legion is our country) demands that soldiers should renounce or forget their family, friends, home country and other loyalties. On the negative side, intellectual ability and knowledge of the French language are not required; colour, creed, nationality and social class have no bearing; and few questions are asked about identity or background.

Enlistment can only take place in France at one of the 23 Foreign Legion information centres. Any gendarmerie in France can direct you to the nearest centre. The obligatory medical, psychological and professional tests are held at Aubagne, near Marseille.

Service

Contracts are initially for five years, starting with sixteen weeks' training at Castelnaudary. Following the training course, soldiers will be classified as specialist combatant, technician or corporal, with promotion prospects to officer status. Service is in one of the parachute, infantry, cavalry or mixed regiments in Corsica or the south of France; all soldiers must also serve for 24-30 months in one of the regiments stationed in Tahiti, Mayotte, Djibouti and French Guiana. Special training can be given in a variety of technical trades, including telecommunications, mechanics and building.

At the end of five years, contracts can be renewed for up to three years at a time, pensionable after a total of fifteen years, Legionnaires are also entitled to acquire French nationality after five years' service, or to obtain a ten-year residents warrant.

Further Details

Le Chef du Poste d'Information de la Légion Etrangère (PILE), Fort de Nogent, 94120 Fontenay-Sous-Bois, France.

The Police

Opportunities for British Policemen and Policewomen do occasionally arise in a few Commonwealth member States, although these have been reduced in recent years.

There are no formal foreign exchange schemes available to Police Officers, but a small number of Officers are seconded abroad each year from the Metropolitan and other Constabularies. Secondments are made to places as far afield as Hong Kong, Bermuda, Papua New Guinea and The Falkland Islands.

Recruitment to forces overseas takes place in two ways: either by secondment from the Metropolitan and other Constabularies; or through direct advertised vacancies.

Police positions overseas are sometimes advertised in *The Police Review,* available on subscription from *The Police Review Publishing Company,* 14 St Cross Street, London EC1.

Examples of recent recruitment drives are those conducted by the Bermuda Police Force, which regularly recruits a "pool" of some 70 Officers for permanent contracts every two years; and that of the Papua New Guinea Police Force which in 1984 recruited some 20 Officers.

The Recruitment Section of the Metropolitan Police (address below) advises that at any one time, some 20 fairly senior Officers will be seconded abroad from this country.

The Metropolitan Police advise that much of this recruitment takes place by word of mouth, but serving Officers interested in the general prospects of contracts with overseas forces might like to contact the *Recruitment Executive,* of the *Overseas Development Administration* at East Kilbride, whose address is Ambercrombie House, Eaglesham Road, East Kilbride, Glasgow G75 8EA.

THE METROPOLITAN POLICE

All Officers recruited to the Met must meet certain minimum entry standards. Officers must be intelligent, physically fit, a British or Commonwealth citizen permanently resident in the UK, and must meet the minimum height requirement of 172 cm for men and 162 cm for women. Good eyesight is also essential.

Prospective Police Officers should ideally have five GCSE passes, including English and Maths; or take a series of written test designed as equivalents. Ideal candidates will be between the ages of 18½-40 years, and have some experience of earning a living.

The Met. also runs a Cadetship scheme for young people aged between 17½ and 18½ years.

Every Metropolitan Police Officer, including ex-Cadets, starts by becoming a Police Constable on two years probation. The first seven months of the probationary period is spent on integrated training, which begins with 20 weeks at the Metropolitan Police Training Centre at Peel Centre, Hendon. Further information about recruitment to the Met. is available from the Recruitment Officer, *Metropolitan Police,* New Scotland Yard, Broadway, London SW1H 0BG.

THE ROYAL HONG KONG POLICE

The Royal Hong Kong Police Force claims the distinction of being one of the oldest and yet most modern police forces in the world. Formed in 1842 it evolved from an extremely broad based role embracing the fire services, prisons, immigration and customs, to that of a traditional police force.

In 1969 the Queen awarded it the title "Royal" in honour of its role during the 1967 disturbances. Today the Force has a total of 26,600 disciplined officers with a civilian staff well in excess of 5,000.

The Force's main headquarters comprises of the following five departments: Operations, Special Branch, Personnel and Training, Management and Inspection Services and Civil Administration. Day-to-day policing is the responsibility of four (soon to become six) police Regions each with their own headquarters.

The Force, which is expanding, continues to recruit candidates for the post of Inspector from the United Kingdom. Applications are invited from suitably qualified serving military and police officers as well as those from industry or Higher Education. The Force's minimum entry requirements are five GCEs (two of which must be at Advanced level including English Language) with slightly lower qualifications being sought from serving military or police officers. Full details and application forms are available from the Police Appointments Officer, *Hong Kong Government Office,* 6 Grafton Street, London W1X 3LB.

Worldwide Employment

Belgium

Belgian Embassy, 103 Eaton Square, London SW1W 9AB
Currency: 1 Belgian franc (BF) = 100 centimes
Rate of exchange: £1 = BF 67.57

Belgium is the seat of the EC, NATO, and over 300 other international organisations which constantly require English and English-speaking personnel. Because it is close to Britain, and transport is cheap and fast, short-term work in Belgium is a realistic proposition, and for long-term work a weekend at home presents little problem.

Although there is still a shortage of skilled labour in some economic sectors, the very high unemployment rate means considerable competition for jobs. A knowledge of French or Dutch may be required.

GENERAL FACTS

Population

Belgium's population is a dense 9.9 million, with an increase of 0.6% per annum. 19.4% of the population is under 15, and 14.0% over 65.

With a total area of 11,783 square miles, Belgium has, after the Netherlands, the second highest population density in Europe — 828 inhabitants per square mile.

Belgium is an essentially flat country, rising above 1,000 ft. only in the Ardennes in the east. Over half the land area is farmland, and industry accounts for a further 25%.

Climate

The climate for most of Belgium is similar to that in the south of England. A more continental climate (colder winters, drier summers) is found in the Ardennes and Luxembourg.

Government

Belgium is a consititutional monarchy. The central legislative system consists of two chambers — the Chamber of Representatives and the Senate. The 212 members of the Chamber of Representatives are elected every four years. In July 1981 the voting age was lowered from 21 to 18. The Senators who also serve four-years terms, fall into three categories: those who are directly elected; those elected by provincial councils; and those co-opted by Senators in the first two categories. At present there are 181 Senators.

The country is divided into nine provinces — Antwerp, Brabant, East Flanders, West Flanders, Hainaut, Liège, Limburg, Luxembourg and Namur. These provinces are administratively divided into 44 arrondissements, 214 cantons, and 2,359 communes.

Cities

Belgium has undergone a higher rate of urbanisation than most other European countries, and industry has created its own towns and suburbs out of agricultural land. Over 30% of the population is concentrated in five main urban areas. Brussels (980,196); Antwerp (486,576); Liege (202,314); Ghent (234,653); and Charleroi (211,943). Antwerp is the world's third largest port after Rotterdam and New York.

Rural Life

Farmland accounts for just under half of the total area of Belgium, but less than 3% of the labour force is employed in agriculture. This figure also covers employees in forestry (a further 20% of the land area) and the fisheries on the North Sea coast.

Religion, Sport and Culture

Belgium is overwhelmingly Roman Catholic, although complete religious freedom is observed.

The country's most popular sport is cycling. Second comes football, which is played, for the most part, on a semi-amateur basis.

The history of Belgian art contains such names as Van Dyck, Breughel and Rubens, most of whose paintings are to be seen in the Brussels Museum of Ancient Arts, and other art galleries. Brussels has a particularly high cultural standard, with a number of art galleries, theatres and concert halls.

FACTORS INFLUENCING EMPLOYMENT

Immigration

The Belgian Embassy, although unable to assist in finding employment, issues a series of leaflets containing general information for aliens wishing to settle in Belgium.

Although work permits are no longer required, all Britons intending to take up employment in Belgium must register their address within one week of arrival at the *maison communale* of the district in which they are staying. The *maison communale* can issue a temporary residence permit, but a permanent residence permit can only be issued later on approval of the Aliens Police.

Language

The racial division of Belgium between the Flemings and the Walloons is a traditional cause of unrest. In 1971, legislation created four sectors of the country, on a racial/linguistic basis. The Flemish-speaking sector, in the north and west, contains 57% of the total population, compared with only 33% in the French-speaking area. Brussels is bi-lingual, with 10% of the population; the fourth sector is the German-speaking Eupen-Malmédy region on the German frontier. This area contains only 62,000 inhabitants.

Cost and Standard of Living

Although Belgium has a scarcity of raw materials, and imports are therefore high, the Belgo-Luxembourg Economic Union (concluded in 1921), which exports about half of its industrial production, has the highest per capita export rate in the world and an economic importance out of proportion to its surface area.

As indicators of the standard of living, there are, for every 1,000 inhabitants: 302 televisions, 328 private cars, and 332 telephones.

Housing and Accommodation

Belgium is one of the few countries in Europe that does not have a housing problem. An average of 33,350 new houses are built annually, which leaves a constant vacancy rate of 3-4%.

Rents vary from area to area and according to size and comfort. A two-bedroomed unfurnished apartment with central heating and a partly equipped kitchen, will cost between BF16,000-25,000 a month in a residential area of Brussels. Deposits of up to three months' rent are normally required.

Health and Welfare

Belgium has a comprehensive welfare system. Workers pay compulsory contributions of about 10% of their earnings; employers pay up to 60%. This covers sickness, disablement and unemployment; pensions of up to 75% of a worker's average earnings; maternity and family allowances; and almost complete medical coverage. 70-80% of medical costs will be reimbursed by the medical insurance.

Education

Education is free and compulsory for all children between the ages of 6 and 15 or 16. Apart from the state schools there are a large number of private schools, most of them religious (Catholic) foundation. Brussels also has a few international schools.

Belgium has four main universities — two bi-lingual, at Brussels and Louvain; one Flemish, at Ghent; and one French, at Liège. There are also two university centres, at Antwerp and Mons. Universities are State-financed or subsidised, and entrance requirements are high. Courses are generally longer than in English universities, with a minimum of four years (five for law and engineering; seven for medicine).

National Service

National Service is compulsory only for male citizens aged 18-33. Aliens are not liable.

British Embassy and Consulates

British Embassy, rue Joseph II 28, 1040 Brussels.

There are also honorary consulates in Antwerp and Liège. The Consular Section of the British Embassy in Brussels issues a leaflet *Coming to Belgium to Work.*

CONDITIONS OF WORK

Wages

There are no standard legal minimum wages in Belgium, but monthly minimum salaries for white-collar workers have been established according to age and skills. The average monthly salary for clerical categories of employees is BF 40,000-45,000. The average weekly wage for a man working in industry is BF 10,000-11,000. Women's wages are, on average, 20% less than men's but equal pay is given to men and women in identical jobs.

Hours

A six-day week (45 hours) is not uncommon in Belgium, but the tendency is towards a standard five-day 40-hour week. Sunday work is prohibited by law except in special circumstances. Double pay is given, and a day of rest in lieu within the next week.

Holidays

There are 10 official public holidays per annum: New Year's Day, Easter Monday, Labour Day (May 1), Ascension Day, Whit Monday, Fête Nationale (July 21), Assumption (August 15), All Saints' Day (Nov. 1) Armistice Day (Nov. 11), Christmas Day. In addition, the legal minimum paid holiday is four weeks in any working year.

Safety and Compensation

The Government appoints Social Inspectors to check the standard of hygiene and safety in major industries. In co-operation with these, large firms must set up their own Hygiene and Safety Committees to inspect premises and recommend improvements.

Sickness, disablement and industrial injuries come under the social security scheme, and benefits are very generous. In the event of disablement, for instance, between 80 and 100% of the worker's average income can be claimed. If the disablement requires the help of another person, 150% can be claimed. Legislation also protects employees by establishing the minimum notice to be given by employers.

Trade Unions

About 65% of Belgian workers belong to unions. Most of the unions (90% of all union membership) are affiliated with one of the three major political parties. Membership is voluntary, and workers will have several unions to choose from.

Labour-management relations are highly organised, with permanent delegations representing both sides at local and national levels. Agreements are usually reached without the necessity for drastic action, but there are special Labour Courts to settle particularly tough disputes.

Taxation

Income tax is deducted from wages at source. The first BF 100,000 is tax free, additional income is taxed at a progressive rate, varying from a minimum rate of 25% to an upper limit of 72%. There are extra allowances for dependants.

WORK AVAILABLE

General

The Belgian Embassy in London, and the British Embassy and Consulates in Belgium are unable to assist in finding employment.

Newspapers

The main French language newspaper, *Le Soir,* is represented by Rossel & Cie. s.a., 112 rue Royale, 1000 Brussels; and by Publicitas Ltd., 525/527 Fulham Road, London SW6 1HF, who can also place advertisements in the major Flemish newspaper *Het Laatste Nieuws. Le Soir* has a special section on Tuesdays for people looking for a job.

Advertisements can also be placed in the English language newspaper *The Bulletin,* 329 avenue Molière, 1060 Brussels.

See also the *Advertisements* section in the chapter *Getting the Job.*

Labour Force

About 40% or 4,200,000 of the population is gainfully employed, one third of the labour force being women. The unemployment rate is 13%. Of the active work force, 33% work in industry, 3.3% in agriculture and fisheries, 63.7% in services.

SPECIFIC CONTACTS

Employment Service

British citizens, once in Belgium, may use the services of the *Office National de l'Emploi (ONEM),* whose Brussels office is at 65 Boulevard Anspach, 1000 Brussels, and which has 30 regional bureaux throughout the country. Bureau addresses are available from *ONEM's* Central Administration, Boulevard de l'Empereur 7, 1000 Brussels.

Consultants and Agencies

As well as the organisations listed in the section *Consultants and Agencies,* the following British and Belgian firms are among those that recruit personnel for positions in Belgium, mostly in Brussels.

ACT Careers, Avenue des Arts 50, Box 3, 1040 Brussels — offers full time employment for office staff and middle management.

Career Secretaries, Avenue des Arts 50, Box 3, 1040 Brussels — offers full time employment for all levels of secretarial positions. Applicants must have secretarial skills plus French, Dutch or German.

International Secretaries, 174 New Bond Street, London W1 (and avenue de Tervuren, 1040 Brussels) — top-level secretarial and PA appointments in Brussels.

Services de la Jeunesse Feminine, 29 rue Faider, 1050 Brussels — au pair agency and all social services.

Teachers

The addresses of Belgian universities and language schools in Brussels are obtainable from the Belgian Embassy, 103 Eaton Square, London SW1W 9AB.

Other Opportunities

Opportunities in Belgium are also referred to in the following chapters (see Contents), which cover a wide range of professions:

Transport, Tourism and Catering
Voluntary Work
British Government Departments
International Organisations
United Nations

SHORT TERM WORK

Belgium still offers a large number of temporary jobs to British people, despite possessing one of the highest rates of unemployment in Europe. Britons are helped both by their right to work in Belgium without a work permit and their ability to make use of the Belgium employment service (T-Service) which has many branches which specialise in finding short term work. These are:
5-7 Jezusstraat, 2000 Antwerp.
2 Pensmarkt (Groentenmarkt), 9000 Ghent.
17 Spanjaardstraat, 8000 Bruges.
47 Thonissenlaan, 3500 Hasselt.
22 Rollewagenstraat, 1801 Vilvoorde.
68 Beheerstraat, 8500 Kortrijk.
86 de Merodelei, 2300 Turnhout.
22 Rue de la Province, 4020 Liege.
91 Rue de Montignies, 6000 Charleroi.
14 Rue Borgniet, 5000 Namur.
24 Rue General Molitor, 6700 Arlon.
69 Boulevard Anspach, 1000 Brussels.

Seasonal Work

Contrary to popular belief Belgium does receive tourists in the summer, and extra staff are taken on to cater for them.

Those looking for jobs should write directly to individual hotels (a list can be obtained from the Belgium Tourist Office, 38 Dover Street, London W1).

International Voluntary Service, and *Christian Movement for Peace* and the *UN Association (Wales)* all arrange voluntary work camps in the summer: see the *Voluntary Work* chapter for details. A Belgian organisation called *Youth Service Nete en AA VZW,* at Oude Steenweg 13A, B-2280

Grobbendonk, also arrange camps lasting for two weeks in July and August. Write to them for details.

Other Work

It is possible to find short term work on various exchange schemes and in Belgian households, see the relevant chapters in the *Specific Careers* section for details. Belgium also offers a number of opportunities in its cities through the branches of the "T-Service". Girls with secretarial experience and a working knowledge of French may be able to get office work, particularly with the multi-national companies based in and around Brussels. For boys, the opportunities are more likely to consist of unskilled manual work, perhaps in warehouses or supermarkets.

LIST OF BRITISH COMPANIES
with branches, affiliates or subsidiaries in Belgium
(see appendix for numerical classification code)

A copy of the Year Book of the British Chamber of Commerce in Belgium containing the names and addresses of its member firms can be obtained from the secretary of the Chamber at 30 rue Joseph II, 1040 Brussels, on advance payment of BF 1,000.

Antwerpse Diamantbank NW 4
(London EC1)
Pelikaansstraat 54
2000 Antwerpen

Atlas Chemical Industries 8
(London SW1)
Everslaan 45
3078 Eversberg

BAT Benelux 47
(London SW1)
rue de Konink 38
1080 Brussels

BP Chemicals Belgium 8
(London SW1W 0SU)
Division of BP NV/SA
Postbus 30
2050 Antwerpen

BTI Ferodo SA 7
(Manchester)
Avenue Reine Astrid 1
1420 Wautier Braine

Black & Decker 26
(Harmondsworth)
Weihock I
3072 Nossegem

Blackwood Hodge (Belgium) 6
(London W1)
Steenweeg op Leuven II
1940 St Stevens Woluwe

Barclays Bank International Ltd 4
(London EC3)
Avenue des Arts 27
1040 Brussels

Beecham SA & Beecham Pharma 8
(Middlesex TW8 9BD)
rue de L'Indendant 59
1020 Brussels

Belgian Shell SA 35
(London SE1)
Cantersteen 47
1000 Brussels

Bowater Philips NV 33
(London SW1)
New Orleansstraat 100
900 Gent

British Leyland Belgium 7
(London W1H 0HQ)
Chaussée de Mons
6198 Seneffe

British Leyland Belgium 7
(Preston)
Leyland Truck & Bus
Luithagen Haven 2
Blok H
2030 Antwerpen

British Steel Corporation 28
(London WC1E 6BB)
rue de la Loi 15
1040 Brussels

British Tourist Authority 48
(London SW1)
Place Rogier 23
1000 Brussels

Brouwery Maes-Watney 16
(London W1)
2571 Waarloos

NV Casco SA (Unilever) 16
(London EC4)
rue Montoyer 46
1040 Brussels

Castrol NV 35
(Glasgow)
Helmstraat 107
2200 Borgerhout

Chloride Belgium NV 8
(Manchester)
Groenstraat 31
2510 Mortsel

Christies Belgium Ltd 50
(London SW1Y 6QT)
Boulevard de Waterloo 33
1000 Brussels

Deloitte Haskins & Sells 1
(London)
Bd du Jarden Botanique 14
1000 Brussels

Derby-Ladbroke 4
(London NW10)
Chaussée de Waterloo 715
1060 Brussels

Dow Jones International 2
(London EC4)
Marketing Services (UK) Ltd
Boulevard de Waterloo 38
1000 Brussels

Dunlop Belgium Ltd 42
(London SW1)
Rue de Sel 86
1070 Brussels

EMI (Belgium) SA 29
(Middlesex)
rue Emile Claus 49
1050 Brussels

The Economist Intelligence 14
Unit (Europe) SA
(London SW1)
Avenue Louise 137
1050 Brussels

The Financial Times 38
(London EC4P 4BY)
Benelus Ltd
Hertogsstraat 39
1000 Brussels

Fison UCB SA 8
(Felixstowe)
Chaussée de Charleroi 138
Bte 6
1060 Brussels

General Accident Fire 23
& Life Assurance Corp Ltd
(Perth)
Meir 14
2000 Antwerpen

Hightons SA 28
(London WC1 2EB)
rue Ortelius 32
Brussels

Hoverspeed Ltd 48
(London WC2R 0HF)
rue do Brabant 13
1030 Brussels

ICI (Europe) 46
(London SW1P 3JF)
Everslaan 45
3078 Eversberg

ICL (Belgium) 10
(London SW18)
Avenue Louise 375
1050 Brussels

King & Co SA 40
(London EC1)
rue de la Loi 26, Bte 17
1040 Brussels

Laura Ashley Ltd 46
(Powys, Wales)
rue de Namur 81/83
1000 Brussels

Lever SA 11
(London EC4P 4BQ)
rue Montoyer 46
1040 Brussels

Lloyds Register of Shipping 23
(London EC3)
Karel Oomsstraat I
2000 Antwerpen

Marks & Spencer SA 13
(London W1)
Bld E Jacqmain 6
1000 Brussels

Max Factor Belgium SA 11
(Bournemouth)
Rue Gachard 90
1050 Brussels

Pitney Bowes Belgium SA 30
(Harlow)
Mercure Centre
rue de la Fusée 100, Bte 2
1130 Brussels

Price Waterhouse & Co 1
(London EC1)
rue Ravenstein 60
1000 Brussels

Proctor & Gamble 11
(Newcastle-upon-Tyne)
1 rue P Le Bon
1040 Brussels

Rank Xerox SA 30
(London N1)
Leuvensebaan 225
1930 Zaventem

Reckitt & Colman SA 8
(London W4 2RW)
rue de la Bienvene 9
1070 Brussels

Renold Continental Belgium Ltd 39
(Manchester M22 5W1)
Allée Verte 1
1000 Brussels

Schweppes SA 16
(London W2)
rue du Cerf 127
1320 Genval

NV Smith & Nephew (Belgium) SA 12
(London WC2R 2BP)
rue Middelbourg 64A
1170 Brussels

W H Smith & Son SA 38
(London WC2)
71-75 Bd A Max
1000 Brussels

J Walter Thompson SA 2
(London W1)
rue Charles Lemaire 1
1160 Brussels

Townsend Car Ferries 48
(Dover)
Doverlaan 7
8380 Zeebrugge

AMERICAN COMPANIES
with branches, affiliates or subsidiaries in Belgium

These are given in the *List of American Companies in Belgium,* price BF 2,050, from the American Chamber of Commerce in Belgium, avenue des Arts 50, BTE 5 B-1040 Brussels. Payment should be made in advance, preferably by transfer, to bank account No. 687-3090000-91 with Morgan Guaranty Trust Co. of New York, avenue des Arts 35, 1040 Brussels.

Luxembourg

Luxembourg Embassy, 27 Wilton Crescent, London SW1X 8SD
Currency: 1 Franc = 100 Centimes
Rate of Exchange: £1 = LF69.4

With an area of only 1,000 square miles, and a total labour force of 165,000, the Grand Duchy of Luxembourg does not, obviously, offer employment opportunities on any grand scale. Luxembourg is, nevertheless, a member of the European Community, and is therefore subject to the Community regulations concerning free movement of labour. Entry requirements are basically the same as for Belgium. All aliens must, however, hold an "Identity Card for Foreign Nationals", which also serves as a residence permit for up to five years (renewable).

Applications for this Identity Card must be made to the relevant municipality office in the place of intended residence.

General information on entry, residence and employment is available from the *Luxembourg Embassy,* 27 Wilton Crescent, London SW1X 8SD.

Language

The official legislative, administrative and judicial language is French, but there is a native language or dialect, known as *letzeburgesch* or *luxembourgeois*. However, French, English and German are the most commonly used languages in business.

British Embassy

14 boulevard Roosevelt, 2450 Luxembourg.

Newspapers

Advertisements can be placed direct in:

Luxemburger Wort, CP 1908, L-2988, Luxembourg.
Tageblatt, PO Box 147, L-4002 Esch/Alzette, Luxembourg.
The Journal, CP 2101, L1021 Luxembourg.

See also the section on *Advertisements* in the chapter *Getting the Job*.

Labour Force

The labour force is divided as follows: 0.9% in agriculture, 39.1%in industry, 74.2% in services.

Work Available

When seeking employment in Luxembourg, it might be helpful to contact the National Employment Office, which is called the *Administration de l'Emploi,* 34 avenue de la Porte-Neuve, Luxembourg.

Opportunities in Luxembourg are sometimes available with the organisations referred to in the following chapters (see Contents):

Banking and Accountancy
International Organisations
Computer Services
British Government Departments
Secretarial, Translating and Interpreting

SHORT TERM WORK

Luxembourg does offer opportunities for short term work, but you will normally need some knowledge of French or German unless you are hoping to work for Radio Luxembourg as a disc jockey.

Two employment agencies in Luxembourg which deal with temporary work are *Manpower-Aide Temporaire, Sarl.,* 19 rue Glesenar, and *Bureau-Service, Sarl.,* 2 allée Leopold Goebel. The former deals with all types of jobs while the latter deals with office jobs.

Seasonal Work

The tourist industry plays a significant part in Luxembourg's small economy, and you may be able to get a temporary job by writing directly to one of its 256 hotels — a list is available from the Luxembourg Embassy in London (enclose a self addressed envelope).

Other Work

Experienced multilingual secretaries may be able to find work with one of the multi-national companies in Luxembourg: *International Secretaries,* described in the *Secretarial, Translating and Interpreting* chapter, sometimes knows of short as well as long term vacancies. British citizens who are prepared to visit Luxembourg to look for work should visit the office of *L'Administration de l'Emploi* at the address given above.

BRITISH AND AMERICAN FIRMS
in Luxembourg

A free list of some 22 British and American companies with operations in Luxembourg is available from the Luxembourg Embassy, 27 Wilton Crescent, London SW1X 8SD.

Denmark

Danish Embassy, 55 Sloane Street, London SW1X 9SR
Currency: 1 Danish krone (Dkr) = 100 øre
Rate of Exchange: £1 = Dkr 12.8

As a rule, it is difficult to obtain any sort of employment in Denmark, and some knowledge of Danish is essential in most jobs. There are no Danish offices operating as labour exchanges or advisory bureaux for foreigners.

GENERAL FACTS

Population

Of Denmark's total population of 5.1 million, 25% are under 19, and 15% over 65.

Denmark covers 16,615 square miles; in addition to the Jutland peninsula, the country consists of 483 islands. Population density is 295 people to the square mile. The country is low-lying, with no important minerals.

Climate

Denmark's climate is similar to that of Britain or West Germany, rather than to the other Scandinavian countries. However, there is generally more sunshine in summer than in England, and winter temperatures tend to be lower.

Government

A constitutional monarchy (the oldest kingdom in Europe), Denmark's *Folketing* (the legislative assembly) contains 179 elected representatives, headed by a Cabinet and a Prime Minister. A referendum in September 1978 reduced the minimum voting age from 20 to 18. Women have had the vote since 1915.

Cities

Copenhagen, the capital and the largest port in Scandinavia, has a population of 1,382,000; other large cities are Aarhus (population: 182,000), famed for its old buildings and museum; Aalborg, the chief city of North Jutland, with a population of 114,000, a gourmet's paradise with 120 restaurants; and Odense (136,000), the old city made famous by Hans Christian Andersen.

Rural Life

About 20% of the population live in rural areas, but this number is steadily decreasing, due to the slow drift to the cities.

The number of farm properties, now about 120,000, is also decreasing, due largely to the amalgamation of small units. Still, the average size of farms has remained small, some 95% of farms covering less than 150 acres.

Denmark is well known in Britain for exports of dairy produce and bacon. Also important to Danish economy are forestry (forests cover 10% of the country's land area), and fruit and vegetable production. Being almost entirely surrounded by water, fishing is also an important industry.

Religion, Sport and Culture

There is complete freedom of religion in Denmark, but 97% of Danes belong to the established Evangelical-Lutheran church.

The most popular sport in Denmark, as in most other European countries, is soccer. Also popular are badminton, rowing, yachting, handball, gymnastics, swimming, athletics and tennis. Keep-fit training has recently become a national pastime.

Danish cultural life is advanced, with many art galleries, museums, theatres, etc. A large number of clubs cater for all leisure pursuits from sport to striptease, and the Danish attitude to censorship is well known.

FACTORS INFLUENCING EMPLOYMENT

Immigration

As a reflection on the high unemployment rate and the general difficulty in finding work in Denmark, the issue of work permits was suspended in November 1973. Despite this immigration ban, the EC agreement on free movement of labour still applies, so Britons are still allowed to look for work. However, all aliens in employment must register with the local civil register (Folkeregister), and residence permits are required for all stays of over three months. These must be applied for at *The Directorate for Aliens,* Absalonagade 9, 1658 Copenhagen V or through the local police.

Language

Non-Danish speaking foreigners may find difficulty in obtaining any sort of well-paid work. Most Danes know basic English, but prospective workers are advised to learn some Danish before they leave Britain. Once in Denmark, the local education authorities arrange cheap language classes with an English-speaking teacher when the need arises. The Universities of Copenhagen and Aarhus hold courses in Danish for beginners and for intermediate students.

Cost and Standard of Living

Because wage levels are adjusted according to the cost of living index, people working in Denmark are assured of a fairly stable standard of living; visitors to the country may find prices high.

For every 1,000 Danes there are 278 private cars, 470 TV sets and 570 telephones.

Housing and Accommodation

Housing is scarce in Denmark, yet one of the conditions behind residence permits is that the applicant must have a suitable dwelling. You are therefore advised to arrange accommodation before you arrive. Rents are high — at least Dkr. 750 a month, even for a single room. On the other hand, home ownership is encouraged by tax relief on mortgages.

Health and Welfare

Denmark was one of the first countries to introduce social welfare schemes: social security is the largest single item of Danish national expenditure, accounting for 48% of the public revenue.

In the majority of cases, it is sufficient merely to be resident in Denmark in order to qualify for social security and welfare assistance. To a large extent, foreigners may therefore obtain such assistance on the same terms as ordinary Danes. Social benefits include retirement pensions from the age of 67, pensions for widows over 55, mothers and children under 18, single mothers and invalids. Benefits are also paid for unemployment, sickness, maternity and industrial injury. All hospitalisation, including periods of convalescence, is provided free. Doctors' and dentists' bills are generally payable in cash, refundable in part or in whole by local municipal offices.

Education

Education is compulsory between the ages of 7 and 16. Most education, including university, is free, although there are some private schools.

Denmark has five universities (at Copenhagen, Aarhus, Aalborg, Odense and Roskilde). There are a number of other specialised training colleges, including art schools, music colleges, etc. State grants are available to Danes and foreigners alike for higher education.

National Service

Foreigners in Denmark are not liable for military service.

British Embassy and Consulates

British Embassy, Kastelsvej 36-40, 2100 Copenhagen Ø.
British Consulate, Sondergade 24, 6200 Aabenraa.
British Consulate, Østeraa 19, 9000 Aalborg.
British Consulate, Vesthavnen, 7000 Fredericia.
British Consulate, Grenaavej 144, 8240 Risskov Aarhus.
British Consulate, Grimsbyvej, 6700 Esbjerg.
British Consulate, Tvaergade 19, 5100 Odense C.

CONDITIONS OF WORK

Wages

Wages and working conditions are fixed by negotiations every two years between worker and employer organisations. Wage adjustments are made at half-yearly intervals to conform to the cost of living index.

Hours

The normal working week in Denmark is 39 hours in a five-day week. Shops generally close early on Saturdays.

Holidays

All employees in Denmark are entitled to five weeks paid holiday per annum. In addition, the following public holidays are observed: New Year's Day, Maundy Thursday, Good Friday, Easter Monday, Great Prayer Day (April or May), Labour Day (May 1), Ascension, Whit Monday, Constitution Day (June 5 — half day only), Christmas Eve, Christmas Day, Boxing Day and New Year's Eve (half day).

Safety and Compensation

Work conditions, including safety standards, are fixed by collective bargaining between workers' and employers' organisations. National legislation sets down a minimum code of safety.

Trade Unions

To safeguard their interests, both workers and employees have organised unions; the majority of trades set wages and conditions by collective agreements between these unions, which are binding on all employees irrespective of membership. Union membership, while not obligatory, extends to 85% of the labour force. Most foreigners join a Danish union; the rules then require contributions to the Unemployment Insurance Fund. This may be joined separately, but contribution rates are higher for non-union members.

Taxation

Government income tax is deducted at source. A foreigner will be subject to unlimited liability upon arrival if he indicates his intention to become a Danish resident, or if his stay exceeds six months. A personal allowance of Dkr 22,000 is tax-free and where a spouse cannot use the whole allowance, the balance is transferred to the other spouse. The total tax rate, which is made up on a mixture of flat and progressive scales, combining State, county, municipal and church taxes, varies between 25 and 70 per cent. Sickness and unemployment insurance contributions are also deducted at source, but are computed separately. Further information can be obtained from the Danish Embassy, which can provide the booklet *Worth Knowing When You Come to Work in Denmark.*

WORK AVAILABLE

General

Despite the freedom of movement within the EC countries, finding work in Denmark is still no easy task, and Britons are advised to check the current situation at a local Labour Exchange before making any definite plans.

With the exception of EC nationals, work permits for foreigners have virtually ceased until the employment situation improves. No foreigner is allowed to take up a post in the Danish Civil Service.

Newspapers

Advertisements can be placed in *Politiken,* a leading Danish paper, through the London agent Frank L. Crane Ltd., 5-15 Cromer Street, Grays Inn Road, London WC1H 8LS.

A leading publishing house is *Teknisk Forlag A/S,* Skelbaekgade 4, Dk-1717 Copenhagen V, who produce many journals covering engineering and electronics to chemistry and plastics.

See also the section on *Advertisements* in the chapter *Getting the Job.*

Labour Force

The labour force numbers nearly 2½ million (half the population), including 36,000 foreigners, 33% work in industry, 8% in agriculture, 59% in services. The current unemployment rate is about 8.5%.

SPECIFIC CONTACTS

Employment Service

The Danish state employment service can help Britons who call at their offices to find a job. A list of all the local offices is available from the head office: *Arbejdsdirektoratet,* Adelgade 13, Dk-1304, Copenhagen K. Alternatively, the addresses of local offices can be found under *Arbejdsformidlingen* in telephone directories.

Local Agencies

There are a number of general employment agencies in Copenhagen that may be able to offer jobs in offices, factories, etc. to personal callers. Two of the largest are *Adia* at N. Volgade 82, and *Western Services* at Kobmagergade 54: alternatively, look up *Vikarbureaux* in the telephone directory.

Medical Staff

Medical personnel wishing to work in Danish hospitals should consult the weekly journal of the *Danish Medical Association* (available from the DMA, Trondhjemsgage 9, 2100 Copenhagen Ø, Denmark) in which all vacant hospital medical posts are advertised. Positions of less than three months duration are handled by the DMA Bureau at the same address. A list of hospitals and other medical institutions is available from the same source for D.Kr.300, as is the free booklet *Information for Doctors Migrating to Denmark.*

With regard to authorisation to work as a doctor in Denmark the *National Board of Health,* 13 Amaliegade, DK-1012, Copenhagen K, should be contacted after employment has been obtained. The National Board of Health emphasises the difficulty of obtaining employment in Danish Hospitals particularly without a solid knowledge of the Danish language. Furthermore, there is a surplus production of doctors for a number of years ahead.

Regulations and methods of application for foreign doctors are set out in the leaflet *Guidance for Foreign Graduates in Medicine who Apply for*

Permission to Practise Medicine in Denmark, available from the Danish National Board of Health (Sundhedsstyrelsen) at the above address.

Oil Industry

A/S Dansk Shell, Kampmannsgade 2, Dk-1604 Copenhagen V, is an operating company in the Royal Dutch/Shell group of companies, with a refinery located at Fredericia in Jutland. Activities include manufacturing, distribution and marketing of oil products.

Other opportunities

Opportunities in Denmark are also referred to in the following chapters (see Contents), which cover a wide range of professions:

Transport, Tourism and Catering British Government Departments
Voluntary Work

SHORT TERM WORK

Denmark offers a comparatively high average wage and few bureaucratic delays to British people looking for short term jobs. It should be borne in mind that although most Danes speak English, preference will generally be given to people who can speak at least a little Danish.

Seasonal Work

It is worth writing directly to hotels for jobs in Denmark's healthy tourist industry, which has its centre in Copenhagen. Casual workers, are also needed to help harvest tomatoes, strawberries, cherries and apples over the summer. There is, unfortunately, no principal fruit-producing area to visit; a picking job may be found by placing an advertisement asking for work in *Landsbladet,* a farming journal published by Landboforeningernes Ugeblad at Vester Farimagsgade 6, 1606 Copenhagen K. Students looking for temporary work around Copenhagen can visit a particular branch of the national employment service: called the *Studenternes Arbejdsformidling* it is at Tøndergade 14, Dk-1752, Copenhagen V.

Other Work

Opportunities for voluntary and domestic work and on exchange schemes are covered under the relevant *Specific Careers* chapters (see also the section Local Agencies above).

LIST OF BRITISH COMPANIES
with branches, affiliates or subsidiaries in Denmark
(see appendix for numerical classification code)

Laura Ashley (Mail Order) 46
(Powys, Wales)
Nyhavn 21
1051 Copenhagen K

The Associated Press 38
(London EC4)
Kristen Bernikows Gade 4ii
1105 Copenhagen K

The Barclays Group of Banks 4
(Representative Office)
(London EC3)
Bredgade 23, iii
1260 Copenhagen K

Baxenden Scandinavia A/S 8
(Accrington BB5 2SL)
Fulbyvej 4
Pederborg 4180 Sorø

Beecham Scandinavia A/S 8
(Brentford)
Transformervej 16
2730 Herlev

Black & Decker A/S 26
(Maidenhead)
Bistrupvej 172
3460 Birkerød

Boeg-Thomsen A/S 16
(London W3)
4390 Vipperød

British Airways 3
(Hounslow)
Vesterbrogade 2B
1620 Copenhagen V

British Caledonian Airways Ltd 3
(London SW1)
Vester Søgade 10
1601 Copenhagen V

British Railways Board 48
(London SW1)
Møntergade 3
1116 Copenhagen K

British Steel Corporation 28
(London SW1)
Dansk Representations
Kontor
Nørre Voldgade 68
1358 Copenhagen K

British Tobacco Co ApS 47
(Woking)
Strandvaeget 43
2100 Copenhagen ø

Castrol A/S 35
(Swindon)
Esplanaden 7
1263 Copenhagen K

Courtaulds Danmark A/S 9
(London W1)
Falkoner Alle 53
2000 Copenhagen

A/S Dansk Shell 35
(London SE1)
Kampmannsgade 2
1604 Copenhagen V

DEB Swarfega Denmark 8
(Derby)
Teglvaerksvej 6
5620 Glamsbjerg

DER A/S 10
(London WC2H 6ED)
Gungevej 17
2650 Hvidovre

DOW Chemical A/S 8
(Hounslow)
Vedbaek Strandvej 350
2950 Vedbaek

Dunlop A/S 42
(London SW1)
Tagensvej 85b
2200 Copenhagen N

EMI (Dansk-Engelsk) A/S 10
(London W1)
Hoffdingsvej
2500 Valby

European Plastic Machinery 37
Manufacturing A/S
(Brentford)
'Euromatic'
Krimsvej 29
2300 Copenhagen S

Ferrymasters A/S 17
(London E11)
Fabriksparken 8
2600 Glostrup

Fisons A/S
(Loughborough)
Rosenkaeret 22A
2860 Søborg

Flymo A/S 10
(Darlington)
Lundtoftevej 160
2800 Lyngby

Hoover El-Udstyr ApS 10
(Perivale)
Gasvaerksvej 16
1656 Copenhagen V

ICI Denmark A/S 8
(London SW1)
Islands Brygge 41
2300 Copenhagen S

Ilford Foto A/S 36
(Ilford)
Gadelander 18
2700 Brøshøj

Int'l Computers Ltd A/S 10
(London SW15 TSW)
Klampenborgvej 232
2800 Lyngby

International Factors A/S 17
(London W1)
Bredgade 29
1260 Copenhagen K

Johnson Matthey A/S 28
(Royston)
Nørre Farumagsgade 33
1364 Copenhagen

Leyland-DAB A/S 7
(London NW1)
Kajlstrupvej 71
8600 Silkeborg

Lloyd's Register of Shipping A/S 23
(London EC3M 4BC)
Kronprinsessgade 26
1264 Copenhagen

Max Factor & Co ApS 11
(Bournemouth)
Naerum Hovedgade 2
2850 Naerum

Nordlund Trading 43
(London W1P 0AA)
St Strandstraede 9
1255 Copenhagen K

John Player ApS 47
(Bristol)
Nrdr. Fasanvej 108
2200 Copenhagen F

Price Waterhouse 1
(London EC2)
Nørre Farimagsgade 64
1364 Copenhagen K

Racal Radar Aktieselsskab 45
(London SE1 7SW)
Mitchellsgade 9
1568 Copenhagen V

Rank Xerox A/S 30
(London NW1 3BH)
Borupvang 5
2750 Ballerup

Reckitt & Colman A/S 16
(London W4)
Industrivej 14
2600 Glostrup

Renold A/S 25
(Manchester)
Skelmarksvej 6
2600 Glostrup

Thorn Electric A/S 10
(London WC2)
Brogrenen 6-8
2635 Ishøj

United Biscuit A/S 16
(Middlesex)
Sdr. Ringvej 41-45
2600 Glostrup

Whitbread & Co (Scandinavia) 16
(London EC1)
Strandboulevarden 130
2100 Copenhagen ø

Wiggins Teape (Danmark) 33
(Basingstoke)
Hovedgaden 49
2970 Hørsolm

France

French Embassy, 58 Knightsbridge, London SW1X 7JT
Currency: 1 Franc (Fr.) = 100 centimes
Rate of Exchange: £1 = Fr. 10.7

Although general work prospects are not particularly good in France, its closeness to England has always made it popular for short-term work, which seems to be constantly available.

GENERAL FACTS

Population

France's population of about 55,406,000 includes roughly 3½ million foreigners. About 30% of the total are under 20. Including Corsica, France covers 213,000 square miles — the biggest country in Europe after Russia, and twice the size of England, Scotland and Wales. The average population distribution is 252 to the square mile.

Climate

France is the only country with all three European climatic subdivisions of Continental, Maritime (wet) and Mediterranean (hot and dry). No part has less than 20″ of rainfall a year, but the wettest parts are the Central Plateau, the Jura, the Alps, the Pyrenees and the coastal Brittany area. The Paris Basin and the Mediterranean coast are the driest.

Government

France is a Republic headed by a President who has considerable power over the French nation. The former overseas French territories are now largely independant: the last to gain autonomy was the Republic of Djibouti.

The Government decides and directs the policy of the nation and is responsible to the elected Parliament, but Ministers must resign their Membership of the National Assembly or the Senate when selected. Four major parties are represented (including the Communists, now much reduced after Francois Mitterand's 1981 Presidential victory) and the referendum is occasionally used in national decision-making.

France is divided into 96 *départments,* in turn sub-divided into 324 *arrondissements,* which break down into 3,509 *cantons;* the smallest unit is the *commune,* which there are 36,394. The *départments* are not autonomous but differ administratively.

Cities

The rural exodus to urban areas has hit France as elsewhere, but towns are still small by British or American standards. Paris has 10,000,000 (metropolitan area); Marseille, Lyon and the Lille metropolitan area exceed the million mark, but only about twenty others have over 200,000 inhabitants.

Rural Life

France's richest natural resources are her fertile farm lands and forests, which combine to make her enviably self-sufficient. Agricultural produce accounts for 5% of GDP, and it is estimated that maximum exploitation of the existing resources could support a population twice the size of the present one.

France is the world's fifth largest wheat producer; barley, oats, rice, grapes, beef and dairy cattle and fisheries are also important. About $1\frac{1}{2}$ billion gallons of wine are produced annually.

Religion, Sport and Culture

90% of the French are baptised into the Roman Catholic Church but only 1 adult in 5 attends church regularly. Protestants number about 800,000 and other evangelical and non-Christian (especially Jewish) faiths are represented. There are two million Moslems.

Sport is not so developed as in Britain since in the past far more emphasis was placed on mental than physical achievement, in school and beyond. Only 7% of French men practise some sport on a regular basis, compared with 14% of English. Yet there is a wide interest in spectator sport, notably soccer, rugby, cycling and horse-racing. Field sports are popular, and about 4 million Frenchmen belong to one of the 7,000 clubs catering for sport of all kinds. Boules is a favourite, especially in the South.

Classical, popular and experimetal theatre are well represented and patronised in France, as is the cinema. Music, ballet and opera are encouraged, also literature and other arts. The Parisians, if not all the French, are certainly more politically, and perhaps more culturally, aware than the average Briton.

FACTORS INFLUENCING EMPLOYMENT

Immigration

EC nationals intending to stay in France for more than three months can only do so if they have an offer of employment. The residence permit (*carte de séjour*) is only issued on production of a *déclaration d'engagement,* signed by the prospective employer. Applications for residence permits should be addressed to the local *Commissariat de Police,* or *Mairie,* or, in Paris, to the *Préfecture de Police.* Persons wishing to set up their own business in France should also apply to the same authorities for a *carte de commerçant.*

The French Consulate in London cannot help British citizens to find work, but enquiries about permits, etc., should be addressed to the *French Consulate General,* Cromwell Road, London SW7 by those resident in Bedfordshire, Berkshire, Buckinghamshire, Cambridgeshire, Cornwall,

Devon, Dorset, Essex, Hampshire, Hertfordshire, Isle of Wight, Kent, Leicetershire, Greater London, Norfolk, Northamptonshire, Nottinghamshire, Oxfordshire, Suffolk, Surrey, East and West Sussex, Wales, Warwickshire, Wiltshire.

Persons living outside this area should contact the French Consulate nearest their home. They are at: 11 Randolph Crescent, Edinburgh EH3 7TT; 523/525 Cunard Building, Pier Head, Liverpool 3; and Philip Le Fuvure House, La Motte Street, St. Helier, Jersey.

Language

Anyone looking for a job in France should be able to speak at least some French, since, although the French learn English in school, the majority only remember a few words five years later. Fluency is essential for most commercial and professional jobs. The French are very proud of their language; it is the official language in 24 countries and the medium of education in seven others. Northern and Southern French dialects are very different, but an average French speaker should not find too much difficulty in understanding them both.

Cost and Standard of Living

The French have increased their standard of living by 80% in the past 15 years. Although the average French family may not seem well equipped with mod. cons. in the home, the increase in spending on these since the war has been enormous, and now for every 1,000 inhabitants there are 344 private cars, 340 television sets and 372 telephones.

Housing and Accommodation

The housing situation in France is not good. Despite the claim that the French are the worst housed nation in Europe, the number of houses per inhabitant built annually (15.7 per 1,000) is better than average. In fact, the total French building programme is, in Europe, second only to West Germany.

70% of all French homes were built before 1948; and nearly ¾ of all rural dwellings are pre-1914. But the cities have more than their fair share of new building projects.

In terms of value for money, rents are no higher than in Britain. For house-buyers there are still some bargains to be found — but certainly not in Paris or on the Cǫte d'Azur.

Health and Welfare

The social security schemes cover almost everyone in France on a compulsory basis (wage earners, salaried and self-employed persons, and their families including aliens) or on a voluntary basis.

The system is financed by employers' and workers' contributions calculated as a percentage of their salaries or wages, the employees' shares being deducted at source. Benefits include medical and unemployment insurance; pensions (amounts dependent on salaries and length of insurance); death, maternity, family and housing allowances; and industrial accident insurance.

Medical treatment and drugs are available to EC citizens under the same conditions as for French nationals.

Education

Education is free and compulsory from the age of 6 to 16. Primary education lasts from 6 to 11, and the first stage of secondary education lasts a further four years.

At the age of 15, those with sufficient ability stay on for another 3 years, ending in the notorious *baccalauréat* examination which determines university entrance. For entrance to the high-status *grandes écoles,* further study is necessary.

French universities are free, apart from low matriculation and examination fees, and grants related to parental income are given for accommodation and living costs.

French education in the past has been directed entirely from the Ministry of Education in Paris, which resulted in a hopelessly bureaucratic and rigid structure. But since 1968 the French Universities have enjoyed a certain extent of self-government.

National Service

All French males between 19 and 36 are liable for national service comprising 12 months of active duty and 8 periods of further duty, none of which may exceed a month. Those with special qualifications may work in schools, hospitals or colleges in the overseas territories instead of the armed services. Foreigners are not eligible.

British Embassy and Consulates

British Embassy, Consular Section, 35 rue du Faubourg St. Honoré, 75838 Paris Cedex 8.
British Consulate General, 15 cours de Verdun, 33081 Bordeaux Cedex.
British Consulate-General, 11 square Dutilleul, 59800 Lille.
British Consulate-General, 24 rue Childebert, 69288 Lyon Cedex 1.
British Consulate-General, 24 avenue du Prado, 13006 Marseille.

There are also British vice-consulates in Blagnac, Cherbourg, Pinard, Nantes, Calais, Boulogne, Dunkirk, Nice, Perpignan and Ajaccio.

CONDITIONS OF WORK

Wages

Wages are based on a 40-hour week, and additional hours must be paid at a higher rate. Pay scales in Paris are about 25% higher than in the rest of the country. Since 1972 when the *Equal Pay for Equal Work* act was passed, differences in wages between men and women doing identical jobs have been considerably reduced. The national minimum hourly wage was FFr28.76 on July 1st 1988: this wage is reviewed several times a year to keep ut with inflation and productivity. The average annual income was FFr 40,600 in May 1984.

Hours

Traditionally, France has worked a 48-hour week, and *le weekend* was regarded as a peculiarly British phenomenon. However, the 40-hour, 5-day week has now become accepted, and now the average working week is just under 41 hours.

The working day used to be much longer than in Britain, but increasingly a typical French day begins at 8.15-8.30 and ends at 4.30-5.00. In Paris, the rush hour is at about 6-6.30 pm; in the provinces it is earlier.

Holidays

There are 10 public holidays annually, and most workers receive 5 weeks in addition. Because annual holidays tend to be taken simultaneously, the yearly 'August madness' results in chaos on the roads. The public holidays are: New Year's Day; Easter Monday; Labour Day; Ascension; Whit Monday; Fête Nationale (July 14); Assumption Day (August 15); All Saints' Day (November 1); Armistice Day (November 11); Christmas Day.

Safety and Compensation

Hygiene and security committees are obligatory in large firms, and industrial health specialists carry out regular inspections, although some feel that these should be more frequent.

Sickness and injury benefits come under the social security code and a worker on sick leave receives half pay. Compensation for industrial accident usually carries the full cost of medical and surgical expenses, functional re-adaptation and professional re-education. Pensions are given to those permanently incapacitated, and to the dependents of those killed at work. Unemployment does not come under the Social Security code, but under a separate scheme run by UNEDIC (Union Nationale pour l'Emploi dans l'Industrie et le Commerce).

Trade Unions

Until 1968 unions were small and less widespread than in Britain; there is no obligation to join, but the four largest (including the Communist-controlled *Confédération générale du travail* with 2.4 million members) have great prestige. Numerous small autonomous unions also exist and are theoretically non-political. Employers' and workers' unions come to collective agreements concerning hours, holidays, minimum wages, etc.

Taxation

About half of all French households are now required to pay income tax, based on the annual declaration and paid in instalments. However, the government relies heavily on indirect tax for its main source of revenue. French income tax is low, certainly lower than that levied in Britain or America, but indirect taxes and value-added tax raise the cost of living considerably. For a single person, the first FFr 13,770 is tax free, then rates rise in steps of 5% up to 65%. Taking into account the various allowances, overall rates rarely rise above 20%. The tax year runs from January to December, and taxes are paid in arrears (usually one lump sum in the autumn) based on a statement of earnings from the previous year.

WORK AVAILABLE

General

The French Embassy in London cannot help the British to find work in France.

Newspapers

Advertisements can be placed in all the leading Paris and provincial newspapers and magazines through the *French Publishing Group,* 21-23 Elizabeth Street, London SW1W 9RW. *The International Herald Tribune* newspaper is published in Paris, and has a worldwide circulation. Advertisements can be placed through their office at 63 Long Acre, London WC2.

See also the section on *Advertisments* in the chapter *Getting the Job.*

Labour Force

The labour force is distributed as follows: 8% in agriculture; 33% in industry and 59% in services. The unemployment rate is 9%, or two million.

SPECIFIC CONTACTS

Employment Service

The official labour exchange in France is the *Agence Nationale pour l'Emploi,* which has over 600 branches in the main French towns. They handle all types of work, but special engineering departments exist in the offices in Paris, Lyon and Marseille. Their main office at 53 rue Général Leclerc F-92136, Issy-les-Moulineaux, can supply the addresses of all the regional labour exchange branches.

Local Agencies

There are a number of private employment agencies in France that may be able to offer jobs in industry or office work to personal callers.

Manpower France S.A.R.L., 9 rue Jacques Bingen, 75017 Paris — one of the largest employment agencies in the country, with branches throughout France. They deal mainly with office and secretarial work, both permanent and temporary.

Select France, 34 Boulevard de Picpus, 75012 Paris — can provide a variety of both full time and temporary work. A good grasp of French is required. There are generally good job opportunities for those with computer skills, office work qualifications and industrial experience, especially in aeronautics and petrochemicals.

Au Pairs

Apart from the organisations listed in the *Au Pair* chapter, au pair positions are arranged throughout France by:

Accueil familial des jeunes Etrangers, 23 rue du Cherche-Midi, 75006 Paris.
L'ARCHE, 7 rue Bargue, 75015 Paris.
CONTACTS, 55 rue Nationale, 37000 Tours.
Inter-Séjours, 179 rue de Caurcelles, 75017 Paris.
Service Social de l'Institut Catholique, 21 rue d'Assas, 75270 Paris Cedex 6.

In addition, *Pro Filia,* 14 B avenue du Mail, 1205 Geneva, Switzerland, can place Au Pair girls for 1 year in the Geneva-Lyon region.

Teachers

The *Berlitz School of Languages Ltd,* 29 rue de la Michodiere, 75063 Paris, occasionally recruit TEFL teachers. See the *Teaching* chapter for details.

Other Opportunites

Opportunities in France are also referred to in the following chapters (see Contents), which cover a wide range of professions:

Transport, Tourism and Catering	Voluntary Work
International Organisations	United Nations
British Government Departments	Military Service

SHORT TERM WORK

France is the country chosen by many people who are looking for their first taste of work abroad. British people do not need work permits to go there, it offers a wide variety of seasonal jobs, and it is cheap to get to. The fact that French is the principal foreign language taught in schools also means that many British people are able to cross the language barrier and take up the sort of general temporary work that they might look for at home.

Seasonal Work

Prospects for finding summer jobs in France are described in depth in the book *Emplois d'Ete en France* (in French) and the substantial chapter on France in *Summer Jobs Abroad* (in English): both of these are revised every year, and list individual vacancies you can apply for. Those prepared to go to France and look for work on the spot should consult *Work Your Way Around the World.* See the Bibliography for information on all these books.

There is great scope for finding work in France's tourist industry, especially in the beach resorts along the Cote d'Azur from June to September and skiing resorts in the Alps from December to March. A number of major employers, including a number of British-owned "packaged" camping holiday organisers, are listed in the chapter on tourism. *Jobs in the Alps,* PO Box 388, London SW1X 8LX, also deal with hotel work. Jobs can also be found in the large number of holiday centres to which the French traditionally send their children during the school summer holidays. This sort of work can be obtained through the following organisers of holidays centres in France: *La Jeunesse en Plein Air* (21 rue d'Artois, 75008 Paris) and *L'Association des Paralyses de France* (17 bld. Blanqui, 75013 Paris).

Thousands of extra workers are needed to help with France's grape harvest early every Autumn. This sort of job can be arranged in advance through *Concordia* and the *Vacation Work International Club:* see the book *Summer Jobs Abroad* for details.

Treat any advertisements placed by other organisations with caution: some of them seem to be offering jobs in the harvest but are in practice only offering one-way travel to the south of France with no regard for the time when the picking begins, or whether there are already enough workers available. Every year more and more machines are introduced to pick grapes, and the competition for work from both local migrant workers does not decrease. But people with the time, money and inclination to travel from region to region asking for work should eventually be successful.

Below are listed the address of major ANPE (Agence Nationale pour l'Emploi, or local employment offices), in the wine producing regions, with rough guidelines as to the dates of the harvest. It should be stressed that these dates can vary by days or weeks from year to year.

September 15th — October 10th
Langeudoc-Roussillon: ANPE, 44 ave des Grande Bretagne, BP 643, 66006 Perpignan

September 20th — October 15th
Bordeaux: ANPE Tour 2000, Terrasse du Front du Médoc, 1 rue H. Labit, 33077 Bordeaux Cedex
Libourne: ANPE, 108 rue du President Carnot, BP 196, 33504 Libourne
Beaujolais: ANPE, 42 rue Paul Bert, BP 295, 69665 Villefranche-sur-Saone

October 1st — 20th
Loire Valley: ANPE, 9 rue du Docteur Herpin, Champ Girault, 37025 Tours Cedex
ANPE, Square Lafayette, BP 2108, 49021 Angers, Cedex
Burgundy: ANLE, clos des Bijonnieres — 1 Cours Moreau, 71000 Macon.
ANPE, 6 boulevard St Jacques, BP 115, 21203 Beaune 3, Cedex
Champagne: ANPE, 40 rue Talleyrand, BP 210, 51097 Reims.

For any information about grape picking, write to the ANPE concerned.

There are many other opportunities for casual farm work in France between May and September: *Work Your Way Around the World* lists the dates and areas of the major harvests. After grape-picking the next largest demand is for help castrating (removing flowers from) maize for periods of about ten days between mid-July and August, in the south west of France and Auvergne. The ANPE branches in Mont de Massan, Clermont-Ferrand and Pau may be able to help people who visit them to ask for this sort of work.

There are two organisations apart from the national employment service that can be of use to people who are looking for temporary work of any kind when in France. The *Centre d'Information et de Documentation Jeunesse* produces a number of leaflets on seasonal work as part of its general information service for young people: for copies of these send three International Reply Coupons to its head office at IOI Quai Branly, 75740 Paris, Cedex 15. There are 25 other regional branches in major town around France that should know of opportunities locally. Similarly, there are 33 *Centres Regional des Oeuvres Universitaires et Scolaire* in French university towns, these are only meant to advise people studying in France on prospects nearby, but in practice they may be helpful if there is a shortage of labour.

Other Work

In addition to the opportunities listed under *Voluntary Work, Au Pair and Domestic, Secretarial, Translating and Interpreting* and *Teaching,* there are, of course, other temporary jobs to be found in France. It is worth visiting private employment agencies as well as ANPE's: see the section on Local Agencies above.

LIST OF BRITISH COMPANIES

with branches, affiliates or subsidiaries in France
(see appendix for numerical classification code)

The *Franco British Chamber of Commerce and Industry,* 8 rue Cimarosa, 75116 Paris, publishes a Year Book, which contains a full list of members of the Chamber, many of which are branches, subsidiaries or agents of British-based companies. The Year Book costs Frs 200 (postage included).

Automotive Products France 22
177 rue des Fauvelles
92404 Courbevoie

Barclays Bank SA 4
(London EC4)
33 rue du Quatre Septembre
75002 Paris

Baring Brothers SA 4
(London)
38 rue de Provence
75009 Paris

British Airways 3
(London)
Tour Winterthur
92085 Paris la Defense

British Caledonian Airways 3
(Surrey)
182 avenue Charles de Gaulle
92522 Neuilly Cedex

Austin Rover France SA 7
(London W1)
rue Ambroise Croizat BP 32
95101 Argenteuil Cedex

British School of Paris
(London)
38 quai de l'Ecluse
78290 Croissy-sur-Seine

British Steel Corporation 28
(France) S.A.R.L.
21 rue des Trois Fontanot
92024 Nauterre Cedex

British Tourist Authority 48
63 rue Pierre Charron
75008 Paris

Charterhouse SA 4
(London EC2)
47 Avenue George V
75008 Paris

Commercial Union Assurances 23
(London)
104 rue de Richelieu
75002 Paris

Cooper France SA 8
(Berkhampstead)
22-24 rue du Chateau
92200 Neuilly-sur-Seine

Courtaulds SA 46
(London W1)
20 boulevard du Parc
92521 Neuilly Cedex

Alfred Dunhill SA 47
(London SW1)
4 rue Roger Bacony
75017 Paris

Financial Times 38
(London)
Centre d'Affaires le Louvre
168 rue de Rivoli
75001 Paris

Fisher School of English
(London)
43 avenue de Wagram
75017 Paris

Gestetner SA 30
(London)
71 rue Camille Goult
94400 Vitry-sur-Seine

Guardian Royal Exchange PLC 23
(London EC2)
42 rue des Mathurins
75008 Paris

Hambros Bank Ltd 4
(London EC2)
16 place Vendome
75001 Paris

ICI France SA 26
(Birmingham)
1 av. Newton
92142 Clamart

ICL France SA 10
(London SW5)
24 av. de l'Europe
78140 Velizy

International Westminster Bank PLC 4
(London EC1)
18 Place Vendome
75021 Paris

JCB France 27
(Rocester)
3 rue de Vignoble
92506 Sarcelles Cedex

Johnson Matthey & CIE 28
(Royston)
80 rue Ardoin
93401 St Ouen Cedex

Laboratories Glaxo 8
(Guildford)
43 rue Vineuse
BP 166 16
75764 Paris

Laboratories Fisons SA 8
(Leicester)
BP 177 Les 4M Chemin du Petit Bois
69132 Ecully

Legal & General Assurance 23
(London)
58 rue de la Victoire
75009 Paris

Lloyds Register of Shipping 23
(London EC3)
32 rue Caumartin
75009 Paris

Lloyds Bank (France) Ltd 4
(London EC4)
43 Bde. des Capacines
75002 Paris

Lucas France SA 2
(Birmingham)
11 rue Lord Byron
75008 Paris

Marks & Spencer (France) SA 1
(London)
6-8 rue des Mathurins
BP 252-09
75424 Paris

Midland Bank SA
(London EC2)
6 rue Piccini
75116 Paris

Pitman Professional English Centres
Pitman Central College
154 Southampton Row
London WC1B 5AX

Powell Duffryn Compagnie Francaise 3
35 avenue de l'Europe
BP 76
78143 Vélizy-Villacoublay Cedex

Rank Precision-Industries (France) SA 22
33 boulevard Dubreuil
91400 Orsay

Rapid English SA
128 rue du Faubourg St. Honoré
75008 Paris

Reckitt & Coleman SA 18
(Hull)
15 rue Ampére
91301 Massy Cedex

Rowntree Mackintosh SA 16
(York)
Noisiel
77422 Marne-la-Vallee

Securicor France SA 43
(London SW3)
12 avenue des Cocquelicots
94380 Bonneuil-sur-Marne

WH Smith & Son SA 13
248 rue de Rivoli
75001 Paris

Standard Chartered Bank Ltd. 4
(London EC4)
4 rue Ventadour
75001 Paris

Thorn EMI Computer Software 10
12/14 rue de l'Eglise
75739 Paris Cedex 15

Trusthouse Forte Hotels 20
23 Place Venedome
75001 Paris

Weatheralls France SA 40
(London WC2)
64 rue de la Boetie
75008 Paris

Wimpey SA 6
72-78 Grande Rue
92310 Sevres

AMERICAN COMPANIES

with branches, affiliates or subsidiaries in France

American Firms in France 1985 is published by the American Chamber of Commerce in France, 21 avenue George V, 75008 Paris and costs Frs 200.

West Germany

Embassy of the Federal Republic of Germany, 23 Belgrave Square, London SW1X 8PZ.
Currency: 1 Deutschmark (DM) = 100 Pfennig
Rate of Exchange: £1 = DM3.21

At present Germany has a continuing demand for skilled foreign workers, but the rate of unemployment is rising.

GENERAL FACTS

Population

Germany's population numbers 61,100,000, including 4½ million foreigners. Women outnumber men by about 3 million. The birth rate is 10.3 per 1,000 inhabitants, the lowest in the world.

Germany covers 95,967 square miles, including West Berlin; average population density throughout the country is 644 inhabitants per square mile, the third highest in Europe, after Belgium and the Netherlands.

Climate

The climate is temperate with prevailing westerly winds. Annual precipitation varies between 20″ in the north, to over 80″ in the Alps. Average summer temperatures are in the seventies. Winters can be very severe, and produce good ski conditions throughout the country.

Government

Since 1949 Germany has been a federal republic, headed nominally by a President whose term of office lasts five years. The Chancellor, like the British Prime Minister, remains in office as long as his government (maximum term four years). The Bundestag, the legislative body of 518 members, is elected every four years by all German citizens over 18. The Bundesrat is the second chamber, the 41 members of which are appointed by the State Governments from among their own members.

West Berlin occupies an anomalous position as the 11th State, which is still under four power military rule. It sends 22 members to the Bundestag and 4 to the Bundesrat, but they may speak only, not vote.

The other states are: Bavaria, Baden-Württemberg, North Rhine-Wesphalia, Hesse, Rhineland-Palatinate, and Saarland — all prosperous industrial states — and the comparatively agricultural states of Lower Saxony and Schleswig-Holstein. Finally there are the city states of Hamburg and Bremen, the two largest ports.

Cities

Twenty one million Germans, or nearly one third of the population, live in the 64 cities that have over 100,000 inhabitants. These include West Berlin, with 1.9 million inhabitants, Hamburg, with 1.57 million, and Munich (1.3 million). Cologne has 916,000 inhabitants, while Bonn, with only 300,000 inhabitants, is the nation's capital.

Rural Life

Although the number of agricultural workers decreases each year, there is a gradual population shift away from the large towns, particularly in the industrialised and overcrowded Ruhr Valley. However, this trend is turning villages into small towns, and there is a consequent fall in the number of communities with less than 2,000 inhabitants.

Religion, Sport and Culture

42% of the Germans are Protestants, 42.5% Catholic; the rest belong to Islamic, Jewish and other faiths.

Football is the most popular sport, followed by gymnastics, rifleshooting, athletics, tennis and swimming. Horse-riding is also favoured, and motor racing interests many. Winter sports are also popular, and include skiing, ski-jumping, skating, ice-hockey, and tobogganning.

Germany has always consisted of a number of more or less autonomous territories. This tradition of decentralisation makes for a wide — and rich — range of cultural diversity. Stereotypes are inevitably inaccurate, but most visitors observe a general difference in atmosphere between North and South. In the North, a hard-working Protestant ethic is noticeable, while the more Catholic South seems given to a more slower pace, and festivals (e.g. the Munich Beer Festival, and the Shrove Tuesday Carnival).

FACTORS INFLUENCING EMPLOYMENT

Immigration

All aliens wishing to work or reside in Germany must register on arrival with the Aliens Authorities (*Ausländerbehörde*) in the town or district residence.

The German Embassy cannot help in finding employment, but can give information to intending workers and residents in Germany. Further information for immigrants can be obtained from the *Bundesverwaltungsamt,* Referat V2-4, Barbarastrasse 1, D-5000 Köln 60. The *German Embassy* is at 23 Belgrave Square, London SW1X 8PZ, but persons residing in the North of England, North Wales, Northern Ireland or the Isle of Man, should contact the *German Consulate General,* Norwich House, 8-12 Water Street, Liverpool L2 8TA. Applicants in Scotland must contact the German Consulate General, 16 Eglinton Crescent, Edinburgh EH12 5DG.

Languages

Most British people find German quite easy to pronounce, but grammar and sentence construction can cause problems. Prospective workers are advised to learn at least a little German before leaving England.

Cost and Standard of Living

Germany's standard of living was extremely low after the war, and the "economic miracle" that followed has now placed Germany fourth on the world table of GNP per capita, with the Deutschmark surviving as one of the world's strongest currencies. However, in the wake of the worldwide economic recession, the *wirtschaftswunder* (economic miracle) has faded away.

Housing and Accommodation

Hardly any other Western nation can boast a housing construction programme as extensive as Germany's. Since 1949, almost two thirds of the present supply — some 16 million dwellings — have been built. Of these, well over six million were state-subsidised. In theory at least, Germany's housing shortage ended in 1974 when, for the first time, the number of available dwellings exceeded the number of private households by 23.2 million to 23.1 million.

Most Germans live in rented accommodation, but home-ownership is encouraged, and there is a steady increase in owner-occupation of both houses and flats. Rents range from 360 DM per month for a small single room, to 1,900 DM per month for a large house in Bonn. Rented flats usually come with all kitchen appliances, and central heating.

Health and Welfare

Germany's general social policy is to help an individual when he is in need through no fault of his own (e.g. through sickness, accident or old age), but not to allow him any absolute claim on the state for subsistence.

About 30% of the national budget goes on social security. Contributions from employer and employee are high — more than 10% of a worker's earnings — half paid by the employee and half by his employer, but benefits are also high (up to 100% of earnings in sickness). Over 90% of the population are covered.

Insurance distinctions are made between manual workers (*Arbeiter*) and office staff (*Angestellte*). The *Arbeiter* is compulsorily insured while above a certain (quite high) level of income the *Angestellte* may choose whether or not to insure himself, and his employer makes no contribution.

The contributions cover maternity and unemployment benefits, death payments, old age and disability pensions, children's allowances, widows' and orphans' pensions, all medical and most dental treatment, and supplementary benefits in all cases of need.

Education

There are a few private schools, but most children attend free State schools, starting with voluntary kindergarten at 3 or 4. Education is compulsory from

6 years old, up to 15 years. Children stay at their first school (*Grundschule*) for four years, then move on to either a *Gymnasium* (grammar school), or a *Realschule* (general secondary school). *Gymnasium* pupils often stay on until they are 18 or 19, then continue with higher education. Pupils from the *Realschule* may leave at 15, but many go on to a *Fachschule* to learn a skill or trade. West Germany has 44 universities, 7 technical colleges, and over 2,918 specialist training colleges.

National Service

The entire armed service (*Bundeswehr*) is commanded by NATO. All German males have to serve 18 months military (or equivalent national) service. Foreigners are exempt.

British Embassy and Consulates

British Embassy, Friedrich-Ebert Allee 77, 5300 Bonn.
British Consulate-General, Uhlandstrasse 7-8, 1000 Berlin 12.
British Consulate-General, Nordsternhaus, Georg-Glock-Strasse 14, 4000 Düsseldorf 20.
British Consulate-General, Bockenheimer Landstrasse 51/53, 6000 Frankfurt/Main.
British Consulate-General, Harvestehuderweg 8A, 2000 Hamburg 13.
British Consulate-General, Amalienstrasse 62, 8000 Munich 40.

The British Chamber of Commerce in Germany (BCCG) publishes a variety of papers relevant to working and setting up business in West Germany. These papers are available, at a cost of 25 DM, from the Secretariat of the BCCG at Heumarkt 14, D-5000 Köln 1.

CONDITIONS OF WORK

Hours

Germany is geared to a five-day, forty-hour week.

Holidays

All employees receive at least 18 days paid holidays per year (24 days for those under 18 years): many employers give their workers more. In addition, there are the following public holidays: New Year's Day; Good Friday; Easter Monday; Labour Day (May 1); Ascension Day; Whit Monday; Corpus Christi (not in Protestant, mainly northern, districts); All Saint's Day (November 1 — again not in Protestant areas); Repentance Day (in November); Christmas Day; Boxing Day; Day of Unity and Carnival/Rose Monday.

Safety and Compensation

Special labour courts protect employees against unfair dismissal, safeguard holiday rights, etc. Accident insurance is paid by all employers, who contribute to an industrial injury society. This covers retraining and rehabilitation, artificial limbs, daily cash allowances and pensions for those totally incapacitated, or for the widows and orphans of men killed at work.

Trade Unions

Of Germany's 25,795,000 workers, about 8.7 million are union members; 7.8 million of these belong to unions affiliated to the German Federation of Trade Unions. However, there are only 17 unions, as one union will embrace all the workers in any given industry.

Compared with other European countries, Germany loses few days in strikes. Before a strike is held, a ballot must be held and show 75% in favour. So unofficial strikes are unknown.

Taxation

All German employees are divided into six income tax classes, based on age, marital status and number of dependants. Class I (single persons under 50 with no dependeants) are taxed at the highest rate. Very low income groups pay no tax at all. After allowance for certain non-taxable sums, income tax comprises at least 22, and at most 56 per cent.

WORK AVAILABLE

General

Prospects of employment in Germany remain good, especially for skilled workers: although recruitment of foreign workers was cut after 1973, when the number of *gastarbeiter* (guest workers) rose above 2.5 million, this has in no way affected EC nationals.

Newspapers

German dailies are published on a regional basis. The following include the most promising possibilities for advertisements:

Die Welt, Welt am Sonntag, Bild, Hamburger Abendblatt, Berliner Morgenpost and *B.Z.* are among the papers published by the Axel Springer Publishing Group, whose UK office is at 58 Jermyn Street, London SW1Y 6PA.

Many German newspapers, including the major local dailies *Kölnische Rundschau, Münchner Merkur, Hannoversche Allgemeine Zeitung* and the *Westdeutsche Allgemeine Group* are represented by International Graphic Press Ltd., 6 Welbeck Street, London W1M 7PB.

The daily with the widest circulation is the *Frankfurter Allgemeine Zeitung,* whose UK office is at 10 Hans Crescent, London SW1X 0LJ; the paper publishes a Situations Wanted section every Wednesday, primarily designed for people seeking full time employment.

Publicitas Ltd., 525/527 Fulham Road, London SW6 1HF represent the *Süddeutsche Zeitung.*

Small ads can also be placed in the British Chamber of Commerce's magazine and bulletin; the cost is 5 DM per line (of 35 spaces), with a minimum charge of 50 DM. Texts should be sent to the Secretariat, Heumarkt 14, D-5000 Köln 1.

See also the section on *Advertisements* in the chapter *Getting the Job.*

Labour Force

The total German work force numbers 25,976,000, 40% of the population. Of these, 6% work in agriculture, 45% in industry, and 49% in services. The number of unemployed is about 2,249,000 or 8.9% of the work force. Foreign workers constitute 8% of the total.

SPECIFIC CONTACTS

Employment Service

Since labour exchange is a government monopoly, the most important contact is the *Zentralstelle für Arbeitsvermittlung,* Feuerbachstr. 42-46, D-6000 Frankfurt 1 (International Department). This office handles enquiries for all types of work, from student vacation employment to permanent professional work. Enquiries addressed to this office should include an international reply coupon and the following detailed information: your full name, address, date and place of birth, marital and family status, and whether you intend to enter Germany alone or with other members of your family; professional or vocational training, qualifications and experience, present employer and occupation; knowledge of the German language; type of employment you are looking for; and the length of your intended stay in Germany.

If you want to work in a particular town in Germany, you can write to the labour exchange (*Arbeitsamt*) in that town, but you must include all the above information in your enquiry. Addresses are available from the Central headquarters at the above address.

Au Pairs

Apart from the agencies listed in the section *Consultants and Agencies,* and the *Zentralstelle fur Arbeitsvermittlung* (above) which handles au pair work for minimum stays of nine months, there are two main agencies that are officially allowed to offer au pair positions, preferably for 1 year (absolute minimum 6 months).

These are: the Catholic organisation *IN VIA, Deutscher Verband Katholischer Mädchensozialarbeit e.V.,* Karlstrasse 40, 7800 Freiburg with branches in Aachen, Augsburg, Bamberg, Braunnschweig, Freiburg, Hildesheim, Köln, München, Nürnberg, Osnabruck, Paderborn, Passan, Stuttgart and Wurzburg (and a Centre with au pair placement service in England: German Catholic Social Centre, "St. Lioba", 40 Exeter Road, London NW2 4SB); and the *Verein für Internationale Jugendarbeit e.V.,* Adenauerallee 37, 5300 Bonn, which has branches in Augsburg, Berlin, Bielefeld, Darmstadt, Düsseldort, Hamburg, Hannover, Karlsruhe, Kassel, Kiel, Köln, Krefeld, München, Oberursel, Nürnberg and Stuttgart; and an office in England at 39 Craven Road, London W2 3BX.

Doctors

Due to legal regulations, arrangements for employment are possible only through the *Zentralstelle für Arbeitsvermittlung,* 6000 Frankfurt/Main, Feuerbachstr. 42-46. The weekly medical journal *Deutsches Arzteblatt* contains a large advertisement section. Details of rates and subscriptions are available from the publishers, Deutscher Arzte-Verlag, Dieselstrasse 2, 5000 Köln 40 (Lövenich).

Teachers

Linguarama, Deichmannhaus IV, Bahnhofsvorplatz 1, 5000 Koln 1 — an English Language school, which can offer permanent positions to graduates qualified in teaching English as a foreign language.

The *Overseas Educational Appointments Department, British Council,* 65 Davis Street, London W1Y 2AA, may be able to supply information about teaching vacancies in German. See the *Teaching* chapter for details.

Positions as *Lektors* in German universities can sometimes be obtained by direct application to the university.

Other Opportunities

Opportunities in West Germany are also referred to in the following chapters (see Contents), which cover a wide range of professions:

Transport, Tourism and Catering
Voluntary Work
Military Service
International Organisations
British Government Departments

SHORT TERM WORK

Although Germany no longer actively seeks casual workers in the way it did in the early 1970's, it still can offer a wide range of well paid temporary jobs.

Seasonal Work

Seasonal opportunities in Germany are mainly to do with the tourist industry and agriculture. Work can be found in hotels and restaurants in the Bavarian Alps and the Black Forest in the summer and over the winter skiing seasons. Summer jobs can also be found in resorts along the Black and North Seas, and in the Bohmer Wald. The chapter on tourism gives advice on how to obtain this sort of job. In addition the agency *Jobs in the Alps,* PO Box 388, London SW1X 8LX, can arrange hotel work.

The *Vacation Work International Club,* at 9, Park End Street, Oxford OX1 1HJ, arranges a number of jobs in hotels, restaurants and factories for students. Those interested must be free to work for at least eight weeks from mid July to mid September, and should contact the above address in January or February.

Fruit-picking jobs can be found on German farms, but finding this sort of work normally depends on being in the right place at the right time. The grape harvest in particular needs extra workers: the harvest in Germany tends to begin in October, slightly later than in France because of the more northerly climate, and continues into November. Vineyards can be found along the Rhine, the Mosel and the Nahe. *Concordia,* of 8, Brunswick Place, Hove, East Sussex BN3 1ET, can arrange grape picking jobs along the Mosel for

British people. Jobs can also be found picking other fruit earlier in the summer. There is a particular concentration of fruit farms in the Altland, a region along the south bank of the Elbe to the west of Hamburg, where cherries are picked in July and August, and apples are picked in September and October.

Other Work

See the relevant chapters in the *Specific Careers* section for information on how to find temporary voluntary, domestic and office work. The German state employment service has a near monopoly of finding work, and there are only a few private employment agenices there, although branches of *Adia, Manpower* and *Interim* can be found in larger cities and are worth visiting.

People who are looking for work when in Germany should also look out for mobile temporary employment offices that are set up by the employment service when there is a special local need for temporary workers. These offices, called *Service-Vermittlung,* may be found when any of the frequent trade fairs or wine or beer festivals are organised, as extra help may be needed to set up and man stalls.

LIST OF BRITISH COMPANIES

with branches, affiliates or subsidiaries in West Germany
(see appendix for numerical classification code)

The British Chamber of Commerce in Germany (BCCG), Heumarkt 14, D-5000 Köln 1, publishes a membership directory costing 60DM post free to non-members. The directory lists about 650 member firms engaged in British-German trade, including about 300 British-controlled companies in the Federal Republic of Germany. The BCCG also publishes an annual survey report on salaries and fringe benefits in the Federal Republic of Germany. The report costs 300DM to non-members (post-free). Both the director and the survey report can be obtained from the BCCG Secretariat, Heumarkt 14, D-5000 Köln 1.

A B Electronic Components 10
(Glamorgan)
Kloechnerstr, 4
47 12 Werne

Acrow (Engineering) Ltd 27
Krabbenkamp 13
4100 Duisburg

Allen Bradley Electronics Ltd 10
(Jarrow)
Karl Hromadnikstr, 3
8000 München 60

Ansvar Insurance Co Ltd 23
(Eastbourne)
Johnsalle 14
2000 Hamburg 13

Balkan & Black Sea Shipping Co Ltd 17
(London EC3M 5EQ)
Schwanenwik
2000 Hamburg 76

Barclays Bank International Ltd 4
(London EC3P 3AH)
Theaterplatz 2
6000 Frankfurt/Main

Beecham Group Ltd 8
Herrmannstr 7
7580 Buühl/Baden

Boosey & Hawkes Ltd 29
(Edgware)
Prinz-Albert-Str 26
5300 Bonn 1

Boots Pure Drug Co 8
(Nottingham)
Gutenbergstr 2
6901 Dossenheim

British Airways 3
(London SW1)
Europe Center
1000 Berlin 30

BAT Co Ltd 47
(London SW1P 3JE)
Esplanade 39
2000 Hamburg 36

British Leyland International Ltd 7
(London NW1 5AA)
Am Fuchsberg 1
4040 Neuss 1

The British Metal Corp Ltd 28
(London EC2)
Flottenstr 25
1000 Berlin 25

British Tourist Authority 48
(London SW1)
Fremdenverkehr
Neue Mainzerstr 22
6000 Frankfurt/Main

Brooke Bond Liebig Ltd 16
(London EC4)
Am Wherberg
2308 Preetz

Cable & Wireless Ltd 45
(London WC1X 8RX)
Gruenstr 32
4005 Meerbusch-Buederich

Cadbury Schweppes Ltd 16
(London W2)
Sonninstr 28
2000 Hamburg 1

Cannon Rubber Ltd 42
(London N17)
Uhrbacherstr 1
5210 Troisdorf-Spich

Thomas Cook & Sons Ltd 48
(London W1A 1EB)
Lyonerstr 44-48
6000 Frankfurt-Niederrad 71

Courtaulds Ltd 46
(London W1A 1BS)
Fuerstenwall 25
4000 Düsseldorf 1

Croda International Ltd 8
(Coole)
Herrenpfad 38
4054 Nettetal-Kaldenkirchen

Alfred Dunhill Ltd 47
(London SW1)
Koenigsallee 28
4000 Düsseldorf

Dunlop Ltd 42
(London SW1)
Dunlopstr 2
6450 Hanau

EMI Ltd 29
(London W1A 1ES)
Maarweg 149
5000 Köln 41

Ferrymasters Ltd 17
(Cheshire)
Graf Adolf Str 64
4000 Düsseldorf

Gestetner Duplicators Ltd 30
(London NW1)
Georg Brauchle Ring 68
8000 München 50

GKN Ltd 25
(London WC2)
Alte Lohmarer Str 59
5200 Siegburg

Glaxo Holdings Ltd 8
(London W1Y 8DH)
Huettenstr 10
6200 Wiesbaden-Schierstein

Ilford Ltd 36
(Ilford)
Dornhofstr 100
6078 Neu Isenburg

International Computers Ltd 10
(London SW15)
Marienstr 10
8500 Nuernberg

Lloyd's Bank International Ltd 4
(London EC4P 4EL)
Westendstr 28
Frankfurt 2

Longman Group Ltd 38
(Harlow)
Neusser Str 3
8000 München 40

Marconi Electronics Ltd 10
(Chelmsford)
Gartenstr 112
6000 Frankfurt/Main 70

Negretti & Zambra Aviation Ltd 3
(Buckingham)
Heilwigstr. 64
2000 Hamburg 20

PA Management Holdings Ltd 10
(London SW1)
Mendelssohnstr 53
6000 Frankfurt/Main

The Plessey Co Ltd 10
(Swindon)
Altheimer Eck 10
8000 München 2

Price Waterhouse Associates 1
(London EC2)
Gaensemarkt 45
2000 Hamburg 36

Rank Xerox Ltd 30
(London NW1)
Emmanuel Leutze Str 20
4000 Düsseldorf 11

Rentokil Group Ltd 8
(East Grinstead)
Ronsdorferstr 77 a
4000 Düsseldorf 1

Securicor Group Ltd 43
(London SW1)
Alter Markt 7
4000 Duesseldorf-Gerresheim

Shell International Petroleum 35
(London SE1)
Ueberseering 35
2000 Hamburg 60

Tarmac Ltd 6
(Wolverhampton)
Koppelstr 13
2870 Delmenhorst

Trust Houses Forte Ltd 20
(London WC1)
Neue Mainzer Str 22
6000 Frankfurt/Main

Vickers Ltd 26
(London SW1P 4RA)
Emanuel-Leutze Str 1
4000 Düsseldorf 11

AMERICAN COMPANIES

with branches, affiliates or subsidiaries in West Germany

These are listed in the *Directory of American Business* (price 105 DM including postage), available from the publishers, Grosse Verlag, Kurfuersten Strasse 112-113, 1000 Berlin 30.

Greece

Greek Embassy, 1A Holland Park, London W11 3TP
Currency: The unit of currency is the drachma
Rate of exchange: £1 = Dr 257

Greece is now an integral part of the EC. Its excellent climate and scenery have made it a popular place for British people to work; however with the rise in unemployment to 8%, opportunities for foreigners to work in Greece have declined.

GENERAL FACTS

Population, Cities and Climate

The population of Greece numbers 10,000,000, spread over 50,960 square miles, of which 9,560 square miles are islands. Although the metropolitan area of Athens has a total of 3,000,000, there are few cities over 100,000: the main ones amongst these are Piraeus (196,000), Patras (142,000) and Thessaloniki (406,413). The climate, as might be expected from the country's geographical location is Mediterranean, with mild winters and hot summers.

The Government

Six years after the *coup d'etat* of 1967, there was a referendum to decide whether Greece should be a republic: 77.2% voted for a republic. However, President Papadopoulus's government collapsed in 1974 and elections had to be held in November of that year, leading to a new Constitution of 1975, under which the President is the Head of State, elected to a five-year term of office: the chamber of deputies (numbering 300) is elected by universal suffrage every four years.

Rural Life

Agriculture remains a vital part of Greece's economy, although there is a move towards industrialisation. In 1960, agriculture accounted for 91.45% of all exports; by the mid Seventies this had dropped to 36%; the number continues to fall. The agrarian sector today comprises 30% of total exports and 18% of Greece's GDP. Wheat, sugar beet, olives, raisins and figs are the main agricultural products. The principal industries are agriculture-based: canned fruit, cigarettes, leather, paper and viniculture.

Religion

The Christian Eastern Orthodox faith has a virtual monopoly, claiming 98% of the population. However, complete religious freedom is recognised by the Constitution, but interference and proselytizing from the Greek Orthodox Church are forbidden.

Holidays

There are eleven public holidays a year: New Year's Day; Epiphany (January 6th); Shrove Monday; National Day (March 25th); The Greek Orthodox Easter (two days); May Day (May 1st); Holy Spirit Day (15th June); Assumption (August 15th); *Ochi* day, celebrating the defiant stand against Italy in 1940 (October 28th); Christmas Day; Boxing Day.

FACTORS INFLUENCING EMPLOYMENT

Immigration

The *Foreign and Commonwealth Office,* Petty France, London, SW1H 9HD, issues a free leaflet called *Notes on Greece for British Passport Holders.* Although since January 1st 1988, nationals of EC countries do not require work permits to work in Greece, a residence permit is required for stays of over three months. Applications for this must be made within the three months period, to the Aliens Department office, 173 Alexandras Avenue, Athens, or the other Aliens Department offices in Amaronsio, Piraeus, Glyfada, Elefsina and Lavrio. Employment must be found within three months of entering Greece.

Language

Greek is not an easy language to learn: the use of a different alphabet often hinders comprehension. There are two branches of modern Greek: *katharevousa,* a formal revival of the classical language; and *demotiki,* the spoken language.

Health, Welfare and Education

A state social insurance system exists, including voluntary staff insurance for salaried people and sickness and old age persons' benefits for nearly everyone. Nursery, primary and secondary education is free for children between the ages of 6 and 15. For higher education there are six universities, one polytechnic and six other university-level independent institutions.

Trade Unions

All trade union activity is regulated by the Associations Act of 1914: the Constitution guarantees union liberty. The National Body is the Greek General Confederation of Labour.

SHORT TERM WORK

There are few "organised" ways of finding a temporary job in Greece, and certainly none which will guarantee that an individual will earn enough in a couple of weeks to cover the cost of getting there and back. Jobs tend to be found simply by approaching a potential employer and asking for work.

Seasonal Work

The chapter on tourism lists a few British travel companies that need staff for the summer and some large hotels needing staff are listed in the book *Summer Jobs Abroad.* Anyone prepared to travel to Greece on the off-chance of finding work should go there in March and April, which is when hotel owners prepare for the annual tourist invasion: jobs can be found cleaning and decorating hotels and bars that have been closed all winter.

Jobs can be found picking grapes, olives and oranges, but again it is necessary to be on the spot. The best regions to look for work are on the Peloponnese (especially around Navplion), Crete and Rhodes.

Vineyards in Greece are generally far smaller and more widely dispersed than in, say, France: in practice this means that not many workers are needed, and that the harvest may only offer a few days' work if a job is found. Prospects are better in both the olive harvest, which starts in late October, and the orange harvest, which begins in November and continues until April.

There are many other harvests that may provide work at various times of the year, from apricots to potatoes: the easiest way of discovering what is being grown locally at any time is to find a sympathetic stall-holder at the vegetable market.

Other Work

There are two employment agencies in Athens that can help to find temporary work around the year. *Working Holidays,* Department of Pioneer Tours, 11 Nikis Street (Sytagma Square), Athens 105 57, finds both governess and mother's help positions with Greek families and jobs in hotels and field work. *Cammenos, International Staff Consultants and Recruiters,* 12 Botasi Street, 147 Athens can also offer short term work. Other sorts of work, such as teaching English or office work, are normally only obtained by people who are in Greece and can keep an eye on advertisements in the English language press.

BRITISH FIRMS

with branches, affiliates or subsidiaries in Greece
(see appendix for numerical classification code)

The British Hellenic Chamber of Commerce, 4 Valaoritou Street, Athens 106 71, publishes a *Directory of Members,* (some of which are British controlled companies in Greece), which is available on remittance of £15 including postage (within Europe) of £15 (outside Europe).

Barclays Bank International Ltd 4
(London EC3)
15 Voukourestiou Street
Athens

BP of Greece Ltd 35
(London)
Kifissias 268
Athens

British Airways 3
(London SW1)
10 Othonos Street
Athens

Cayzer Steel Bowater International Ltd 28
Akti Miaouli 73
185 37 Piraeus

Coats (Hellas) Ltd 46
Advianiou 25
115 25 N Psychiko, Athens

Commercial Union Assurance Co Ltd 23
Sina 2-4
106 72 Athens

Commissioners International 14
84 Ethnikis Antistasseos
N Psychico
Athens

Coopers & Lybrand 1
(London)
Abacus House
Semitelou 9
Athens

EMI Greece SA 29
Heracliou 127
111 42 Rizopolis
Athens

Ernst & Whinney O.E. 1
(London EC1)
10-12 Dorileou St
Athens

General Accident Fire & Life Assurance 23
Corp PLC
Zalacosta 8
106 71 Athens

Glaxo AEBE 16
(London W14)
226 Ionias Avenue
111 43 Athens

Group 4 Securitas Hellas Ltd 43
15 Omirou Street
106 72 Athens

Heinemann Educational Books Ltd 38
Hoida 2
106 76 Marasleioun
Athens

Hellas Can SA 17
(Reading)
135 Solonos Street
176 75 Kallithea
Athens

Horizon Travel Tours Co Ltd 48
Nikis 14
105 57 Athens

ICI Hellas SA 8
(London SW1)
231 Syngrou Avenue
171 21 Athens

ICL International Computers Ltd 10
ICL House
Putney
London SW5 1SW

International Paint Ltd (Hellas) SA 25
Efplias 4-6
185 37 Piraeus

Legal & General Assurance Society Ltd 23
Vouchourestiou 16
106 71 Athens

Lloyds Register of Shipping 23
(London EC3)
87 Akti Miaouli
Piraeus

Lucas Service Hellas SA 26
(Birmingham)
84 Constantinoupoleous Street
104 35 Athens

Midland Bank Group 4
(London EC3)
Sekeri 1a
106 83 Athens

Miller Limited EPE 23
(London EC3)
117 Notara Street
Piraeus

Morgan Grenfell Ltd 4
(London EC3)
19-20 Kolonaki Square
106 73 Athens

National Westminster Bank Ltd 4
(London EC2)
Stadion 24
105 61 Athens

Oxford University Press 38
Amerikas 9
2nd Floor
106 72 Athens

P&O Containers Ltd 17
Beagle House
Braham Street
London E1 8EP

Peat Marwick Mitchell & Co 1
(London EC4)
Vas Sofias 120
115 26 Athens

Price Waterhouse & Co 1
(London EC2)
Athens Tower
2 Messogion Avenue
115 27 Athens

Rank Xerox Hellas Ltd 30
(London NW1)
154 Syngrou Avenue
176 71 Athens

Reckitt & Colman SA 16
(London W4)
Spyrou Mercouri 21
144 52 Metamorphossis Street
Attikis

Reuters News Agency (Hellas) SA 38
Vouchourestiou 15
106 71 Athens

Royal Bank of Scotland PLC 4
Akti Miaouli 61
185 36 Piraeus

Shell Company Hellas 35
(London SE1)
2 El Venizelou Street
176 76 Kallithea
Athens

Touche Ross & Co 1
Syngrou 108
176 71 Athens

P Wigham Richardson Co Ltd 5
67 Akti Miaouli
Piraeus

Willis Faber Hellas SA 23
Ermou 44
105 63 Athens

AMERICAN FIRMS

with branches, affiliates or subsidiaries in Greece

The American Hellenic Chamber of Commerce, 17 Valaoritou Street, Athens 106 71, publishes a Directory, in which American firms established in Greece are listed separately. The Directory is available from the Chamber on remittance of $40 (airmail), including postage.

Ireland

Irish Embassy, 17 Grosvenor Place, London SW1X 7HR
Currency: The unit of currency is the Irish Pound (Punt)
Rate of Exchange: £1 = IR£1.20

Although the level of unemployment in Ireland is high, its proximity to England and its membership of the EC make it a popular place for British citizens seeking long-term work abroad. For those interested primarily in short-term work, there is a strong demand for summer staff in the tourist industry of the southern and coastal county areas.

GENERAL FACTS

Population, Cities and Climate

The population of Ireland numbers 3,547,000, spread over 27,127 square miles. The capital city, Dublin, has a total of some 530,000, and the only other large city is Cork, the metropolitan area of which contains 140,000 inhabitants.

Ireland consists of a central plateau surrounded by isolated groups of mountains and hills. The climate is similar to that of the UK, although the Republic's Atlantic exposure makes it windier and liable to slightly greater rainfall.

Government

Following seven centuries of bitterly oppressive English domination, and the failed Easter Rebellion of 1916, the constitution of the Irish Free State was adopted in December 1922. Northern Ireland remained part of the UK. Successive Irish governments have favoured peaceful unification of all of Ireland; in 1985 the Anglo-Irish Agreement, signed by Britain and Ireland, gave Ireland a say in the affairs of Northern Ireland.

Religion, Sport and Culture

Although freedom of worship is practised in the Republic, 94% of the people are Roman Catholic, with a further 4% Anglican. The English language predominates, with the mother tongue, Gaelic, spoken by a minority.

The Irish have a distinct predilection for rugby and soccer, but their own variant, Gaelic football (a spectacular combination of both), is extremely popular.

Ireland is particularly gifted with a fine and rich cultural history, nowhere more so than in its literature. Famous Irish writers include Jonathan Swift, Oliver Goldsmith, George Bernard Shaw, Oscar Wilde, James Joyce, W. B. Yeats and Seamus Heaney.

FACTORS INFLUENCING EMPLOYMENT

Immigration

Persons born in an EC member State, and those who can show at least one Irish born parent or grand-parent, are free to live in the country without restriction. Those who do not fall under these categories shoud consult the *Department of Justice,* at 72, St Stephen's Green, Dublin 2.

Citizens of EC members States do not require permits to work in Ireland. Citizens of other countries may be employed only where the Ministry of Labour has issued work permits to prospective employers in Ireland. The Irish authorities state that the need to protect employment opportunities for EC citizens is a key factor in determining whether or not work permits are thus issued.

Language

The two official languages are Irish (Gaelic) and English. Gaelic, a Celtic language, is the first official language and is one of the oldest written languages in Europe.

Health, Welfare and Education

A state social insurance system, funded partly by both employees' and employers' contributions, and partly by general taxation, provides a security net of unemployment, disability, maternity, occupational injury, medical treatment, widow's, old age and retirement, and orphan's benefits.

Persons with an income of less than IR£12,000 per annum, and persons over 66, are entitled to a full range of hospital and treatment services. Those on higher earnings are liable to pay hospital consultant's fees.

School attendance is compulsory for children between the ages of 6 and 15, and primary education is provided free in national schools. Some 212,000 children are currently in second level education, which is provided free of charge in secondary, community, and comprehensive and vocational schools.

Direct government financial assistance is available, under certain conditions, for students in higher education. The main universitites are Trinity College, Dublin and Cork.

Trade Unions

The Irish Trade Unions Congress was established in 1894. Freedom to form a trade association or union is guaranteed under article 40.6.1 of the Irish Constitution. More than half of the Irish workforce belong to unions. The Irish Congress of Trade Unions has some 71 affiliated unions, accounting for over 90% of the total union membership. There are also 16 licensed employer's organisations, with a total membership of 10,500.

National Service

Military service is voluntary and aliens are not liable.

British Embassy

British Embassy, 33 Merrion Road, Dublin 4.

Newspapers

The Irish authorities advise prospective foreign workers to place advertisements in or consult the national newspapers:

Irish Independent, 90 Middle Abbey Street, Dublin 1.
Irish Press, Burgh Quay, Dublin 2
The Irish Times, 11 D'Olier Street, Dublin 2.

See also the section *Advertisements* in the chapter *Getting the Job.*

Labour Force

The total labour force of 1,473,000 is divided as follows: 17% in agriculture; 29% in industry; and 53% in services. The current unemployment rate is 19%, one of the highest in Europe.

SPECIFIC CONTACTS

Those interested in working in Ireland should consult the national *Training and Employment Authority (FAS),* 27-33 Upper Baggot Street, Dublin 4. The Authority supplies a free booklet called *Working in Ireland,* available from the same address, although it is currently being revised. Individual inquiries should be made through the local offices of FAS, the addresses of which are available from the above address.

The main source of working opportunities is the tourist industry, and those seeking longer term jobs may well have to settle for seasonal work before using the creative job seach to find what they are looking for.

The largest demand is in the south western counties of Cork and Kerry. For a list of hotels contact the Irish Tourist Board, 150 New Bond Street, London W1.

Apart from FAS, there are a number of private employment agencies listed in the Irish *Golden Pages* with whom they may register in addition to FAS.

Further possibilities for employment in Ireland may be found in the various chapters of the *Specific Careers* section, and in the section on *Consultants and Agencies* in the chapter *Getting the Job.* It may also be worth contacting the various British firms with branches, affiliates and subsidiaries in the country, listed below.

Au Pairs

American & European Au Pair Service, 60 Haddington Road, Ballsbridge, Dublin 4 — has a few positions for au pairs over the summer.

Language Centre of Ireland, 9-11 Grafton Street, Dublin 2 — can place au pairs in Ireland for a minimum of six months. Age limits 18-23.

Camp Counsellors

Camp 2000 Adventure Holidays, 200 Rathamham Road, Dublin 14 — organises summer camp programmes for children aged 3-16. The following staff are required to help run the camps from April to September: activity leaders, administrators, group counsellors, language teachers, managers, nurses and team leaders. All positions include board and lodging.

Voluntary Work

Sherkin Island Marine Station, Sherkin Island, Co. Cork — requires graduates for research into various aspects of the marine environment, from April until October.

Other Opportunities

Opportunities in Ireland are also referred to in the following chapters (see Contents):

Banking and Accountancy
British Government Departments
Computer Services
Teaching

BRITISH FIRMS

with branches, affiliates or subsidiaries in Ireland
(see appendix for numerical classification code)

The Irish Industrial Development Authority publishes a list of *Overseas Companies in Ireland,* available at a cost of £5.00 from the IDA, 150 New Bond Street, London W1Y 9FE.

David Ball Ltd (Irl.) 36
(Cambridge)
Blackrock Road
Cork

Beecham of Ireland Ltd 16
(Middx)
Long Mile Road
Dublin 12

Berger Paints (Irl.) Ltd 32
(London)
Malahide Road
Dublin 5

Cadbury (Irl.) Ltd 16
(London)
Malahide Road
Coolock, Dublin 5

CAL (Irl.) Ltd 10
(Surrey)
Clanwilliam Court
Mount Street
Dublin 2

Brian Colquhoun & Partners 22
(London)
16 Upper Fitzwilliam Street
Dublin 2

Concrete Products of Ireland Ltd 6
(Sevenoaks)
Lucan
Co Dublin

Concrete Pipes Ltd 6
(London)
Maudlings Works
Naas, Co Kildare

Dehymeats Ltd 16
(Croydon)
Ballast Quay
Sligo

ETA Ltd 22
(Staffordshire)
Kinsale
Co Cork

Fleet Parts (Irl.) Ltd 39
(Warrington)
Clondalkin
Co Dublin

Gallaher (Dublin) Ltd 47
(London)
Tallaght
Co Dublin

Gilbeys of Ireland Ltd 16
(London NW1)
Naas Road
Dublin 12

Glaxo Labs (Irl.) Ltd 8
(London W1)
Grange Road
Rathfarnham
Dublin 14

Guinness Peat Aviation Ltd 3
(London EC3)
Shannon Airport House
Shannon, Co Clare

Irish Industrial Gases Ltd 39
(London)
PO Box 201
Bluebell
Dublin 12

Laura Ashley (I) Ltd 9
(Powys, Wales)
Kylemore Park North
Dublin 10

James North & Sons (I) Ltd 9
(Hyde)
Dartry
Dublin 6

Northern Cartons Ltd 33
(Isle of Man)
Rossmore Park
Co Monaghan

The Ormond Printing Co Ltd 38
(Leeds)
16-17 Lower Ormond Quay
Dublin 1

Peerage Ireland Ltd 18
(Birmingham)
Syngefield
Birr
Co Offaly

Player & Wills Ireland Ltd 47
(Nottingham)
South Circular Road
Dublin 8

Pretty Polly (Killarney) Ltd 9
(Nottingham)
Park Road, Killarney
Co Kerry

Reckitts (Ire) Ltd 18
(London W4)
Bluebell
Dublin 12

Reliance Precision Mfg Ireland Ltd 22
(Huddersfield)
Parnell Street, Bandon
Co Cork

Rowntree-Mackintosh (Ireland) Ltd 16
(York)
34 Inchicore Road
Dublin 8

Stewarts & Lloyds of Ireland Ltd 25
(Huntingdon)
East Wall Road
Dublin 3

Turner Grain (Irl.) Ltd 27
(Ipswich)
Sandyford Industrial Estate
Leopardstown, Dublin 18

United Photofinish 38
(Hemel Hempstead)
8 York Road
Dun Laoghaire
Co Dublin

Whessoe (Ireland) Ltd 28
(Darlington)
Jamestown Road, Finglas
Dublin 11

Wiggins Teape (Ireland) Ltd 33
(Chadwell Heath)
Gateway House
East Wall Road
Dublin 3

AMERICAN COMPANIES

with branches, affiliates or subsidiaries in Ireland

A list of American companies is contained in the Irish Idevelopment Authority's *Overseas Companies in Ireland,* price £5.00, available from the IDA, 150 New Bond Street, London W14 9FE.

Italy

Italian Embassy, 14 Three Kings Yard, London W1.
Currency: the unit of currency is the lira
Rate of Exchange: £1 = 2386 lire

Work in Italy may be hard to find, but some qualified people, such as secretaries and teachers of English, are much in demand.

GENERAL FACTS

Population

Italy's population of 57,291,000 increases annually by 0.4%. The country covers 117,578 square miles including the islands of Sicily, Sardinia, Elba and others; and the Vatican City, containing 1,000 inhabitants in 0.44 square kilometres. The average population density throughout the country is 480 people per square mile, but this is unevenly distributed, the industrial North being most crowded, while the central mountainous region is much emptier. The predominantly agricultural South has the highest birth-rate and lowest death-rate, but the southern population has increased little since the war, due to the shift to the Northern industrial cities.

Climate

There is a vast difference in climate between North and South. In the North the average winter temperature is 36°F, summer 75°F. The central regions of Italy, divided by the Appenines, have average temperatures of 43°F (Venice) or 49°F (Rome) in winter, 77°F (Venice) or 82°F (Rome) in summer. The South, including Sicily and Sardinia, are hottest — average temperatures in winter range from 50°F (Naples) to 55°F (Amalfi), in summer from 83°F (Naples) to 85°F (Amalfi).

Government

Italy is a democratic republic. The President is elected by an electoral college to serve the country for seven years; the Chamber of Deputies (630 members) and the Senate (315) are elected by direct suffrage to legislate and to advise the Council of Ministers which has administrative powers and is headed by a Prime Minister.

The 20 regions of Italy are financially autonomous and have their own administrative structures, supervised by a government commission. These are divided into provinces, which are responsible for health and similar matters and are managed by elected councils. The commune is the traditional basis of State organisation, and deals with all local interests.

The Italian judiciary deserves comment in that suspects may be held for months or years without trial, particularly foreigners on drug or political cases. It is not a country to be arrested in.

Cities

Rome, the capital, has about three million inhabitants; there are in all 48 cities with populations above 100,000. Milan, Turin and Genoa form the "industrial triangle" of the North; Florence, Venice, Bologna, Naples, and many other smaller towns such as Cremona and Pisa are internationally famous for their cultural or historical attractions.

Rural Life

The Italian population is more evenly distributed between town and country than that of most European countries. About 50% of Italians live in muncipalities with less than 25,000 inhabitants, and 21% in towns and villages with less than 5,000. About 58% of the land surface is used for agriculture.

Religion, Sport and Culture

98% of Italians are baptised into the Roman Catholic faith, and Catholicism obviously has a great influence on Italian life, but there is freedom of religion, and numbers of atheists, protestants, Jews and members of other churches live in Italy.

Popular sports in Italy include fishing, golf, shooting, horse racing and jumping, motor racing, bowls, football and yachting. All winter sports are popular in the Alpine regions.

The annual absolute number of visits made to the cinema is second only to the United States. Opera, theatre and music flourish in all forms. Italy has played a major role in history of art and architecture, and has many galleries, particularly in Rome, Florence and Venice, to display its art treasures.

FACTORS INFLUENCING EMPLOYMENT

Immigration

The *Italian Consulate General,* 38 Eaton Place, London SW1, cannot assist in finding work, but will advise on entry requirements, customs etc., for nationals who require a visa to enter Italy.

All visitors to Italy are required to register with the police within three days of arrival. Registration entitles you to a stay of the same validity as your visa. For a longer stay, a residence permit is necessary, available from the *questura* (police station), of the area of intended residence.

Language

Prospective workers in Italy are strongly advised to learn Italian, as English is not widely spoken or understood except among professional people. Most British people find Italian quite easy, especially if they have studied French and Latin.

Cost and Standard of Living

Italy used to be a very poor country, but is now approaching a consumer economy. The industrial population is paid best, though wages still tend to be low by British standards, especially for skilled tradesmen.

Italians spend 45% of their income on food and drink, which are cheaper than in Britain, especially in markets. The cost of producing an article and its retail price are closer than in any Common Market country, since distribution costs are low.

Living standards have risen considerably since the war but are still low in the south. For every 1,000 Italians there are: 380 telephones, 250 television sets, and 345 private cars.

Housing and Accommodation

Recent building programmes have concentrated on blocks of flats, and in Rome there is now a surplus, but Naples and the South generally are still short of accommodation.

Rents are highest in cities, and higher in the North than the South. A typical two-bedroom flat in Rome would cost about 800,000 lire a month.

Health and Welfare

Contributory medical benefits insurance now covers the whole of the working population, including foreigners; but private medical services continue. Many hospitals are run by the church, but their numbers are insufficient for the population. The government has brought in a social assurance scheme to administer existing invalid and old age pensions. Family allowances, unemployment and sickness benefits are also covered.

Education

Schooling is compulsory and free (apart from registration fees) for all children aged between 6 and 14, and lessons are usually held in the morning only. Nursery schools cater for over 1½ million children aged 3 and over; elementary schools take pupils between 6 and 11, 90% of these proceed to a lower secondary school (*scuola media*), providing a three-year general course, ending in the lower secondary school certificate. Those who pass (roughly 80% of those sitting) go on to a higher secondary school which offers a five-year course. The final school leaving certificate grants entry to higher education in one of the 49 universities or colleges. Grants are available for those with low-income parents.

There are two English schools in Rome for the use of the British residents' children, and various other international schools for foreign communities.

National Service

Military service of 12-18 months is compulsory for all Italian males. Conscientious objection is treated as a civil crime, so many Italians emigrate to avoid it. Foreigners are not liable.

British Embassy and Consulates

British Embassy, Via XX Settembre 80/A, Rome.
British Consulate, Via XII Ottobre 2, Genoa.
British Consulate-General, Via San Paolo 7, Milan.
British Consulate-General, Via Francesco Crispi 122, Naples.
British Consulate, Lungarno Corsini 2, Florence.
British Consulate, Accademia 1051, PO Box 679, Venice.
British Consulate, Via San Lucifero 87, Cagliari.
British Government Trade Office, Corso Massimo d'Azeglio 60, 10126 Turin.

CONDITIONS OF WORK

Wages

Wages are low compared to those in Britain, but the cost of living is lower, as are taxes. Basic minimum wages are set down by law for specific types of work. Although wage levels look low on paper in comparison with other European countries, it is common practice to augment wages with generous fringe benefits.

Women are paid considerably less than men for the same work. Career women are not generally favoured in Italy, and the number of women who have managed to break away from the family stranglehold is still small.

Hours

The five day week has become standard. Many workers still do more than a 48-hour week, but the average is 44 hours. The long lunch break for a siesta is common practice, so the working day may drag on until 7 pm.

Holidays

Most employees receive between 20 and 30 days holiday a year. In addition, there are the following public holidays: New Year's Day; Epiphany (January 6); 11 February (half day); St. Joseph's Day (March 19); Easter Monday; Liberation Day (April 25); Labour Day (May 1); Ascension Day; Corpus Christi; Proclamation of the Republic Day (June 2); Sts. Peter and Paul (June 29); Assumption Day (August 15); October 4 (half day); All Saints' Day (November 1); Victory Day (November 4); Conception Day (December 8); Christmas Day; Boxing Day.

Safety and Compensation

Workers have the right to enforce the regulations covering accident prevention and occupational diseases. All workers are insured against sickness and industrial injury under the social security code.

Trade Unions

The three major unions — CGIL, CISL and UIL — are grouped together as the General Conference of Labour, along with several smaller unions. Total union membership is about 10,000,000.

The unions work to make collective contracts and in 1970 enacted a new labour charter bringing a certain freedom and security to all workers. Union membership is voluntary.

Taxation

Taxes are imposed by the Treasury, the Ministry of Finance, the Minister of the Budget and by regions, provinces and communes. The rate of income tax, which varies according to income, ranges from 18% up to 65% on income over 500 million lire. The first 360,000 lire is tax-free.

WORK AVAILABLE

General

The Italian Consulate General cannot help in finding work; nor is it in a position to offer much useful advice.

Newspapers

Publicitas Ltd., 525/527 Fulham Road, London SW6 1HF, represent a number of Italian newspapers, including *Corriere della Sera* (Milan) and *Il Messaggero* (Rome).

See also the section on *Advertisements* in the chapter *Getting the Job*.

Labour Force

The work force numbers about 23 million, or 40% of the population. 13% work in agriculture; 36% in industry; and 51% in services. The unemployment rate is 11.3%.

SPECIFIC CONTACTS

Employment Service

Applications, typewritten and in Italian, could be addressed to the *Ufficio del Lavoro* in the provincial capital of the area of intended residence. The addresses can be found by consulting the Yellow Pages.

Teachers

Italy has many English, American and international schools and institutes, that have a steady demand for teachers. Teachers of English are frequently required by the four British College schools in southern Italy. Applications should be addressed to the Director of Studies, British College, Via Luigi Rizzo 18, 95131 Catania.

Posts in Italian state schools are not open to foreigners, except in conjunction with the Central Bureau for Educational Visits and Exchanges (see the section on *Student Working Exchanges* in the chapter *Getting the Job*). However, there are a number of one-year posts for assistants in English faculties of Italian universities. Applications should be made direct to the university.

There are many opportunities for English teachers in Italy, mainly because the standard of English teaching there is very inadequate. The British Council at Palazzo del Drago, Via 4 Fontane 20, 00184 Rome, will be able to offer useful advice. See under *Scuole de Lingua* in the Italian Yellow Pages.

Other Opportunities

Opportunities in Italy are also referred to in the following chapters (see Contents), which cover a wide range of professions:

Transport, Tourism and Catering
International Organisations
British Government Departments
Voluntary Work
United Nations

SHORT TERM WORK

Italy has a high rate of unemployment, so English-speaking people should look for temporary jobs where their language is a positive advantage, such as in hotels or offices, or teaching English.

Seasonal Work

Over the summer Italy's tourist industry can offer employment both in the inland cities such as Rome, Florence and Venice and in the coastal resorts along the Italian Riviera and the Adriatic and to the south of Naples. Many of the camping holiday organisers in the chapter on tourism operate in Italy: details of specific vacancies in Italian hotels can be found in *Summer Jobs Abroad.* Work can also be found in ski resorts in the Alps of Lombardy, the Dolomites, the Apennines north of Florence, and in the region to the north east of Turin.

Italy is the world's largest producer of wine, but work on the grape harvest is traditionally done by local workers and a large number of migrant workers from north Africa. But the comparatively high wages (sometimes 50% more than for the equivalent job in France) still make this sort of work worth looking for by travellers in Italy in September or early October. Vineyards can be found all over Italy, but chances of finding work should be best in the north of the country, where unemployment is not as high as in the south.

Other Work

Short-term domestic jobs in Italy can be found through the agency *Au Pairs — Italy* (see the *Au Pair* chapter). Most types of casual work can only be found by people who are already in Italy and can visit employment offices and follow up newspaper advertisements.

LIST OF BRITISH COMPANIES

with branches, affiliates or subsidiaries in Italy
(see appendix for numerical classification code)

The British Chamber of Commerce for Italy, Via Agnello 8, 20121 Milan, publishes a trade directory which contains not only a list of members, but also an "alphbetical list of British firms present in the Italian market", obtainable for L 72,000 (including postage).

Amstrad SpA 10
(Essex CH14 4EF)
Via Riccione 4
20156 Milano (MI)

APV Italia 27
(Crawley)
Via Molise 9
20098 San Guiliano Milanese MI

Austin Rover Italia SpA 7
(London NW1 5AA)
Via Paolo di Dono 73
00143 Roma

Automotive Products (Borg & Beck) SpA 22
Via Montenarottses 2
60030 Moie di Maiolati (AN)

Avdel Stl 25
(Welwyn Garden City)
Via G di Vittorio 307/10
20099 Sesto S Giovanni MI

Beecham Italia SpA 11
(Brentford)
Via Pirelli 19
20124 Milan

Brit European Transport Ltd 17
Scholar Green
Stoke on Trent

British Airways 3
(London SW1W 9SR)
Via Bissolati 76
00187 Roma

British Caledonian Airways 3
(London)
Via Larga 3
20122 Milano (MI)

British Railways Board 35
(London W1)
Via GB Pirelli II
20121 Milano

British Tourist Authority 48
(London SW1A 1NF)
Cso Vittorio Emanuele II, 337
00186 Roma

BSR Italia SpA 10
(Warley)
Via Quintiliano 25
20138 Milano

Bunzl Pulp & Paper (Italy) SrL 33
(London)
Via Caradosso
18-20123 Milano

Castrol Italiana SpA 35
(London NW1)
Via Aosta 4/a
20155 Milano

Clarkson Italiano SpA 26
(Nuneaton)
Via 1 Nievo 41
20145 Milano

Coopers & Lybrand 4
Via Vittor Pisani, 20
20124 Milano

Courtlands Ltd 46
(London W1A 2BB)
Viale Piemonte 66
20013 Magenta MI

Croda Italiana SpA 8
(Humberside)
Via P. Grocco 917/919
27036 Mortara (PV)

De Beers Industrial Diamond Division 25
Via Pisacane 1
20129 Milano

EMI Italiano SpA 29
(London W1A 1ES)
Via Nomentana
1015-00137 Roma

Feroda Italiana SpA 22
Corso Inghilterra 2
12085 Mondivi (CN)

Flexibox SpA 31
Viale Spagna, 106
20093 Colgno Monzesa (MI)

Foseco SpA 8
Via Roma, 151
20010 Marcallo con Casone (MI)

Gestetner Duplicatori SpA 38
Viale Vittorio Veneto, 14
20124 Milano

Guiness Italia SpA 16
(London NW10)
Via Leopardi I
20123 Milano MI

Imperial Chemicals Industires 8
(London SW1P 3JF)
V.W. le Isonzo 25
20135 Milano

Italia Srl 20
(London W1)
Via 6 Fara 39
20124 Milano

Jones & Shipman Ltd 26
(South Leicester)
Via GB Morganilo
20129 Milano

Letraset Italia Srl 38
Via M Pagano
37/29 - 20145 Milano

Lloyds Register of Shipping 23
(London EC3 4BS)
Via Sottoripa 1/A
16126 Genova

Longman Italia Srl 38
Via Felice Casati
20-20124 Milano

Lucas SpA 10
(Birmingham)
Via Palazzi 2/A
20124 Milano

Marconi Italiana SpA 45
(Chelmsford)
Via A Negtone 1/A
16152 Genova

Massey Ferguson SpA 25
(Coventry)
Via Silvio D'Amico 40
00145 Roma

PA Personnel Services Srl 14
(London SW1X 7LA)
Via Turati 40
20121 Milano

Prudential Assurance Co Ltd 23
Via M Polo 59
00154 Roma

Racal Precision Industries SpA 22
(Newbridge EH28 8LP)
Via Vassallo 31
20125 Milano

Rank Xerox Ltd 30
(London NW1 3BH)
Via Andrea Costa 17
20131 Milano

Reckitt & Colman Ltd 16
(London W4)
Via Piave 6/10
16145 Genova

Rowntree Mackintosh Ltd 16
(York YO1 1XY)
Via Boccardo 1/20
16121 Genova

Sun Alliance Office Ltd 23
(London W1)
Via Martin Piaggiol
16122 Genova

AMERICAN COMPANIES

with branches, affiliates and subsidiaries in Italy

American business concerns in Italy are full listed in the *Italian-American Business Directory*, published by the American Chamber of Commerce in Italy, Via Cantu 1, 20123 Milan. Price $90 including airmail postage.

Netherlands

Royal Netherlands Embassy, 38 Hyde Park Gate, London SW7 5DP
Currency: 1 gulden (guilder or florin, written: fl.) = 100 cents
Rate of Exchange: £1 = fl. 3.63

Prospects for work and residence in the Netherlands are very poor, due to high unemployment and an increasingly severe housing shortage.

GENERAL FACTS

Population

Holland has a population of 14.7 million, including about 558,000 foreigners. In an area of 15,900 square miles, over half of which is below sea level, the population density is over 1,000per square mile, the highest in Europe.

Climate

Not much need be said of the Netherlands' climate, since it is so similar to that in Britain. Temperate is the word to describe it — mild winters and cool summers. August is the month with the highest rainfall. Average monthly winter temperatures rarely fall below freezing, although snow and ice are both more common and more intense than in the typical British winter.

Government

The Netherlands is a constitutional monarchy: the sovereign exercises nominal executive power through a Council of Ministers, or Cabinet, with the Prime Minister at its head.

Legislative power rests with the Parliament, (known as the States General), of which there are two chambers. The First Chamber has 75 members, elected every four years by Provincial Legislative Councils. The Second Chamber has 150 members, elected every four years on a basis of proportional representation. Suffrage extends to all citizens aged 18 and over.

Holland is divided into eleven provinces, with a twelfth planned to include the land reclaimed from the Zuider Zee. There are about 820 municipalities — governed by a burgomaster, aldermen and a council — which have the right to pass local regulations.

Cities

The Hague (population: 671,830) is the seat of government, but the capital city is Amsterdam (998,130), which is the principal commercial and cultural centre. The second largest city is Rotterdam (568,000), which ranks as the world's largest port. There are 17 other towns with over 100,000 inhabitants.

Rural Life

Cheese and tulips are perhaps the best known products of Holland's fields — and both make a major contribution to the national economy. Since the war, 420,000 acres of land have been reclaimed from the sea, most of which is now being used as pasture land.

Religion, Sport and Culture

There is complete freedom of religion in the Netherlands. 40.4% of the population is Roman Catholic; 30.7% Protestant. The largest Protestant denomination is the Dutch Reformed Church, to which the Royal Family belongs.

Considering their past World Cup successes, football is not surprisingly the Netherlands' favourite sport, followed closely by gymnastics and water sports. Cycling is not so much a sport as a way of life. For winter sports, skating tops the bill; there are 5,579 miles of canals. Weather permitting, the year's greatest skating event is the 200 km. "Eleven Towns" race held on the canals of Friesland.

Culturally, the Netherlands has a treasure-house of art galleries and museums, and the larger towns have a full programme of concerts, opera, ballet and theatre. Amsterdam's recently acquired reputation (no doubt well founded) as a hotbed of pornography and psychedelia, is in reality, balanced by the more sedate and traditional entertainments it has to offer.

FACTORS INFLUENCING EMPLOYMENT

Immigration

The Royal Netherlands Embassy (Consular Section) cannot help in finding accommodation or employment. The extent of their assistance is the issuance of a circular stating visa requirements, etc. Paragraph III of the circular (printed in capitals), reads: "In view of considerable unemployment, a seemingly permanent housing problem and the increasing density of the population, immigration is not encouraged and permanent residence is only rarely granted."

This should not, however, deter any stout-hearted Britons who are determined to live and work there. No visas are required for stays of up to 3 months, whereafter a residence permit will normally be granted to persons with guaranteed employment. Applications for residence permits should be addressed to the local police authorities. Permits may be refused on grounds of public security or public health.

Language

It is possible to get by in the Netherlands with only a knowledge of English, since the standard of language teaching in Dutch schools is so high. Still, fluency in English is perhaps not widespread enough to be relied on completely. Dutch is not a difficult language, being closely related to German and less closely to English. The intonation of the spoken language bears a very close resemblance to English.

Cost and Standard of Living

Although consumer prices, for food and other goods, are comparable to those in Britain, wages tend to be considerably higher. The standard of living indicators show lower figures: for every 1,000 inhabitants there are 320 television sets and 424 telephones.

Housing and Accommodation

The Netherlands has a fairly permanent housing shortage, owing to the extreme density of population. Over half of all Dutch homes are of post-war construction, and the building programme increases each year. All new constructions have central heating installed. Local municipalities control housing distribution by issuing permits allowing holders to occupy accommodation of a size stipulated in the permit.

Health and Welfare

Health insurance is compulsory for all wage earners and contributions are shared by employers and employees. Three Social Insurance Acts cover old age, widows' and orphans' pensions and family allowances. Workers are covered by another four Social Security Acts, including health insurance, disablement insurance, unemployment benefits and sickness benefits. A further act provides for exceptional medical expenses, such as long term treatment in specialised institutions.

Education

Education is free and compulsory from the ages of 6 to 16; part-time education is also compulsory for another year. Only 40% of schoolchildren go to state schools; the rest attend private (mostly denominational) schools, subsidised up to 100% by the state.

Primary schools lasts 6 years, after which several types of secondary school are available. General secondary schools provide a general education up to school leaving age, and beyond if required. Vocational schools give special technical or trade training. The *gymnasium* (grammar school) gives a longer and more specialised education, leading up to university entrance. There are state universities at Rotterdam, Utrecht, Leiden, Groningen, and Maastricht; a free municipal university at Amsterdam; an agricultural university at Wageningen; a Catholic University at Nymegen, as well as a number of technical colleges and institutes.

National Service

All Dutch males between the ages of 18 and 25 must undergo military service for 14-17 months. Aliens are not liable.

British Embassy and Consulate

British Embassy, Lange Voorhout 10, 2514 ED The Hague.
British Consulate-General, Koningslaan 44, Postbus 5488, 1007 AL Amsterdam.

CONDITIONS OF WORK

Wages

There is a legal minimum wage for all workers aged 23-65. All wages are reviewed at six-month intervals, and adjusted in accordance with the cost of living index. The Wages and Salaries Act of 1970 allows for free wage bargaining between employers and workers. In 1987, skilled workers averaged about fl. 45,000 a year. Executives can expect some of the highest salaries in Europe.

Hours

The 38-hour, five day week is standard, although the average number of hours worked is higher. The maximum permitted hours of work are $8\frac{1}{2}$ per day, 48 hour week.

Holidays

All Dutch workers are entitled to at least two weeks paid holiday a year, but many workers receive more. In addition there are the following public holidays: New Year's Day; Easter Monday; Queen's Day (April 30); Liberation Day (May 5 — only every five years, 1985, 1990, etc.); Ascension Day; Whit Monday; Christmas Day; Boxing Day.

Safety and Compensation

Safety standards are set down by the Industrial Safety Act, and it is the right of every worker to see that they are enforced. The Netherlands has a comprehensive series of laws and safety decrees covering industrial accidents, etc. The cost of benefits are met by employers, employees and the government.

Trade Unions

Union membership is not compulsory, and only 40% of the working population belongs to a union. There are two federations of trade unions (one Protestant, one Catholic).

Taxation

Any foreign national who obtains both work and residence in the Netherlands is subject to unlimited tax liability. In 1988 there was a personal income tax allowance of Dfl. 7,392.- with additional allowances for unmarried people over 27 and married persons whose partners are low income earners. Unmarried couples who share a household are also entitled to certain tax concessions. After all allowances have been made, there is a progressive scale of taxation which ranges from 14% for the first Dfl. 9,652.- to 72% for everything earned after Dfl. 108,764.

WORK AVAILABLE

General

Beyond the normal channels little general advice can be given. The Royal Netherlands Embassy is unable to help actively, but can provide background information for intended immigrants.

Newspapers

As in Britain, Holland has many national newspapers, with regional papers concentrating on events of local interest. Among the national dailies, *Haagsche Courant* and *De Telegraaf* are represented in London by Publicitas Ltd., 525/527 Fulham Road, London SW6 1HF.

Het Parool, Trouw and *de Volkskrant* are represented by Frank L. Crane Ltd., 5-15 Cromer Street, Grays Inn Road, London WC1H 8LS.

See also the section on *Advertisements* in the chapter *Getting the Job.*

Labour Force

The work force of 6 million includes 200,000 foreigners. The number of unemployed 1987 was 680,000 (12.5%) — one of the highest in the EC. The division of labour is 5.1% in agriculture, 27.8% in industry and 67.1% in the service sector.

SPECIFIC CONTACTS

Employment Service

The Dutch National Employment Office is at *Directoraat-Generaal voor de Arbeidsvoorziening (DG-ARBVO),* Visseringlaan 26, Postbus 5814, 2280 HV Rijswijk (2-H). It can supply the addresses of all the government's regional employment offices.

Medicine and Nursing

Information on existing vacancies in Dutch hospitals can be obtained from the *Geneeskundige Vereniging tot Bevordering van het Ziehenhuiswezen,* Postbus 9696, 3506 GR to Utrecht.

On obtaining an appointment, a licence must be secured. Applications should be sent to the *Ministry of Welfare, Health and Culture, Public Health Section,* Dr. Reijersstraat 10, Leidschendam.

BNA International, 3rd Floor, 443 Oxford Street, London W1R 2NA — recruits nurses for hospitals in the Netherlands. Contracts are for six months with the possibility of a permanent post. RGNs and ENs must be qualified in either operating theatre or intensive care unit nursing; ODA's and Radiographers must have at least one years experience.

Other Opportunities

Opportunities in the Netherlands are also referred to in the following chapters (see Contents), which cover a wide range of professions:

Agriculture, Conservation and Forestry
Transport, Tourism and Catering
Voluntary Work
International Organisations
United Nations
British Government Departments.

SHORT TERM WORK

Dutch employers are accustomed to taking on British and Irish people for temporary jobs. Language is not normally a problem, as most Dutch people speak good English, but knowing just a few Dutch phrases will help to influence an employer in your favour as unemployment causes the competition for jobs to grow more intense.

Seasonal Work

Holland has a comparatively long tourist season, as the bulb fields attract tourists from April onwards. There are no agencies in Britain that find jobs in Dutch hotels, and so it is necessary to write directly to potential employers. The Dutch tourist office, 25-28 Buckingham Gate, London SW1, produces a free map of Holland showing the bulb producing areas, which is a useful guide to where to apply; the most important single region is between Leiden and Haarlem.

The bulb industry itself can provide employment between May and October. Workers are needed both to work in the fields and to process bulbs in the bulb-packing factories. The towns of Hillegom, Lisse and Sassenheim are especially recommended to people who are prepared to go to Holland to look for this sort of work.

Information on summer jobs in the Netherlands can be obtained from the DG-ARBVO (address above), Internationale Arbeidsbemiddeling en Stagiaires section.

Other Work

Holland's ubiquitous private employment agencies are the best source of unskilled jobs in factories, offices, laundries, etc. They can be found in most large cities: for their addresses look up *Uitzendbureaux* in the local yellow pages.

Other opportunities are covered in the chapters on secretarial, agricultural and voluntary work.

LIST OF BRITISH COMPANIES

with branches, affiliates or subsidiaries in the Netherlands
(see appendix for numerical classification code)

A full and detailed list of about 240 majority-owned British subsidiaries operating in the Netherlands is contained in the publication *Britain in the Netherlands,* obtainable at £10.00 (including postage) from the Netherlands-British Chamber of Commerce, The Dutch House, 307-308 High Holborn, London WC1V 7LS

Accles & Pollock BV (Warley) 27
Derde Broekdijk 1, POB 14
Aalten

Atkins BV 10
(Epsom)
Banstraat 2, The Hague

Austin Rover Nederland BV
Goudsepoort OX 40
PO Box 204
2800 AE Gouda

J C Bamford (Rochester) 3
Bamfordweg 1
Ulestraten

Barclays Bank plc 4
Weteringschans 109
PO Box 160
1000 AD Amsterdam

Beecham Nederland BV (Brentford) 8
Sportlaan 198, PO Box 394
Amsterdam

British Airways 3
Stadhouderskade 4
1054 ES Amsterdam

British Petroleum Mig Nederland 35
(London EC2)
Frederikslpein 42
Amsterdam

British School in Netherlands
Jan van Hooflaan 3
2252 BG Voorschoten

British Tourist Authority 48
Aurora Gebouw 5e
Stadhouderskade 2
1054 ES Amsterdam

John Brown Engineers & Constructors BV 6
Bredewater 4
PO Box 5254
2701 GG Zoetermeer

Caligon Europa BV 37
(Accrington)
Konijnenberg 59
PO Box 2154
Breda

Clarkson Holland BV (Nuneaton) 22
Sttombootweg 31
Amsterdam

Equity & Law Levensverzeeringen 4
(London WC2)
Korte Voorhout 20
2501 The Hague

Ernst & Whinney Nederland 4
Kon Julianaplein 10
PO Box 11649
2502 AP The Hague

GEC Computers (Nederland) BV 10
Antwerpseweg 1
2803 PG Gouda

Gestetner BV 30
Muiderstraatweg 14/15
PO Box 163
1110 AD Diemen

Glaxo BV 8
Wattbaan 51
PO Box 2190
3430 CZ Nieuwegein

Hamworthy Engineering Ltd 39
(Poole)
Goudsesingel 12
POB 129
Rotterdam

Hawker Siddeley Electric 10
Export Ltd
(London WC2)
Wassenaarseweg 19
The Hague

Howard BV (Borehamwood) 2
Den Biest 22-31
Eindhaven

WH Howson Algraphy BV 38
(Leeds)
Koningweg 24
Soest

ICI (Holland) BV 46
(London SW1)
Wijnhaven 10
Rotterdam

ICL Nederland BV 10
(London SW15)
Zwaansvliet 20
Amsterdam

George Jowitt & Sons (Holland) BV 22
(Sheffield)
Industrieweg 157-159
Best

Ladbrooke Hotels 20
Stadhouderskade 25
PO Box 50600
1007 DC Amsterdam

Lansing Benelux BV 39
(Basingstoke)
Haarlemmerstraat 39
PO Box 140, Hillegom

Reuter Nederland BV 38
Hobbemastraat 20
1071 ZC Amsterdam

Linguarama Nederland
Kantoorencentrum Pasadenha
Venestraat 27
2511 AR The Hague

Lloyds Bank International Ltd 4
(London)
Leidseplein 29
Amsterdam

Matthew Hall Keynes Engineering BV 6
(London W1)
Gerrit Verboonstraat 14
Schiedam

Midland Bank Ltd 4
International Division
Rokin 9-15, 3rd Floor
PO Box 1209
1000 BE Amsterdam

National Westminster Bank plc 4
p/a F van Lanschot Bankiers
Hoge Steenweg 27-31
5211 JN 's-Hertogenbosch

Oxford Instruments Benelux BV 22
Avelingen West 42
4202 MS Gorinchem

PA Personnel Services 34
Sophialaan 1a
2514 JP The Hague

Peat Marwick Nederland 4
Laan van Nieuw Oost-Indie 127
PO Box 93210
2509 AE The Hague

Pergamon TSI Nederland 38
Zwaluwlaan 1
2211 LD Noordwijkerhout

Phillips' International BV 10
PO Box 218
5600 MD Eindhoven

Plessey Fabrieken BV 10
(Ilford)
v d Mortelstraat 6
Noordwijk

Reed Corrugated Cases BV 31
(London SW1)
Coldenhovenseweg 130
Eerbeek

Renold Continental Ltd 22
Kabelweg 42
PO Box 8019
1005 AA Amsterdam

Shell International Petroleum 35
Maatschapping BV
Group Materials Division
Larel van Bylandtlaan 30
PO Box 650
2501 CR The Hague

Topjobs Consultants BV 14
Hotplein 33
3011 AJ Rotterdam

Transalpino BV 48
Wildenbroch 1
PO Box 299
1110 AG Diemen

Trusthouse Forte Hotels Ltd 20
Apollolaan 2
1077 BA Amsterdam

Nederlands Unilever Bedrijven BV 8
Burg s'Jacobplein 1
PO Box 760
3000 DK Rotterdam

Wellcome Nederland BV 8
(London NW1)
Ysselmeerlaan 2
Weesp

World Trade Centre Amsterdam 4
Strawinskylaan 1
PO Box 7030
1007 JA Amsterdam

AMERICAN COMPANIES

with branches, affiliates or subsidiaries in the Netherlands

The Netherlands-American Trade Directory offers a complete picture of the American presence in the Netherlands and the Dutch presence in the United States. The listings of parent companies and their subsidiaries, branches and affiliates in the two countries give full details about address, telephone and telex numbers, cable address, name of chief executive, size of workforce, date of establishment, activities and European headquarter operations, if any. The Directory is available, on remittance of Dfl. 230.-, from the American Chamber of Commerce in The Netherlands, Carnegieplein 5, 2517 KJ The Hague.

Portugal

Portuguese Embassy, 11 Belgrave Square, London SW12 8PP
Currency: The unit of currency is the Escudo
Exchange Rate: £1 = Esc 261

Portugal, with a population of 10 million, has been an independent state since the 12th century, when it ceded from Spain. It covers an area of 34,000 miles, which includes the two archipelagos in the Atlantic Ocean, the Azores and Madeira.

Although Portugal has joined the EC, British citizens intending to work there will be subject to the full range of Portuguese immigration and employment controls until 1993, when the free movement of labour legislation is brought into effect.

Persons intending to work on a long-term basis in the country require a visa, a residence permit and a work permit. Applications for visas should be addressed to the *Consular Section, Portuguese Embassy,* 11 Belgrave Square, London SW1X 8PP.

For stays of longer than thirty days permission should be obtained through the Portuguese Embassy from the authorities in Portugal.

Your prospective employer in Portugal must obtain a work permit from the Ministry of Labour there, unless the job concerned lasts for less than 30 days.

A leaflet entitled *Some Hints on Taking Up Residence and Living Conditions in Portugal* is available from the *Foreign and Commonwealth Office,* Clive House, Petty France, London SW1H 9HD.

British Embassy and Consulates

British Embassy, Rua de S. Domingos a Lapa 35-37, 1296 Lisbon .
British Consulate, Avenue do Zarco 2, 9000 Funchal , Madeira.
British Consulate, Rua de Santa Isabel 21-29 Esq, 8500 Portimao.
British Consulate, Rua Dr. Bruno Tavares Carreiro 26, 9500 Ponta Delgada.
British Consulate, Avenida da Boavista 3072, 4100 Oporto.

Newspapers

Advertisements can be placed direct in:
The *Anglo-Portuguese News,* Avenida Sao Pedro 17, 2765, Monte Estoril.

See also the section *Advertisements* in the chapter Getting the Job.

Labour Force

The labour force of 4,476,000 is divided as follows: 23% in agriculture; 35.7% in industry; and 40.7% in services. The unemployment level was 8.0% in 1987.

SPECIFIC CONTACTS

The major industries in the Portuguese economy are textiles, pottery, shipbuilding, oil products, paper, glassware and tourism. Portugal is the world leader in cork production.

In general, working opportunities in Portugal are not very good. Its relatively high level of unemployment and its status as a semi-developed country means that there is usually an abundance of willing local (unemployed) labour for unskilled jobs in both urban and rural areas.

Some opportunities are, however, available in hotels and restaurants in tourist areas such as the Costa del Sol and the Algarve.

Apart from contacting the British firms below, intending workers might approach the *British-Portuguese Chamber of Commerce,* which may be able to offer general advice on the prospects of gaining long-term work there. Their address is Rua da Estrela 8, 1200 Lisbon.

The Hispanic and Luso Brazilian Council, Canning House, 2 Belgrave Square, London SW1X 8PJ, can provide information and advice on job opportunities in Portugal. Their leaflet, *Notes on Employment, Travel and Opportunities in Portugal for Foreigners and Students,* can be obtained for £1 (non members).

Agriculture

The Regional Agricultural Directorates in the provincial capitals may be able to advise on opportunities in agriculture. Prospective applicants in this field may write to the *Dir. Regional de Agricultura* Beira Interior, Rua Dr. Francisco Prazeres, Guarda; or to the *Dr. Regional* de Agricultura do Alentejo, Rua Cicioso 18-20, Evora.

Teaching

A list of English-speaking schools in Portugal can be obtained from the *Portuguese Consulate-General,* Silver City House, 62 Brompton Road, London SW3 1BJ, to which applications can be made.

Voluntary Work

Some of the major workcamp organisations listed in the *Voluntary Work* chapter (e.g. Christian Movement for Peace, Quaker Workcamps and IVS) run projects in Portugal.

Other Opportunities

Opportunities in Portugal may also be available with some of the organisations listed under the following chapters (see Contents):

Banking and Accountancy
Computer Services
Medicine and Nursing
Teaching
Transport, Tourism and Catering
British Government Departments

LIST OF BRITISH COMPANIES

with branches, affiliates and subsidiaries in Portugal
(see appendix for numerical classification code)

Austin Rover Portugal 7
(London)
Quinta de Vitoria
ENIO
2685 Sacavem

Barclays Bank International Ltd 4
(London)
Av de Republica 50
1000 Lisboa

Bank Of London & South America 4
(London)
Rua do Ouro 40-48
1100 Lisboa

Building Design Partnership 6
(London)
Sitio do Castelo 1-1
2750 Cascais

Beecham Portuguesa Produtos 11
(Middx)
Rua Sebastio e Silva 56
2745 Queluz

Bells & Cia Lda 25
(Nottingham)
Av de Roma 42
1700 Lisboa

Berec Portuguesa Lda 7
(London)
Rua Goncalves Zarco 6 G/J
1400 Lisboa

Black & Decker 26
(Maidenhead)
Quinta Carreira Lote 78
S Joao do Estoril
2765 Estoril

Blackwood Hodge Lda 6
(London W1)
Av Infante D Henrique 306
Cabo Ruivo
1800 Lisboa

BP Ltd 8
(London)
Praca Marques de Pombal 13
1298 Lisboa

Coopers & Lybrand Ltd 1
(London)
Av Antonio Jose de Almeida 3
1000 Lisboa

Cambridge School
Instituto de Linguas
Av da Liberdale 173-4
1000 Lisboa

Commercial Union Assurance 23
(London)
Av da Libevdade 38-4
1200 Lisboa

Companhia de Seguros Prudential 23
(London)
Rua Madalena 191-4
1100 Lisboa

Cia de Linhas Coats & Clarke Lda 46
(London)
Santo Ovidio
4401 Vila Nova de Gaia

Deloitte Haskins & Sells Lda 1
(London)
Rua Silva Carvalho 234-4
1200 Lisboa

Ernst & Whinney 1
(London)
Av Antonio Augusto de Aguir 19-4
1000 Lisboa

Eastecnica Electronica e Tecnica Ltd 41
Praca Prof Santos Andrea
1500 Lisboa

Glaxo Farmaceutica Lda 8
(London)
Rua S Sebastiao da Pedreira 82-1
1000 Lisboa

Hoover Electrica Portuguesa Lda 10
(Perivale)
Rua D Estefania 90 A
1000 Lisboa

ICI Portuguesa SARL 8
Rua Fillipe Folque 2-1
1000 Lisbon

ICL Computadores Lda 10
(London)
Av Estados Unidos da America 57 A/B
1700 Lisboa

Industrias de Alimentacao (Heinz) 16
(London)
Av da Republica 52-7
1000 Lisboa

James Rawes & Cia Lda 4
(London)
Rua Bernardino Costa 47
1200 Lisboa

Laing Portuguesa Lda 6
(London)
Rua Augusto dos Santos 2-2
1000 Lisboa

Laboratorios Wellcome de Portugal 8
(London)
Rua Visconde de Seabra 4-4
1700 Lisboa

Lloyds Register of Shipping 23
(London)
Av 24 de Julho 60-2
1200 Lisboa

Metal Box of Portugal 17
(Reading)
Av Conselheiro Fernando de Sousa 19-5
1000 Lisboa

PA Consultores 10
(London)
Rua Castilho 211-5
1000 Lisboa

Peat Marwick Mitchell & Co 1
(London)
Av do Brasil 1-8
1700 Lisboa

Price Waterhouse & Co 1
(London)
Av 5 de Outubro 35-8
1000 Lisboa

Pillar Portuguesa (RTZ) 8
(London SW1)
S Marcos
Apartado 23
2736 Cacem

Rank Xerox Ltd 20
(London NW1)
Av Antonio Augusto de Aguiar 106
1000 Lisboa

Robbialac Portuguesa 32
Rua da do Conde Redondo 46
1100 Lisboa

Reckitt Portuguesa Lda 16
(London W4)
Rua S Sebastiao da Pedreira 122-1
1000 Lisboa

Reuter Portuguesa Lda 38
(London)
Praca da Alegria 58-1
1200 Lisboa

Royal Exchange Assurance 23
(London)
Rua Jose Estevao 87
Caixa Postar 1234
1007 Lisboa

Shell Portuguesa SARL 35
(London)
Av da Liberdale 249
1200 Lisboa

Arthur Young & Co 1
(London)
Rua Marques Subserra 10-1
1000 Lisboa

Spain

Spanish Embassy, 20 Draycott Place, London SW3 2RZ
Currency: 1 Peseta = 100 Centimos
Rate of Exchange: £1 = 211 pts

Since joining the EC in 1986, Spain has undergone a buoyant economic recovery; however unemployment is still one of the highest in Europe, and foreigners wishing to work in Spain will only be granted a work permit when the work to be performed cannot be done equally well by a Spaniard. Work restrictions on EC nationals will stay in force until 1993, when Spain becomes a full member of the EC.

GENERAL FACTS

With its area of 189,950 square miles, Spain is the second largest country in Europe. A democratic government was established in 1978, with the King as head of state, and the 17 provinces enjoying a great deal of autonomy.

The population of Spain is 38,818,000; this makes for a low population density of 199.2 inhabitants per square mile. Madrid (population 4 million) is the capital, although Barcelona and Seville both have more inhabitants (6,000,000 and 6,730,000 respectively). Barcelona has been chosen to host the 1992 Olympic games.

In addition to the mainland, Spain also comprises of the Balearic Islands, an archipelago off the east coast of mainland Spain, the Canary Islands in the Atlantic Ocean, and Ceuta and Melilla, two small enclaves on the North African coast. 62% of the land surface is used for agriculture and 31% is wooded.

The main exports from Spain are cars, iron and steel products, machinery and fruit. Tourism is of major importance, with over 50 million tourists arriving each year, bringing in US $8,000 million in foreign currency. Spain is also host to a large number of foreign workers; there are at present over 300,000 foreign residents, more than half of them from EC countries.

FACTORS INFLUENCING EMPLOYMENT

Since 1986, residency and work by foreigners in Spain has been subject to two different rulings, according to the country of origin and the type of work.

EC Ruling — applies to those who are members of the EC, and their families. Those working on their own behalf (self-employed) do not need a visa and can work in Spain on an equal basis with Spaniards. Those who wish to work under the aegis of someone else, until 1993, will need a visa and will have to live and work, at least for a year, under the restrictions of the Regular Ruling before being eligible for the EC Ruling.

Regular Ruling — applies to those foreigners who are not included in the above category, who will need a visa to work in Spain. They may obtain combined residence/work permits of the following types:

Workers who work for someone else —

Permit A: for seasonal/temporary work (maximum duration of nine months).

Permit B: for work that is fixed in a geographical boundary (maximum duration of one year).

Permit C: for any kind of work (maximum duration of five years).

Workers who are self-employed —

Permit D: for fixed work and locality (maximum duration of one year).

Permit E: for any activity in any area (maximum duration of five years).

Applications for work permits are made through the offices of the Provincial Commissioner of Police to the Civil Governor of the province where the work is to be carried out. They must then be sent by the prospective employer to the Spanish Ministry of Labour in Madrid. Self-employed workers, however, must take their own application to the Ministry of Labour after arriving in Spain. Otherwise, intending workers must not enter Spain before receiving their work permit from the Spanish authorities.

Spanish consular offices in Britain are in no way involved in the issuance of work permits and can offer no assistance with employment. Any queries they receive will be answered by their circular *Work Permits for Spain.* The Spanish authorities increasingly require that anyone, for whatever purposes, who wishes to spend more than 90 days in Spain should obtain a special visa before entry from a Spanish consulate in the country in which they reside.

British Embassy and Consulates

British Embassy, Calle de Fernando el Santo 16, Madrid 4.

British Consulate General, Edificio Torre de Barcelona, Avda. Diagonal 477 (13th floor), Apartado des Correos 12111, Barcelona 36.

British Consulate General, Alameda Urquijo 2-8, Bilbao 8.

There are also British consulates in Algeciras, Alicante, Las Palmas (Grand Canary), Malaga, Palma (Majorca), Seville and Santa Cruz (Tenerife), Tarragona and Vigo; and a vice-consulate in Ibiza and Menorca.

The Consular Section of the British Embassy in Madrid issues two leaflets, *Employment of Foreigners in Spain* and *Settling in Spain.*

Newspapers

Advertisements can be placed direct in:

ABC, Serrano 61, Madrid.

El Pais, Miguel Yuste 40, Madrid.

La Vanguardia, Pelayo 28, Barcelona, 1.

See also the section on *Advertisements* in the chapter *Getting the Job.*

Labour Force

The labour force of 13.2 million is divided as follows: 17.3% in agriculture, 32.2% in industry, 50.4% in services. The unemployment level is some 3,000,000 — a rate of 20.3%.

SPECIFIC CONTACTS

Employment Service

General enquiries on working in Spain should be addressed to the *Ministerio de Trabajo,* Departamento de Extranjeros, Agustin Bethencourt 4, Madrid.

Enquiries about vacancies — although most unlikely to produce a job offer — can be sent optimistically to the Centro Nacional de Colocación, General Pardinas 5, Madrid; or to the Delegación Provincial de Trabajo in the provincial capitals.

All such enquiries should be in Spanish and include an international reply coupon.

Consultants and Agencies

English Educational Services, Alcedá 30, 28014 Madrid — interviews, assesses and recommends qualified teachers to private schools all over Spain. Interviews are held regularly in London and occasionally in Dublin for client schools in Spain; from time to time Primary and Secondary School teachers are also helped to find jobs in equivalent schools in Spain. Most candidates have as a minimum qualification the RSA (Royal Society of Arts) preparatory certificate in TEFL.

In addition to recruiting teachers, EES also offers advice and guidance to teachers, and helps with work permits and residences. Teachers should send their *curricula vitae* to the above address, together with an International Reply Coupon to ensure a reply.

Human Resources Management (HRM), Jose Abascal 45, 28003 Madrid — an executive search consultancy specialising in the selection and location of high level managers for the Spanish, Portuguese and Latin American markets. Interested applicants who speak fluent Spanish should send their curricula vitae.

Teaching

As in the case of Italy, there is a considerable demand for English language tuition and this is not always met by the supply of locally trained teachers.

The *Briam Instituto SA,* Calle Tetuán 5, 28013 Madrid — offers a minimum of nine months teaching contracts, in any subject to graduates. Applicants should preferably have a degree in modern languages, especially Spanish.

The *Centro de Idiomas Oxford,* San Miguel 16, 50001 Zaragoza — is a private educational institution where English is taught as a foreign language by the Streamline English method. Its academic year runs from September to June and teachers with TEFL qualifications aged 23-30 are required.

English American College, Calle Obispo Hurtado 21-1A, 18002 Granada — recruits graduates with TEFL or similar qualifications for one year contracts to teach English at the college. The minimum age is 21 years. In order to apply for work and residence permits, a special visa, a medical certificate and a good conduct sheet signed by a Justice of the Peace should be obtained before arriving in Spain. Enquiries should be directed to the Director of Studies at the above address.

The National Association of British Schools, Runnymede College, Calle del Arga 9, El Viso, 28002 Madrid — can be contacted for work as qualified teachers in British primary or secondary schools.

A useful source of information on language schools in Spain is the *British Council Institute* at Calle Almagro 5, Madrid and Calle Amigo 83, Barcelona. These two offices keep lists of the language schools throughout Spain. It is also possible to advertise your availability on the British Council's notice boards. The *Spanish Institute* at 102 Eaton Square, London SW1, can also supply a list of language schools to which applications can be made.

Other Opportunities

Another source of information dealing with job opportunities in Spain is the Hispanic and Luso Brazilian Council, Canning House, 2 Belgrave Square, London SW1X 8PJ. The council produces a leaflet, *Notes on Employment, Travel and opportunities in Spain for Foreigners and Students,* available for £1 to non-members.

Other opportunities can be found in the *Specific Careers* chapters, as well as in the chapter *Getting the Job.*

SHORT TERM WORK

Spain has a high rate of unemployment, especially among the young, and work permits are not normally granted for jobs which a Spanish citizen could do. But opportunities still exist for British people, particularly in the tourist industry or teaching English, and British people continue to take them up, whether legally or illegally.

Seasonal Work

Spain is the most popular holiday destination abroad for the British, and many Spanish hotelliers are happy to employ British people to look after them. Jobs in the tourist industry can be found legally by contacting hotels and campsites before the start of the summer season (see the chapter on tourism), or illegally by calling in on potential employers, especially those along the Costa Brava and the Costa Blanca.

Seasonal farm jobs such as orange or grape picking are fiercely competed for by Spanish workers, and foreigners have little chance of obtaining them.

Other Work

The other major source of casual work in Spain involves teaching English.

Short-term teaching jobs may be pre-arranged through organisations such as the *Mangold Institute* at Avenida Marques de Sotelo 5, Pasaje Rex-2, 46002 Valencia, or *Relaciones Cultuales,* at Ferraj 82, 28008 Madrid, which can also place au pairs and nannies. Alternatively, many British people have found jobs in Spain simply by heading for the major cities and placing or following up advertisements for teaching work.

LIST OF BRITISH FIRMS

with branches, affiliates or subsidiaries in Spain
(See appendix for numerical classification code)

The British Chamber of Commerce, Pl. Santa Barbra, 10-1°, 28004 Madrid 4, publishes a *List of British Firms in Spain and Spanish Firms with British Capital,* costing £30, payable in advance to the Chamber.

APV Iberica SA 25
(Crawley)
Miguel Yuste 15
Madrid 17

Blackwood Hodge (Espana) SA 25
(London W1)
Velazquez 75
Madrid 6

BP Espanola de Petroleos SA 35
(London EC2)
Cea Bermudez 66, 3
Madrid 3

British Steel Corporation Spain Ltd 28
(London WC1)
Serrano Jover 5,5
Madrid 15

Brent Iberica SA 35
(Brentford)
Ctra de Loeches Km 1 300
Torrejon de Ardoz
Madrid

British Airways SA 3
(London SW1)
San Bernardo 17
Madrid 8

British Caledonian Airways 3
(Surrey)
Torre de Madrid
Princesa I
Madrid 13

British Tourist Authority 48
(London SE1)
Torre de Madrid, Planta 6a
Plaza de Espana
Madrid 13

Brooke Bond Liebig Espana SA 16
(London EC4)
Avda Jose Antonio 497, 1
Barcelona 15

Cadbury Schweppes Espana SA 16
Lagasca 88
Madrid 3

Commercial Union Assurance 23
(London EC3)
Via Augusta 23
Barcelona 6

Cory Bros Y CIA SL 17
(London W1)
Expl Torres Quevedo
Muelle Grande
Las Palmas de Gran Canaria

Ernst & Whinney 1
(London WC1)
Alberto Alcocer 24
Madrid 16

Expandite Asociada Iberica SA 6
(Kingston upon Thames)
Avda General Peron 4, 3 b
Madrid 20

Ferodo Espanola SA 7
(Stockport)
Aptdo 231
Alcala de Henares
Madrid

Fisons Ltd 8
(Leicester)
Capitan Haya 22, 1 b
Madrid 16

Flexibox de Espana 25
(Manchester)
C/ Canada s/n
Torrejon de Ardoz
Madrid

Formica Espanola SA 18
(London W1)
Aptdo 1031
Galdacano, Bilbao

Foseco Espanola SA 28
(London SW1)
Pedro IV, 345
Barcelona 5

Guardian Royal Exchange 23
(London EC3)
Avda Diagonal 523
Barcelona 7

Guest Keen & Nettlefold International 28
Trading (London) Ltd
Paseo de la Castellana 62
Madrid 1

Hawker Siddeley International 7
(London WC2)
Rey Francisco 8
Madrid 20

ICI Espana SA 8
Gran Via Sur km 22
Hospitalet Barcelona

International Nickel Iberica Ltd 28
(London W1)
Alberto Alcocer 46, 3 a
Madrid 16

JCB Sales Ltd 27
(Rocester)
Dr Esquerdo 136, 7
Madrid 7

Kompass Espana SA 38
(East Grinstead)
Avde General Peron 26, 4
Madrid 20

Laboratories Beecham SA 8
(Middx)
Edificio Mirasierra
Costa Brava 13
Madrid 34

Leyland Espana SA 7
Avda Mar Mediterraneo S/n
Aptdo 14.845
Torrejon de Ardoz, Madrid

Lucas Service Espana SA 25
(Coventry)
Poligono Industrial de Coslada
Avda de Fuentemar 23
Coslada, Madrid

Marston Iberica SA 25
(Liverpool)
Talleronde Aldé
Sopelana, Vizcaya

Mather & Platt Espanola SA 25
(Manchester)
Tuset 23-25
Barcelona

Midland Bank 4
(London EC1)
Serrano 45, 3
Madrid 1

Pearl Assurance Co Ltd 23
(London)
Via Layetana 120
Barcelona

Peat Marwick Mitchell & Co 1
(London EC4)
Serrano Jover 5, 1
Madrid 8

Perkins Hispania SA 25
(Peterborough)
Hermosilla 1 17
Madrid 9

Phoenix Assurance Co 13
(London EC4)
Ronda Universidad 20
Barcelona 7

Company	No.
Plessey Co Ltd (Swindon) Martires de Alcala 4-3 Madrid 8	10
Price Waterhouse & Co (London EC2) Princesa 3 Madrid 8	1
Pritchard Espanola SA (London W1) Vicente Muzas II Madrid 33	24
Rio Tinto Minera SA (London SW1) Zurbano 76 Madrid 3	8
Royal Insurance Co (Liverpool) Paseo de la Castellena 36/38, 4 Madrid 1	23
Sandeman Hermanos Y CIA SRC (Harlow) Pizarro 10 Jerez de la Frontera, Cadiz	16
Shell Espanola SA (London SE1) Barquillo 17 Madrid 4	35
Touche Ross SA (London EC2) Orense 2, 9 Madrid 20	1
Wilkinson Sword SAE (Middx) Avda de Brasil 17 Madrid 20	18
Wimpy Espanola SA Orense 20 Madrid 20	40

Austria

Austria Embassy: 18 Belgrave Mews West, London SW1X 8HU
Currency: The unit of currency is the Schilling
Rate of Exchange: £1 = S22.6

In view of the current unemployment situation, the prospects of finding work in Austria are extremely limited. Work permits are required for all kinds of full-time employment, including au pairs. The Austrian Embassy states that the permit can only be applied for by the future employer in Austria, and prior to the prospective employee's intended departure from Great Britain. In principle, work permits are no longer issued to foreign passport holders visiting Austria. Excepting Au Pair positions, a sound knowledge of German is a basic requirement.

Once the offer of work is secured, the employer obtains the work permit from the *Arbeitsamt* (see below) who then forwards it to the employee. The employee then sends the work permit application to the Consular Section of the Austrian Embassy, 18 Belgrave Mews West, London SW1X 8HU. The special visa will then be issued upon approval.

In the case of short-term Student Exchange schemes (see below) the relevant documents are issued by the agency concerned.

In addition to work permits, foreign nationals (and Austrians as well) who intend to set up business in Austria require a permit from the head of the provincial government (*Landeshauptmann*). For certain trades and professions a licence must be obtained, or proof of qualifications given.

All aliens are required to register with the police within 24 hours of arrival. Britons staying more than six months also need a residence permit (to be obtained in advance), which usually covers the period for which a work permit has been issued. After ten years residence in Austria, aliens may apply for Austrian nationality. Nationality enquiries should be addressed to the Austrian Ministry of the Interior in Vienna.

The British Embassy's Consular Section in Reisnerstrasse 40, 1030 Vienna, issues a *Memorandum for British Subjects Seeking Employment in Austria,* which says: "Applications for work permits must be made by the employer, who is required to satisfy the Regional Labour Office that he is unable to fill the vacancy except by employment of a foreigner not already resident in Austria. It follows that work permits are extremely difficult to obtain unless the prospective employee has some special technical or professional qualification. They are seldom, if ever, issued for clerical or unskilled manual work."

British Embassy and Consulates

British Embassy, Reisnerstr. 40, 1030 Vienna.
British Consulate, Matthias-Schmid-Strasse 12/WUB, A-6021, Innsbruck.
British Consulate, Alter Markt 4, A-5020 Salzburg.
British Consulate, Schmiedgasse 8-12, A-8010 Graz.
British Consulate, Bundesstrasse 110, A-6923 Lauterach.

Newspapers

Austrian newspapers can be consulted in the reading-room of the Austrian Institute, 28 Rutland Gate, London SW7.

Advertisements can be placed in the daily *Die Presse* through Publicitas Ltd., 525/527 Fulham Road, London SW6 1HF.

See also the section on *Advertisements* in the chapter *Getting the Job.*

Labour Force

The number of economically active people in Austria is 2,780,200, including 146,300 foreigners and 151,973 unemployed. The division of labour is roughly: 1.2% in agriculture and forestry; 38.6% in industry and manufacture; 58.9% in the service sector; and 19.6% pensioners.

SPECIFIC CONTACTS

Employment Service

None of the Austrian consular offices in Britain can help in finding employment. Information on work prospects can be obtained from Jobcentres in Britain under the OECD clearance of vacancies schemes; or from the relevant regional employment office (*Landesarbeitsamt*) in Austria. The Landesarbeitsamt addresses are:

Permayerstrasse 10, 7001 Eisenstadt;	(for Burgenland)
Kumpfgasse 25, 9010 Klagenfurt;	(for Carinthia)
Hohenstaufengasse 2, 1013 Vienna;	(for Lower Austria)
Gruberstrasse 67-69, 4010 Linz	(for Upper Austria)
Auerspergstrasse 67-69, 5020 Salzburg;	(for Salzburg)
Bahnhofgurtel 95, 8021 Graz;	(for Styria)
Schoepfstrasse 5, 6010 Innsbruck;	(for Tyrol)
Rheinstrasse 32, 6901 Bregenz;	(for Voralberg)
Weihburggasse 30, 1010 Vienna;	(for Vienna)

Applications should be made to one of these Arbeitsamt as Austria is equipped with a nationwide computer based labour exchange system. They should be typed in German and contain the following details: name and address; date of birth; education; profession; type of present employment; knowledge of foreign languages; length of intended stay; and type of job required in Austria.

Members of most nations need special permits for entering and working in Austria, which are nowadays nearly impossible to get, as the labour market situation is rather unfavourable and further immigration of foreign workers is not desired.

Au Pairs

Girls seeking Au Pair work are advised to look at private advertising (or advertise their availability) in newspapers or they can contact *Auslands-Sozialdienst,* Johannesgasse 16, A - 1010 Vienna, Austria. The British Embassy warns that Au Pair positions are often difficult to obtain and that prospective Au Pairs should be over 18. It also advises that they join a private Insurance Scheme.

Au pairs need work permits, and positions lasting more than six months require a residence permit, which must be obtained in advance from the Austrian Embassy in London; applications to include a letter of invitation from the host family.

International Agencies

An exception to the rigid work permit and visa requirements is made in the case of the international agencies in the Vienna-UNO city area. The Consular Section of the British Embassy advises that these agencies may employ foreign staff without a work permit and vacancies do occasionally arise for secretarial staff, accountants and computer programmers. Details can be obtained direct from *The Division of Personnel,* UNIDO-IAEA, Vienna International Centre, PO Box 100, A 1400, Vienna, Austria (see the *United Nations* chapter).

Teachers

Persons seeking teaching work are advised that teachers in the Austrian State School System have civil servant status and therefore have to be Austrian citizens. However, a limited programme for the exchange of teachers is being run by the *Central Bureau for Educational Visits and Exchanges* (see their entry in *Teaching* chapter). There may also be some possibility of work in private schools.

Other Opportunities

Opportunities in Austria may also be available with some of the organisations listed in the following chapters (see Contents):

Banking and Accountancy
Computer Services
Medicine and Nursing

SHORT TERM WORK

Although the Austrian authorities have made it more difficult for foreign temporary workers to obtain work permits in recent years, there are still opportunities for finding legal temporary work there.

Seasonal Work

Austria's hotels need extra staff to cover both the summer and winter tourist seasons. For hotel work the best single area is the Tyrol, particularly in resorts around Innsbruck. Campsite companies such as *Canvas Holidays* and *Next Travel* can also offer jobs over the summer: see the tourism chapter for details.

Students and teachers can find jobs as teachers or monitors in the camps that are arranged for Austrian children every summer around Salzburg. These camps take place from mid June to mid September, and need workers for periods of three weeks or more. Details can be obtained from the *Central Bureau for Educational Visits and Exchanges* at Seymour Mews House, Seymour Mews, London W1H 9PE.

Other Work

There are many opportunities for both au pair and voluntary work in Austria: see the relevant chapters for details.

LIST OF BRITISH COMPANIES

with branches, affiliates or subsidiaries in Austria
(see appendix for numerical classification code)

Beecham Pharmaceuticals 8
(Brentford)
Kupelwiesergasse 16
1131 Vienna

Borax Chemicals GmbH 8
(London)
Hofzeile 3
1191 Vienna

BP Austria AG 35
(London EC2)
Schwarzenbergplatz 13
1041 Vienna

British Airways 3
(London)
Karntne Ring 10
1010 Vienna

British Bookshop, 38
Blackwell & Hardwiger GMBH
Weihburggasse 8/Blumenstrasse 2
A-1010 Vienna

Castrol GmbH 35
(London NW1)
Schwarzenbergplatz 6
1030 Vienna

Croda DLS Chemicals GmbH 8
(Goole)
Alois Keller Strasse 63
A-2324 Rannersdorf bei Schwectat

Desoutter GmbH 8
Benatzkygasse 2-6
1220 Vienna

EMI Columbia GmbH 10
(Hayes)
Webgasse 43
1060 Vienna

Gestetner GmbH 30
(London NW1)
Siemensstrasse 160
1210 Vienna

Glaxo Pharmaceuticals GmbH 8
(London)
Dornbacherstrasse 63
1170 Vienna

Hoover Austria GmbH 18
(Perivale)
Forstergasse 6
1025 Vienna

ICI Austria GmbH 10
(London SW1)
Schwarzenbergplatz 7
1037 Vienna

ICL International Computers Ltd 10
(London SW15)
12 Heidlinger Hauptstrasse 51
1120 Vienna

Johnson Matthey & Co 28
(Royston)
Sandwirtgasse 10
1061 Vienna

Kenwood GmbH 18
(Havant)
Erzherzog Strasse 57
1221 Vienna

London Rubber Co 42
(Chingford)
2 Josenfinengasse 10
1021 Vienna

Martonair 26
(Twickenham)
Industriezentrum
N. O-Sud
Strasse 2
2351 Vienna Neudorf

Mothercare GES MBH 9
Mariahilferstrasse 20
A-1070 Vienna

Rank Xerox GmbH 30
(London NW1)
Nussdorferlande 29
1190 Vienna

Redicut Wood GES MBH 46
Mollardgasse 69
A-1061 Vienna

Reuters Ltd 38
Zweigniederlassung Wien
Borsegasse 11
A-1010 Vienna

Schweppes AG 16
Halleinerstrasse
A-5411 Oberalm
PO Box 12

Shell Austria AG 35
(London SE1)
Rennweg 12
1030 Vienna

Standard Chartered Bank (Austrian) AG 4
Karntner Ring 10
A-1010 Vienna

Sun Insurance Office Ltd 23
Dr Karl Leuger Ring 10
A-1010 Vienna

Thorn EMI Licht GES MBH 10
Erzherzog-karlstrasse 57
A-1220 Vienna

Unilever GmbH 8
(London EC4)
Schenkenstrasse 8-10
1011 Vienna

Wellcome Foundation Ltd 8
(London NW1)
Kostlergasse 7
1061 Vienna

Wiggins Teape GmbH 33
(London EC4)
Glanzinggasse 20/7
1190 Vienna

AMERICAN COMPANIES

with branches, affiliates or subsidiaries in Austria

American companies operating in Austria are comprehensively listed in the *US List 1983*, published by the American Chamber of Commerce in Austria, Türkenstr. 9, A-1090 Vienna. Price for the *1986 edition: AS 350,--*, postage: AS 50 (surface), AS 150 (airmail). A new edition was due to appear at the end of 1988.

Finland

Finnish Embassy, 38 Chesham Place, London SW1X 8HW
Currency: 1 Markka (Mk) = 100 Penniä
Rate of Exchange: £1 = 7.58 Mk

All foreign nationals intending to work in the Republic of Finland require a Labour Permit before they will be allowed to enter the country. A Labour Permit will only be granted for a specific job, and a letter of recommendation from the prospective employer must be included with the application. Applications should be addressed to the *Finnish Embassy,* 38 Chesham Place, London SW1X 8HW, from where they will be forwarded to the relevant authorities in Finland. Processing of applications takes about four weeks. The Finnish Embassy wishes to point out that it is unable to give assistance in finding Finnish employers.

A residence permit must be obtained from the Ministry of Interior Affairs before going to Finland. It is not possible to apply for a Labour Permit after arriving in Finland on a tourist visa.

Language

Finland has two official languages; Finnish, spoken by 93% of the population, and Swedish. English and German are widely understood.

British Embassy and Consulates

British Embassy, 16-20 Uudenmaankatu, Helsinki 12.

There are also consulates in Kotka, Kuopio, Oulu, Pori, Tampere, Turku and Vaasa.

Newspapers

Frank L. Crane Ltd., 5-15 Cromer Street, Grays Inn Road, London WC1H 8LS, represent *Helsingin Sanomat (Helsinki), Turun Sanomat* (Turku) and *Aamulehti* (Tamperi).

See also the section on *Advertisements* in the chapter *Getting the Job.*

Labour Force

The labour force of 2,600,000 million is divided as follows: 14.9% in agriculture, 30% in industry, 53% in services. The unemployment rate is 6.5%.

Work Available

Most of the opportunities for finding work in Finland will be found in the chapter *Getting the Job* especially the section *Consultants and Agencies,* and many of the chapters in section on *Specific Careers.*

SHORT TERM WORK

Apart from the *Finnish Family Programme,* organised by the Ministry of Labour in Helsinki and enabling young people aged 18-23 whose mother tongue is English, French or German to spend the summer months teaching the language to a Finnish family, opportunities for temporary work in Finland have been largely limited to those available through the organisations in the chapter on voluntary work and the scheme organised by the *International Farm Experience Programme:* see the chapter on agriculture, forestry and conservation for details. Information concerning the Finnish Family Programme can be obtained from the *Central Bureau for Educational Visits and Exchanges,* Seymour Mews House, Seymour Mews, London W1H 9PE. Some knowledge of a Scandinavian language is normally required for other types of paid work, and the authorities are strict in enforcing the regulations that state that no foreigner should take on a job that a local could do.

LIST OF BRITISH COMPANIES

with branches, affiliates or subsidiaries in Finland
(see appendix for numerical classification code)

Albright & Wilson Oy 8
(London SW1)
Tyomiehenkatu 2 B 31
00180 Helsinki 18

British Airways 3
(London SW1)
Keskuskatu 5
00100 Helsinki 10

Coats Patons Oy 46
(Glasgow)
Hankasuontie 5
PL 30
00391 Helsinki 39

Courtaulds Finland Oy 46
(Coventry)
Fredrikinkatu 48 a
00100 Helsinki 10

ECC International Oy 16
(London ED1)
Etelaesplanadi 20
PL 171
00131 Helsinki 13

Oy EMI Finland Ab 29
(London WC2)
Arinatie 6E
00370 Helsinki 37

Fisons 8
(Leicester)
Hameentie 6 A 11
00530 Helsinki 53

Glaxo Pharmaceuticals Oy 8
(Guildford)
Ahventie 4 B
02170 Espoo 17

Oy Hardy Spicer Ab 22
(Birmingham)
Pulttitie 3-5
PL 11
00811 Helsinki 81

Hambros Bank Ltd 4
(London EC2)
Aleksanterinkatu 48 B
00100 Helsinki 10

Hoover Oy 18
(Perivale)
Saunatontuntie 18
02200 Espoo 20

Oy Hudson's Bay & Annings Ab
(London EC4)
Vasaratie 5
65350 Vassa 35

ICI Pharma Oy 8
(Macclesfield)
Kutojantie 8
02630 Espoo 63

ICL Finland 10
(London)
International Computers Oy
Annankatu 12 A
00120 Helsinki 12

Lloyds Register of Shipping 23
(London EC3)
Aleksanterinkatu 48 A
00100 Helsinki 10

Mather & Platt Oy 25
(Manchester)
Kuriiritie 46
01300 Vantaa 30

PA International Finland Oy 14
(London SW7)
Korkeavuorenkatu 41 A
PL 54
00131 Helsinki 13

Pilkington Floatglass Oy 19
(St. Helens)
Mannerheimintie 60 A 2
00260 Helsinki 26

Rank Xerox Oy 20
(London NW1)
Sinimaentie 8
PL 55
02631 Espoo 63

Sedgwick Payne Finland 25
(London EC3)
Asemamiehenkatu 3
00520 Helsinki 52

Spirax Oy 25
(Cheltenham)
Valimontie 13
00380 Helsinki 38

Suomen ICI Oy 47
(London SW1)
Nuijamiestentie 1-3 A
00400 Helsinki 40

Suomen Tupakka Oy 47
(London SW1)
Vattuniemenkatu 10
00210 Helsinki 21

Thorn Video & TV Oy 45
(London WC2)
Aleksanterinkatu 36
00100 Helsinki 10

Woods Puhallin Oy 10
(Colchester)
Ritarikatu 7
00170 Helsinki 17

Norway

Royal Norwegian Embassy, 25 Belgrave Square, London SW1
Currency: 1 Krone (Kr) = 100 øre
Rate of Exchange: £1 = Kr 11.7

Because of a swollen immigrant population, the Norwegian government has imposed a ban on aliens seeking employment and residence in Norway. This ban started in February, 1975, and, when reviewed in July, 1976, it was extended indefinitely. The purpose of the ban is to allow the authorities time to improve conditions for foreigners already resident in Norway, and to develop a positive programme for their educational, housing, social and cultural needs. Even when the ban is lifted, work permits will be severely restricted.

Among the exemptions from the ban are people who were previously exempt from work permit requirements, including foreign diplomatic representatives and consular staff; aliens employed in international traffic on trains, buses, lorries or aircraft; foreign seamen employed on Norwegian ships in overseas trade; certain employees of foreign firms that have no business premises in Norway; and travelling salesmen working for firms based abroad. This general exemption is also extended to work on mobile drilling rigs on the Norwegian continental shelf; and part time and holiday work undertaken by foreigners studying in Norway. However, because of the difficult labour situation in Norway, work permits will usually not be given to foreign nationals seeking seasonal employment there.

Of the people normally required to obtain a work permit, the ban is waived only for Norwegian born aliens; spouses and children of Norwegian citizens or legal residents, and other aliens with special links with Norway; refugees and stateless persons; au pairs; certain exchange workers on the OECD placement scheme; trainees admitted under existing agreements with other countries; artists and musicians; scientists; and a limited quota of specialists and skilled workers employed in work that is considered essential and cannot be done by a Norwegian citizen or resident.

Even those entitled to exemption from the ban are still subject to the following conditions: initial work permits will only be granted for a specific job with a specific employer at a specific place; applications for work permits must be filed in the applicant's native country or country of permanent residence; the employer must file a definite job offer on the approved form; and the employer must provide or arrange suitable accommodation for at least a year; applicants must be physically fit and literate in their native language — in Norwegian, too, for certain types of work.

A report issued by the Ministry of Labour revealed that most of those granted permits had obtained jobs in Norway by themselves, either by corresponding directly with Norwegian employers, or through family, friends or compatriots already in Norway.

A leaflet explaining the ban on immigration is available from the *Royal Norwegian Embassy,* 25 Belgrave Square, London SW1X 8QD.

Language

There are two official forms of Norwegian in use; the older Bokmal which is the principle language, and the newer Nynorsk (Neo-Norwegian), based on Norwegian dialects and developed in the aftermath of Norwegian independence from Denmark in 1814. English is also widely spoken.

British Embassy and Consulates

British Embassy, Thomas Heftyesgate 8, 0264 Oslo 2.

There are also consulates in Alesund, Bergen, Harstad, Havgesund, Kristiansand, Kristiansund, Oslo, Stavanger, Tromsø and Trondheim.

Newspapers

Oslo's leading daily *Dagbladet* is represented by Frank L. Crane Ltd., 5-15 Cromer Street, Grays Inn Road, London WC1H 8LS.

Vacancies for teachers, engineers and lawyers are advertised daily in *Norsk Lysingblad,* Postboks 177, 8501 Narvik, to which anyone may subscribe. The cost is 125 Norwegian kroner a quarter (Europe).

Engineers and other technical staff could place advertisements in *Teknisk Ukeblad,* Postboks 2476 Solli, 0202 Oslo 2.

Labour Force

The labour force is 2,064,000, with only a 2.5% unemployment rate. The division of labour is 7.4% in agriculture, forestry and fishing; 20.5% in manufacturing, mining and power supply services; 11.1% in employment and construction industries; 61% in service industries.

SPECIFIC CONTACTS

Employment Service

Private employment bureaux are prohibited by law, so the principal contact is the official government Directorate of Labour, *Arbeidsdirektoratet,* Holbergs Plass 7, Postboks 8127, Dep., Oslo 1. However, foreigners must channel applications through their own local Jobcentre under the OECD clearing scheme. The *Arbeidsdirektoratet* issues two useful leaflets; *Summer Employment in Norway* and *Employment in Norway under the OECD Clearing Scheme.* They can also supply copies of *Immigrant in Norway,* published by the Ministry of Local Government and the Central Information Service, which contains information on requirements for settling, taxes, insurance, education, community life and important addresses for prospective immigrants. In addition there is a special department of the Norwegian

Employment Service, especially for foreigners, at Trondheimsveien 2, Oslo 1.

The *Arbeidsdirektorate* advises, however, that owing to the halt in immigration, the OECD Clearing Scheme is practically not functioning any more, and only those who conform to the current immigrational restrictions can be helped.

Nurses

Under the ICN (International Council of Nurses) Nursing Abroad Scheme, the *Royal College of Nursing,* 20 Cavendish Square, London W1M 0AB can arrange employment in Norway for RCN members only.

Oil and Gas Exploration

Job prospects in the Norwegian sector of the North Sea are covered in the chapter *Oil, Mining and Engineering.*

Teaching

Although prospects are not good, a useful leaflet, *Information for Foreign Teachers Seeking Positions in the Norwegian School System,* is issued free by the *Norwegian Ministry of Church and Education,* Postboks 8119, Dep 0032, Oslo 1.

A number of foreign teachers have been able to find temporary and part-time employment within one of the Norwegian voluntary adult education organisations: *Friundervisning i Oslo,* Postboks 496 Sentrun, 0105 Oslo 1; or *Arbeidernes Opplysningsforbund,* Postboks 8703 Youngstorget, 0028 Oslo 1.

However, foreign teachers still have to conform to the current immigration restrictions.

Other Opportunities

Other work qualifying for exemption from the ban on immigration will be found in the chapters on *Transport and Tourism, British Government Departments, Voluntary Work* (for summer work camps), and (for au pair and professional positions) the section *Consultants and Agencies,* and the chapter *Au Pair and Domestic.*

SHORT TERM WORK

Paid temporary employment has become steadily more difficult to obtain in recent years, especially as the authorities no longer allow foreigners to enter Norway to look for jobs. But people who plan ahead may be able to obtain some of the best paid casual work in Europe there: when accepting a job remember that the cost of living is high and check whether food and accommodation are provided.

Seasonal Work

Norway's tourist hotels need a number of English-speaking staff over the summer: the greatest density of hotels can be found along the south coast around Kristiansand, and inland along the fjords north of Bergen. *The*

Directory of Summer Jobs Abroad lists many specific vacancies in individual hotels.

The *Norwegian Foundation for Youth Exchange,* Rolf Hofmosgt. 18, oppg. 1, 0655 Oslo 6 — arranges individual stays for young foreigners aged 18-30, as working guests on Norwegian farms. Free board and lodging plus an allowance (min. 300 Kroner in 1988) is provided. Those taking part are involved in the daily life and work on the farm. Applications for such work should arrive by 15th April if possible.

There are also opportunities for short-term voluntary work in Norway, see the entry for *International Voluntary Service* in the *Voluntary Work* chapter.

Other Work

Norway has the reputation of offering well paid work in the fish processing factories around ports such as Trondheim, Bergen and Vardo, but there is no established procedure for arranging such jobs in advance.

LIST OF BRITISH COMPANIES

with branches, affiliates or subsidiaries in Norway
(see appendix for numerical classification code)

BP Norge A/S 35
(London EC2 79B)
Arbiensgate 11
Oslo 2

BP Petroleum Development Ltd 35
(London EC2 79B)
Forusbeen 35
PO Box 197
4033 Forus

British Airways 3
Postboks 1715
Oslo 2

British Steel Corporation A/S 28
(London WC1E 6BB)
PO Box 2145
Grunerlokka
Oslo 5

Castrol Norge A/S 35
Drammensvein 97
Oslo 2

Chubb Fire Norge A/S 35
(Middlesex)
Postboks 5042 Dusavik
4001 Stavanger

Chloride A/S 8
(London SW1W 0AU)
Ostre Akervei 203
0975 Oslo 9

Duracell-Hellesens A/S 8
(W Sussex)
Lorenvangen 21
Postboks 45 Okern
0508 Oslo 5

Gillette Norge A/S 11
(Middlesex)
Rolf Hofmosgate 24
0655 Oslo 6

Hamworthy Engineering Ltd 25
(Poole)
Stronmsvein 312
Olso 1

ICI Norge A/S 37
(London SW1)
Drammensveien 126
Oslo 2

ICI Pharma A/S 8
(London SW1)
Drammensvein 126
Oslo 2

ICL Norge A/S 10
(London SW8)
Ostensjøveien 39
Oslo 6

Letraset Norge A/S 30
(London SE1 8KJ)
Pottemakerveien 2
0954 Oslo 9

LRC Norge A/S 42
(London EC1)
Sandakerveien 33C
Oslo 4

Lloyd's Register of Shipping 23
Tollbugate 24
Oslo 1

Samuel Montagu A/S 4
(London EC2P 2HY)
Karl Johans gate 45
0162 Oslo 1

Newage Norge A/S 25
(Stamford)
Stalfjaera 12
Oslo 9

Norsk Marconi A/S 45
(Chelmsford)
Ryensvigen 5
Oslo 6

A/S Norske Shell 35
(London WC2)
Tullings gate 2
Oslo 1

PA International Consultants A/S 14
(London SW1)
Langkaia 1
Havnelgaeret

Peat, Marwick Mitchell & Co 1
(London EC4)
Ostensjoveien 43
Oslo 6

Price Waterhouse & Co 1
(London EC2)
Welhavensgate 1-3
Oslo 1

Reckitt & Colman Norge A/S 16
(London W4 2RW)
Trondheimsveien 80
0565 Oslo 5

Salvesen Drilling Services A/S 25
(Edinburgh)
PO Box 5010 Dusavik
4001 Stavanger

Smith & Nephew Scandinavia A/S 8
(Essex CM20 2RQ)
Postboks 68
Fanaveien 200
5046 Radal

Stanley Norge AS 26
(Sheffield)
Okernveien 145
0580 Oslo 5

Storey of Lancaster A/S 9
(Lancaster)
Hvamsvingen 7
2013 Skjetten

Tate & Lyle Norge Ltd 16
Tollbugate 8
Oslo 8

Thorn EMI Belysning A/S 18
Brobekkveien 107
0583 Oslo 5

Woods of Colchester Scandinavia A/S 18
Brynsveien 5
0667 Oslo 6

Sweden

Swedish Embassy, 11 Montagu Place, London W1H 2AL
Currency: The unit of currency is the kronor
Rate of Exchange: £1 = Kr 11

All aliens from non-Nordic countries seeking temporary or permanent employment or residence in Sweden are subject to controls designed to adjust immigration to current labour market policy and resources. In practice, this means that the prospective immigrant must obtain either a work or residence permit (or both, since they are usually applied for together) prior to arrival in Sweden. Both must be applied for at the nearest Swedish consular office. The work permit application must be accompanied by a written offer of employment in Sweden, including details of working hours, pay, duration of employment and accommodation arrangements.

Under the law, aliens share many rights with Swedish citizens, including freedom of speech, worship and association, plus many social welfare benefits. Voting in general elections is a right reserved for citizens only.

Work permit applications are usually assessed with reference to the state of the labour market by the National Labour Markets Board (AMS) and the associations of employers and workers. Work permits are generally valid for one year, renewable by the Police.

Any person wishing to stay in Sweden for more than three months must apply in advance for a residence permit. An alien who has held such a permit for one year and who has immigrant status, or one who has had an A-marked residence permit (implying deferment of immigrant status assessment) for two years, may obtain a permanent residence permit. Under recently introduced provisions, an immigrant can acquire Swedish citizenship after five years residence in that country.

For general information on immigration, write to the National Immigration Board (*Statens Invandrarverk*), Box 6113, S-600 06 Norrköping. Once in Sweden, you can turn for advice to the immigration bureaux (*invandrarbyraer*) that have been set up in about 125 communities all over Sweden. The Stockholm office is at Kungsbroplan 1.

British Embassy and Consulate

British Embassy, Skarpögatan 6, S-115 27 Stockholm.
British Consulate, Götgatan 15, S-411 05 Gothenburg.

WORK AVAILABLE

General

The Swedish Embassy is not in a position to assist with finding employment, and their *General Guide to Immigration Reguilations and Procedures* contains little more than instructions for obtaining work permits.

Newspapers

Frank L. Crane Ltd., 5-15 Cromer Street, Grays Inn Road, London WC1H 8LS, represent *Dagens Nyheter* (the largest morning daily), *Sydsvenska Dagbladet* and *Göteborgs Posten.*

See also the section on *Advertisements* in the chapter *Getting the Job.*

Labour Force

The Swedish work force numbers about 4,400,000 or nearly 50% of the population. About 213,000 aliens are employed in Sweden, mostly from other Nordic countries. Of the total work force, 4% are employed in agriculture; 27.7% industry; and 65.7% in services. The unemployment rate is 2.3%.

SPECIFIC CONTACTS

Employment Service

There are no private employment agencies in Sweden, but intending workers may write to the Swedish Labour market Board (*Arbetsmarknadsstyrelsen*), S-171 99 Solna, for general information on the employment scene. However, this agency only works in cooperation with the British Employment Service Agency, and cannot offer much assistance to individual enquirers. Applications should be channelled through Jobcentres in Britain, under the OECD clearance of vacancies scheme. Once in Sweden, the local Employment Service offices are the first contacts when changing jobs.

Medical and Nursing Personnel

Information on registration requirements for foreign doctors and nurses are available from the *Swedish Board of Health and Welfare,* FAP 1, 106 30 Stockholm. However, the Board advises that the possibilities for foreign medical personnel to work in Sweden are extremely limited due to the lack of resources to provide the necessary complementary training.

Teachers

International Language Services, 14 Rollestone Street, Salisbury, Wilts. SP1 1ED, annually recruit about 40 British teachers to teach English for the British Centre in Sweden, part of Folk University. Most of the work involves adult classes, but teachers may also be required to assist in Swedish state schools. See the *teaching* chapter for further information.

Other Opportunities

Reference to other opportunities in Sweden will be found under *Getting the Job,* especially the section *Agencies and Consultants,* and in the various chapters of the section on *Specific Careers.*

SHORT TERM WORK

Sweden has severe restrictions which limit the employment of foreigners, although exceptions are made for foreign students under 30 looking for jobs lasting for up to three months between May 15th and October 15th. Even they, however, need to find jobs and arrange work permits before entering the country, and possibilities are limited by the general requirement that they speak some Swedish.

Seasonal Work

People who cannot speak any Swedish may be able to find jobs in tourist hotels by writing direct to possible employers selected from hotel guides. People who are already in Sweden may be able to find "informal" farm jobs picking fruit and vegetables, especially in the county of Skane.

Voluntary work in Sweden can be obtained through the British organisation *International Voluntary Service:* see the chapter on voluntary work for details.

LIST OF BRITISH COMPANIES

with branches, affiliates or subsidiaries in Sweden
(see appendix for numerical classification code)

A list of British business organisations and their subsidiaries can be obtained from the British-Swedish Chamber of Commerce in Sweden, Grevgatan 34, Box 5512, 11485 Stockholm.

Albright & Wilson Scandinavia AB 8
(London SW1)
Box 2111
421 02 Västra Frölunda

Atlantica Insurance Co Ltd 23
(London)
Box 2251
S-403 14 Göteborg

Barclays Group of Banks 4
(London)
Biblioteksgatan 6-8
111 46 Stockholm

BOC Ohmeda 12
(Chester-le-Street)
Frötallsgatan 30
Box 140
421 22 Västra Frölunda

Boosey & Hawkes Svenska AB 29
(London W1)
Krytongatan 7
Box 98
431 22 Mölndal 1

BP Raffinaderi (Göteborg) AB 35
(London EC2Y 9BU)
Raffinaderivägen 1
Box 23037
400 73 Goteborg

Bristol Babcock AB 25
Fallhammargatan 2A
721 33 Västeras

British Airways 3
(London SW1)
Norrmalmstorg 1
111 46 Stockholm

British Steel Corp Svenska AB 28
(London WC1E 6BB)
Norra Hamngatan 32
S-411 06 Göteborg

British Timkin Scandinavian 25
Liaison Office
(Northampton)
Virvelvindsgaten 6
Box 8819
402 71 Goteborg

British Turistbyran 3
Malmskillnadsgatan 42
Box 7293
103 90 Stockholm

BTR Industries AB 39
(London)
Kistinge Industriomrade
Box 536
301 80 Halmstad

Castrol AB 35
(London)
Box 45168
104 30 Stockholm 35

Chloride Batteri AB 22
(London SW1)
Box 260
651 07 Karlstad

EMI Svenska AB 29
(Middlesex)
Box 1289
171 25 Solna

Ferrymasters AB 17
(London EC3)
Gjutarnsgatan 10
Box 8978
402 74 Göteborg

Fisons Sweden AB 8
(Ipswich)
Box 42063
126 12 Stockholm

Ford Motor Co AB 7
(Dagenham)
Tullvaktsvägen 11
10254 Stockholm

Foseco AB 8
(Tamworth)
Hökedalen 3007
668 00 Ed

Gestetner AB 30
(London NW1)
Maria Skolgata 83
116 52 Stockholm

GKN International AB 28
(Smethwick)
Harpsundsvägen 185
Box 85
124 21 Bandhagen

Glaxo Läkemedel AB 8
(Middlesex)
Box 263
Idrottsvägen 14
431 23 Molndal

GRE-Försäkring
Motor Union Assuransfirma AB
(London EC3V 3LS)
Sibyllegatan 32
Box 5071
102 42 Stockholm

Hamworthy Sweden AB 39
(Poole)
Box 115
162 12 Vällingby

ICL Data AB 10
(London SW18)
Kanalvägen 18
194 85 Upplands-Vasby

Ilford AB 36
(Ilford)
Frofastegayan 69
Box 3052
400 10 Göteborg

International Färg AB 32
(London NW1)
Box 44
424 21 Augered

Lansing AB 27
Fabriksvägen
175 12 Järfälla

Lloyds Register of Shipping 23
(London EC3)
Första Langgatan 28B
Box 31177
400 32 Göteberg

Lucas Nordiska AB 3
(Birmingham 19)
Gustaf Daiensgatan 8B
417 05 Göteberg

Johnsson Matthey AB 22
Rosenlundsgatan 54
Box 17129
104 62 Stockholm

Ogilvy, Mather 2
Gustavslundsvägan 145
105 13 Stockholm

Pilkington Floatglas AB 19
(St Helens)
Box 530
Kistinge
301 80 Halmstad

Racal Svenska AB 10
Sandhamnsgatan 65
Box 27105
105 52 Stockholm

Rank Xerox AB 30
(London W1)
163 87
Stockholm

Rentokil Svenska AB 8
Landskronavägen 28
Box 5025
250 05 Helsingborg

Reuters Svenska 38
Sveavägen 17
Box 1732
111 87 Stockholm

Schenker & Co Transport AB 17
(London EC2)
Box 81580
104 82 Stockholm

Southeby Scandinavia AB 4
(London)
Arsenalsgatan 4
111 47 Stockholm

Stanley Svenska AB 26
(Woodside)
Datavägen 31
Box 1054
436 00 Askim

Svenska BP AB 35
Västavägen 67
115 83 Stockholm

Svenska Dunlop AB 28
(London SW1)
Metalastik Sweden
Box 260
151 23 Sodertalje

Svenska GEC AB 10
Kungsholmsgatan 10
Box 111
101 21 Stockholm

Svenska ICI AB 8
(London SW1)
Fröfästsgatan 79
Box 184
401 23 Göteborg

Svenska Plessey AB 45
Box 2044
172 02 Sundbyberg

Svenska Readicut Wool AB 46
Verkstadsgatan 14
434 00 Kungsbacka

Svenska Unilever AB 8
(London EC4)
Box 7838
103 98 Stockholm

Thorn Belysning AB 10
Box 4203
171 04 Solna

Trusthouse Forte Hotels 20
Linnégatan 7
114 47 Stockholm

Wellcome Foundation Ltd 8
Kanalvägan 17
Box 2118, 183 02 Taby

Wormald Fire Systems Ltd 2
(Manchester)
Box 3065
122 03 Enskede

Switzerland

Swiss Embassy, 16-18 Montagu Place, London W1H 2BQ
Currency: The unit of currency is the Swiss Franc
Rate of Exchange: £1 = 2.71

It is very difficult at present to obtain permits to settle in Switzerland, as the current policy of the Swiss authorities is to stabilise the number of foreigners. Aliens wishing to settle in Switzerland are subject to a numerical limitation. The quota that are allowed in each year are selected on the basis of their skills and qualifications.

All foreigners must have a work permit to enter Switzerland to take a job, and for this it is necessary to have a definite offer of employment. The future employer must apply to the Aliens Police of the canton where the applicant wants to work. The cantonal authorities will decide each case on its merits, and successful applicants will receive an *assurance d'autorisation de séjour.* This and a valid passport are sufficient for the immigration authorities; the only other formality is a medical examination at the point of entry. Persons who enter Switzerland as tourists, visitors or on business and then look for work will not be granted a permit whilst in the country.

Temporary work permits are available in limited numbers for seasonal work, mainly in the hotel and catering trades. Students on exchange schemes or wishing to train (for a maximum of six months) in a Swiss enterprise, or gain experience with machines and production procedures used in Swiss firms, are also subject to quota limitations.

The *Swiss Embassy,* 16-18 Montagu Place, London W1H 2BQ, can offer no assistance or information on the subject of employment. Nor will the Swiss consular office in Manchester. Note that there is no consular involvement in the issue of work and residence permits. Enquiries about employment addressed to any consular office will be replied with the circular *Note for Persons wishing to take up Employment in Switzerland,* which explains the reasons for the virtual ban on foreign workers.

The British Embassy's Consular section (address below) issues a free note on *Employment for British Subjects* which says that work applicants should have a good knowledge of German, French or Italian, and that males should normally be less than 45 years of age and females less than 40 years of age. The leaflet also contains a number of useful addresses for those interested in nursing, teaching, hotels, agriculture, au pairing, medicine and printing. It advises, however, that Swiss immigration policy is being very rigorously enforced.

British Embassy and Consulates
British Embassy, Thunstr. 50, Berne.
British Consulate General, Dufourstrasse 56, Zurich.
British Consulate General, rue de Vermont 37-39, Geneva.

There are also vice-consulates in Lugano and Montreux.

British Residents' Association
Although unable to assist in any way with employment, the British Residents' Association of Switzerland, is a useful contact for advice and information. The Association's Handbook, which costs SFr. 10.- to non-members, contains information on Swiss taxation, law and social security, and lists various clubs, schools and contact points for British residents. For further information contact the Honorary Secretary, Ponfilet 74, 1093 La Conversation, Vaud.

Newspapers
Publicitas Ltd., 525/527 Fulham Road, London SW6 1HF are agents for the most important Swiss newspapers, including *Neue Zurcher Zeitung, Tages Anzeiger, Basler-Zeitung, La Suisse* and *Tribune de Geneve.*

See also the section on *Advertisements* in the chapter *Getting the Job.*

Labour Force
The Swiss labour force numbers 3 million, or 48% of the population. This includes 700,000 foreign workers, 95,000 of whom are "frontier commuters", who live in neighbouring countries, but work in Switzerland. The division of the work force is: 7% in agriculture, 45% in industry, 55% in services. There are only 25,000 registered unemployed (or 0.8%, one of lowest unemployment rates in the world).

SPECIFIC CONTACTS

Despite the massive clamp-down on immigrant labour, the following organisations are still expressing an interest on foreign personnel for long-term posts.

Qualified nurses with a good working knowledge of either French or German can apply to work in Swiss hospitals through the *Schweizerische Vermittlungsstelle für Spitalpersonal* (Swiss Employment Office for Qualified Foreign Hospital Personnel), Weinbergstrasse 29, CH-8006 Zurich. This office is affiliated to the Swiss Hospital Federation VESKA, Swiss Association of Graduate Nurses and Male Nurses SBK, Swiss Association of Laboratory Technicians, Swiss Society of Radiographers and Swiss Midwifes' Association.

Under the ICN (International Council of Nurses) Nursing Abroad Scheme, the *Royal College of Nursing,* 20 Cavendish Square, London W1M 0AB can arrange employment in Switzerland for RCN members only.

In addition *BNA International,* 3rd Floor, 443 Oxford Street, London W1R 2NA, recruits nurses for hospitals throughout the French speaking part of Switzerland; the majority are at the University Hospital in Lausanne. RGN's should have a minimum of six months post-registration experience. Contracts are for a year.

Personal Sigma AG, Gotthardstr. 14, 6300 Zug — is a recruitment agency for management and professional appointments, with offices in Zug, Lucerne, Chur, St. Gallen, Basel, Zurich, Winterthur, Bern, Aarau, Sursee and Lugano.

Verein der Freundinnen junger Mädchen, Zähringerstrasse 36, 8001 Zurich — offer au pair and mother's help positions for a minimum of one year.

Other Opportunities

Other opportunities for work (short or long term) in Switzerland, will be found in the earlier sections of the directory. Particularly relvant references appear in the following chapters and section:

Au Pair and Domestic
Getting the Job
Consultants and Agencies
Banking and Accountancy
United Nations
Voluntary Work

SHORT TERM WORK

Like Austria, Switzerland has a need for large numbers of temporary workers at certain times of year, and yet limits their numbers by imposing and enforcing strict regulations about work permits.

Seasonal Work

Switzerland has a healthy tourist industry over both the summer and winter seasons which needs to import many temporary workers from abroad, as the many pages of vacancies in *Summer Jobs Abroad* attest. This work is normally more than adequately paid, but the hours can be long and hard.

Hotel work can be arranged by the agency *Jobs in the Alps,* PO Box 388, London SW1X 8LX for the summer and winter seasons, and by the *Vacation Work International Club* in Oxford for the summer only: see *Summer Jobs Abroad* for details. *Canvas Holidays* and *Next Travel* in the same book can offer summer jobs on campsites.

Swiss farms also offer temporary jobs over the summer. The Vacation Work International Club can arrange working stays on Swiss farms for between three and eight weeks from July and August, and also arranges jobs on the Swiss grape harvest around Lac Leman in October. Informal jobs may also be found on farms in the summer picking anything from cherries to hazelnuts: the area along the Rhone between Martigny and Saxon is especially recommended.

Other Work

The other opportunities for temporary work are largely limited to those covered in the chapters on voluntary and au pair and domestic work.

BRITISH FIRMS

with branches, affiliates or subsidiaries in Switzerland

A list of British concerns operating in Switzerland is not included here, as many of the companies are merely registered in the country for tax purposes and are not actively engaged in business there. However, the 1988 list can be obtained from: The British-Swiss Chamber of Commerce in Switzerland, 51 Dufourstrasse, CH-8008 Zürich.

Australia

Australian High Commission, Australia House, Strand, London WC2B 4LU
Currency: Australian $1 = 100 cents
Rate of Exchange: £1 = $2.06

Although some 4,200,000 migrants have settled in Australia since World War II, the number of newly admitted immigrants has declined steadily in recent years and the Australian government no longer offers assisted passages. Permanent settlers fall into five categories which are very restricted because of the current high rate of unemployment. Additionally, there is provision under the Goverment's Temporary Residence policy for certain top professional and specialist personnel. Young people may also obtain some casual work there under the Working Holiday Scheme.

GENERAL FACTS

Population

Australia's total population is 16.2 million, with a yearly increase of 2%, two fifths of this through net migration. Spread over 3 million square miles, the average population density is a mere 5 people to the square mile. Distribution is very uneven, however, with only one person per square mile in Western Australia, which covers one third of the continent, and only 150,000 inhabitants in the 500,000 square miles of the Northern Territory.

Climate

Because of its enormous area, Australia's climate varies considerably, ranging from tropical and sub-tropical conditions in Queensland and other northern areas to temperate, cooler weather in the south. In the western and central regions, desert conditions prevail.

In general, Australia is warm and sunny (Perth has a daily average of almost 8 hours sunshine); summer temperatures often exceed 38°C (100°F) and humidity is high in the north-east. Snow falls on the Australian Alps and in Tasmania, but is rare elsewhere.

Annual rainfall varies from 160″ (tropical north-east coast) to below 5″ in the Lake Eyre region of northern South Australia. Annual rainfall in the capital cities is less extreme varying between Darwin with 58.7″ and Adelaide with 21.1″.

Government

Australia is divided into six states — New South Wales, Victoria,

Queensland, South Australia, Western Australia and Tasmania — and has a three-tier structure of Government. Matters of national concern are the responsibilty of the Australian Parliament and Government. Six State Governments and legislatures have responsibilities within their own boundaries which complement the activities of the national government (the Northern Territory is similar to the States in that it is largely self-governing). About 900 "Local Government" bodies are concerned with matters of local or regional nature at city, town, municipal or shire level. The Australian Parliament, formed by the federation of the Australian States, has powers laid down in the written Constitution which can be changed only by referendum and then only if a majority vote in at least four of the six states as well as an overall majority favour it. State parliaments are subject to the provisions of both their own Constitutions and the Australian Constitution. Broadly, the division of powers between the Australian and State Parliaments follows the American model, the powers to be exercised by the federal authorities being specified with all other powers left to the States.

Close institutional links are retained with Britain and the Commonwealth of Nations. Queen Elizabeth II of Great Britain and Northern Ireland is also Queen of Australia and is represented in Australia by a Governor-General (at the national level) and six State Governors. The Governor-General is the head of State and formally the chief executive. The six Governors perform a similar constitutional role in the States.

Voting in parliamentary and state elections are compulsory for all Australians over 18, and eligible people who fail to do so are liable for a fine.

Cities

The majority (65%) of the Australian population live in urban metropolitan areas, with a further 20% in provincial towns. Australian cities cover a much larger area than comparable European towns, due to the tendency of most Australians to live in detached houses set in their own gardens, rather than flats or terraced houses. The suburbs of Sydney (the largest of Australia's cities with 3,430,600 inhabitants) stretch out to cover a radius of over 20 miles. Other capital cities have populations ranging from Melbourne's 2,942,000 to Darwin with 68,500. Canberra, the national capital, has 285,800.

Rural Life

Only about 13% of Australians live in rural areas; some of these are farmers, while others are engaged in mining or devlopment projects. Most aboriginies also live on the land, but in reserves or settlements.

Recently, however, some secondary industries in Tasmania, Victoria, New South Wales and coastal Queensland have been decentralised and communities have evolved in the irrigation areas. The more progressive settlements resemble towns in the southern states of America.

Religion, Sport and Culture

73% of Australians are Christian; the Church of England claims 24% of the population, while 26% are Roman Catholics.

Hot summers and a largely sandy coastline have made swimming Australia's favourite pastime, closely followed by yachting, power boat racing, surfing and other water sports. British settlers introduced traditional sports such as cricket, tennis, rugby and athletics — in all of which Australians have excelled. Other sports include Australian Rules football (a mixture of rugby and Gaelic football), squash, basketball, the martial arts and skiing

Australia is blessed with a strong and rapidly developing arts scene, which derives much of its potency from the culture of Australian aboriginals. A tradition of fine artists (Nolan, Drysdale, Boyd) and opera singers (Joan Sutherland), plus international success in literature (Patrick White's Nobel Prize and Peter Carey's Booker Prize for example) reveals the growth of vigour and originality in the arts. In particular a new generation of Australian film makers have made their mark over the last decade: pictures such as *Picnic at Hanging Rock, Breaker Morant, Gallipoli* and *The Getting* of Wisdom have gained worldwide critical acclaim, while the exploits of Crocodile Dundee have entertained cinema audiences worldwide.

Immigration

Current Australian immigration policy stems from the basic principle that employment opportunities must be available as a first priority to Australian citizens and migrants admitted for permanent settlement. (The further condition that migrant intake should not jeopardise social stability in the resident community makes high unemployment a casual factor in diminished immigration prospects). Nevertheless, some 113,000 settlers arrived in 1986-7.

Eligibility for permanent settlement falls into five categories, including those with close family connections who must be sponsored by their relatives; people whose occupations are in the labour shortage category; those nominated by an Australian employer for a specific job under the Employment Nomination Scheme; and experienced business people with definite proposals and sufficient capital (at least $500,000) to establish viable enterprises which will aid Australia's economic development.

There are currently few opportunities for unskilled or semi-skilled workers. Details of occupations in current demand are available, together with the free leaflets *Australian Immigration* and *Emigration to Australia: What Are The Requirements?,* from the Migration Branch, Australia High Commission.

Under the Government's Temporary Residence policy there is provision for people from overseas who are top management, other executive, professional, technical and specialist personnel to enter Australia for a specific employment period where it can be shown that the job cannot be filled by an existing resident. Other categories included under this policy are sports people and entertainers. Further details appear in the note *Entry to Australia for Temporary Residence for Employment or Other Specified Purposes,* available free from the Migration Branch, Australian High Commission.

Persons living outside the London area are advised to contact their nearest Australian Consulate (Migration):

Chatsworth House, Lever Street, Manchester M1 2DL.
Hobart House, 80 Hanover Street, Edinburgh EH2 2DL.

The Financial and Migrant Information Service of the *Commonwealth Bank of Australia,* 3rd Floor, 1 Kingsway, London WC2B 6DU, conducts special Information Days for approved migrants at venues in London, Manchester, Edinburgh and Dublin. To obtain further details of these promotions as well as further information on such aspects as housing, cost of living, taxation, health insurance, household expenses, transfer of capital and banking/investment facilities, contact the Bank at the above address.

Citizenship will normally be granted after at least two years residence in Australia. A total of 68,658 people were granted Australian citizenship in the year 1980-1.

Cost of Standard of Living

As an indication of the standard of living, latest figures show that the statistically average home in Australia has more than five rooms, with less than one person per room; 99% of all homes have gas or electricity, or both; 80% have television; and most own at least one radio, a refrigerator, a washing machine and telephone. Australia is one of the most highly motorised countries in the world, with 396 cars per 1,000 inhabitants.

Housing

More than 60% of the Australian population live in the five major cities of Brisbane, Sydney, Melbourne, Adelaide and Perth. Most of the others live in cities and towns along the coastal fringe. The cost of housing varies considerably from state to state and is affected by various factors such as whether residence is in or near to the city centre or in the outlying districts. Those seeking temporary residence in Australia, particularly on a working basis, will think in terms of rental costs which again vary considerably; it is difficult therefore to quote prices, but it probably would be realistic to think in terms of paying from a quarter to a third of your gross income for rent. It could be less — or more — depending on individual circumstances. The Financial and Migrant Service of the Commonwealth Bank of Australia, (address above), issues a comprehensive *Cost of Living and Housing Survey,* free to prospective migrants to Australia.

Health

Persons who are approved to live in Australia for a period more than six months are entitled to enrol for, and receive, basic hospital and medical cover under the National Health Insurance scheme, Medicare. Funded by a 1.25% income surcharge, Medicare covers hospital accommodation and treatment as well as 85% of the scheduled fee charged by general practioners. Supplementary insurance for services not covered by Medicare such as dental and optical treatment or treatment in hospital as a private patient is available from the private health organisations.

Education

Education is free in both primary and secondary schools, though some fee-paying schools exist, usually denominational, attended by one out of four children. Compulsory schooling ages are 6-15 in all states except Tasmania where the leaving age is 16. The school year begins in February.

School education culminates with the examination for the High School Certificate, conducted in the sixth year of secondary school.

There are 21 universities and over 200 specialist or technical colleges. The Australian Government operates a number of student assistance schemes and some grants are subject to a means test.

British High Commission and Consulates

British High Commission, Commonwealth Avenue, Canberra, ACT 2600.

British Consulate-General, Gold Fields House, Sydney Cove, Sydney, NSW 2000.

British Consulate-General, CML Building, 330 Collins Street Melbourne, Victoria 3000.

British Consulate-General, BP House, 193 North Quay, Brisbane, Queensland 4000.

British Consulate-General, Prudential Building, 95 St. George's Terrace, Perth, WA 6000.

CONDITIONS OF WORK

Hours

Hours of work are fixed by awards or legislation and are usually 38 per week, based on the 5-day week, except for the retail trade ($5\frac{1}{2}$-day week) or those who work on a shift basis.

Holidays

Most employees receive four weeks paid holiday per annum. In addition, there are seven national public holidays — New Year's Day; Australia Day (January 26); Good Friday; Easter Monday; Anzac Day (April 25); Christmas Day; and Boxing Day — but extra state and local holidays mean that everywhere has at least ten holidays a year.

Safety and Compensation

State and national laws protect workers by laying down strict conditions concerning standards of safety, sanitation, heat and lighting, applicable to all workplaces. Frequent inspections are carried out by officers of each State's Department of Labour and Industry. All employers are required to insure their workers against industrial accidents; compensation is paid either in weekly amounts or as a lump sum, based on the workers normal earnings.

Trade Unions

Membership of unions is not compulsory in Australia but fifty-five per cent of employees have joined one of the 326 in existence, whose total membership is 3,186,200. Unions are similar in structure to those in Britain, and bi-ennial Congress of the Australian Council of Trade Union fills the role of the TUC in Britain. Industrial disputes are settled by arbitration.

Taxation

Income tax is deduced on a PAYE basis, and adjusted at the end of the tax year (June 30). Deductions are allowed for dependants, life insurance schemes, etc. The first $5,100 is tax free and there is a 29% rate on the tax band between $4,596 to $19,500; followed by 40% for the next band up to $35,000. All additional income is taxed at 49%. The Government is currently changing the system of taxation. Further details can be obtained from the Australian High Commission.

WORK AVAILABLE

General

Prospective migrants are advised to contact the Chief Migration Officer at the Australian High Commission. The Migration Department can supply a free factsheet on the *Australian Labour Force* which contains details of minimum and basic wages, recent wage increases by geographical area and the latest information on job vacancies.

In many professions, eligibility for work in Australia depends on acceptance of English qualifications. Agreement has been reached on the mutual acceptance of many qualifications, but in some fields the membership of an Australian professional association, or the passing of an extra examination may be necessary.

Individual assessments of qualifications and employment prospects are referred back to the Department of Immigration and Ethnic Affairs, whose Committee on Professional Qualifications decides what recommendation to make concerning would-be migrants or temporary residents. Emigrants should take with them to Australia as much documentary evidence of their qualifications as is available. In principle, it is not possible to move to Australia without a pre-arranged job.

The Agents General for the Australian states can offer information on all aspects of life in their respective states, but in general recruitment is confined to specific requests from employers. Their methods of recruitment usually hinge on advertising campaigns in the national press. Their addresses in London are:

New South Wales, 66 Strand, WC2N 5LZ.
Queensland, 392-393 Strand, WC2R 0LZ.
South Australia, 50 Strand, WC2N 5LW.
Victoria, Victoria House, Melbourne Place, WC2B 4LG.
Western Australia, 115 Strand, WC2R 0AJ.

Newspapers

Regional newspapers can be consulted at the Agents General listed above, and at Australia House.

See also the section on *Advertisements* in the chapter *Getting the Job.*

Labour Force

The labour force numbers about 7,800,000, some 63% of the population aged 15 or more and including a steadily increasing proportion of women. The division is: 8% in primary industries; 33% in industry; 59% in services and construction. The present unemployment rate is about 8.3%.

SPECIFIC CONTACTS

Chiropodists

In general, graduates of the British *Society of Chiropodists* who have completed a three year full-time training are eligible for chiropody work in Australia.

Registration with a chiropody board is a prerequisite for practising as a chiropodist (now known as a 'Podiatrist' in Australia) in all Australian States. Enquiries should be made either to the *Migration Branch* of the Australian High Commission (address above); the Council on Overseas Professional Qualifications, PO Box 1407, Canberra City, Act 2601; or to the Executive Secretary, the *Australian Podiatry Council,* Suite 26, 456 St. Kilda Road, Melbourne, Victoria 3004, who will also make available a list of the State Registration Boards and the Podiatry Schools.

Consultants and Agencies

AB Secretariat Pty. Ltd., 8b Borrack Square, Altona North, Victoria 3025 — offer temporary and permanent office staff placements in major oil, chemical, manufacturing, transport and meat industries, and professional and engineering companies.

Centacom Staff Pty. Ltd., 72 Pitt Street, Sydney 2000 — has a network of 44 city and local branches in Australia (there are branches in capital cities of every state). Placements are in secretarial, word processing, computer and accounting positions.

Staffing Centre Personnel Services, Suite 3403, 60 Margaret Street, Sydney 2000, and 24th Level, State Bank Centre, 385 Bourke Street, Melbourne — places people with office or computer experience in full or temporary positions.

Nursing

The Royal Women's Hospital, 132 Grattan Street, Carlton, Victoria 3123 — has a Staff Development Programme to whom nurses may apply. Applicants must have an appropriate visa for employment in Australia and be eligible for registration as a general nurse and midwife in Victoria. The two major areas of employment possibilities are the Operating Theatres and Special Care Nurseries of the hospital.

Secretarial

The major agencies include *Centacom Staff, Drake Personnel, Western Staff Service, Allstaff, Lorraine Martin Personnel* and *Kelly Girls.* Addresses are available from the Information Office, Australia High Commission.

Other Opportunities

Anglo Australian Services, Altrincham Business Centre, Howard House, Lloyd Street, Altrincham W14 2DE, can provide a staff and executive recruitment service to UK professionals wishing to work and live in Australia.

Opportunities in Australia are also referred to in the following chapters (see Contents), which cover a wide range of professions:

Banking and Accountancy
Computer Services
Transport, Tourism and Catering
British Government Departments
Voluntary Work

SHORT TERM WORK

There are some schemes that enable people to pre-arrange short term work in Australia, but many of the most interesting — and lucrative — jobs are available only for those who are prepared to make the journey to Australia and then look for work on the spot. Those aged between 18 and 25 who are not deterred by the cost of getting there can obtain a "working holiday" visa that will enable them to work legally for up to six months.

Seasonal Work

Students may be able to find short term work over the English summer through the *British Australia Vocational Scheme,* which is organised by the *Careers Research and Advisory Centre (CRAC),* 2nd Floor, Sheraton House, Castle Park, Cambridge CB3 0AX. This scheme attempts to match students with jobs related to the course they are studying: participants work eight weeks over July and August and then have four weeks free time to travel around Australia. The GAP scheme also operates in Australia: see the section on student working exchanges for details.

It is possible to take part in voluntary work camps lasting for three weeks over the Australian summer, beginning in late December. These are arranged by *Christian Work Camps,* who can be contacted through the *Australian Council of Churches,* Box C199, Clarence Street Post Office, Sydney 2000.

Other Work

The Australian government's *Commonwealth Employment Service* is normally helpful to those looking for work: its branches notify each other of any vacancies by computer, and in some major cities there are even branches which specialise in temporary work. These offices are particularly helpful to those looking for seasonal work on farms, and issue a booklet that gives the locations and dates of various harvests around the country. Two of the most important of these are the tobacco harvest, which begins in the Atherton Tablelands of Northern Queensland in late September and around Myrtleford in central Victoria in late January, and the grape harvest, which takes place in February and March: two particular regions to head for are Griffith in New South Wales and the Barossa Valley in South Australia. There are also possibilities for working as ranch hands in the outback, especially on sheep farms when shearing takes place in October and November or February and March.

The lack of any language barrier means that people can try for the same sort of temporary jobs they might look for at home, in offices, shops, bars, petrol stations etc. The *Commonwealth Employment Service* may be able to help people find such work, as may the private employment agencies such as *Drake Industrial Overload* which can be found in many cities.

LIST OF BRITISH COMPANIES

with branches, affiliates or subsidiaries in Australia

The *Australian British Business Directory* is published by International Public Relations Pty. Ltd., 33 Walsh Street, West Melbourne, Victoria 3003 for $200, which includes a free update service four times a year.

New Zealand

New Zealand High Commission, New Zealand House, Haymarket, London SW1Y 4TQ
Currency: NZ$1 = 100 cents
Rate of Exchange: £1 = NZ$2.62

The main thrust of New Zealand's current immigration policy is directed towards attracting migrants who have skills and experience which are urgently needed in New Zealand. Assisted passages are not provided by the Government but in some cases employers may offer to pay or subsidise an applicant's fare.

GENERAL FACTS

Population

The total population is about 3,303,000 including some 296,400 Maoris. The natural yearly increase is about 1.1%.

New Zealand comprises two large islands and some smaller islands covering 103,736 square miles. The total area is slightly larger than that of the UK; average population density is 31 people to the square mile.

Climate

While generally similar to the climate in Britain, New Zealand's average temperatures throughout the year are a little higher. The north is warmer than the south, and, of course, the seasons are reversed. Annual rainfall is heavier, but hours of sunshine greater.

Government

New Zealand is a parliamentary democracy; a Governor-General represents the Queen, but is politically insignificant. The House of Representatives has 97 members, including four Maoris. The Parliament, headed by a Prime Minister, is elected by all citizens and permanent residents aged 18 and over.

Cities

84% of the population live in urban areas, and more than 1,500,000 inhabit the four main cities.

Auckland (pop. 829,200) is New Zealand's largest city: one-third of manufacturing employees work there in the developing secondary industries.

Wellington (pop. 324,400 including Hutt Valley), the capital and centre for government, famous for its fine harbour, contains many commercial firms, national organisations and the chief manufacturing industries.

Christchurch (pop. 229,400), the largest city in South Island, is a beautiful, open city, set in lush farmland and well known for its parks, botanical gardens and sports grounds.

Dunedin (pop. 106,864), was founded by Scotsmen; as well as being an important educational centre, it also provides an outlet port for the wool and fruit produced in surrounding Otago.

Rural Life

Pasture and arable land accounts for 53.5% of New Zealand's land area; forests cover a further 26%. Both are essential to the country's economy. Although acreage is large, not much manpower is required, due to the high level of mechanisation, so that a typical farm would utilise the farmer, his wife and an agricultural labourer only, with occasional extra help.

Religion, Sport and Culture

There is complete religious freedom, and no state-aided church. The majority (24%) belong to the Church of England; the remainder include Presbyterians (18%), Catholics (15.2%) and Methodists (4.7%).

Cinemas, libraries, museums and theatres exist in New Zealand, and outdoor recreation is popular. New Zealand is ideal for sports, with facilities for rugby (the national game), soccer, golf, hockey, cricket, tennis, skiing, fishing, hunting, yachting and horse racing and many others.

FACTORS INFLUENCING EMPLOYMENT

All persons who are not New Zealand or Australian citizens require permits to enter the country. Those intending to remain in New Zealand for more than 12 months must apply for a residence visa. A separate category exists for tourists and short-term visitors, described in leaflet UK30 (see below). Generally, applicants are required to be aged 18-45, and be of good health and character.

The New Zealand Government must be satisfied that employment will be available for applicants when they arrive. In some cases applicants may be required to provide accommodation guarantees. Consideration is currently only given to applicants with urgently required skills, for which see the Migration Branch's Occupational Priority List. A leaflet entitled *Applying for Residence* explains all these conditions. Those possessing professional or technical qualifications may need to have them recognised by the appropriate registration authorities in New Zealand.

Recognising that it is often difficult for prospective migrants to make contact with an employer in New Zealand, the New Zealand High Commission in London operates an Immigration Placement Service with the Department of Labour in New Zealand. Migrants may complete a "Personal History Card" which is referred to New Zealand for circulation to employers who are interested in recruiting staff overseas. If a guarantee of employment is given an immigration application may be lodged.

Entrepreneurs and Businessmen

Migrants who are applying for residence on the basis of their business skills will be assessed on their potential contribution to New Zealand and account will be taken of: their business record and skills; the amount of investment capital they have available (in addition to the funds required for personal establishment costs in New Zealand); and their intended business activities in New Zealand.

Migrants and their families will also need to satisfy routine immigration, health, character and interview requirements.

In approving a residence application under the business skills category, the New Zealand authorities expect that migrants will move to New Zealand within a reasonable period of time and establish a base of family and business operations in New Zealand. The migrant is expected to become a genuine resident who contributes fully to the New Zealand community, but who may wish to maintain business and family connections outside New Zealand which will involve travel overseas. If extended periods are spent outside New Zealand and there is reason to doubt that a substantial and continuing connection with New Zealand has been established, any returning resident's visa has expired and the applicant is outside New Zealand, a new application for residence may be required and all current requirements for migration to New Zealand would have to be satisfied.

Applicants will need to supply the following information to the nearest New Zealand Diplomatic or Consular office:

Business background; work history including details of the business enterprises worked in or owned, their size and position in the market, and an indication of the applicant's responsibilities in those enterprises. Business references from sources such as banks, accountants and business contacts as well as a credit report will be required.

Details of investment capital and evidence of personal funds; the amount of investment capital available for transfer to New Zealand will be a factor in assessing the application but there is no minimum figure. It is expected that at least NZ $200,000 (November 1987) will be available for transfer to New Zealand to meet housing and personal establishment costs *in addition* to investment capital.

Statement of intent for the business venture in New Zealand; the statement should outline the applicant's reasons for wishing to migrate to and invest in New Zealand and an indication of the intended business venture.

All applicants for entry to New Zealand are interviewed and are required to meet strict standards in respect of their health and character.

Applications for residence permits, and all enquiries about immigration, should be addressed to the *Migration Branch,* New Zealand House, Haymarket, London SW1Y 4TQ. Leaflets are available on various aspects of residence and employment:-

	Applying for Residence
L34	Education in New Zealand
L35	Foreign Exchange and Banks
L36	Storage, Handling and Rail Charges in New Zealand on Household Effects

L37 Importing Firearms into New Zealand
L38 New Zealand Income Tax
L39 Plunket Infant Care
L43 New Zealand Retail Prices
L78 Electrical Apparatus for use in New Zealand
L82 Housing and Home Ownership in New Zealand
L84 Social Security
L102 Labour Relations
L200 Health Care in New Zealand
UK30 Visiting New Zealand
UK83 Subscriptions to New Zealand Newspapers

Housing and Accommodation

In some cases intending immigrants must have accommodation arranged before leaving for New Zealand. All residents are encouraged to build or buy their own house, but existing homes for rent are in short supply, especially in Wellington (and are expensive). Mortgages can be obtained from building societies, banks and terminating societies, but the interest rates are high. Migrants are not likely to secure loans from the Government Housing Corporation.

Health and Welfare

New Zealand's comprehensive social security system is financed by taxation, and no special contributions are required. As in Britain, the New Zealand social security scheme provides unemployment, family, maternity, sickness, old age, widow's, invalids' and orphans' benefits. Hospital and medical treatment is free but visits to dentists must be paid in full. Visits to doctors are only partially subsidised.

Education

Education is compulsory between the ages of 6 and 15, and free from 3 (kindergarten) to 19, unless a private school is attended. Most children start co-educational primary school at 5, and at 12 or 13 go on to secondary school, where a two-year general course is followed by one year's specialisation leading to the School Certificate examination.

University entrance is by examination or by a certificate of fitness issued by a recognised school; most students remain at school one extra year after qualifying to obtain the Higher School Certificate, which entitles the holder to a university grant covering tuition fees and an annual allowance. New Zealand has universities in Auckland, Christchurch, Dunedin, Hamilton, Palmerston North and Wellington; there are also 13 technical institutes and 6 teacher training colleges, as well as a number of community colleges covering technical and adult education courses.

National Service

At the end of 1972 New Zealand abolished compulsory military service, and now maintains a purely voluntary defence system. Aliens therefore have no liability to conscription.

British High Commissions
9th Floor, Reserve Bank Building, 2 The Terrace, PO Box 369, Wellington.
9th Floor, Norwich Union Building, 179 Queen Street, Auckland 1.

CONDITIONS OF WORK

Wages

Although there is a minimum wage fixed by national legislation, each profession or industry also has sets of minimum wages which are usually higher. The minimum weekly wage is about NZ$210 — but the average wage is considerably higher (NZ$10.50 per hour). Under the Equal Pay Act of 1972, women now receive equal pay for all types of work.

Hours

Wages are based universally on the 40 hour, 5 day week. Overtime is paid at 150% for the first three hours, 200% for every hour thereafter.

Holidays

Most employees receive at least three weeks paid holiday per annum. In addition, there are the following public holidays; New Year's Day; Waitangi Day (February 6); Good Friday; Easter Monday; Anzac Day (April 25); Queen's Birthday (first Monday in June); Labour Day (fourth Monday in October); Christmas Day; and Boxing Day. Each province also celebrates its own Anniversary Day.

Safety and Compensation

Industrial awards lay down certain standards, but conditions are usually far above the minimum. Employers are obliged to insure their workers against industrial accidents resulting in temporary incapacity disablement or death.

Trade Unions

Union membership is not obligatory under national legislation. There are 250 registered unions of workers and about 220 employers unions in the private sector. Most worker unions are represented at the National level by the Federation of Labour, an unregistered organisation formed to co-ordinate worker interests. In the public sector there are 21 trade unions, of which the collective organisation is called the Combined State Union. The Federation of Labour and the Combined State Union are in the process of amalgamating.

Taxation

A direct tax on personal income is deducted on a PAYE basis and includes social security contributions. Allowances are made for dependants, life insurance premiums, school fees, charitable donations, etc. See Leaflet L38 for further details.

WORK AVAILABLE

General

Within the immigration limitations, qualified people listed under the approved occupations should have little difficulty in obtaining a work permit, provided that an offer of work is guaranteed.

Newspapers

Advertisements for insertion in the New Zealand press can be placed with any of the following agencies, which act on behalf of the dailies with the widest circulation:

New Zealand Associated Press, Ludgate House, 107 Fleet Street, London EC4A 2AN *(New Zealand Herald, Evening Post, The Press, Otago Daily Times).*

PA Overseas Media Ltd, 40 Roseberry Avenue, London EC1R 4RN. (*The Dominion* and the *Sunday Times,* which has national circulation).

Subscription to New Zealand newspapers can be arranged through these agencies, which also sell specimen copies on request. The Saturday editions of the major New Zealand dailies are available for inspection at the Migration Branch on the first floor of New Zealand House. Also available from New Zealand House is leaflet L86 Subscriptions to New Zealand Newspapers.

See also the section on *Advertisements* in the chapter *Getting The Job.*

Labour Force

The New Zealand labour force of about 1,325,000 is divided as follows: 11% in primary industries; 30% in manufacturing and commerce; and 59% in service industries. There are 101,393 unemployed: a rate of almost 7.6%. The following sectors in the manufacturing industry are areas where a significant rate of growth is expected to occur in the next few years: tanning and leather; ceramics and glass; chemicals and chemical products; furniture; plastic and rubber products; woollen goods and carpets; machinery and appliances; and electronics and computer software.

SPECIFIC CONTACTS

Accountants

An accountant wishing to practise in New Zealand must be a member of the New Zealand Society of Accountants. Under a reciprocal agreement, membership of this society is automatically granted to members of the Association of Certified Accountants, or of any of the three British Associations of Chartered Accountants.

There are good prospects for qualified accountants in New Zealand, both in public accountancy and in other fields. There are also excellent opportunities for young people (up to age 25) who are almost qualified and intend to complete their academic training in New Zealand.

Further information on prospects and eligibility for registration is available from the Executive Director, *New Zealand Society of Accountants,* 57 Willis Street, Box 11342, Wellington.

For NZ$59.50 per 25 mm column, advertisements can be placed in the Society's official publication *The Accountants' Journal.* Contact Professional Media Limited, PO Box 14502, Kilbirnie, Wellington.

For job-hunting the Society recommends:

Lampen Management Group, 16th Floor, Stock Exchange Building, 191 Queen Street, Auckland.

Lampen Management Group, 107 Customhouse Quay, Wellington.

PA Management Consultants Ltd., 53-59 Cook Street, Auckland 1.

PA Management Consultants Ltd., Wellington Trade Centre, 173-175 Victoria Street, Wellington.

Professional Careers Auckland Ltd., 75 Great South Road, Remuera, Auckland 5.

Chartered Secretaries

Information on registration and employment prospects can be obtained from the Executive Director, *New Zealand Institute of Chartered Secretaries and Administators,* PO Box 444, Auckland 1.

Consultants and Agencies

Lampen Associates, 16th Floor, Stock Exchange Building, 191 Queen Street, Auckland — deal with temporary staff, specialising in secretarial, accounts, computer, marketing and clerical assignments, as well as some labouring and warehouse work; and permanent office staff. All applicants must have at least three years work experience, and are usually interviewed with their references checked before they can be employed.

People seeking temporary work with secretarial, accounts and computer skills can be given assistance with obtaining work permits.

Morgan & Banks, level 9, AA Centre, 342 Lambton Quay, Wellington — provides a permanent and executive leasing service in the senior accounts, computer and sales areas, providing long and short term assignments for accountants, computer specialists and specialist consultants.

PA Management Consultants, PO Box 11540, Wellington — deals with management and accounting, computers and telecommunications, technology and personnel services.

Doctors and Medical Staff

Doctors registered in the UK or Eire by virtue of a university degree obtained in either of these two countries are eligible for registration in New Zealand. Queries on eligibility should be addressed to the Secretary, *Medical Council of New Zealand,* PO Box 9249 Courtenay Place, Wellington.

Qualified radiologists and radiotherapists, as well as specialists in anaesthetics, community medicine, dermatology, ophthamology, psychiatry and venerology are currently in demand in New Zealand. To ascertain for registration, contact the Secretary, *Medical Council of New Zealand* (address above).

Fully qualified radiologists wishing to work in New Zealand can obtain advice and information from the Honorary Secretary, *New Zealand Branch of the Royal Australasian College of Radiologists,* Department of Radiology, Waikato Hospital, Private Bag, New Zealand.

Engineers

Intended emigrants could advertise in *New Zealand Engineering,* the monthly journal of the *Institution of Professional Engineers,* New Zealand. The publishers are Engineering Publications Co Ltd., PO Box 12241, Wellington.

Industrial Chemists

Opportunities exist in industries such as meat freezing and preserving, pulp and paper, tanning, petroleum refining and marketing, pottery and ceramics, fertilisers, soap and detergents, paint and varnish, rubber, brewing, timber products, general chemical products, cement, and others.

Information on conditions and prospects can be obtained from the Administrative Secretary, *New Zealand Institute of Chemistry,* PO Box 29-183, Christchurch.

Public Service Appointments

The *State Services Commission,* PO Box 329, Wellington, is a convenient source of information on the functions of the New Zealand Public Service Departments. These departments have an occasional need for persons with high technical, scientific or managerial qualifications and experience, but demand for such staff needs to be taken up from each individual department as they individually function as an employing organisation in their own right.

Other Opportunities

Opportunities in New Zealand are also referred to in the following chapters (see Contents), which cover a wide range of professions:

Au Pair and Domestic
British Government Departments
Transport, Tourism and Catering
Voluntary Work

SHORT TERM WORK

Opportunities for temporary work in New Zealand are very similar to those in Australia. There is no direct equivalent to Australia's "working holiday" visa, but people who enter the country as tourists may be able to obtain work permits if they can persuade the local District Superintendent of the Department of Labour that they are not depriving a local resident of a job (see leaflet UK30, *Visiting New Zealand*). British students can work in New Zealand from July to September under the vocational exchange scheme administered by the *Careers Research and Advisory Council (CRAC),* Sheraton House, Castle Park, Cambridge CB3 0AX.

Seasonal Work

The *British Australia Vocational Scheme* can find summer jobs for students in New Zealand: see the section on summer jobs in the *Australia* chapter for details.

People already in the country may be able to get jobs over the English summer in hotels in New Zealand's expanding skiing resorts. Areas to head for include Mount Hutt and Coronet Peak in the Southern Alps on the South Island and Mount Ruapehu on the North Island. Jobs over the New Zealand summer may be found in Nelson and Christchurch on the South Island or Tuaranga or the Bay of Islands on the North Island.

Casual fruit picking jobs may be found around New Zealand, from picking peaches and apricots around Kerikeri in December to picking kiwifruit in May around the Bay of Plenty. The dates and locations of different harvests are covered in detail in the book *Work Your Way Around the World.*

Other Work

GAP Activity Projects can arrange jobs lasting for six months on farms in the Christchurch area for school leavers: see the chapter on exchanges for details. The *International Farm Experience Programme,* described in the chapter on agriculture and conservation, can find farm jobs lasting for six or eight months to students of agriculture.

Canada

Canadian High Commission, Canada House, Trafalgar Square, London SW1Y 5BJ and Macdonald House 1 Grosvenor Square, London W1X 0AB
Currency: $ (Canadian) 1 = 100 cents
Rate of Exchange: £1 = $2.06

Since the war, Canada has accepted an estimated four million immigrants, more than a million of them coming from Britain and Ireland. Since 1967, unacceptably high (8-9%) unemployment levels have necessitated stricter immigration controls, and the flow of immigrants is now limited to those possessing skills and qualifications in major demand in Canada's developing economy.

GENERAL FACTS

Population

In 1986, Canada's population was estimated at 25,354,064. In 1985, the birth rate was 14.8 per 1,000.

Canada is one of the world's two largest countries in area, covering 3,851,809 square miles, 291,571 square miles of which is water. Overall population density is 6.4 persons per square mile. However, the population is unevenly distributed and all except the maritime provinces have large, almost uninhabited areas. Eighty per cent of the total population is concentrated in the four provinces of Quebec, Ontario, Alberta and British Columbia. By contrast, the Yukon and Northwest Territories contain 0.3% of the population, yet cover one third of Canada's total area. Approximately 80% of the population is also concentrated in the southernmost 200 miles of the country.

Climate

The climate varies widely from severe Arctic conditions in the north to the English climates of the temperature coastal regions, with extremes of heat and cold experienced in the central provinces. The Pacific coast has the highest rainfall and, inland, snow covers all regions during three to five of the winter months. Temperatures this century have ranged from a summer high of 115 degrees Fahrenheit in Alberta to minus 81 degrees in the Yukon. In general, Canadian winters are cold but dry, springs short but dramatic, summers quite warm and sunny for two or three months, autumn usually clear and crisp.

Government

Canada is a confederation of ten provinces (Ontario, Nova Scotia, British Columbia, Alberta, Saskatchewan, Manitoba, New Brunswick, Prince Edward Island and Newfoundland) and two territories. The Queen is the head of state of Canada, and is represented by a Governor General nominated by the Canadian Prime Minister.

The federal government legislates over matters of national and general concern, including defence, external affairs, trade, the postal services, navigation and shipping. Provinces have jurisdiction over matters of local interest, including municipal institutions, the law relating to property and civil rights, health care and education. Federal legislative power is vested in the Parliament of Canada which consists of the Queen, an appointed upper house called the Senate, and a lower house, the House of Commons, elected by universal adult suffrage.

Since the September 1984 general election, there were four parties represented in the House of Commons: the Progressive Conservatives, who form the government; the Liberals, who are the official opposition; the New Democratic Party; and one Independent.

Cities

The major cities are Toronto, with a population of 3,427,168; followed by Montreal (2,921,357); Vancouver (1,380,729); the capital Ottawa (819,263); Edmonton (785,465); Calgary (671,326) and Winnipeg (625,304). Altogether there are over 25 metropolitan areas with over 100,000 inhabitants.

Rural Life

Only 24.3% of the population lives in the country, and the continuing decrease is mainly from farms. However, agriculture is still Canada's most important primary industry: occupied land exceeds 174 million acres and there are 318,361 farms, all highly commercialised, mechanised and specialised, cultivating mainly wheat, other field crops, dairy products, livestock, fruit, vegetables, tobacco, honey, maple syrup and furs.

Forestry is another major rural occupation: forests cover 800 million acres; pulp and paper manufacture are the most important related industries.

Fishing, mining and electric power (75% water-generated) are among the other imporant rural occupations.

Canada is rich in mineral wealth with vast reserves of petroleum and natural gas, and is a major world producer of nickel, iron ore, copper and zinc. Exports of crude and fabricted mineral products account for nearly 25% of Canada's total exports.

Religion, Sport and Culture

According to the 1986 census, 44.6% of Canada's population was of British origin, 28.7% were French, and the remaining 26.7% were of other origins. The native peoples, Indians and Inuit (Eskimos), number approximately 323,000, or 1.4% of the population, and there are 54 different Indian languages or dialects in Canada, plus Inuktitut, the language of the Inuit.

47.3% of Canadians are Catholic: 17.5% belong to the United Church of Canada (Methodists, Congregationalists and Presbyterians); and 13% to the Anglican Church. The other Protestant denominations and the Jewish faith are also well represented.

The arts in Canada have developed rapidly in recent decades and exhibit a growing sense of a unique identity distinguishable from both Europe and the United States. Theatre, ballet and music performance are held in all major centres; crafts thrive in the smallest communities, and both cinema and television claim large audiences. Canadia produced films and television programmes, in English or French, are competitive in quality, if not quantity, with those produced in the USA, but the United States still exerts a strong cultural influence, particularly in the major population centres close to the border with the USA.

The multicultural nature of Canadian society is recognised and supported by government policy. A Multicultural Directorate was established in 1971 and provides assistance to a wide range of activities organised by various cultural groups.

Canadians spend a lot of their free time out of doors. Most provinces have set aside vast areas for parks for the conservation of the environment and the enjoyment of visitors. Most of the national and provincial parks provide camping facilities and hiking trails. Skiing, swimming, ice skating, ice hockey, tennis and golf are amongst the most popular recreational activities, and sports facilities are generally excellent.

FACTORS INFLUENCING EMPLOYMENT

Immigration

Since the war, Canada has accepted over four million immigrants, most of whom settled in Ontario. Although British citizens do not require a visa to visit Canada, visitors cannot change their status from visitor to worker while in Canada. Persons who wish to work in Canada must obtain the appropriate documentation prior to entering Canada/leaving the UK.

Under current immigration regulations, the flow of immigrants is tied closely to labour market demands. There are two ways permanent residence, known as landed immigrant status, is obtained — through sponsorship, or by independent application. Sponsored applicants must be dependent relatives (i.e. spouses, retired parents, or unmarried children) of Canadian citizens or residents.

Applicants in the independent category are assessed according to several factors including age, education, knowledge of English and French, training and occupation. Under current immigration regulations, persons in certain occupations are able to meet the selection criteria without arranged employment; others require a job offer which has been certified by employment officials in Canada as a position for which no qualified Canadians are available. In some cases the presence of relatives — brother, sister, uncle or aunt — can assist a person's application.

In addition to the sponsored and independent categories, Canada is encouraging applications from business persons who have a proven ability in business and substantial capital available to invest in/or set up a business which will be of significant economic benefit to Canada.

Since the closure of the immigration sections at the Canadian Consulates in Glasgow and Birmingham, the Canadian High Commission in London deals with immigration matters for England, Scotland, Wales and Northern Ireland. The address is:

Canadian High Commission, MacDonald House, 38 Grosvenor Street, London W1X 0AA.

For the province of Quebec the approval of Quebec House (address below) must be obtained before applying for a visa from the Canadian High Commision.

Language

Canada is officially bilingual in French and English and all federal government publications and federal court decisions are published in both languages. French and English language radio and television are available throughout Canada, and it is the intention to make state financed schooling available in both languages wherever numbers warrant. In Quebec French is the official language.

Cost and Standard of Living

British visitors to Canada find the standard of living fairly high; many articles are much cheaper in terms of hours of work and salaries received. So that there are 413 private cars, 639 telephones and 427 televisions per 1,000 inhabitants.

Housing and Accommodation

Although there is no actual housing shortage in Canada, there is a shortage of low-cost housing and it is for this reason that the Immigration Department recommends immigrants to have accommodation pre-arranged if possible. Government loans are available for home building and buying.

Rents vary greatly from province to province, and from house to house. Unfurnished one-bedroom apartments cost anything over $400-500 per month. A three-bedroom apartment (unfurnished) can cost over $900 per month.

Health and Welfare

Each provincial government has primary responsibility for health, and operates two insurance programmes — one for hospital treatment, one for medical care. There are also supplementary private insurance schemes, often operated through payroll deductions.

Family allowances are paid for all dependent children under 18. All persons aged 65 and over who have lived in Canada for at least 10 years (regardless of citizenship) receive a monthly old age pension; if their income is limited, they receive an additional guaranteed income supplement. There is also a contributory pension scheme whereby employees pay up to 1.8 per cent of their income while working.

Social assistance is provided by a shared-cost programme to people in need. The federal government provides 50% of the cost to each province by agreement. There is also a separate unemployment insurance scheme, contributions for which are shared by workers and employers.

Education

Education is compulsory for all children for about 10 years in every province and is free up to the end of secondary school. The starting age is 6 or 7 and the minimum leaving age, 15 or 16. Most schools are co-educational, and few are privately educated (3% in English-speaking provinces, 7% in Quebec). Despite the multiplicity of educational systems and authorities, co-operation has produced a surprising uniformity. In some provinces French-speaking pupils are entitled by law to receive instruction in French. In Quebec, the policy is to register the children of immigrants in French schools.

Higher education is provided by 68 universities and some 200colleges; students may receive financial aid and loans. Annual fees are $1,200 for tuition in Ontario, plus $7,000 for living accommodation. Federal or provincial loans are available, repayable over a period of up to ten years.

National Service

There is no military conscription in force in Canada.

British High Commission and Consulates

British High Commission, 80 Elgin St., Ottawa, Ontario K1P 5K7.

Consulate General, Suite 1404, 3 McCauley Plaza, 10025 Jasper Avenue, Edmonton, Alberta T5J 1S6Quebec

Consulate General: 1155 University Street, Montreal, Quebec, H3B 3A7.

Consulate General: 777 Bay Street, Suite 1910, College Park, Toronto, Ontario M5G 2G2.

Consulate General: 1111 Melville Street, Suite 800, Vancouver, BC, V6E 3V6

Consulate: Suite 1501, Purdy's Wharf Bldg, 1959 Upper Water Street, PO Box 310, Halifax, Nova Scotia, B3J 2X1

Consulate: 34 Glencoe Drive, PO Box 8833, St John's, Newfoundland, A1B 3T2

Consulate: c/o Hignell Printing Ltd, 488 Burnell Street, Winnipeg, Manitoba R3G 2B4.

CONDITIONS OF WORK

Wages

The only federal law governing wages is the Canada Labour (Standards) Code, which covers only government employees and workers in industries under federal jurisdiction. This Code, which also prohibits unequal pay and discrimination based on sex, race, colour or religion, is the basis for the different provincial laws covering all professions and workers. However, there are wide variations from province to province. Minimum wages do not fall below $4 an hour. An average yearly salary for a skilled worker would be in the region of $25,000.

Hours

For government employees and workers in industries under federal jurisdiction, the working week is five days of eight hours each. Hours above eight in a day or forty in a week must be paid at 150%, up to a maximum of 48 hours a week. Provincial rulings vary slightly, but 48 hours (in Nova Scotia) is the maximum without overtime pay.

Holidays

Annual paid holidays vary from two to four weeks. There are also ten national public holidays: New Year's Day; Good Friday; Easter Monday; Victoria Day (May 25, or the Monday immediately preceding); Canada Day (July 1); Labour Day (first Monday in September); Thanksgiving (second Monday in October); Remembrance Day (November 11); Christmas Day; and Boxing Day. The different provinces also observe local holidays.

Safety and Compensation

Canadian industry is proud of its low injury rate, and is very safety-conscious. Many large firms conduct constant safety programmes, supplementing the minimum safety standards laid down in most provinces.

All employees in industries and workplaces covered by Workmen's Compensation Funds are entitled to free medical aid and payment of up to 75% of regular earnings. Benefits are also provided for widows and dependent children of workers killed on the job.

Trade Unions

Union membership represents about a third of the labour force. The collective bargaining system between employers and unions functions under the federal Industrial Relations and Disputes Investigation Act, and under labour relations acts in all provinces. The government has the ultimate duty of conciliation when parties are unable to reach an agreement. In some provinces, legislation forbids strikes by workers in essential services, such as firemen, policemen and hospital employees.

Taxation

Income tax is deducted on a PAYE basis, with allowances for dependent children, pension contributions etc. As examples of tax rates, a single man earning $25,000 would pay $5,500 in tax. On the same salary, a married man with two children under 16 and a dependent wife would pay $4,000. Tax is paid in two parts — federal and provincial, so total tax rates vary from province to province.

Municipal authorities also levy taxes, especially on corporate incomes. Some provinces have variable purchase taxes on consumer goods and services.

WORK AVAILABLE

General

The government offices for the various provinces provide similar services to the diplomatic missions (see above), but do not necessarily handle recruitment. However, they can provide prospective immigrants and job-seekers with specific information about the provinces they represent. Their London addresses are:

Alberta — 1 Mount Street, W1Y 5AA.
British Columbia — 1 Regent Street, SW1Y 4NS.
Nova Scotia — 14 Pall Mall, SW1Y 5LU.
Ontario — 21 Knightsbridge, London SW1X 7LY.
Quebec — 59 Pall Mall, SW1 5JH.
Saskatchewan — 16 Berkeley Street, London W1X 5AE.

Members of the professions should ascertain whether their qualifications are acceptable in Canada, or whether they must attend further courses. Assessment of qualifications is carried out by the relevant professional associations in Canada, whose addresses can be obtained from any Canadian Consulate, High Commission or Embassy.

A list of the professional associations is also given in the *Canadian Almanac and Directory,* available in public reference libraries. This also gives the addresses of many potential employers, such as colleges, universities, law firms, insurance companies, libraries, publishers and broadcasting companies.

Newspapers

Newspapers are available for reference at Canada House in Trafalgar Square, which also contains a great deal of other useful information for emigrants. Local city and regional newspapers can be consulted at the offices of the provincial government offices, where information will be given on subscriptions and advertising.

A list of the names and addresses of the main newspapers is included in the free booklet *Teaching in Canada,* issued by the *Canadian Teachers' Federation,* 110 Argyle, Ottawa, Ontario K2P 1B4, although this service is intended only for the benefit of teachers seeking work in Canada. The *Globe and Mail,* Canada's only national newspaper, contains a daily employment and careers section, with a special supplement on Saturdays. Their UK address for advertising purposes is 167 Temple Chambers, Temple Avenue, London EC4Y 0EA.

See also the section on *Advertisements* in the chapter *Getting the Job.*

Labour Force

The Canadian labour force numbers about 13,000,000, about 43% of whom are women. The division of the work is: 8% in the primary sector; 27% in industry; 65% in services. The current unemployment rate is 8.9%.

SPECIFIC CONTACTS

Landed immigrants can use the services of the Canada Manpower Centres, which display lists of vacancies in their "job banks". There are 400 Manpower Centres across the country. Addresses are available through the High Commissions.

Dietitians

Although unable to help individual enquirers to find work, the *Canadian Dietetic Association,* 480 University Avenue, Suite 604, Toronto, M5G 1VZ, publishes a list of regulations and educational and experience requirements for employment in Canada.

Doctors

The *Canadian Medical Association,* Box 8650, Ottawa, Ontario K1G 0G8, publishes the *Candian Medical Association Journal,* which has a large classified section. The Association also issues a free leaflet *Medical Practice in Canada,* which gives information on registration and appointments and lists the addresses of the provincial Medical Associations and their respective registration requirements.

Domestic Staff

Many of the organisations listed in the chapter *Au Pair and Domestic* find domestic work (nannies and mother's helps) in Canada on one-year contracts.

Engineers

The *Canadian Council of Professional Engineers,* 116 Albert Street, Suite 401, Ottawa, Ontario, can advise on procedures used in evaluating foreign engineering education qualifications. For Quebec the address is *Ordre des Ingenieurs du Quebec,* 2020 University, 14th Floor, Montreal, Quebec H3A 2A5.

Hospital Staff

The *Grenfell Regional Health Services* operates and staffs two hospitals and nineteen nursing stations and health centres. The staff consists of doctors, dentists, nurses, occupational therapists, physiotherapists and volunteers. Employment is for negotiable periods, preferably a minimum of two years. GRHS has short appointments for medical students in their clinical electives. Interested applicants should write to: *Grenfell Regional Health Services,* Charles Curtis Memorial Hospital, St. Anthony, Newfoundland and AOK 4SO, Canada.

Pharmacists

Licensing of foreign pharmacists is a provincial responsibility. Candidates are advised to contact first the *Pharmacy Examining Board of Canada,* Suite 603, 123 Edward Street, Toronto, Ontario M5G 1E2. For Quebec the address is *Pharmaciens du Quebec,* 266 Notre Dame Ouest, Montreal, Quebec H2Y 1T5.

Teachers

The *Canadian Teacher's Federation,* 110 Argyle Avenue, Ottawa, Ontario K2P 1B4, cannot help in finding work, but issues the free booklet *Teaching in Canada,* which includes a lot of useful information for immigrants, such as details of entry requirements, and a list of the provincial authorities, from whom permission to teach must be obtained before an appointment can be taken up.

The *Canadian Education Association*, 252 Bloor Street W, 8th Floor, Toronto, Ontario M5S 1V5 issues the leaflet *Information for teachers thinking of coming to Canada,* but cannot otherwise assist in finding work.

Those teachers wishing to work in British Columbia, Manitoba, New Brunswick and the North West Territories should seek information from the following bodies:

Computerised Teacher Registry, British Columbia School Trustees' Association, 1155 West 8th Avenue, Vancouver, British Columbia, V6H 1C5.
Administration and Professional Certification, Professional Certification Section, 227-1200 Portage Avenue, Winnipeg, Manitoba R3G 0T5.
Department of Education, PO Box 6000, Fredericton, New Brunswick E3B 5HI.
The Director of Personnel, Government of the Northwest Territories, Yellowknife, NWT X1A 2L9.

Teachers interested in appointments in private schools should contact the Executive Secretary, *Canadian Association of Independent Schools,* c/o Stanstead College, Stanstead, Quebec J0B 3E0.

University Staff

Information on academic and administrative vacancies in the universities can be obtained from the *CAUT Bulletin,* the news and information magazine published ten times during the academic year by the *Canadian Association of University Teachers.* Publication Office: 75 Albert Street, Suite 1001, Ottawa, Ontario, Canada, K1P 5E7. (Subscription: Yearly) (September-June) 1st Class Air Mail — $30.00. Canadian Funds Only Accepted.

Universities advertise their academic and administrative vacancies in *University Affairs,* the news magazine published ten times a year by the *Association of Universities and Colleges of Canada,* Publications Office, 151 Slater Street, Ottawa, Canada K1P 5N1. ($20 surface mail; $45 air mail). Lists of specific university departments and addresses are also available from AUCC Information.

Other Opportunities

Opportunities in Canada are also referred to in the following chapters (see Contents), which cover a wide range of professions:

Agriculture, Conservation and Forestry
British Government Departments
Oil, Mining and Engineering
Transport, Tourism and Catering

SHORT TERM WORK

Foreigners looking for legal temporary work in Canada must either apply for specific jobs before they arrive and then wait for the employer to arrange a work permit or, in some cases, take part in an approved "educational" scheme such as that offered by BUNAC. People looking for unauthorised work when in Canada risk exposure because they will not be able to provide a prospective employer with a Canadian social insurance number, which is required by law.

Seasonal Work

Students can obtain Employment Authorisations which will allow them to look for jobs in Canada and make use of the government's *Canada Employment Centres* from the *British Universities North America Club (BUNAC),* 232 Vauxhall Bridge Road, London SW1V 1AU. BUNAC's *Work Canada Programme* allows students to work for up to 6 months. BUNAC can also directly arrange for students to work on the tobacco harvest.

Non-students can apply for the various jobs listed in the chapters on Canada in *The Summer Employment Directory of the United States* and *Summer Jobs Abroad.* Alternatively, they can try writing directly to hotels listed in tourist guides: those in resorts in the Rocky Mountains are especially recommended, as many of them can offer work on the winter skiing season (from November to May) as well as in the summer.

Students with "Employment Authorisations" can look for work picking fruit or tobacco in the Okanagan Valley in British Columbia, where a succession of harvests take place, beginning with cherries in June and ending with applies in September and October. Jobs can be found through local "Farm Labour Pool" offices, which specialise in helping people to find this sort of work. See *Work Your Way Around the World* for further details.

Other Work

It is possible to take part in various voluntary construction projects in Indian communities around the year. These are arranged by "Frontiers Foundation", of 2615 Danforth Avenue, Suite 203, Toronto, Ontario M4C IL6. Participants need to pay for their own travel expenses as far as Toronto, and must be free to work for at least two months (see the Voluntary Work Chapter).

BRITISH FIRMS

with branches, affiliates or subsidiaries in Canada

The Canadian High Commission, address above, can issue a free list of many British companies operating in Canada.

United States of America

American Embassy, 5 Upper Grosvenor Street, London W1A 2JB
Currency: (US) $1 = 100 cents
Rate of Exchange: £1 = 1.68

At present it is not at all easy for British citizens to find work in the USA, due to the situation regarding immigration and work permits. Although work may be offered, a work permit can take up to 18 months to be issued.

GENERAL FACTS

Population

The resident population of the USA in 1986 was 241,077,000, including 28,000,000 blacks. Women outnumber men by about 6.5 million.

The total area of the USA is 3,536,855 square miles. Excluding Alaska, the continental United States measures about 2,500 miles from east to west, and, at the narrowest point (Cleveland to Tallahassee), 800 miles from north to south. Including Alaska and Hawaii, the country spans seven time zones.

The population density is about 65 per square mile, but, because of the deserts and mountains, and the great uninhabited expanses of Alaska, distribution is uneven. 53% of the population live in counties within 50 miles of a coastal shoreline. The population density in Alaska is 0.9, compared with 978 in New Jersey.

Climate

The climate of the United States can be classed as continental, with cold winters and hot summers. Hawaii and Florida, the only states that get no frost, come into the sub-tropical zone.

Average January temperatures are below freezing in all but the southern states, and in Alaska and the northern mid-west states, the average is often below 0°F.

Summer, on the other hand, can be unbearably hot, with average July temperatures rising into the 70's and 80's and 100°F being no rare event.

Precipitation is about twice as high as in Britain, but most of it is accounted for by heavy snowfalls, rainstorms and hurricanes, rather than constant drizzle. In the desert areas, however (New Mexico, Arizona, Nevada), annual rainfall is only 7-8″.

Government

The United States is a federal republic led by a President, who is elected by all citizens aged 18 and over, for a four-year term of office. No president may serve for more than two terms. The president, and the cabinet which he appoints, form the executive branch of the government.

The Congress is the seat of the legislature, and consists of the Senate and the House of Representatives. Each state elects two senators, who serve a six-year term, and one third of the membership is renewed every two years. There are only two major parties — Democrats and Republicans.

The USA is a confederation of 50 states, each of which has its own governor and legislature (this takes different forms in different states). The States have considerable autonomy and legislative power; they run their own courts and police forces and levy their own taxes. The states are further subdivided into counties, which are responsible for local government.

Cities

As the world's leading industrial power, the USA has built its economy on large industrial cities. 73.7% of the population live in urban areas, and there are 39 metropolitan areas with over a million inhabitants.

The largest cities and conurbations are: New York, the world's largest port, with 7,183,000 inhabitants; Chicago and Los Angeles, each with about three million; Houston (1,705,000), Philadelphia (1,646,000); and Detroit (1,088,000); the capital Washington, DC has 626,000 inhabitants.

American cities tend to have very concentrated and over-crowded centres, with tall office and apartment blocks dominating the skyline. Traffic congestion is a major problem, but it is eased slightly by the gigantic network of highways that extend over, under and around all large towns.

Rural Life

Cultivated land covers 47% of America's total land area; forests another 21%. The farm population of some 6 million is only 2.5% of the country's population, yet the USA leads the world in both production and export of meat and agricultural produce. The size of some farms in the mid-west is enormous, and although the average size is only 415 acres, over 42% of the country's farmland is contained in farms of 2,000 acres and more.

Religion, Sport and Culture

All major religious faiths are represented in the USA. In general the many denominations of the Protestant church form the predominant religious body, but Catholicism comes out stronger where certain ethnic groups prevail, such as the Mexican-influenced south-west, and the French-Canadian elements in Maine. Industrial regions settled by immigrants from Southern and Eastern Europe also have large Catholic populations.

The US is one of the few countries in the world where soccer is not a major sport, although its popularity is growing (the US will host the World Cup in 1994). The four main sports are baseball, American football, ice-hockey, and basketball. Tennis and skiing are also popular, and there are facilities for almost any sport imaginable.

The cultural standard is very high, with cinemas, theatres, concert halls and art galleries in all large towns.

FACTORS INFLUENCING EMPLOYMENT

Immigration

The processing of United States visas involves a long and complicated ritual, and quite a large outlay in application and other fees. The flow of immigrants has been reduced over the last few years by the establishment of numerical quotas, which has allowed the Immigration Service to be quite selective. Those wishing to enter the country solely for the purpose of employment must have a definite job offer (petitions must be filed by the prospective employer) and must obtain a certification from the US Department of Labour that there are no able, willing and qualified workers in the USA for that particular type of employment. Only workers with really valuable skills will be considered for work permits.

Immigrants fall into two categories — those subject to numerical limitations and those exempt. The exempt are: parents, spouses and unmarried children under 21 of US citizens; persons who have lost citizenship or resident status; past and present government employees and their families; and ministers of religion (and their families), if they are working for a bona fide religious organisation.

The annual quota of all other immigrants is 270,000, within which there is an annual limitation of 20,000 for each country. Visas are issued on the following preference basis. After each preference category the percentage of the overall limitation for May 1984 is cited in brackets.

First, second, fourth and fifth preferences are given to various relatives of US citizens and resident aliens (80%).

Third preference is for members of the professions or persons of exceptional ability in the sciences and arts (10%).

Sixth preference goes to skilled and unskilled workers in short supply (10%).

There is additional provision for refugees.

There are also various types of "non-immigrant" visa, issued to people wishing to take up short term work in the US. These are only issued for the following categories: lecturers and performing artists; trainees and exchange visitors on approved programmes; intra-company transferees on short term transfers; and other temporary workers fulfilling limited term contracts. Non-immigrant and tourist visas cannot be changed to immigrant visas once you are in the US, except in special circumstances, such as marriage to an American. Holders of exchange visitor visas, issued to medical doctors and exchange visitors sponsored by the US government, are normally required to spend at least two years outside the US before being considered for an immigrant visa.

Although vaccination against smallpox is no longer generally required, good health is still prerequisite for a visa, as is sound moral character. Thus certain aliens are totally ineligible to receive visas. These include: narcotics addicts or traffickers; members of the Communist party; persons with mental deficiencies or contagious diseases; ex-convicts; offenders against public morals; illiterates; and anyone likely to become a public charge.

When considering emigration to the United States, the first step is to contact the *US Embassy (immigrant Visa branch),* 55/56 Upper Brook Street, London W1A 2JB. Because of the strong possibility of an application being rejected or taking longer than expected, it is unwise to make any definite plans until the visa is issued. All immigrant Visa applications in the UK are now processed at the Embassy in London.

Cost and Standard of Living

Although British visitors to the USA may find life there very expensive, the myth of the high cost of living is largely unfounded. Retail food prices, for instance, compare very favourably with British prices, because so much is home-produced. Petrol (gasoline) is about half as cheap. Entertainment, apartment rents and certain luxury items tend to be more expensive than in Britain, but because wages are two to three times higher, they are well within the reach of most of the population.

As indicators of the standard of living there are, for every 1,000 inhabitants, 531 private cars, 680 television sets and 788 telephones.

Housing and Accommodation

On average, rents are far higher than in Britain, but so too is the average size and quality of the property. Housing of all kinds is generally readily available in the United States. There is relatively little public housing, the equivalent of council housing in the United Kingdom, and most people either own their own houses or rent privately-owned houses or flats. Even the lowest rents ordinarily exceed $100 per month for a very small flat and the average price of a house now exceeds $40,000.

Health and Welfare

While there is no equivalent to the NHS in the USA, the Social Security Department provides, against contributions from an employee's wage (half paid by the employer), benefits for old age, disability, unemployment and injury.

Personal medical insurance is the responsibility of the individual, who must insure himself privately. Many employers give advisory and financial assistance in this. Because medical fees are high, insurance premiums are also high, and can account for 5-10% of a week's pay packet. This is a very worthwhile investment.

Education

State laws vary concerning the ages of compulsory school attendance, but the highest minimum age is 7, and nearly all states set the upper age at 16 although obtaining a high school diploma usually requires attendance at school until the age of 18. Public schools are free, but there are also a number of private, fee-paying schools.

With over 2,500 universities and specialised training colleges, entrance to higher education is easier than in the UK. Each state controls at least one university, which gives preference to state residents. University courses are completed on the basis of credits, which offer students the chance to change courses, even colleges, or drop out for a year or two, without damaging their chance of obtaining a degree. On the whole, university courses last longer than in Britain, the usual minimum period of study being four years. University fees, including tuition and accommodation, can amount to $10,000 a year, but government loans are available, repayable over a period of up to ten years.

National Service

Although the draft was ended in 1973, the Selective Service System is still functioning and requires all men aged 18-26 to register for possible call-up in the case of a national emergency. This also applies to alien residents, who must register with their local Selective Service Board within 60 days after arriving in the US, or, if application for residence is granted after arrival, within 60 days after registration as a resident.

British Embassy and Consulates

British Embassy, 3100 Massachusetts Ave NW, Washington DC 20008.
Consulates General:
Suite 912, 225 Peachtree St NE, Atlanta, Ga 30303.
Suite 4740, Prudential Tower, Prudential Center, Boston Mass 02199.
33 N Dearborn St, Chicago I11. 60602.
1828 Illuminating Bldg, 55 Public Sq, Cleveland, Ohio 44113.
Suite 2250, 601 Jefferson Avenue, Houston, Texas 77002.
3701 Wilshire Blvd, Los Angeles, California 90010.
845 Third Ave, New York, NY 10022.
Suite 850, 1 Sansome Street, San Franscisco, California 94104.

There are also consulates in New Orleans, Dallas, Kansas City, Anchorage, Portland, Seattle, St Louis, Philadelphia and Norfolk.

CONDITIONS OF WORK

Wages

Minimum wages are laid down by state and Federal laws, and never fall below $3.35 an hour. Average weekly earnings are about $315.

Equality of pay for women is fast becoming a reality, thanks to the activities of the woman's movement. In matters of employment, advertising vacancies, etc., discrimination based on sex, age, colour, creed or national origin is banned by law. Members of minority groups are protected by law to the extent that employers must maintain a certain quota of them on their payrolls.

Hours

The standard is a 40-hour, 5-day week, but many offices get by with a 35 or 37½-hour week. Banks and shops keep longer hours than in Britain, and all-night shops are no rarity in large towns. Sunday work and shop-opening is generally forbidden, but laws vary from state to state, and essential services are excluded.

Holidays

Most employees are given at least two weeks' paid holiday a year. There are also nine nationally observed public holidays: New Year's Day; President's Day (third Monday in February); Memorial Day (last Monday in May); Independence Day (July 4); Labour Day (first Monday in September); Columbus Day (second Monday in October); Veterans' Day (fourth Monday in October); Thanksgiving (fourth Thursday in November); and Christmas. Other holidays vary from state to state but Lincoln's Birthday (February 12); St. Patrick's Day (March 17); and Arbor Day (April 26) are quite widely observed.

Safety and Compensation

Safety standards are set down by federal and state laws, and are rigidly enforced. Compensations are paid for injury, accident, death and disability. Very few benefits, even in the cases of permanent disability, are payable for an indefinite period, but short-term payments are quite adequate.

Trade Unions

Roughly 25% of the American labour force are union members, and union membership is compulsory in very few trades. Altogether there are 175 unions, of which 93 are affiliated to the American Federation of Labour and Congress of Industrial Organisations (AFL-C10). Despite the Labour Courts, which exist to effect conciliations between employers and employed, the figures for industrial disputes are still high.

Taxation

Federal and state income tax is deducted on a PAYE basis at fixed rates, and adjusted at the end of the tax year. Total tax deductions are generally less than 25% of the total income.

Sales tax (between 3% and 12%, varying from state to state) is payable on most goods and services. State variations make for big differences in the prices of many items, for instance, cigarettes, alcohol and cars.

WORK AVAILABLE

General

Details of the types of labour likely to qualify for a work permit cannot be precisely defined, but the American Department of Labour has given advance certification for persons with an advanced degree in dietetics, nursing, pharmacy, physical therapy, or medicine and surgery. With the excepetion of medicine and surgery, the advanced degree requirement is sometimes waived if the applicant has a combination of a regular degree and experience in one of the special fields. Advance certification is also given to members of bona fide religious organisations, entering the United States to perform non-profit duties on behalf of such an organisation. The US

Embassy's Visa Branch issues a free leaflet, Optional Form 172, dealing with the varies categories, of Labour Certification. The US Embassy is not in a position to help applicants to find work. They suggest contacting friends or relatives already resident in the United States.

Newspapers

USA Today International Corporation, 184 High Holborn, London WC1V 7AP, can place advertisements in the nationwide newspaper *USA Today*. Another useful newspaper is the *New York Times,* which has a large help wanted section on Sundays. Advertisements for this paper can be placed through Joshua B. Powers Ltd., 46 Keys House, Dolphin Square, London SW1V 3NA.

See also the section on *Advertisements* in the chapter *Getting the Job*.

Labour Force

The labour force of about 117,167,000 is divided as follows: 3.1% in agriculture; 23% in industry; and 73.9% in services. There is an unemployment rate of about 7.1%.

SPECIFIC CONTACTS

Au Pairs

There are two long-term programmes in the UK which enable au pairs to work in the USA for a year:

Au Pair in America, 37 Queens Gate, London SW7 5HR.

CBR Au Pair, 63 Forest Street, Worcester WR1 1DX.

See the *Au Pair* chapter for further details.

Librarians

The generally accepted qualification nation-wide is possession of a Master's degree, obtained at a school whose programme is accepted by the *American Library Association,* 50 East Huron Street, Chicago, Illinois 60611, USA. In addition certain states may have additional requirements for employment in certain positions. These may require the holding of United States citizenship or the possession of qualifications in addition to a Master's degree. For example, school library positions often call for qualification as a teacher in the state in which the school librarian is employed. For further information, write to the American Library Association at the above address.

Nurses

To practice professional nursing in the USA one must pass a licensing examination in one of the 50 states, the District of Columbia, Guam, American Samoa, Northern Mariana Islands or the Virgin Islands. Passing an examination given in the applicant's home country by the Commission on Graduates of Foreign Nursing Schools (CGFNS) is a requirement to sit for the National Council of State Boards of Nursing Licensure Examination (NCLEX). Obtaining a CGFNS Certificate, signifying a passing grade, is a requirement to obtain a non-immigrant occupational preference visa (H-1) from the United States Immigration and Naturalization Service. Also, the

CGFNS Certificate will be required in order to obtain an immigrant occupational (third) preference visa and a work permit from a US Labor Department regional office.

Information and application forms may be secured by writing to:

Commission on Graduates of Foreign Nursing Schools (CGFNS), 3624 Market Street, Philadelphia, Pennsylvania 19104.

Addresses of state boards of nursing are available from:

National Council of State Boards of Nursing, 625 North Michigan Avenue, Suite 1544, Chicago, Illinois 60611.

BNA International, 3rd Floor, 443 Oxford Road, London W1R 2NA, has vacancies in hospitals throughout the USA, the most popular areas being Boston, California, New York, New Jersey, and Florida. Contracts for all hospitals are for a minimum of one year, one way tickets to the USA or subsidised accommodation is normally provided.

Teachers

Apart from special teacher exchange programmes (see the section on *Exchanges* in the *Teaching* chapters), opportunities in public schools are rare. However, teaching agencies can register applicants for positions in both public and private schools. A list of agencies is available from the *National Association of Teachers' Agencies,* 1100 NW Loop 410, Suite 219, San Antonio, Texas 78213, USA.

University Staff

Applications for university places are usually made direct. The *Education Directory: Colleges and Universities, 1988-1989* is a complete list of American universities and institutes of higher education. It is available for $15.00 from the Superintendent of Documents, *US Government Printing Office,* Washington DC 20402.

Lists of vacancies in university Modern Language Departments and English Departments are supplied by the *Modern Language Association Job Information Service,* 10 Astor Place, New York, NY 10003, for an annual subscription of $40 (for five issues, overseas subscriptions).

Female, minority and handicapped people can contact the *Affirmative Action Register,* 8356 Olive Boulevard, St. Louis, Missouri 63132, which registers applicants and provides free lists of business, industrial, university and academic vacancies.

Other Opportunities

Opportunities in the USA are also referred to in the following chapters (see Contents), which cover a wide range of professions:

Agriculture, Conservation and Forestry
Computer Services
Transport, Tourism and Catering
Voluntary Work
International Organisations
United Nations
British Government Departments

SHORT TERM WORK

America, like Canada, presents a number of obstacles for foreigners who are looking for work there. Students have a defininte advantage as they can obtain work visas as part of approved *Exchange Visitor Programmes* with comparative ease: these enable them to look for work inside America. Others wanting to work legally must first obtain an offer of a job, then wait several months while the employer applies for a *Temporary Worker Visa* for them. These temporary visas apply only for specific jobs: they can not be transferred if you come across a better job when in America.

Seasonal Work

An enormous range of summer jobs exists in America: the *Summer Employment Directory of the United States* each year lists some 50,000 specific vacancies in hotels, offices, children's holiday camps, amusement parks, ranches, etc. and should be consulted by anyone looking for this sort of work. (See bibliography). Two of the most important organisations for British people are described below.

British Universities North America Club (BUNAC), 232 Vauxhall Bridge Road, London SW1V 1AU, can help full time students aged between 19 and 35 by placing them in jobs as supervisors or in the catering staff of the summer camps that are organised for American children each year: these jobs last for nine weeks. BUNAC also operates a *Work America Programme* that enables students to look for and take up any temporary work of his or her choosing in America between June and October.

Camp America, at 37 Queen's Gate, London SW7 5HR, also places students in jobs lasting for nine weeks in summer camps for children, but will consider applications from teachers, sports coaches and social workers as well. There are also vacancies for nurses. Their minimum age for applicants is 18. In addition, they offer a limited number of places for students who are interested in spending the summer in an American family as a working guest, or "family companion".

BRITISH FIRMS

with branches, affiliates or subsidiaries in the USA

The Anglo-American Trade Directory, (£85 or $150, including postage), available in economics, business or public reference libraries, is published by the American Chamber of Commerce (United Kingdom), 75 Brook Street, London W1Y 2EB. It contains the addresses of Anglo-American associations, a list of members of the Chamber, and a Trade Register aimed "at listing all British and American businesses having trade and/or investment relations with each other, and at indicating the nature of the relationship". This register includes about 18,000 British and American firms.

China

Embassy of the People's Republic of China, 31 Portland Place, London W1N 3AG
The unit of currency is the yuan

Working in China is, for the most part, fascinating, especially as the country is undergoing continual change from year to year. But it can prove immensely frustrating at times — in particular for the newcomer. Working with a top-heavy, all-powerful and often strikingly inefficient bureaucracy can wear down even the most enthusiastic China buff. However, the frustrations can be considerably lessened by a little foreknowledge.

GENERAL FACTS

Population

China is the world's third largest country, with an estimated population (in 1986) of 1,060,390,000, spread over 9.6 million square kilometres, which is roughly 7% of the land surface area of the world. Its territory has a land border that stretches 20,000 kilometres and includes 5,500 islands. The average population density is 110 persons per square kilometre, although 80% of the population is concentrated in the east, especially the north-east, due to the high mountain ranges on the western side of the country.

Climate

The climate in China varies hugely, spanning the worst extremes in weather. While the whole of north China has harsh winters with cultivation only possible in the summer which is generally hot and dry, the south is humid with very mild winters and hot summers that last five to eight months. In the very south the climate is tropical and year-round cultivation is possible, which is also true of the sub-tropical areas of central China. Temperatures during winter vary from 46.4°F in the Yangtse Valley to –40°F in Inner Mongolia. The hottest temperature in China is about 100°F (over the summer) depending on the area. In both the north and south the greatest rainfall is during the summer, but while Tibet, the north-west and Inner Mongolia are fairly arid, central and southern China has a moderate to heavy rainfall.

Government

Under the new Constitution of 1982, the National People's Congress (NPC) became the most powerful organ in the state hierarchy. Its 2,798 (in

1986) deputies are elected by each region for a five year term. The NPC elects the head of state, the President of the People's Republic of China, and the national Government — the State Council — to administer the country.

This basic principle of administration, with each level being answerable to the level immediately above, works for local government too. China is divided into 22 provinces, three municipalities (Beijing, Shanghai and Tianjin) which continue to come directly under the Central Government, and five autonomous regions including Xizang (Tibet). The latter regions, forming 50-60% of the total land, are home largely to minority nationalities including some 55 different races, compared to the Han Chinese stock which comprises 94% of the rest of the population.

Cities

Population censuses in China tend to be rough estimates only, due to the large numbers in question and to the varying definitions of city boundaries. Shanghai is the largest city with an approximate population of 12,050,000, followed by Beijing with 9,470,000 and Tianjin with 7,990,000. Spasmodic efforts that began in the 1950s to halt migration from the country into the cities, have met with little success.

Rural Life

China consists largely of high mountain ranges, vast deserts and steppeland. Only 11 per cent of the country is under systematic cultivation, although a survey in 1984 showed that the agricultural sector employed about 70% of China's labour force. The main crops are cereals, rice, tea and cotton. Livestock is raised in large numbers and minerals and coal are also important sources of income. Most agricultural production is carried out on collectively-owned fields and income is distributed according to individual output. The administrative functions of these people's communes were abolished by the new Constitution leaving them as just economic enterprises.

Religion, Sport and Culture

The indigenous religions of China are Confucianism, Taoism and Buddhism. The first two especially are more a combination of ancient supersition and philosophy than a ritualised religion. During the Cultural Revolution places of worship were ransacked, but the 1982 Constitution granted the people freedom of religious activity, although the extent of this freedom is debatable. There are also estimated to be 12 million Moslems and 50 million Christians in China, the latter largely the result of relentless missionary work in the 19th and early 20th century.

There is an ancient tradition of physical fitness in China, and every school, factory etc. has sports facilities. Fitness also forms part of a general awareness of civil defence; during the day people, prompted by the radio, will stop work to "keep fit and defend the mother country". Various Western sports are popular, such as football, table tennis and badminton but China is best known for its martial arts (*wushu*) such as *taijiquan* (shadow boxing) and *tai chi.*

In 1942 Mao Tse-tung, developing Lenin's idea that art was the cog-wheel of the revolution, declared that "Art should serve the people" and artists were encouraged to deal with the efforts of China to create a socialist state, although traditional arts were used as well. China's cultural heritage is very rich, its literature going back 2,000 years owing to the early invention of paper in the country. The 20th century has seen a great spread of literacy, and modern works of a more popular nature, as well as Marxist classics, have been added to the older literary tradition.

Calligraphy and painting are the two most respected art forms, evidence of which can be seen wherever you go in China. Dancing, singing, theatre and opera are all part of China's cultural scene, the Peking opera deserving worldwide fame. Finally, acrobatics, which have been the most popular form of art for about 2,000 years and indeed is one of the few art forms to be condoned by Mao, are performed all over China, either on their own, or incorporated into theatre and opera.

FACTORS INFLUENCING EMPLOYMENT

Immigration

Although procedures tend to change constantly, tourist visas are easy to obtain from the Chinese embassy. They are valid for three months and cost £20 (1988). These visas can be extended once in China, but only under certain circumstances.

Foreign workers, once informed that they have a job in China, will be requested to apply for a visa. They will be supplied with an interim visa which, on arrival in China, they take to the Public Security Office where they will be given a resident's permit.

Language

The official language of China is Mandarin (known as *putonghua* to the Chinese), a regularised dialect spoken originally in the northern parts of the country. Although roughly 70% of the population speak Mandarin, there are eight major dialects of which Cantonese is the most important.

Chinese is a tonal language, therefore one character may have three or four different meanings depending on the way you say it. The ideographic system comprises some 60,000 characters, of which about 7,000 are in current use. In 1956, the Government introduced 2,000 simplified characters in an attempt to make the written script easier to learn and then, in 1958, continuing their battle against illiteracy, the NPC adopted a system of Romanisation, known as *pinyin.* This is used especially to help children learn the pronunciation of Mandarin since that is the particular pronunciation which was used in the creation of *pinyin.*

In 1979, *pinyin* became the official language in diplomatic documents and street names and other information in the more tourist oriented areas are in both forms. The important step of using the spoken language in writing is not a key to communication however, since Westerners still find it very hard to get the tones or pronunciation correct.

Currency

There is a dual currency system in China. This was instigated in an attempt to prevent foreign currency leaving the country and to restrict the domestic purchase of consumer imports. *Renminbi* (Rmb) and Foreign Exchange Certificates (FEC) are both produced in units of *Yuan*. *Renminbi* is the local currency for Chinese use only. FECs are issued in exchange for foreign currency and are therefore only available to foreigners. No money of either sort may be taken out of the country; however, FEC may be exchanged back into hard currency on leaving, unlike *Renminbi*. Therefore, if you wish to save money to take home, it must be in the form of FEC. Most imported goods and Western luxury goods in general, such as film and foreign newspapers, as well as air tickets, cannot be bought with *Renminbi*. Although officially one FEC is equivalent of one *Renminbi*, due to their unequal purchasing power there is a thriving blackmarket.

Salaries are paid monthly, in cash. Sending money back home can be done through the Bank of China and some Units (see below) will arrange this directly for you. It is possible to open an account at the Bank of China, but this offers no advantages. It is also possible to transfer money to China fairly easily, (at least in Beijing) involving a bank draft from a UK bank to the Bank of China.

Housing and Accommodation

There are two types of housing available for foreigners: at the place of work and in a hotel. There is a policy to move everyone to the former eventually, but this entails an extensive building programme and there is unlikely to be any major changes for the next few years. For the present a great many people in the larger cities are housed in hotel complexes. While it is possible to move from a hotel to the place of work, it is virtually unheard of vice versa.

At the place of work, flats are usually provided which are comfortable enough, if a little spartan. Obviously a good deal will depend on where you are working — flats in the provinces can be very basic indeed and hot water and electricity will certainly be rationed. The main benefits of such housing are the proximity to work and the full involvement with it this implies. The disadvantages include never being able to get away from work (particularly important for teachers, who may be inundated with "visitors").

Hotels offer the advantages of a larger foreign community with the chance to meet workers from different fields. Although the foreign workers live in a special area, with their own flats, they can use the facilities of the rest of the hotel. These can include tennis courts, swimming pools and so on. There are also courses in Chinese, martial arts, calligraphy and various other traditional skills. The existence is undoubtedly more comfortable than in the place of work, but one can begin to feel cut off from the Chinese themselves.

The Unit

The Unit is the administrative division of any place of work. Its responsibilities spread much further than mere work, however, and covers just about every aspect of its employees' lives. It is the Unit that employs, arranges housing, gives permission for marriages, study and travel. For the foreign worker, almost as much as for his Chinese colleague, the Unit determines the quality of life.

Units vary from institute to institute, especially in their political colouring. Whilst most welcome foreigners sincerely and openly, there are still some which resent the priviledges foreigners are given and they make no secret of this. Try not to antagonise your Unit. If they take against you they can very easily make your life extremely difficult. Conversely, they can be very helpful in arranging extra visas, travel permits and even interpreters.

The Unit will assign you an interpreter to help with day-to-day problems. How useful they prove depends on the luck of the draw; it is worth complaining if they are of no use since the post is a coveted one and can lead to study abroad.

Most Units employing foreigners have a Foreign Affairs Office, and it is through this that most things are arranged. All problems should be directed through it. In the case of finding yourself up against a truly hostile Unit it is possible to appeal direct to the Ministry of Education and to arrange a transfer.

Each foreigner is issued with four cards by the Unit. These are:

(a) White card: This enables you to buy goods with *Renminbi* and allows discounts on trains, planes and in hotels.
(b) Green card: Resident's permit, used mostly when travelling.
(c) Red card: Work permit.
(d) Blue card: Medical card.

Education

School in China begins at the age of seven. Five years in Primary School are followed by five years in Secondary School (three years at Junior Middle and two years at Senior Middle). 1985 saw the end of free higher education except for teacher training. Higher education rewards academic ability by being open to students who compete for scholarships.

Children of foreign workers, if of school age, would benefit by being in the cities or Beijing itself. Only Shanghai and Beijing have English speaking schools, run by diplomatic missions for the children of their staff and a few others. Space is limited and it is best to write to the embassy or consulate in advance. They take children up to 13 and charge at least $3,000 a year. The alternatives are Chinese schools and self-help groups. In Beijing there are two middle and one primary school which accept foreign children. All classes are in Chinese, but they do run special language lessons. Most parents have been surprised at how quickly and easily their children pick up the language. The host institute will organise enrolment. Formal classes are usually supplemented by parents themselves, who group together to run their own lessons. Clearly this is only possible in a city supporting a number of Westerners.

Families

Many foreigners wish to bring their families with them to China and the Government recognises this, although they do not provide any official facilities for them.

The ideal position is for both partners to arrange employment before leaving. However, if this is not possible spouses can often be found jobs once they have arrived, although it is by no means certain. In Beijing there are an increasing number of Western companies that take on part-time and temporary workers, which can be contacted directly (approach embassies for lists). Otherwise it is usually the case of becoming an English teacher. Such positions can be arranged on the spot through an institute or by keeping one's ears open.

It is possible for one partner not to be employed at all; however, choosing not to work can quickly lead to intense boredom, loneliness and frustration which puts great strain on any marriage.

China is an easy place to take babies and young children. The Chinese love children, and nannies can be hired without problem. Medical care is good in the large cities and Hong Kong is easily accessible for any major health problems.

WORK AVAILABLE

Since the Chinese instigated the 'open-door' policy in the late '70s, it has employed an increasing number of foreigners to supplement its modernisation programme. Most of these have been in academic institutions, but recently they have been employed in other fields too. In 1988, there were well over 2,000 foreigners in Beijing alone and over the next few years the figure is expected to rise. The new policy is administered by *The Foreign Experts Bureau* of the State Council (FEB) but actual recruitment and day-to-day affairs are handled by the *Bureau of Foreign Affairs* of the Ministry of Education (BFA). The BFA puts out a pamphlet outlining its requirements and policies entitled, *Information for the Recruitment of Foreign Experts,* that can be obtained from the BFA itself or local embassies. In short, they are interested in three types of personnel: genuine experts in particular fields, media people and teachers.

General

There are a number of jobs which do not involve teaching, although one should always be prepared to do some teaching whatever field you happen to be working in. It is never a bad idea to pack a few English Language books before you go.

Most non-teaching jobs are presently in the media, although the market is expanding. All these jobs confer Foreign Expert (FE) status, the status given to most foreigners who work for the Chinese government (see below, under *Teaching*), and therefore enjoy much the same terms and conditions. However, these FEs are expected to work a full year with just one month's holiday and they also usually work a longer day and a six day week. The majority of jobs are in the capital and can begin at any time of the year.

Anyone who thinks their skills could be useful to the country's modernisation programme should write to the *Bureau of Foreign Affairs* (see below, under *Addresses*) enquiring about possible openings. In general, however, most jobs are in publishing or journalism.

The *Foreign Language Press* (FLP) in Beijing, (see below under *Addresses*) employs a fair number of FEs to work on its various publications. These divide into two categories: books and magazines. The FLP publishes a wide list of books in a number of languages. They include translations of classics, contemporary literature, history, political texts and so on. The magazines are basically propaganda aimed at the outside world to give a glowing impression of Chinese Socialism, although recently they have become a little less strident and more realistic. Titles include *China Reconstructs, China Women* and *Beijing Now*. They are produced in English, German, Spanish and Japanese. The work in both areas consists of 'editing and polishing' which in practice means taking literally translated copy and making it read properly. The work, while sometimes interesting, can become tedious as one wades through virtually incomprehensible "Chinglish".

There is also a daily English Language newspaper, the *China Daily,* and a news agency/wire service, *Xinhua*. Both these employ FEs as journalists and editors but do not expect to be a roving reporter, the work is basically the same as at the FLP, i.e. polishing.

CTV (China Television) broadcasts a few hours each day in English, both English lessons and the news, and Beijing Radio has a more extensive English service, including broadcasts to the rest of the world. Again, both employ FEs as polishers, although there is more scope here to get involved in other aspects of the work. They also require technicians and experienced producers to help upgrade their service.

Translators, polishers and editors should have several years experience in journalism, editing etc. and a good command of English or Chinese if the former is not their mother tongue.

The British Council

While the Council is active in China it employs relatively few people (ten in Beijing in 1988). Most of these are engaged in teacher training or lecturing rather than straight language teaching. The conditions are good, with FE status and pay plus an additional £6,000 or so deposited in a UK bank account. Candidates require at least the Royal Society of Arts qualification and several years experience and, more usually, an MA in a relevant subject. Applications should be made direct to the Council in London (see *Addresses* below).

Teaching

There are literally hundreds of higher education establishments in China, including universities, colleges, foreign language institutes, institutes of science and technology and so on. It is difficult to assess the relative status of these, but in general the universities are top of the pile. Nearly all of them hire foreigners, although the majority are taken on as language teachers. Each year there are nearly 700 posts, of which 400 are to teach English. Other languages taught include, in order of numbers employed: German, Japanese, French, Spanish and Italian. While there are opportunities to teach languages such as Arabic and Greek, these are rare. Other disciplines include literature, history, law, economics and all the sciences and technology. There is also an increasing demand for management training and any discipline connected with business.

Non-language teaching posts are generally under the auspices of various agencies, such as the UN and the EC, but there are opportunities for the independent teacher too. To teach the hard sciences or the arts one really needs to be a true expert with the appropriate qualifications, and to be perceived as such by the Chinese. Such is the interest in everything from the West that it is probably worth applying whatever one's speciality.

Most teachers in China end up teaching English, regardless of their original brief. Although some do teach their own subject it is quite common to go believing you are to teach one subject and end up teaching another. This is a result both of bureaucratic confusion and the very real need for language teachers. It is no defence to plead ignorance or lack of expertise.

The Chinese pedagogic tradition places great value on literature and written language. The result is an astounding imbalance in the curriculum for language teaching which has the absurd effect of producing tourist guides who can read Milton but who cannot tell you the way to the station.

The hierarchy of the various departments within an institute is as difficult to follow as the internal politics. There is usually no central office or secretary, but rather a bewildering Kafkaesque array of deans, vice-deans, year-heads and so on. It can make the simplest operation, such as photocopying, a lengthy business. One's best hope is to find the most senior person available.

The majority of teachers are contracted to teach 14 to 16 hours a week, but most people end up doing between 10 and 12 hours in the classroom. To this can be added office hours and the occasional unofficial lecture or seminar and everyone asks for help with translations, recordings, singing clubs and so on. These can be accepted at your discretion.

A large proportion of foreigners are employed in Beijing, but there are a great many opportunities elsewhere. (Most Foreign Teachers tend to work in the provinces). Although there is no guarantee, it is possible to state a preference for an area when applying. Choosing the capital, a big city or smaller town depends on your attitude to the work and expectations of the Chinese experience.

The academic year begins in early September. The year is divided into two semesters, running from September 1st to February 4th, and March 4th to July 31st.

The Chinese Government classifies teachers either as Foreign Teachers (FT) or Foreign Experts (FE). These are degrees of status, conferred usually according to qualifications and experience, which bring different conditions and privileges set by the BFA. Out of 400 English teachers employed in 1984, 240 were FEs and the rest FTs.

Foreign Teachers: FTs are very much the poor relations of FEs in terms of pay, conditions and privileges; indeed, they are virtually volunteer workers. FTs are usually under 25 and/or without an MA, although there is flexbility here. Some go straight from university, but it is unlikely that non-graduates will be accepted unless they show wide experience or true expertise in some area.

Foreign Teachers are recruited directly by institutions many of which are in the provinces, and by local education departments as well as by the Ministry of Education; all of these can be contacted through the Bureau of Foreign Affairs. Unlike Foreign Expert contracts, those of FTs are not standard and vary from institute to institute. This allows for a certain flexibility and it is worth negotiating over a number of points. It is quite possible, and normal practice, to change status once in China, especially if staying a second year (it is therefore inadvisable to sign a two year contract as an FT).

Foreign Teachers are expected to pay their own return fare to China. They are funded by the hiring institutes and not, like the Foreign Experts, by central government. Consequently their salaries are considerably lower. An FT can expect in the range of 350 to 450 *Yuan* a month (£115-£150) which is just about enough to live on. An FT's salary is paid entirely in the local money, *Renminbi,* which cannot be exchanged for Foreign Exchange Certificates (FEC) or hard currency (see *Currency,* above). In effect, your stay in China as an FT could actually cost you money, but while the FT's life may not be as comfortable as that of an FE, it would be wrong to think of it as a misery.

Most FTs are housed, rent free, usually in a flat on 'campus'. These flats are luxurious by Chinese standards but seem fairly spartan to Europeans (see the section, *Housing and Accommodation,* above).

Foreign Experts: FEs are paid according to qualifications and experience; salaries range from 650 to 1,000 *Yuan* a month (£165-£355). A single person can exchange 50% of this into Foreign Exchange Certificates but the figure drops for married couples, to 30% each. Since, in general the more FEC you have the better, if your spouse is working it is a good idea for him or her to acquire independent status so that they can exchange 50% too. This should be negotiated with the institute before leaving for China and confirmed in writing. Although FE contracts are standardised there is still room for negotiation. You will not be expected to sign a definitive contract until at least two months into the first semester, to give both sides a trial period. By this time you should be well aware of what to ask for. Sometimes FEs are asked to sign a provisional contract before leaving; if so, make sure this is only provisional and not the final agreement.

Foreign Experts are housed either on campus or, in the larger cities, in hotel complexes. As well as paying the rent and providing facilities, the Government will also pay for the full round trip airfare.

For those whose term of service is a year or longer, a spouse and children under 12 will be paid for if they accompany you for the full term, i.e. not just for a visit. It is possible to bring them out later, but this has to be negotiated with the hiring institute.

Those who work for a calendar (or academic) year are entitled to one month's vacation. Those who have worked half a year (or two semesters in succession but less than one year) will be entitled to a two-week vacation. The vacation time of those working in colleges and universities will correspond with the Chinese academic vacation in those institutions. Most teachers, by arranging their exams or classes carefully, manage to begin both their spring and summer breaks slightly early.

Foreign Experts also receive a vacation allowance (800 *Yuan* in 1986). Those who work just half a year will be given half the stipulated allowance. This allowance cannot be exchanged for foreign currency, and FEs who work for less than six months are not entitled to any allowance and will also have to pay for their fare back home as well as reimbursing the host institute for the expenses of their outward journey.

Other privileges of the FE include: income tax exemption, free transport to and from work and free medical treatment.

In theory, FE language teachers should have at least three years' experience of teaching a language or literature in a university or college, or five years' experience of teaching in senior schools. Experience can count for more than qualifications and thus it is not strictly necessary to have a PGCE (Post Graduate Certificate of Education) or RSA (Royal Society of Arts) and nor, for British applicants, is an MA mandatory (although it is preferred for American and Australian candidates). It is enough, for an FE, to have had some teaching experience and be over 25. However, having said this, the Chinese do greatly respect qualifications and they will certainly use them, as well as experience, to determine pay and conditions.

Application

The Bureau of Foreign Affairs recruits Foreign Teachers and Foreign Experts through China's embassies abroad. There is no publicity or advertising in the belief that China needs dedicated, genuinely interested workers who will, by definition, discover the opportunities for themselves. The country does not want people just out for the ride.

The individual establishments send requests for FTs and FEs to the BFA in Beijing, which is then responsible for recruitment. The BFA in turn informs the various embassies around the world, which handle incoming applications. Unfortunately this process allows room for much bureaucratic bungling and applicants can even find themselves teaching something totally removed from their own field.

When an application is received by an embassy it is screened to see if it fits the basic criteria. If so, the applicant is generally invited for an interview; if this goes well, you may be offered a job there and then, (although no specific job will have been marked out for you) and asked to decide. It is at this stage that one should stress any preference as to job location. It is best to accept tentatively. The application is forwarded to the BFA in Beijing where it is matched to a request by an institute. The institute is then informed of this and contacts the applicant directly. There can be a considerable time lag between these two stages of the process and a wait of several months is not unknown. When you do receive notification of the job it is best to ask for more details, such as your status, salary and conditions. This is an important stage, especially for the FT, as it sets the terms of employment. Having accepted formally you may be asked to sign a provisional contract, but it is quite normal to have very little in writing before you go.

You will be requested to apply for a visa from the embassy, often another lengthy process. You will probably hear nothing else at this stage, until a few weeks, even days, before your departure. Even the departure date won't be announced long in advance.

Once in China many issues, such as teaching hours, are open to negotiation. Usually a full contract will not be signed until after a two month probationary period. Any disagreement can be referred to the BFA in Beijing, although a threat to do so is usually enough. Similarly, a threat to write to the papers or to resign, should be sufficient if desperate. In general, try to clarify as many details as you can before leaving. Make sure you have agreed all points before signing a contract. It becomes virtually impossible to negotiate after you have put your name to one. Similarly, having negotiated successfully over an issue, ask for it to be written down immediately before memories blur. Always try to talk to the highest authority, since one of the reasons for any hedging is a fear of taking responsibility.

Applicants who do not receive a reply from an institute after three months can assume that the application has not been accepted. It is possible to apply at any time for the non-academic positions, while teaching jobs generally begin in September. Recruiting starts in January and it is advisable to begin early, both because this offers a wider choice and because it allows plenty of time for the lengthy bureaucracy to function. It is possible to apply later, indeed there are nearly always some last-minute posts available in July and August, but they could be anywhere.

Application can be made either direct to the BFA or through the embassy. The latter is preferred since you have a contact in this country with whom to discuss things and negotiate. In the UK the Chinese embassy has a special Education Section in Ealing, where all enquiries should be sent (see *Addresses,* below).

ADDRESSES

UK

Embassy of the People's Republic of China, Section of Education, 51 Drayton Green, West Ealing, London W13

Society for Anglo-Chinese Understanding, 152 Camden High Street, London NW1

The British Council, Overseas Education Appointment Department, 65 Davis Street, London W1Y 2AA.

China

Bureau of Foreign Affairs of the Ministry of Education (BFA), Ministry of Education, Beijing 100806, People's Republic of China

The External Relations Secretary, Chief of Recruiting and Placement Division, Box 300, Beijing, PRC (for general enquiries)

The British Council, The British Embassy, 11 Kwanghua Lu, Beijing

The Foreign Languages Press, 24 Baixwenxhuang Road, Beijing

China Daily, 2 Jintai Xilu, Beijing

Japan

Japanese Embassy, 43-46 Grosvenor Street, London W1 0BA.
The unit of currency is the yen (Y)
Rate of exchange: £1 = Y225.3

Japan has undergone massive development over the last 50 years and is now one of the world's major industrial nations with an ever-increasing efficiency rate as productivity levels keep ahead of labour costs. Japan is also the world's top creditor.

Working in Japan, although not such an easy option now that more and more foreigners are heading out there, can be rewarding, especially for those who are willing to stay for at least a year. The Japanese are becoming less insular and many find their sense of community refreshing. However, they can be difficult to get to know as their renowned politeness can lead to superficiality and they do have a tendency to be fairly conservative in their attitudes.

GENERAL FACTS

Population

Japan is one of the world's most crowded countries, with just over 122 million inhabitants spread over 377,800 square kilometres. There are four large islands — Hokkaido, Honshu, Shikoku and Kyushu — and several hundred smaller islands. The average population density is 323 persons per square kilometre, unevenly distributed between the sparsely populated island of Hokkaido in the north, and the dense conurbation of Tokyo.

Climate

Japan lies at the north-east corner of the Asian monsoon area, so the months of June and July are extremely wet and humid. Temperatures range from 22.1°F in Sapporo in winter to 80.2°F in Kagoshima in summer. The temperature range in Tokyo is 38.7°F in winter to 77.2°F in summer. In the winter months, snow is heavy in the island of Hokkaido and the north of Honshu, but is relatively unknown in Tokyo and further south.

Government

Under the new constitution of 1947, Japan renounced war and the threat and use of force. The constitution also withdrew power from the emperor, who remains as a symbol of the state and the unity of the people. The legislative power now lies in the hands of the Diet, composed of the House of Representatives and the House of Councillors. Representatives are elected for four years, councillors for six. The Prime Minister, who is nominated by the Diet, heads the 20-member Cabinet, which forms the executive branch of the government. The Conservatives have governed Japan almost without interruption since World War II.

Regional government is based on 47 prefectures, which are divided into 3,262 local administrations — 644 cities (*shi*) 1,974 towns (*machi*) and 644 villages (*mura*).

Cities

76.2% of Japan's population live in cities, well over half in the four metropolitan areas of Tokyo, Osaka, Nagoya and Kitakyushu. The largest cities are Tokyo, the capital, (11,806,729), Osaka (2,629,135), Yokohama (2,925,877), Nagoya (2,103,460), Kyoto (1,486,873), Kobe (1,401,928), Kitakyushu (1,060,470) and Sapporo (1,515,582). There are nine other cities with over 500,000 inhabitants.

Rural Life

Japan is a mountainous country, and only 16% of the land is cultivated. The farming population numbers about 24 million, living on some five million farms. The main crop is rice, of which twelve million tons are produced a year. Other crops include tea, tobacco, potatoes and wheat. Forestry accounts for 70% of the land area. The other major primary industry is fishing: with a catch of 14,000,000 tons a year, Japan has the world's most lucrative fishing fleet.

Labour Force

The work force numbers 59,270,000 or 47.5% of the population aged 15 and over. The distribution is 10% in agriculture; 64.5% in industry; 25.5% in services. The shortage of labour during the 60s has resolved itself, and now there are 1,610,000 unemployed. However, as a percentage of the labour force (about 2.7%), this compares favourably with most western countries.

Religion, Sport and Culture

Shintoism, the worship of nature and ancestors, is the traditional Japanese cult, which had a tremendous effect on the fighting spirit in World War II. However, it is not really a religion and most Japanese consider themselves to be adherents of both Shinto (93.4%) and Buddhism (74.1%). All religions are tolerated and Christianity is actively practised, but claims just 1% of the population.

Most western sports are represented, including athletics, soccer, rugby, baseball, and skiing with tennis and golf being the most popular and the most expensive. But the traditional Japanese sports are *sumo* (wrestling), *kendo* (fencing), *kyudo* (archery), as well as the more familiar martial arts of *judo, karate* and *aikido*.

Literature, theatre, art and music are also heavily influenced by the west, but the traditional Japanese forms are still alive — such as *noh* and *kabuku* drama, *bunraku* puppet theatre, *haiku* poetry, and music played on the *shakuhaci* (wind instrument), *koto* or *shamisen* (stringed instruments). Two other traditional art forms are flower arranging *(ikebana* or *kado*) and the tea ceremony (*chanoyu*).

FACTORS INFLUENCING EMPLOYMENT

Immigration

Britons require no visa to enter Japan and stay for up to six months as tourists, and it is possible to extend a tourist visa by applying to one of the immigration offices at least ten days before its expiry.

Work permits will only be issued for a specific job, and proof of the job offer must be shown. Application forms can be obtained from any Japanese embassy or consulate outside Japan.

As well as two complete application forms and two passport photographs, every application for a work permit must include two copies of each of the following documents: the applicant's curriculum vitae, and, where relevant, professional qualification certificate; a letter of guarantee from the employer, and a letter stating why it is necessary to employ an alien; the employment contract; the employing company's official brochure or prospectus, giving company information including commercial registration and a tax report; and a list of all the non-Japanese nationals already employed by the company. Processing the visa takes 6-8 weeks.

Because of the leniency in granting extensions to tourist visas, widespread abuse of the law has led to many "tourists" living and working in Japan. The penalty is a fine of up to Y100,000 or three years in prison. However, it is permissible to look for work on a tourist visa, and those who do find a job usually go to Korea, Hong Kong or Taiwan to get a work permit; this generally involves two trips, one to apply for and one to collect the permit.

It is also possible to apply for a cultural visa. These visas cater for those wishing to go to Japan to study but they also allow 10 to 15 hours work per week (as long as you attend a minimum of 20 hours of classes a week too), which brings in just about enough money to live on.

For information on visas and work permits, contact the *Japan Information Centre,* 9 Grosvenor Square, London W1X 9LB. Applications should be sent to the Visa Unit, *Japanese Embassy,* 43-46 Grosvenor Street, London W1.

Language

Japanese is a difficult language to learn, partly because it has three alphabets and bears absolutely no resemblance to any western language. Like Chinese, it is based on a series of picture symbols, each one representing a syllable. Although most Japanese can read the Roman alphabet, few can speak English outside Tokyo.

Cost and Standard of Living

The cost of living is very high, and like most industrialised countries there is an inflation problem. However, wages manage to keep up with prices, but it still comes as a shock to many foreigners how much of a month's pay cheque instantly goes on rent. In a city, it is normal to spend about £15 a day. Looking for work can take time and it would be unwise to go to Japan without a cushion of £400-£500. It may take about six months to begin to save some money.

Housing and Accommodation

For newcomers, home ownership in a Japanese city is a virtual impossiblity, since urban life is so solidly concentrated into apartment blocks. Even rented accommodation is hard to find, the scarcity being reflected in the virtually prohibitive rents. Heavy deposits (non-returnable) must always be paid when moving into rented accommodation, and it is quite normal to be asked for a six month deposit. Since contracts are theoretically renewed every 12 months the deposit must also be paid annually. This is known as "thank-you" money and is an accepted fact of life. Whenever possible take a Japanese friend with you when meeting the landlord.

Employers may help with finding accommodation, but otherwise estate agent windows are the best place to look. Sometimes it is possible to find free rent in exchange for English conversation lessons.

In Tokyo, most foreigners (*gaijins*) stay in *Gaijin Houses* (most of which advertise in the *Tokyo Journal*) which offer the best value, providing a bed in a dormitory for a minimum of £10 a night. These tend to get extremely full in the summer.

Health and Welfare

Japan's social welfare programme has taken enormous strides since the war, and the Social Insurance Act of 1961 laid down programmes for health insurance, pension insurance, unemployment insurance and industrial accident insurance. The Daily Life Protection Law of 1950 provides national assistance to those unable to earn a living wage, in order to maintain a minimum standard of living. Resident aliens are required to enrol with the local health insurance office (*kokuho*), unless they are covered by some other insurance scheme. Medical expenses tend to be high, but facilities are good in the cities.

Education

Education is free and compulsory between the ages of six and fifteen, but 95% of pupils stay on after the age of 15. Education is divided into five basic stages — kindergarden (up to the age of six); elementary school (six years); junior high school (three years); senior high school (three years), and college or university. As an alternative to senior high school, there are several technical colleges offering courses lasting up to four years. Japan has nine major universities — seven State-run (Tokyo, Kyoto, Sapporo, Sendai, Osaka, Kyushu and Nagoya), and two private (Keio and Waseda).

National Service

According to post-war treaties with the USA, Japan has been allowed to build up a self-defence force, which numbers over 260,000. Enlistment is purely voluntary, so aliens are not liable to conscription.

British Embassy and Consulate General

British Embassy, 1 Ichiban-cho, Chiyoda-ku, Tokyo 102.

British Consulate General, Hong Kong & Shanghai Bank Bldg., 45 Awajimachi 4-chome, Higashi-ku, Osaka 541.

CONDITIONS OF WORK

Wages

There is little legislative control over wages, which nevertheless manage to keep up with the retail price index. The pattern of Japanese wage levels contain some unique features, such as the generous fringe benefits, which amount to an average of 20% of a worker's actual wage. Another feature is the employers' response to company loyalty. Most Japanese will join a company on leaving school, and stay with the same employer until retirement. Thus wage increases are given regularly on the basis of length of service. Bonuses are also given as lump sums usually at six month intervals. These bonuses boost the average annual salary by about 25%. Because of these additional benefits, the wage levels vary as much with age and seniority as they do with skills and qualifications.

Hours

Since 1960, when the average working week was 44.7 hours, the five-day, 40-hour week has been slowly phased in. Most industries and offices now open only five days a week, and the average working week is already below 40 hours.

Holidays

As with wages, the allocation of annual paid holidays is often based on length of service within the company, but two weeks is usually the minimum. In addition the following national public holidays are observed: New Year's Day; Adults' Day (January 15); National Foundation Day (February 11); Spring Equinox (March 20); Emperor's Birthday (April 29); Constitution Memorial Day (May 3); Children's Day (May 5); Respect for the Aged Day (September 15); Autumnal Equinox (September 23); Health Sports Day (October 10); Culture Day (November 3); Labour Thanksgiving Day (November 23).

Safety and Compensation

Workmen's accident insurance is covered in the broad welfare programme. Enterprises with more than five workers are all compulsorily insured, with contributions shared by employers and employees. Smaller enterprises are required to provide their own insurance cover, with contributions paid entirely by the employers.

Trade Unions

National unions are virtually unknown in Japan: the union structure is based on individual enterprises, rather than on trades or professions. Thus there are over 73,700 unions, membership of which is not compulsory. About 12.5 million workers belong to unions, or 29% of the labour force. The main functions of unions is to take part in the annual collective bargaining negotiations held each spring.

Taxation

Tax is deducted at source and, if necessary, adjusted at the end of the tax year. Tax deductions — which rarely rise above 25% — also include social security payments. Temporary workers from abroad do not generally have to pay income tax in Japan, although it depends on the nature of the work.

WORK AVAILABLE

General

Looking for work in Japan from abroad can be a difficult process and the Japanese embassy cannot often help. However, it is possible to apply directly to companies and schools.

Work is easier to find once you are in Japan, since the Japanese prefer to deal with prospective foreign workers in person. Employment agencies are beginning to spring up in Japan, but on the whole the best method for seeking work is to read the English newspapers or contact companies or schools in person or by telephone. In Tokyo, many *Gaijin Houses* have notice boards with advertisements and they are often willing for you to use their phone number as a contact.

With the export industry growing at such a fast rate in Japan, there are opportunities for managerial, technical and professional staff as well as openings in the fields of finance and banking. Japanese companies and British companies that have branches or subsidiaries in Japan are increasingly willing to take foreigners on as regular employees.

There is also a lot of scope for editorial work, as well as translation, where English, other European and some Middle Eastern languages can all be used to varying degrees. Advertising agencies, together with publishers of newspapers, magazines and books, require proof-readers, editors and so on. A specialist knowledge of a language, with familiarity with legal or technical terminology for example, could be a great asset. Editorial work can be well paid but editing experience is probably necessary in most cases.

Non-teaching jobs tend to be scarce outside the big cities and it is worthwhile being willing to do some teaching while looking around. Teaching businessmen privately is a possible source of useful contacts.

Teaching

Teaching English is probably the most reliable full-time work to be found in Japan although, as in other fields of work, the competition is stiff, especially as a lot of money can be earned in this way. Experience is nearly always necessary and with more and more qualified teachers venturing out to Japan, it has become virtually impossible to get a work permit if you do not have a degree or TEFL qualifications.

There are about 450 English schools in Tokyo alone and over 225 in the rest of Japan. It is possible to write to them in advance and the bigger language schools send representatives abroad to recruit teachers, but the majority do not and those that do tend to give lower wages. It is usually better to seek work on the spot which allows you the chance to go to a selection of schools and compare conditions and so on. Some people manage to work for a number of schools at the same time.

For those looking for work once in Japan, most hiring is done in March and September. School terms begin in September, January and April and it is best to go a month or so before term starts.

There are a limited number of openings in Japanese state schools as teachers' assistants, but these are rare, as are vacancies at Japanese universities.

Teaching can be very well paid, £10-£15 being a fairly normal, good hourly wage. Salaried teaching in a language school tends to bring in less money than free-lance work but involves less travel around town which is an important consideration with transport costs being so expensive. Most schools will pay local transportation costs too. Teachers' pay varies from school to school so that a teacher with ten years' experience in one school could be paid less than a totally inexperienced teacher in another.

Besides the language schools, companies also organise classes for businessmen. These classes may take place actually within the company building or on school premises etc. Lessons are either very early in the morning or in the evening, to fit around working hours.

Lessons tend to be conversational more than theoretical, since Japanese students receive very thorough English grammar instruction for six years at school. This applies to private lessons too, whether with businessmen or university students etc. Private lessons of all kinds can be found by word of mouth, by advertising in the English papers, or by putting fliers through letter boxes (although the Japanese do prefer personal contact) and you can sometimes inherit work from foreigners who are leaving the country. Those with a flat may find it possible to organise group classes at home which can be very lucrative.

Jobs in Japan by John Wharton, published in the USA and distributed in Europe by Vacation Work Publications, includes an extensive directory of private schools and other organisations useful to the job-seeker. As well as giving advice on teaching prospects it gives advice on all types of work available and explains how to negotiate with employers etc. Vacation Work also distributes John Wharton's *Teaching Tactics for Japan's English Classrooms,* which is full of advice and material for those wishing to teach in Japan, including hints on grammar, activities, general methods and how to cope with Japanese students.

Newspapers

Publicitas Ltd., 525/527 Fulham Road, London SW6 1HF, represent Japan's leading financial and business daily *Nihon Keizai Shimbun* and the weekly trade and technical publications *Nikkei Ryutsu Shimbun* and *Nikkei Sangyo Shimbun.*

There are various English-language daily newspapers in Japan: the *Japan Times,* the *Daily Yomiuri,* the *Mainichi Daily News* and the *Asachi Evening News.* There is also the *Tokyo Journal* which appears monthly. Both *Nihon Keizai* (Japan Economic Journal) and *Toyo Keizai* (*Tokyo Business Today*) release certain editions in English and they both give information on Japanese business and industry.

See also the section on *Advertisements in the chapter Getting the Job.*

Labour Force

The work force numbers 59,000,000, or 48% of the population aged 15 and over. The distribution is 10% in agriculture; 64.5% in industry; 25.5% in services. The shortage of labour during the sixties has resolved itself, and unemployment rate is down to 2.8%.

SPECIFIC CONTACTS

English Teachers

Each year, about 200 UK nationals are recruited as teaching assistants of EFL by the Japanese Government, under its Japan Exchange and Teaching (JET) programme to work in secondary schools, technical schools, universities, local education authorities and private companies. Contracts are for one year.

The Programme is open to UK citizens under the age of 35 holding a Bachelor's degree from a UK university or polytechnic or college of higher education. Teaching qualifications and experience are an advantage but not essential.

Contracts begin in August. For recruitment, the period of application is usually from October to mid December.

For more information and application forms contact the JET Programme Officer, *Japan Information Centre,* 9 Grosvenor Square, London W1X 9LB.

Teachers are also needed to teach the resident British and American children in Japan, for whom a number of special international schools exist. A list of these schools is available from the Japan Information Centre, above address.

The *Overseas Educational Appointments Department, The British Council,*65 Davis Street, London W1Y 2AA, are notified of vacancies in Japanese state schools and also advertise their own vacancies in Japan in the UK press.

The Foreign Language Institute of Japan, Ikedayama House, 5-14-22 Higashi Gotanda, Shinagawa-Ku, Tokyo 141, Japan. FLI can offer work on a full time or casual basis to qualified TEFL teachers. Applicants should contact the Director, Mr M. Jack Sacripante.

The Japan Association of Language Teachers (JALT), c/o K.E.C., Sumitomo Seimei Building, 8F, Shijo Karasuma Nishi-Iru, Shimogyo-Ku Kyoto 600, runs a Job Information Centre for its members and publishes a monthly newsletter which lists jobs as well.

The Language Institute of Japan, Asia Centre, 4-14-1 Shiroyama Odawara, Kanagawa, 250 Japan, recruits teachers to teach adults on residential courses. Other full-time opportunities are available and LIOJ also runs Summer Workcamps for the training of Japanese teachers of English

TEFL qualifications or similar are required, or a background in business, economics, law etc., together with experience. Applicants should apply to the Director, at the above address.

Other Opportunities

JAC Recruitment (Japan Agency and Consultancy), 3rd Floor, College Hill Chambers, 23 College Hill, London EC4R 2RT, specialises in the recruitment of personnel for Japanese companies (in Japan and the UK). They are interested in graduates qualified in the following areas: management, finance, marketing and research, administration and secretarial. They also offer some temporary assignments as well as dealing with TEFL qualified English teachers. A good command of a foreign language is an advantage and casual inquiries are not encouraged.

Opportunties in Japan are also referred to in the following chapters (see Contents), which cover a wide range of professions:

British Government Departments   Transport, Tourism and Catering
Teaching

SHORT TERM WORK

The high cost of travelling to Japan prevents most Europeans from looking for temporary work there. Even if a job can be found in advance, it can easily take two months for an application for a work permit to be processed. But once you are in Japan, it it quite easy to pick up casual part-time employment, either as a main source of income, or to supplement the income for another job. A general meeting point and grapevine for young people in Tokyo is a hostel called *Okuba House* at 1-11-32, Hyakunin-cho, Shinjuku-ku. Their notice boards advertise vacancies that might interest foreigners. Another notice board is at English House, Ryokan, 2-23-8 Nishi-Ikebukuro, Toshima-ku too.

As with longer term work the competition is becoming increasingly fierce, but there are a wide variety of jobs on offer, as models, movie extras, teachers, waiter/waitresses, hosts/hostesses and other jobs in clubs, bars and restaurants etc.

Modelling jobs are not such an easy option as employers are more likely to ask for experience as the number of prospective models increases. Waiting and hosting jobs can be easier to come by but the work (and the pay) varies enormously, especially with hostessing which generally involves chatting to and dancing with Japanese businessmen. Acting can be an attractive prospect, but is fun rather than good money. Both radio and television networks may require foreigners to help with language programmes etc. There are about 150 broadcasting companies in Japan, the most important being the *Nippon Television Network* (NTV), the *Tokyo Broadcasting System* (TBS) and *TV Asahi; Nippon Hoso Kyokai* (NHK) is the only state network.

BRITISH COMPANIES
with branches, affiliates or subsidiaries in Japan

The British Chamber of Commerce in Japan, 3rd Floor, Kowa Building, No. 16, 9-20 Akasaka 1-Chome, Minato-Ku, Tokyo 107, produces a list of its members costing Y3020 (including air mail postage to the UK) to non-members. Payment is by bank draft payable to the Chamber.

Middle East and North Africa

In terms of the international labour situation, the oil producing countries of the Middle East and North Africa occupy a unique position. Fifty years ago, they were struggling economically and the only hope for development appeared to lie in some miraculous reclamation of the desert. The discovery and exploitation of oil has changed all that, and the revenue is now being ploughed back into development programmes and industry. Oil has been able to provide the money to pay wages that are among the highest in the world, particularly when the lenient tax systems are taken into consideration.

As would be expected of a sudden rise in revenue, the rate of development has been inconsistent with the boom in the economy, resulting in the familiar pattern: while there is money to invest in hospitals, roads, airports, defence systems, irrigation and so on, there is still a time lag in the training of native personnel to fill the labour needs, particularly among the managerial and skilled positions. Add this lack of training to the deeply ingrained absence of ambition (sometimes called "laziness") that seems to typify the Arab outlook on life, and it is clear to see why the American and European press is constantly flooded with advertisements for work in this part of the world.

An analysis of the personnel needs of the Arab countries reveals that the highest demands are in the countries that dominate the oil producing cartel i.e. Saudi Arabia, Libya, Iran, Bahrain, Qatar, Kuwait, Oman and the United Arab Emirates (particularly Dubai and Abu Dhabi, although the wealth of these two states also benefits the other five sheikhdoms, which would otherwise still be economically dependent on pearl diving, fishing and dates). Because opportunities in Saudia Arabia seem to be especially fruitful for the British expatriate, a special section is devoted to that country in this chapter.

The other countries in the Middle East and North Africa have more slowly developing economies, and therefore have far more limited opportunities for employment. Of these, the country with the strongest economy is possibly Israel, which — a Zionist state surrounded by Arab neighbours — does not fit into the general pattern, and is therefore not discussed in this chapter except to say that immigration is not encouraged (mainly for demographic reasons), and that some of the short term opportunities that exist (or kibbutzim and archaeological sites) are dealt with in the chapter on *Vountary Work.*

Returning to the richer nations — where oil is cheaper than water and foreign workers are in constant demand — the main attraction of working there is the extraordinarily high rate of pay that can be offered. In addition, income tax is universally low, and completely non-existent in Bahrain, Qatar, Saudi Arabia and the United Arab Emirates. What the advertisements sometimes fail to point out is the very different way of life that foreigners will be confronted with. Many of those who are lured by the high wages and other benefits, return home through boredom or loneliness, or else fall foul of the law or social taboos, or they find they cannot get used to the climate or to living without alcohol.

It should be pointed out too that the days of limitless oil reserves are over. With oil revenues in these states in decline, governments are coming under pressure to reduce their countries' dependence on foreign workers, while wages are not what they used to be; in some cases, were it not for the low or non-existent income tax, wages would be quite similar to what expatriates could command back home.

With regard to the types of work being offered, the situation is similar to the rest of the international labour market: the main needs are for top level management and qualified technical and professional staff. The range of technical and professional needs is enormous — accountants, computer staff, doctors, nurses, all types of engineers, technicians and fitters, and anyone with qualifications relating to the petro-chemical and construction industries. Mainly for social reasons, most of the jobs are offered on bachelor terms, and the number of jobs open to women is very restricted. Men are often preferred even as secretaries and nurses.

However, a redeeming feature of employment patterns in this area is that whole contracts are often put into the hands of foreign companies. This creates artificial communities which serve to protect the immigrant workers from the society for which they are working, as well as providing their own entertainments and sports and leisure facilities to offset the boredom that might otherwise occur. It is within these contract communities that the few vacancies for women exist, and there may also be provision for non-working wives and children to reside *en famille.*

Languages

The languages of the Middle East all belong to the Semitic group and are therefore related to each other. Arabic is the most widespread, and is spoken in Saudi Arabia, the Gulf States and North Africa. Within this area there are many linguistic variations — both written and spoken — and the most noticeable dividing line is that between the Maghreb areas (Morocco, Algeria, Tunisia and the western part of Libya) and countries to the east. The other major languages are Farsi (or Persian) and Hebrew (spoken only in Israel), both of which bear certain similarities to Arabic.

A knowledge of the appropriate native language is important, although all the countries in this area have a widely spoken European language as a stand-by — for instance English in Egypt and the Gulf States; French in Syria, Jordan and Algeria; Italian in Libya.

Customs and Culture

It is in the Arab world, perhaps more than anywhere else, that the expatriate westerner is forced to accept a totally alien way of life. As well as the strict code of social behaviour, the Arabs are very strongly governed by the Islamic religion, on which the laws of all Moslem countries are based. The North African countries have experienced sufficient European influence (French, Italian or British) to be able to cushion the blow for foreign workers. But it is in Saudi Arabia and some of the Gulf States that the new arrival must reconcile himself to a new and strange lifestyle. The newspaper stories of Britons receiving corporal punishment for manufacturing and selling alcohol — horrifying as the are to the majority of the British public — are not so much examples of "the uncivilised legal and penal system", as an indication of the inability of many westeners to integrate themselves into the Arab world. In isolated cases, Europeans have been given the same punishment ever since they were first allowed into Saudi Arabia. Only the recent largescale influx of foreign workers has brought these cases to the attention of the outside world. As other examples of the Saudi legal system: the penalty for petty theft is to have your right hand cut off; the penalty for rape is to be stoned to death, using small stones to prolong the punishment. The death penalty is statutory for many crimes involving violence as well as serious cases of theft, etc.

Saudi Arabia

Opportunities for British citizens interested in professional, skilled and semi-skilled work exist on a relatively large and continually expanding scale in Saudi Arabia.

The UK in particular is seen as an ideal source of talented senior staff for recruitment to the Kingdom. English is the main language of commerce, and British educational and professional qualifications are highly respected there The historical tie which the British have with the Arab world is also an important factor.

Saudi Arabia's economic development began with the discovery of the first oilfield in Damman in 1938. With the flow of oil and the formation of the Organisation of Petroleum Exporting Countries (OPEC) in 1973, major and long-standing changes have occurred in the economic, political and social spheres. In addition to oil, Saudi Arabia has also started to produce gold silver and copper.

Foreigners seeking work in the Kingdom must first obtain a work permit The work permit must be applied for by the prospective employee's employer or sponsor in Saudi Arabia. When this has been obtained it should then be forwarded to the *Royal Embassy of Saudi Arabia,* 30 Belgrave Square London SW1, which will then issue a visa.

Work Available

Saudi Arabia's economy continues to grow with a continuing demand fo properly qualified and suitably experienced personnel, although th government has recently taken steps to reduce the number of foreign workers in the country. As the mainstay of the Kingdom's national economy, oil accounts for some 70% of the Gross National Product, and 90% of its exports. With the introduction of the fourth Five Year Plan in 1985, emphasis has been placed on the development of an expanding economic base that is not so dependent on the sale of crude oil; and which depends on the implementation of large-scale capital projects. The Saudi Industrial Development Fund (SIDF) was established to provide investors with 50% of the basic costs of industrial projects and it has financed over 600 major projects in the last five years.

In these circumstances it is hardly surprising that nearly one fifth of the Saudi workforce is involved in the construction business, which is also the biggest single source of expatriate employment. A useful list of current tenders is published in the *Middle East Economic Digest,* available on subscription from MEED, 21 St. John Street, London WC1.

Areas where the largest contacts are currently being secured are: road construction and drainage, school and office construction, airconditioning, telecommunications systems, and street networks and water reservoirs.

The *British Embassy's Commercial Department,* PO Box 94351, Riyadh, may be able to offer general advice on working opportunities in Saudi Arabia.

British Embassy and Liaison Office

British Embassy, Al Hamra, PO Box 94351, Riyadh 11693.
British Consulate General, PO Box 393, Jedda 21411.

Newspapers

Advertisements may be placed in the English language daily:

Arab News, Saudi Research and Marketing Building, Jeddah, PO Box 4556, Saudi Arabia.

See also the section on *Advertisements* in the chapter *Getting the Job.*

SPECIFIC CONTACTS

Consultants and Agencies

ARA International, Edman House, 17-19 Maddox Street, London W1R 0EY — the largest management recruitment company for Saudi Arabia, recruits a wide range of engineers, managerial, professional, technical and craftsmen personnel for major developments in oil, petrochemicals, telecommunications, marine, medical and defence, throughout the Middle East.

Atkinson Compton Associates Ltd., ACA House, 177 Moulsham Street, Chelmsford, Essex CM2 0LD — occasionally offer work to experienced quantity surveyors, including pre and post contract duties. Contracts are for one year, renewable.

Echo Consulting Services Ltd., Braconash Road, Leyland, Preston, Lancs. PR5 1ZE — recruits technical people for Al Hoty Establishment in Saudi Arabia, which services ARAMCo (Arabian American Oil Co). Echo also recruits for other Middle East companies on an *ad hoc* basis as well.

Medicine and Nursing

ARA International, Edman House, 17-19 Maddox Street, London W1R 0EY — serves the requirements of private and public sector hospital staffing mainly in the Middle East and has vacancies for all levels of medical personnel.

Al Mouwasat Hospital, PO Box 282, Damman 31411 — offers one and two year contracts to doctors, head nurses and supervisors, and other administrative department heads. All certificates should be certified by the Saudi Arabian Embassy.

BNA International, 3rd Floor, 443 Oxford Street, London W1R 2NA — recruit nurses for hospitals in Dhahran, Jedda, Khamis Mushayt and Riyadh. RGNs must have a minimum of two years post registration, with some opportunities for ENs with two years post-enrolment experience as well as for midwives, lab technicians, radiographers etc. Contracts are for a year.

Other Countries

IMMIGRATION AND WORK PERMITS

Methods of obtaining the necessary work and residence permits vary from country to country, but the embassies in London are usually not involved in the procedure. In every country in this part of the world, immigrants will be amazed at the amount of bureaucratic paperwork that has to be filled out (usually in triplicate, with photos) at each stage of the application. Most of the forms will be printed in several languages, but in some cases they must be completed in Arabic, or accompanied by an official translation into Arabic.

A few guidelines are given below for each of the countries offering a substantial amount of work, along with the addresses of the embassies in London, although in most cases these are not involved in processing work or residence permits.

Bahrain

Application for a work permit is made by the employer to the Immigration Authorities in Bahrain. *The Embassy of the State of Bahrain* is at 98 Gloucester Road, London SW7 4AU.

Kuwait

Work permits are obtained in advance by the employer in Kuwait. *The Embassy of the State of Kuwait,* 45 Queen's Gate, London SW7, cannot offer assistance, and suggests placing an advertisement in the classified section of a Kuwaiti newspaper through the *Arab Advertising Agency,* PO Box 2221, 13023 Safat, Kuwait.

Morocco

Anyone wishing to take up employment in Morocco must obtain a work permit, issued by the Ministry of Labour in Morocco on request of the prospective employer. No one can enter paid or unpaid employment without authorisation from the Ministry. Applications should be addressed to the *Ministère de l'Emploi,* Shellah, Rabat, Morocco. Students who want information about work camps should contact *Chantier Jeunesse Maroc,* 24 avenue Madagascar, Rabat, Morocco. The *Moroccan Embassy* is at 49 Queen's Gate Gardens, London SW7 5NE.

Oman

The employer must first obtain a Labour Clearance from the Directorate General of Labour, *Ministry of Social Affairs & Labour,* PO Box 560, Muscat and a "No Objection Certificate" from the Directorate General of Immigration, Oman. Upon arrival, a residence permit (valid for two years renewable) must be obtained.

Further details from the *Embassy of the Sultanate of Oman,* 44A/B, Montpelier Square, London SW7 1JJ.

United Arab Emirates

The Embassy of the United Arab Emirates, 48 Prince's Gate, London SW7, suggests that those considering employment in the UAE should write to the *Ministry of Labour,* PO Box 809, Abu Dhabi; or to *ARA International,* 17-19 Maddox Street, London W1R 0EY — but are otherwise unable to help.

Other Countries

There is far less demand for British workers in the other countries of the Middle East and North Africa, but the embassies listed below may be able to provide information on procedures, etc. In many cases, however, the reply will be that they are not involved in the issuance of work permits.

Algerian Embassy, 54 Holland Park, London W11.
Embassy of the Arab Republic of Egypt, 19 Kensington Palace Gardens, London W8.
Iraqi Embassy, 21 Queen's Gate, London SW7.
Embassy of Israel, 2 Palace Green, London W8.
Jordan Embassy, 6 Upper Phillimore Gardens, London W8.
Lebanese Embassy, 21 Kensington Palace Gardens, London W8.
Embassy of the Syrian Arab Republic, 8 Belgrave Square, London SW1.
Tunisian Embassy, 29 Prince's Gate, London SW7.

BRITISH EMBASSIES AND CONSULATES

In the list below, E = Embassy, CG = Consulate General.

Résidence Cassiopée, Bâtiment B, 7 Chemin des Glycines, Algiers, Algeria (E).

Ahmed Ragheb Street, Garden City, Cairo, Egypt (E).
3 Mina Street, Roushdy, Alexandria, Egypt (CG).

PO Box 114, 21 Government Avenue, Manama, Bahrain (E).

PO Box 248, Abu Dhabi, United Arab Emirates (E).

PO Box 65, Dubai, United Arab Emirates (E).

PO Box 3, Doha, Qatar (E).

Sharia Salah Ud-Din, Karkh, Baghdad, Iraq (E).

192 Rehov Hayarkon, Tel Aviv, Israel (E).

PO Box 87, Abdoun, Amman, Jordan (E).

6 Kuwait Investment Company Building, Fifth Floor, Ahmad Al-Jabir Street, Kuwait (E).

PO Box 300, 13003 Safat (E).

17 boulevard de la Tour Hassan, BP 45, Rabat, Morocco (E).
60 Boulevard d'Anfa, BP 762, Casablanca, Morocco (CG).

British Interests Section, Australian Embassy, Quartier Malki, 11 Rue Mohammed Kurd Ali, Kotob, PO Box 37,Damascus, Syria.

5 Place de la Victoire, Tunis, Tunisia (E).

PO Box 1287, Sana'a, Yemen Arab Republic (E).

WORK AVAILABLE

Because of the vast amount of work available in the Middle East and North Africa, these opportunities are dispersed among the chapters in the first two sections of the book, namely *Getting the Job,* especially the section *Consultants and Agencies,* and every chapter in the section on *Specific Careers* (with the most specific references appearing in the chapters *Computer Services, Medicine and Nursing, Oil, Mining and Engineering* and *Military Service (Foreign Armed Forces).* As already stated jobs on kibbutzim and archaelogical sites in Israel are dealt with in the chapter on *Voluntary Work,* as are opportunities for other unpaid work in the less developed areas.

Latin America

In spite of Latin America's extremely rapid economic growth during recent years, the registered growth has not yet enabled national economies to absorb and fully utilise the potential human resources. In 1970, of the entire population of Latin America, an average of only 31% was economically active, compared with 45% in the developed regions of the world. In other words, the utilisation of the potential of human resources in Latin America is still significantly small.

A detailed study of the structure of the labour market and of the professional structure of the active population reveals that Latin America's labour is characterised by a fundamental disequilibrium. On the one hand there is a large unskilled or semi-skilled workforce which is very often under-utilised especially in agriculture, while on the other hand there is a persistent demand for high-level and skilled technical and managerial manpower.

Despite the efforts made by some Latin American Governments to fight against illiteracy, to improve the education of the working population and to expand the capacity of their educational systems, a number of countries are not yet in a position to prepare a sufficient number of students for the various professional tasks in demand. The educational system often has difficulty in providing the requisite occupational skills. This is caused in part by the fact that a considerable proportion of the children or young students leave school at an early stage, without reaching a minimum level of education or a minimum level of skill.

There is also a lack of teaching personnel, especially in the highest-level technical and scientific field. Even at the operating level, the need for medium-level technicians is growing faster than the ability of the educational systems to produce them. Medium-level education, apart from the necessity to be continuously extended, needs also to be more oriented towards technical professions.

Vocational training programmes — despite valuable assistance offered by international organisations, especially the ILO — have still to be improved, including training of instructors, managers and personnel for rural development, taking into account also the important functions of on-the-job training in public and private services and undertakings.

As with many other developing countries those in Latin America have been, and continue to be, confronted with a considerable outflow of highly qualified personnel. The phenomenon concerns in particular scientists, engineers and physicians, professions for which education and training are necessarily of a long-term, capital intensive nature. It is often difficult to replace those persons from within the local labour market.

It emerges from the above analysis and it is confirmed by governments and private firms that there is a general continuous lack of highly-qualified personnel in many sectors of the economy. Scientists, university professors (and other teaching personnel and vocational training instructors), engineers, technicians, medical and para-medical personnel, agricultural economists, as well as managerial personnel are constantly needed in a number of Latin American countries.

Confronted with this problem of immediate needs for special skills, Latin American governments have pursued supplementary policies for obtaining the additional highly qualified manpower required. One method is through multilateral and/or bilateral technical co-operation programmes which place experts at the disposal of developing countries for a fixed period of time. Another is by sending national workers abroad to be trained in developed countries, however, this sometimes has the disadvantage that the worker chooses to settle in the country where he has received his training. The third method is immigration, which enables specific needs to be met through the recruitment abroad of high and medium-level manpower who will complement, but not compete with, the national human resources.

It was in pursuit of this last method that the Latin American member governments requested the Intergovernmental Committee for Migration to initiate its Selective Programme in 1965. The principle aim is to transfer highly-qualified human resources from developed countries to priority sectors of the economy where they are lacking. It is a vital element in the overall transfer of science and technology to developing countries in order to enable those countries to realise their own development strategy and to make possible their economic and social growth.

Permanent job vacancies exist for the following occupations: industrial engineers (mechanical, electrical, electronics), engineering technicians in the same branches, physical scientists and related technicians, life scientists, economists, university teachers (in scientific branches), high-level production technicians. Details of the main receiving countries' immigration and employment policies are outlined below under the heading *Immigration and Work Permits*.

Languages

Apart from the many native Amerindian languages, the almost universal language of Latin America is Spanish. The main exceptions are Brazil — where the official language is Portuguese — and the few former colonies and possessions of other European countries (i.e. French, English and Dutch). Apart from the former British territories (e.g. Guyana, Belize), English is not widely spoken. Those who already speak Spanish or Portuguese should be warned that there are many variations between the European languages and their South American counterparts.

Politics and Ideology

Despite the undeniable attractions of emigrating to South America, many

Europeans are unwilling to take this step because of an inability to reconcile themselves to the political and social policies that exist in some of the countries. Because of the rapid turnover of governments and the consequent changeability of policies, full consideration of the various political regimes is not given here, but in recent years many political and social practices have been exposed which may be unacceptable to potential immigrants. These practices include serious and widespread violation of human rights (particularly the detention and torture of political prisoners), exploitation of the native Indian population, support of nuclear power, and destruction of the ecology. Many countries have military regimes or dictatorships which do not tolerate freedom of speech or anything that smacks of political opposition.

If you have strong political or social views, and would like to know whether your work and residence in South America might be supporting these policies, you can check the situation with one of the interested pressure groups, such as *Amnesty International* (British Section, 5 Roberts Place, London EC1R 0EJ), *Friends of the Earth, Survival International,* etc.

IMMIGRATION AND WORK PERMITS

Employment in all Latin American countries is subject to obtaining work and/or residence permits. In general, the procedure is to find a job, then the employer applies for a work permit on your behalf. Residence permits will normally be issued on production of a valid work permit. For some countries, residence permits may be issued without a firm job offer, provided certain other criteria are fulfilled, e.g. financial viability, character references, health certificates and political testimonies. In most cases, residence permits must be obtained before arriving in the country.

In general, the embassies and consulates in Britain tend not to be very helpful, even in supplying the simplest information, and none of them is in any way involved in finding or offering employment. If pressed, most will send at least a circular describing the red tape involved, and refer enquirers to other addresses for further information.

Argentina

Enquiries about visa requirements should be addressed to the Argentine interests section at the Brazilian Embassy, 111 Cadogan Gardens, London SW3.

Bolivia

Immigration is no longer encouraged. All enquiries should be made to *Consejo Nacional de Immigración,* Ministerio de Migración, Avenida Arce esq. Belisario Salinas, La Paz, Bolivia.

Brazil

Work permits can be obtained in any of the following ways: through a contract of employment with a Brazilian employer, certified by the Brazilian Ministry of Justice; through an application by a prospective employer in Brazil to the Brazilian Ministry of Labour for permanent stay in the country; or through capital transfer of US$100,000 in order to establish commercial or industrial activities. Details are set out in a circular issued by the *Brazilian Embassy, Consular Section,* 6 St. Alban's Street, London SW1Y 4SG.

Chile

Residence permits are required by all those who wish to work in Chile or stay more than 90 days for any purpose. Applications for residence permits will be considered individually by the *Chile Embassy, Consular Section,* 12 Devonshire Street, London W1N 2DS. Enquiries about employment, accompanied by information on your qualifications, experience and type of employment being sought, should be addressed to the *Servicio Nacional de Empleo,* Avenida Independencia 2, 3er Pabellón, Santiago, Chile.

Columbia

Enquiries about immigration and work permits should be addressed to the *Columbian Consulate,* Suite 10, 140 Park Lane, London W1Y 3DF. Procedures for obtaining visas are set out in the circulars *Documentation Required when Applying for Residents' Visas.*

Guyana

Information on immigration is obtainable from the Passport and Consular Section, *Guyana High Commission,* 3 Palace Court, Bayswater Road, London W2 4LP, from whom the leaflet *Notes on Conditions in the Republic of Guyana* is also available. Although preference in employment is given to Guyanese nationals, non-nationals who possess certain skills can secure employment on contractual bases.

Paraguay

Opportunities for work and residence are excellent, and the requirements for establishing residence are minimal — a passport, a health certificate and character references (an offer of work is not essential). The *Paraguay Embassy, Consular Section,* Braemar Lodge, Cornwall Gardens, London SW7, is not involved in issuing visas.

Peru

A definite job offer is a pre-requisite to obtaining a work permit. Applications for work permits must be made by the employer through the *Peruvian Ministry of Foreign Relations.* Information and assistance can be offered by the *Peruvian Consulate General,* 52 Sloane Street, London SW1X 9SP.

Uruguay

Residence permits are issued upon submission of a variety of documents testifying physical, mental, political and financial soundness. The details are set out in the circular *Formalities to be Complied with by Applicants for Permanent Residence in Uruguay,* available from either the *Uruguay Embassy, Consular Section,* 48 Lennox Gardens, London SW1 or the *Consulate of Uruguay,* Room 216, Royal Liver Building, Liverpool.

Venezuela

Despite the enormous revenue from oil, Venezuela has resisted the large-scale development that is characteristic of many of the Middle East states. Immigration, even of high level technical and managerial personnel, is therefore still restricted, and is controlled on a quota basis. Application for a work permit must in the first instance be made by the employer in Venezuela, and he must also act as sponsor for obtaining a residence permit. *The Venezuelan Embassy, Consular Section,* 56 Grafton Way, "Bello Lodge", London W1P 5LB, can offer little practical help or advice, and tends to refer enquirers to ICM (see below).

BRITISH EMBASSIES AND CONSULATES

In the list below, E = Embassy; HC = High Commission; CG = Consulate General; C = Consulate. Vice-Consulates are not listed.

British Interests Section, Swiss Embassy, Dr. Luis Agote 2412-52, Buenos Aires, Argentina.

Avenida Arce 2732-54, Casilla 694, La Paz, Bolivia. (E).

SES, Quadra 801, Conj. K, Lote 8 (Caixa Postal 07-0586), 70 408 Brasilia, DF, Brazil (E).
Avenida Paulista 1938/17, Caixa Postal 846, Saõ Paulo, Brazil (C).
Praia de Flamengo 284, Caixa Postal 669, 20 010 Rio de Janeiro, Brazil (C).

La Concepción 177, Casilla 72-D, Santiago, Chile (E).
There are also British Consulates in Arica, Punta Arenas and Valparaiso.

Calle 98, No. 3-9, Piso 4, Box 4508, Bogota, Colombia (E).
Carrera 44, No. 45-57, Box 706, Barranquilla, Colombia (C).
Edificio Garces No. 410, Box 1326, Cali, Colombia (C).

Apartado 815, Edificio Centro Colon 1007, San Jose, Costa Rica (E).

Avenida Independencia 506, PO Box 818, Santo Domingo, Dominican Republic (C).
PO Box 314, Avenida Gonzalex Suarez 111, Quito, Ecuador (E).
Casilla 8598, Guayaquil, Ecuador (C).

Edificio Financielo, Torre II, Nivel 7, Zona 4, Guatemala City (E).

3rd Floor, Edificio Palmira, Apartado Postal 290, Tegucigalpa, Honduras (E).
Terminales de Puerto Cortes, Aptdo. 298, San Pedro Sula, Honduras (C).

Lerma 71, Col. Cuauhtémoc, Mexico City 0 6500, PO Box 96 bis, Mexico (E).
There are also British Consulates in Acapulco, Cuidad Juarez, Guadalajara, Merida, Monterrey and Tampico.

El Raparto "Los Robles", Iera Etapa, Carretara de Masaya, Managua, Nicaragua (E).

Via Espãna 120, Aptdo. 889, Panama City (E).

Calle Presidente Franco, Casill de Corre 404, Asunciòn, Paraguay (E).

Edificio Pacifico Washington, Avenida Arequipa, PO Box 854, Lima, Peru (E).

Andres Martinez 400, Casilla 265, Arequipa, Peru (C).

Calle Marco Bruto 1073, Montevideo, Uruguay (E).

Edificio Torre Las Mercedes, Pwo 3, Cuidad Comercial Tamanaco, PO Apartado 1246, Caracas 1010A, Venezuela (E).

WORK AVAILABLE

Newspapers

Argentina's principal English language paper *The Buenos Aires Herald* is represented by Frank L. Crane Ltd., 5-15 Cromer Street, Grays Inn Road, London WC1H 8LS, as are the Brazilian newspapers *O'Estado de S. Paulo* (Sao Paulo) and *Jornal do Brasil* (Rio de Janeiro). See also the section on *Advertisements* in the chapter *Geting the Job.*

Specific Contacts

Apart from the various addresses quoted under *Immigration and Work Permits,* above, the following organisations are involved in migration and employment in Latin America.

Intergovernmental Committee for Migration (ICM), 17 route des Morillons, 1211 Geneva 19, Switzerland — runs a programme for assisting in the emigration of European technical and professional workers to Latin American countries. ICM has offices throughout Latin America, and issues free booklets and fact sheets on aspects of life and work in all these countries. (See the *International Organisations* chapter).

Human Resources Management (HRM), Jose Abascal 45, 28003, Madrid, Spain — an executive search consultancy specialising in the selection and location of high level managers for the Spanish, Portugese and Latin American markets. Interested applicants who speak fluent Spanish and/or Portugese should send their curricula vitae.

Other Opportunities

Information and advice on job opportunities in Latin America can be obtained from the *Hispanic and Luso Brazilian Council,* Canning House, 2 Belgrave Square, London SW1X 8PJ, which produces a leaflet entitled *Latin America: Notes on opportunities and Travel,* available to non-members for £1.

Journey Latin America Ltd., 16 Devonshire Road, Chiswick, London W4 2HZ, recruits personnel for its overland tours in South America; see the *Transport, Tourism and Catering* chapter for further details.

Other references to employment in Latin America will be found in the various chapters of the *Specific Careers* section, and in the chapter *Getting the Job,* especially the section *Consultants and Agencies.*

Hong Kong

Hong Kong Government Office, 6 Grafton Street, London W1X 3LB
Currency: HK$ = 100 cents
Rate of Exchange: £1 = HK$ 13.1

The success of Hong Kong as a leading manufacturing and commercial centre in Asia, and its strong links with the UK, make for a number of employment opportunities for British citizens in the colony.

GENERAL FACTS

Hong Kong consists of more than 200 islands and islets, and a part of the mainland coast east of the Pearl River estuary adjoining the Chinese province of Guangdong (Kwangtung). The total land area is only 409 square miles. Victoria, on Hong Kong island, is the capital and commercial centre.

The New Territories, leased from China in 1898, are to be returned to Chinese control in 1997. Under the Sino-British Joint Declaration, signed in 1985 by the British and Chinese governments, Hong Kong will become a Special Administrative Region (SAR) within China, although the Declaration guarantees "to preserve Hong Kong's unique economic position and way of life for 50 years after 1997" Hong Kong will exercise a high degree of autonomy (except in such areas as defence and foreign affairs), with little change in its economy. Although the situation after this is far from clear, the general consensus is that it is in Chinese interests to maintain Hong Kong's position as an important manufacturing and commercial centre. At present, a draft Basic Law is being drawn up to determine the constitutional framework under which the SAR will be governed.

Hong Kong's land area is mostly steep, unproductive hillside. There is 9.2% agricultural land and some 16% built-up area.

The climate is sub-tropical and monsoonal, the winter is cool and dry, the summer, hot and humid.

The colony is one of the most densely populated areas in the world, there are roughly 17,000 people per square mile.

The total population in 1986 was about 5,533,000, 98% of whom are Chinese. Cantonese is the spoken language of the majority of the people, but several other Chinese dialects are also spoken. The English and Chinese languages have been given equal status and use in government business.

Religions practised in Hong Kong are predominatly Buddhist and Toaist but include the Christian, Hindu, Islamic, Jewish and Sikh faiths.

FACTORS INFLUENCING EMPLOYMENT

British citizens have an automatic right to land in Hong Kong, and do not require visas for employment, for education, to establish or join in any business, or for residence.

An outline of the Hong Kong visa requirements for those who are not British Citizens appears in a free leaflet called *Do You Need a Visa For Hong Kong?,* available from the *Hong Kong Immigration Department,* 61 Mody Road, Kowloon, Hong Kong; or from the *Hong Kong Government Office,* 6 Grafton Street, London W1X 3LB.

Advice on individual cases should be addressed to the *British Passport Office,* Clive House, Petty France, London SW1.

British Trade Commission

British Trade Commission, PO Box 528, Bank of America Tower, 12 Harcourt Road, Hong Kong.

Trade Unions

In 1987 there were 458 trade unions consisting of 415 employees' unions, 29 employers' associations and 16 mixed organisations of employees and employers. The total trade union membership was roughly 405,000.

WORK AVAILABLE

Hong Kong's industries are mainly export-oriented, with light manufacturing industries — producing mainly consumer goods — predominating. The colony's exports account for roughly 95% of domestic production.

The main manufacturing industries include: textiles and clothing; electronics; watches, clocks and accessories; plastics; light metals; machinery and machine tools; shipbuilding and repairing; and aircraft engineering. One third of the workforce is employed in the manufacturing sector.

Newspapers

Advertisements can be placed direct in the English language daily: *South China Morning Post,* Classified Advertising Department, 6/F Morning Post Building, Tong Chong Street, Quarry Bay, Hong Kong.

See also the section on *Advertisements* in the chapter *Getting the Job.*

Labour Force

In 1987 the total labour force was reported at 2,790,000. The labour force is divided as follows: 1.4% in agriculture; 41.5% in industry; and 32.4% in services. The unemployment level in 1987 was 1.7%.

SPECIFIC CONTACTS

Inquiries about specific contacts in Hong Kong may be addressed to *The Hong Kong Government Office* (address above); or *The Hong Kong Association,* 43 King William Street, London EC4; or the *Hong Kong Trade*

Development Council, 14 Cockspur Street, London SW1, who may also be able to help with general inquiries.

Banking

N M Rothschild and Sons Ltd., 16th Floor, Alexandra House, Chater Road, Central Hong Kong — occasionally requires staff for its offices in Hong Kong (see the chapter on *Banking and Accountancy* for further details).

Civil Service

Hong Kong Government Office, 6 Grafton Street, London W1X 3LB — recruits graduates for positions in public administration, personnel management, economic services, environmental control, finance, housing, monetary affairs, security, social services, education, and trade and industry in the Hong Kong civil service. However, their policy is to recruit first locally, and then abroad if they cannot find a suitably qualified candidate.

Computers

Kramer Westfield Associates Ltd., 5 The Avenue, Egham, Surrey TW20 9AB — recruit computer designers with specialised experience for contracts in Hong Kong.

Higher Education

The Association of Commonwealth Universities, John Foster House, 36 Gordon Square, London WC1H 0PF — provides a service through which both The Hong Kong Polytechnic and the City Polytechnic of Hong Kong invite applications for recruitment to their teaching staff.

Nursing

International Private Nursing Service Ltd., Room 1620, Prince's Building, Central Hong Kong — recruit SRN's for nursing work in the colony.

Police

The Royal Hong Kong Police Force, Hong Kong Government Office, Police Appointments, 6 Grafton Street, London W1X 3LB, recruits suitably qualified single male applicants from the UK Police, Armed Services, Industry and Higher Education. See *The Police* in the *Specific Careers* section.

Other Opportunities

See the chapters on *Au Pair and Domestic, Banking and Accountancy, Military Service* and *International Organisations,* and the section *Consultants and Agencies* in *Getting the Job* for other opportunities.

BRITISH FIRMS

with branches, affiliates or subsidiaries in Hong Kong

The British Trade Commission, PO Box 528, Bank of America Tower, 12 Harcourt Road, Hong Kong, issues a free list of British companies on request.

Singapore

Singapore High Commission, 2 Wilton Crescent, London SW1
Currency: Singapore $1 = 100 cents
Rate of Exchange: £1 = S$3.4

The collapse of oil prices in 1986 has checked Singapore's rapid economic expansion; however, strong historical ties with the UK and a series of special employment and residence schemes have created good opportunities for Britons seeking long term work in Singapore.

GENERAL FACTS

Singapore consists of the island of Singapore and 57 islets inside its territorial waters. Singapore's total land area is about 225 square miles, 90% of which is occupied by the main island. Some 40% of the total land area is built-up area, with a further 11% farming land, and some 4% forests.

The island can be divided into three regions: the central hilly region; the relatively flat eastern region; and the western area of hills and valleys.

Singapore has a fairly uniform temperature, high humidity and abundant rainfall. Average daily temperature is 26.6° C.

The population of Singapore is about 2,590,000, increasing at an annual rate of 1.1%. There are about 10,380 people per square mile.

The population consists of 76.3% Chinese, 15% Malay, 6.4% Indians, and 2.3% from other ethnic groups. 55% of the population is under 30.

The people of Singapore enjoy freedom of worship, the main religious faiths being Islam, Buddhism, Christianity and Hinduism. The official languages are Malay, Chinese (Mandarin), Tamil and English. Malay is the national language, with English as the language of administration.

Singapore was accorded British Crown Colony status after the Second World War, and was declared an independent Republic in December 1965. It has been ruled by the People's Action Party, led by Prime Minister Lee Kuan Yew, since 1959.

FACTORS INFLUENCING EMPLOYMENT

Foreigners seeking work in Singapore may apply for an Employment Pass, Permanent Residence or Citizenship, according to their status in the Republic.

Aliens who come to Singapore on Social Visit Passes may take up work there provided they first obtain either a Work Permit issued by the Ministry of Labour, or an Employment Pass or Professional Visit Pass issued by the Immigration Department (address below). Any foreigner who is not a permanent resident, and who has a gross salary over S$1,500 per month, requires an Employment Pass to work in Singapore. Employment Passes are usually issued for a three year period, application form available from *The Immigration Department,* South Bridge Centre, 7th & 8th Storey, 95 South Bridge Road, Singapore 0105.

Employment Pass holders who wish to reside permanently in Singapore may apply for an Entry Permit. There are a number of schemes whereby foreigners can obtain permanent resident status (Entry Permit) before coming to Singapore. Under the Profession/Technical Personnel and Skilled Workers Scheme, any person working in Singapore, who is below 50 years of age, and who has professional or specialist or technical skills which would enable him to pursue his trade or profession in Singapore may apply for permanent residence.

Under the Economic Benefit Schemes, persons identified as having entrepreneurial skills and financial resources likely to benefit the Republic may also apply for permanent residence. Information on both schemes is available on request from the *High Commissioner of the Republic of Singapore,* 2 Wilton Crescent, London SW1.

Generally, only permanent residents may apply for Singapore citizenship. In 1982, 11,784 persons applied for citizenship; 10,467 were approved and 6,887 rejected.

In 1986, 5,798 persons applied for citizenship, of which 3,893 were approved.

British High Commission

British High Commission, PO Box 19, Tanglin Circus, Singapore 1024.

Trade Unions

In 1986 there were 83 registered trade unions, five employer unions and a federation of employee trade unions, the National Trades Union Congress. Total membership of employee trade unions was 200,613, with the employer unions having a total of 1,146.

WORK AVAILABLE

The Singapore economy is still one of the fastest growing in Asia, with the second highesta per capita GNP in Asia after Japan.

The economy has progressively diversified. Transport and communications have expanded rapidly to join trade and manufacturing as the mainstays of the economy. Financial and business services have slumped since 1986, but are now picking up again.

Newspapers

Advertisements can be placed direct in the English language paper: *Straits Times,* 390 Kim Seng Road, Singapore 0923.

See also the section on *Advertisements* in the chapter *Getting the Job.*

Labour Force

The total labour force is 1,228,600 and is divided as follows: 1.1% in agriculture; 35.8% in industry; and 47% in services. The unemployment level was 6.5% in 1986.

SPECIFIC CONTACTS

Employment Service

The Ministry of Labour runs an employment service at 78 Prinsep, Singapore. It assists employers in securing workers and job-seekers in obtaining work, It also monitors the labour market and disseminates information on job vacancies. In 1987, it registered 16,039 job-seekers and successfully placed 3,314 in work.

Employment Agency

JAC Property & Employment Pte. Ltd., 14-10 Hong Leong Centre, 138 Robinson Road, Singapore 0104 — recruits qualified management, marketing and financial people.

Teaching

The *World-wide Education Service,* Strode House, 44-50 Osnaburgh Street, London NW1 3NN — occasionally recruits specialist teachers for expatriate schools in Singapore (see the teaching chapter).

See also the chapters on *Au Pair and Domestic, Banking and Accountancy, Medicine and Nursing, Teaching* and *Secretarial, Translating and Interpreting* for other possible openings in Singapore.

BRITISH FIRMS

with branches, affiliates or subsidiaries in Singapore

The British Business Association, 9th Storey, Inchcape House 450-452 Alexandra Road, Singapore 0511, can provide the BBA trade directory, listing British companies in Singapore. The price is S$40 (plus S$14.90 for postage to the UK).

South Korea

Embassy of the Republic of Korea, 4 Palace Gate, London W8 5NF
Currency: 1 Won = 100 Jeon
Rate of Exchange: £1 = 1175 Won

Despite the enormity of its national debt, and a very fragile external geo-political environment, the Korean economy has made remarkable progress over the last two years. From a declining growth rate of 5.4% in 1985, its economic growth has reached 12-13% in 1987, with inflation down to an impressive 3%. Employment opportunities for properly qualified British personnel are, therefore, quite good.

In 1988 South Korea hosted the Olympic Games; this, together with its new found democracy (President Roe Tae Woo was elected through direct elections in December 1987), has focused world attention on South Korea. The impact of this has yet to be felt, although it is expected to have beneficial effects on trade and the economy, and consequently on future employment.

GENERAL FACTS

South Korea, or the Republic of Korea as it is known, has a population of roughly 41,569,000 people, some 34% of whom are under 14. The country has a population density of 973.4 people per square mile. 65% live in urban areas, the largest of which is the capital, Seoul, with 9,000,000, followed by Pusan with 3,516,000, and Tague with 2,000,000.

The Republic covers a land area of 38,211 square miles. The country is mountainous with a rugged east coast.

The main language and ethnic group is Korean. The major religious faiths are Buddhism, Confucianism, Christianity and Chondokyo.

FACTORS INFLUENCING EMPLOYMENT

Any alien wishing to work in Korea must have a visa. Applications should be addressed to the Korean Embassy, 4 Palace Gate, London W8 5NF.

Any foreigner who wishes to stay for more than 60 days is required to apply for a residence certificate at the District Immigration Office in Korea, address available from the Korean Embassy at the above address.

British Embassy and Consulate
British Embassy, 4 Chung Dong, Chung-Ku, Seoul.

British Consulate, 12th Floor, Yoochang Building, 25-2, 4-Ka, Chungang-dong, Chung-Ku, Pusan.

Trade Unions

Trade union activity has been strictly controlled by the Government following the bloody uprising of 1980 in protest against the seizure of power by President Chun. Regional union organisation is banned, strikes are almost impossible, and unions are only allowed to operate individually on a single company basis.

WORK AVAILABLE

Korea's major industries are electronics, shipping, textile, clothing, and vehicles. The agrarian sector is very strong with 22% arable land, the major chief crops are rice, barley and vegetables.

What concerns the economic planners at the moment is the engineering of more diversification in Korea's export-oriented economy. This requires the exploration and opening-up of more European markets (a fact which prospective British immigrants should note) and the absorption of more technology, enabling the Republic to become as much a supplier of parts as of finished products.

Newspapers

The two English language daily papers take advertisements direct:

The Korea Herald, 11-3 3-ga, Hoehyou-dong, Jung-Gu, Seoul.

Korea Times, 14 Junghak-dong, Jongno-gu, Seoul (there is also a London office at Airwork House, 35 Picaddilly, London W1V 9PB).

Labour Force

The total economically active population is 16,116,000. The labour force is divided as follows: 36% in agriculture; 24% in manufacturing; and 40% in services. The unemployment level is about 3.8%.

SPECIFIC CONTACTS

The *Korea Trade Centre,* Vincent House, Vincent Square, London SW1P 2NB, advises that British citizens seeking specific contacts for long term work in Korea should contact the Commercial section of the British Embassy in Seoul, address above.

Engineers

Overseas Technical Services (Harrow) Ltd, 1st Floor, 100 College Road, Harrow HA1 1BJ — occasionally act as recruitment consultants for companies seeking instrument engineers for a variety of positions in South East Asia.

See also the chapters on *Au Pair and Domestic, Medicine and Nursing, Oil, Mining and Engineering* and the section on *Consultants and Agencies* in the chapter *Getting the Job.*

Appendix One
Bibliography

The Au Pair and Nanny's Guide to Working Abroad, Susan Griffith, Vacation Work Publications, 9 Park End Street, Oxford OX1 1HJ.

Brits Abroad: A Guide to Living and Working in the Developing Countries, Harry Brown and Rosemary Thomas, Express Books.

Careers Encyclopaedia, A. Segal (ed.), Cassell Plc., Artillery House, Artillery Row, London SW1P 1RT.

Careers Working Abroad, Helen Steadman, Kogan Page Ltd., 120 Pentonville Road, London N1 9JN.

CEPEC Recruitment Guide, CEPEC, Plaistow Lane, Bromley, Kent BR1 3JW.

Changing Your Job After 35, Godfrey Golzen and Philip Plumbley, Kogan Page Ltd., 120 Pentonville Road, London N1.

The Directory of Opportunities for Graduates, The Newpoint Publishing Company Ltd., London.

The Directory of Work and Study in Developing Countries, Vacation Work Publications.

Emplois d'Ete en France, Vacation Work Publications.

Equal Opportunities: A Career Guide, Anna Alston, Penguin Books Ltd., 27 Wrights Lane, London W8 5TZ.

Job Hunting Made Easy, John Bramham and David Cox, Kogan Page Ltd., 120 Pentonville Road, London N1.

Jobs in Japan, John Wharton, Vacation Work Publications.

How to Live and Work in America, Steve Mills, Northcote House Publishers Ltd., Harper & Row House, Estover Road, Plymouth PL6 7PZ.

How to Live and Work in Australia, Laura Veltman, Northcote House Publishers Ltd., Harper & Row House, Estover Road, Plymouth PL6 7PZ.

The International Directory of Voluntary Work, Vacation Work Publications.

Internships USA, Vacation Work Publications.

Kibbutz Volunteer, Vacation Work Publications.

Summer Employment Directory of the United States, Vacation Work Publications.

Summer Jobs Abroad, Vacation Work Publications.

Teaching Tactics for Japan's English Classrooms, John Wharton, Vacation Work Publications.

Volunteer Work Abroad, Central Bureau for Educational Visits and Exchange, Seymour Mews House, Seymour Mews, London W1H 9PE.

What Color Is Your Parachute?, Richard Nelson Bolles, Ten Speed Press, P.O. Box 7123, Berkeley, California 94707, USA.

Work, Study, Travel Abroad, Council on International Educational Exchange, 205 East 42nd Street, New York, NY 10017, USA.

Work Your Way Around the World, Susan Griffith, Vacation Work Publications.

Working Abroad, Godfrey Golzen, Kogan Page Ltd., 120 Pentonville Road, London N1.

Working Holidays, Central Bureau for Educational Visits and Exchanges, Seymour Mews House, Seymour Mews, London W1H 9PE.

Working in Ski Resorts — Europe, Vacation Work Publications.

Working in the European Communities, A. J. Raban, Hobsons Publishing Plc., Bateman Street, Cambridge CB2 1LZ.

Writer's And Artist's Yearbook, A. & C. Black Ltd., 35 Bedford Row, London WC1R 4SH.

Yearbook of Recruitment and Employment Services, Federation of Recruitment and Employment Services Ltd., 10 Belgrave Square, London SW1X 8PH.

Appendix Two
Application Procedure

The process of applying for an overseas vacancy, whether advertised in the press, through a job centre or a consultant or agency, or by direct application, demands the successful construction of the curriculum vitae. The first impression you make on an employer is often, rightly or wrongly, the one that sticks, and it it therefore important to take your time over the applications you send in. Additionally, when asking for information about a job, make sure you include in your enquiry all the points you wish to have explained.

Curricula Vitae

Any formal application, unless it is made on a very detailed application form, should include a curriculum vitae (or résumé). If you apply for a number of jobs at the same time, it is quite acceptable to send photocopies of these, but for isolated applications an original copy is obviously preferable. They should be typed and carefully spaced and laid out so that the essential information stands out yet remains in a logical and methodical order. The normal format for a curriculum vitae is as follows:

Personal — nationality, age, date of birth, marital status, special extra-curricular interests or activities, address and telephone number(s).

Employment — names and addresses of past employers, dates of employment, positions held, reasons for leaving.

Education — dates of schools attended, examinations passed, other qualifications obtained.

When setting out the employment and education sections, it is normal to start with the present and work back. If you keep the column for the dates on the left, this should be quite evident to the reader. Also, if your employment record is not particularly impressive (e.g. if you are still a student or have only recently left university or college), it is more usual to put the education details above employment.

Two sample copies of curricula vitae appear at the end of this appendix. Remember, if you are applying for a job abroad, your c.v. and any covering letter should be written in the language of the person to whom it is addressed.

Don't be afraid to apply for more than one job at a time, but if you are trying to find work through an agency, only one application should be necessary. However, don't expect people to hold job offers open indefinitely, while you wait to see if a better off materialises. If you *are* offered a job, either accept it or turn it down as soon as possible.

Return Postage

If you require a reply to your application, or to your requests for information, brochures, etc., you should enclose return postage, whether this be in the form of postage stamps, a stamped addressed envelope, or, for letters sent abroad, the required number of International Reply Coupons (one for a letter, perhaps two or more for brochures). In the course of researching this book, many companies and organisations have unequivocally stated that they will not reply to letters that do not enclose return postage. Not through any impoliteness or meanness, but simply through economic necessity.

Accepting Jobs

Before you accept a job abroad, make sure you know as many of the following points as are relevant to your situation:

—acceptability of your professional qualifications
—arrangements for obtaining a work permit or visa
—length of contract, if any
—wages, and how and when they are paid
—approximate rates of deductions from wages
—hours, overtime rates and holiday arrangements
—accommodation arrangements and travel to and from work
—pension arrangements and provisions for sickness
—any conditions you must meet before being allowed to take up employment, e.g. medical, psychological or academic examinations, any probationary period on the job.

CURRICULUM VITAE

Name:	Janet Susan Brown
Address:	46 Lyall Way, Newtown, Kent
Telephone:	Newtown 37246
Date of Birth:	8th May 1970
Nationality:	British
Education: 1981-1987	Newtown Grammar School, Taunton Lane, Newtown, Kent. 'O' Levels, 1986: English Language (B), Mathematics (B), History (B), Geography (C), Physics (C), Biology (C), French (B). 'A' Levels (to be taken May 1989): Pure Mathematics, History, English.
Positions of Responsibility:	Captain of School Hockey Team School Prefect (my responsibilities included the supervising of sport in the lower school and looking after the finances of the school shop).
Work Experience:	W H Smith, High Street, Newtown (Saturday Assistant) — from January 1986 to July 1986. My responsibilities included stock control, cashier work and other general duties.
Interests and Activities:	Member of School Youth Club. I am on the committee and organise social events. I own a microcomputer and I am developing my knowledge of programming.
Other Information:	Clean current driving licence (for motor cycle and car).
Available to start work:	August 1989
Referees:	Mr G Ralph, Headmaster, Newtown Grammar School, Taunton Lane, Newtown, Kent. Mr R Bishop, 66 Bredbere Avenue, Preston, Kent. (Mr Bishop is the Manager of W H Smith in Newtown).

(Source: Clive Tucker, Kent Careers Service)

CAREER HISTORY

Name:	James Roger Leeper
Address:	23 Clefton Road, Newtown, Yorkshire
Telephone:	Newtown (0871) 432111
Date of Birth:	September 11 1950
Nationality:	British Citizen
Family:	Married with two children, ages 12 and 9 years.
Professional:	Member of Institute of Hydraulic Engineers, 1979 Member of Institute of Technical Managers, 1981
Work Experience	
1982-present	As Engineering Manager with the Whiteside Engineering Company, I head the design and quality control departments with a staff of over 20 people. The machinery built by the company is purchased by firms manufacturing consumer durables at home and abroad.
1978-82	First appointed Production Controller with the Phoenix Manufacturing company. Then, within eighteen months, I was promoted to Production Manager with a staff of 30 engaged in manufacturing components for the makers of a range of domestic and office appliances.
1977-78	Technical Manager with Rogerson and Brown Ltd. With this company, I was responsible for a department of four people engaged in designing machines for industry to be produced at the lowest possible cost to the purchaser without loss of reliability. A fall in demand for new equipment caused the company to close.
Objective:	An overseas engineering management appointment with genuine career opportunity and challenge. I am qualified to contribute to the management team and the engineering technology at senior level in an organisation.
Leisure:	Member of local computer club Member of local drama society Occasional tennis player

Appendix Three
Worldwide Taxation

Below is a table which shows the relative taxation burdens of some of the major countries in the developed world. Taxation is taken to include all compulsory payments to both central and local governments.

Total tax revenue as percentage of GDP 1985

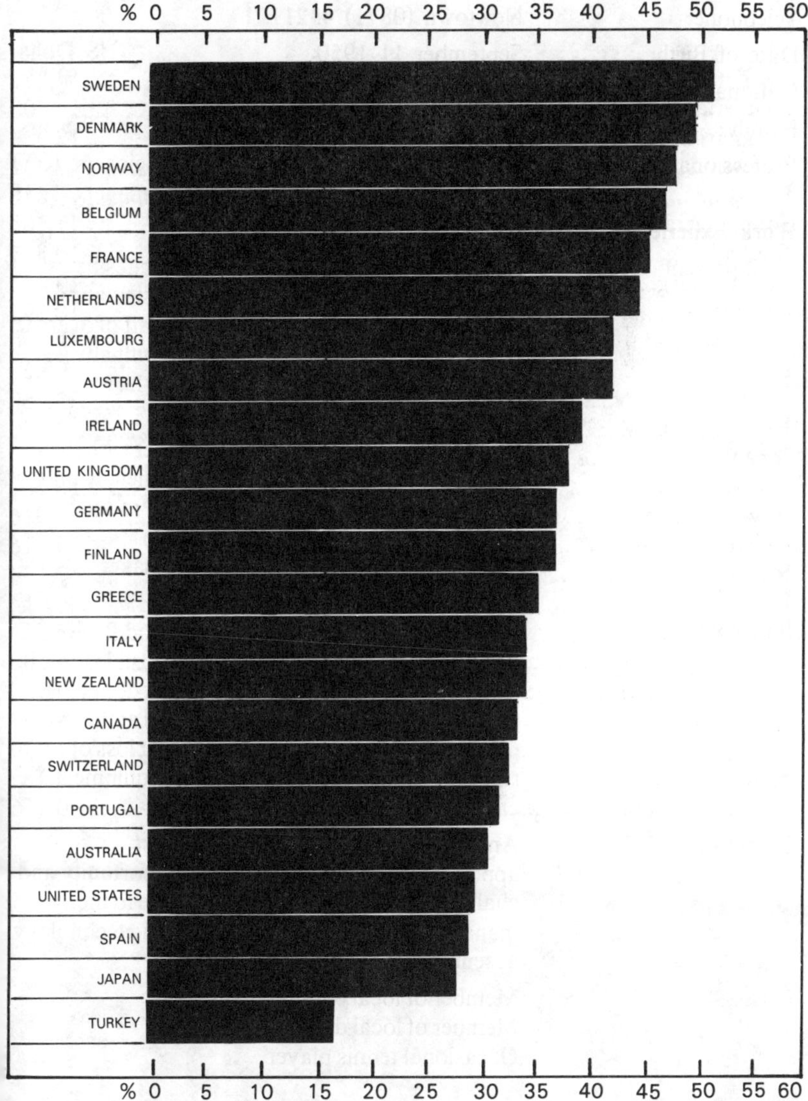

Countries have been ranked by their total tax GDP rations. Source: Revenue Statistics of OECD Member Countries 1965-1986 (OECD, Paris, 1987)

Appendix Four
Worldwide Living Standards

The following table represents the average per capita income in the twenty-six countries dealt with in this book.

	US Dollars
Sweden	14,821
Switzerland	14,408
Denmark	12,956
Norway	12,432
USA	11,675
Saudi Arabia	11,500
Finland	10,477
Luxembourg	10,444
Canada	10,193
Australia	9,960
Belgium	9,827
West Germany	9,450
Netherlands	9,175
Japan	8,460
Austria	8,280
New Zealand	7,916
United Kingdom	7,216
France	7,179
Italy	6,914
Singapore	6,526
Spain	5,500
Ireland	4,750
Greece	4,590
Portugal	1,930
South Korea	1,187
China	0,566

(Source: The World Almanac 1986)

Appendix Five
Key to Company Classifications

1 Accounting and Auditing

2 Advertising and Public Relations

3 Airlines and Aerospace Products

4 Banking, Finance and Investment

5 Boats

6 Building materials

7 Cars, Caravans and other Vehicles

8 Chemicals and Pharmaceuticals

9 Clothing

10 Computers, Electrical and Electronic Equipment

11 Cosmetics and Toiletries

12 Dental, Medical and Optical Supplies

13 Department Stores

14 Executive and Management Consultants

15 Export and Import Trading

16 Foodstuffs and Beverages

17 Freight Storage and Transport

18 Furnishings and Domestic Applicances

19 Glassware and Tiles

20 Hotels and Restaurants

21 Hotel Supplies

22 Industrial Instruments and Precision Engineering

23 Insurance

24 Lawyers

25 Machinery and Industrial Equipment

26 Machine Tools

27 Mechanical Handling Equipment

28 Metal Products

29 Music and Musical Instruments

30 Office Equipment

31 Packaging

32 Paints

33 Paper Products

34 Personnel Agencies

35 Petrochemicals

36 Photographic Equipment

37 Plastics

38 Printing, Publishing and Graphics

39 Pumps and Hydraulic Equipment

40 Real Estate

41 Ropes and Cables

42 Rubber Goods

43 Security

44 Shoes

45 Telecommunications

46 Textiles

47 Tobacco and Tobacco Machinery

48 Tourist Agencies and Travel Services

49 Toy Manufacture

50 Watches and Jewellery

Index to Organisations

List of Advertisers